The Pearson
Custom Program for **CIS**

CIS118
Introduction to PC Applications
Book - 1

D1403823

PEARSON

Senior Vice President, Editorial: Patrick F. Boles
Sponsoring Editors: Ana Díaz-Caneja and David J. Maltby
Development Editor: Christina Martin
Editorial Assistant: Hannah Coker
Operations Manager: Eric M. Kenney
Production Manager: Jennifer Berry
Art Director: Renée Sartell
Cover Designers: Blair Brown and Kristen Kiley

Cover Art: Jerry Driendl/Getty Images, Inc.; Steve Bloom/Getty Images, Inc.; "Cheetah" courtesy of Marvin Mattelson/Getty Images; "Tabs" courtesy of Andrey Prokhorov/iStockphoto; "Open Doors" courtesy of Spectral-Design/iStockphoto; "Compass" courtesy of Laurent Hamels/Getty Images; "Fortune Teller" courtesy of Ingvald Kaldhussaeter/iStockphoto; "Ladder of Success" courtesy of iStockphoto; "Global Communication in Blue" courtesy of iStockphoto.

This special edition published in cooperation with Pearson Learning Solutions.

Printed in the United States of America.

Please visit our website at *www.pearsonlearningsolutions.com*.

Attention bookstores: For permission to return any unsold stock, contact us at *pe-uscustomreturns@pearson.com*.

Pearson Learning Solutions, 501 Boylston Street, Suite 900, Boston, MA 02116
A Pearson Education Company
www.pearsoned.com

ISBN 10: 1-256-22588-6
ISBN 13: 978-1-256-22588-1

Contents

Creating Documents with Microsoft Word 2010

OUTCOMES
At the end of this chapter you will be able to:

OBJECTIVES
Mastering these objectives will enable you to:

PROJECT 1A
Create a flyer with a picture.

1. Create a New Document and Insert Text
2. Insert and Format Graphics
3. Insert and Modify Text Boxes and Shapes
4. Preview and Print a Document

PROJECT 1B
Format text, paragraphs, and documents.

5. Change Document and Paragraph Layout
6. Create and Modify Lists
7. Set and Modify Tab Stops
8. Insert a SmartArt Graphic

Joy Brown/Shutterstock

In This Chapter

In this chapter, you will use Microsoft Word, which is one of the most common programs found on computers and one that almost everyone has a reason to use. You will use many of the new tools found in Word 2010. When you learn word processing, you are also learning skills and techniques that you need to work efficiently on a computer. You can use Microsoft Word to perform basic word processing tasks such as writing a memo, a report, or a letter. You can also use Word to complete complex word processing tasks, such as creating sophisticated tables, embedding graphics, writing blogs, creating publications, and inserting links into other documents and the Internet. Word is a program that you can learn gradually, and then add more advanced skills one at a time.

The projects in this chapter relate to **Laurel College**. The college offers this diverse geographic area a wide range of academic and career programs, including associate degrees, certificate programs, and non-credit continuing education and personal development courses. The college makes positive contributions to the community through cultural and athletic programs and partnerships with businesses and nonprofit organizations. The college also provides industry-specific training programs for local businesses through its growing Economic Development Center.

From Word Chapter 1 of *GO! with Microsoft® Office 2010 Volume 1*, First Edition, Shelley Gaskin, Robert L. Ferrett, Alicia Vargas, Carolyn McClennan. Copyright © 2011 by Pearson Education, Inc. Published by Pearson Prentice Hall. All rights reserved.

Project 1A Flyer

Project Activities

In Activities 1.01 through 1.12, you will create a flyer announcing a new rock climbing class offered by the Physical Education Department at Laurel College. Your completed document will look similar to Figure 1.1.

Project Files

For Project 1A, you will need the following files:

New blank Word document
w01A_Fitness_Flyer
w01A_Rock_Climber

You will save your document as:

Lastname_Firstname_1A_Fitness_Flyer

Project Results

Figure 1.1
Project 1A Fitness Flyer

Word | Creating Documents with Microsoft Word 2010

Objective 1 | Create a New Document and Insert Text

When you create a new document, you can type all of the text, or you can type some of the text and then insert additional text from another source.

Activity 1.01 | Starting a New Word Document and Inserting Text

1 **Start** Word and display a new blank document. On the **Home tab**, in the **Paragraph group**, if necessary click the Show/Hide button ¶ so that it is active (glows orange) to display the formatting marks. If the rulers do not display, click the View tab, and then in the Show group, select the Ruler check box.

2 Type **Rock Climbing 101** and then press Enter two times. As you type the following text, press the Spacebar only one time at the end of a sentence: **Increase your fitness level by learning basic rock climbing using the new Laurel College Gymnasium rock climbing wall. The Physical Education Department is offering Rock Climbing 101 as part of its Recreational Fitness Program.**

As you type, the insertion point moves to the right, and when it approaches the right margin, Word determines whether the next word in the line will fit within the established right margin. If the word does not fit, Word moves the entire word down to the next line. This feature is called **wordwrap** and means that you press Enter *only* when you reach the end of a paragraph—it is not necessary to press Enter at the end of each line of text.

Note | Spacing Between Sentences

Although you might have learned to add two spaces following end-of-sentence punctuation, the common practice now is to space only one time at the end of a sentence.

---

3 Press Enter one time. Take a moment to study the table in Figure 1.2 to become familiar with the default document settings in Microsoft Word, and then compare your screen with Figure 1.3.

When you press Enter, Spacebar, or Tab on your keyboard, characters display in your document to represent these keystrokes. These characters do not print and are referred to as **formatting marks** or **nonprinting characters**. These marks will display throughout this instruction.

Default Document Settings in a New Word Document

Setting	Default format
Font and font size	The default font is Calibri and the default font size is 11.
Margins	The default left, right, top, and bottom page margins are 1 inch.
Line spacing	The default line spacing is 1.15, which provides slightly more space between lines than single spacing does—an extra 1/6 of a line added between lines than single spacing.
Paragraph spacing	The default spacing after a paragraph is 10 points, which is slightly less than the height of one blank line of text.
View	The default view is Print Layout view, which displays the page borders and displays the document as it will appear when printed.

Figure 1.2

Figure 1.3

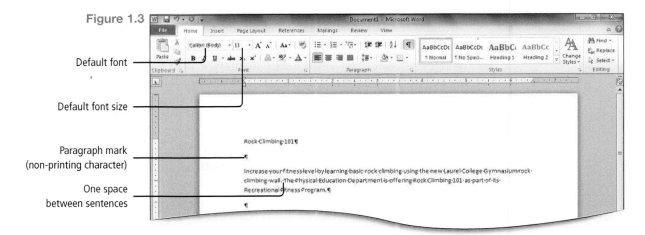

Default font

Default font size

Paragraph mark
(non-printing character)

One space
between sentences

4 On the Ribbon, click the **Insert tab**. In the **Text group**, click the **Object button arrow**, and then click **Text from File**.

> **Alert!** | Does the Object Dialog Box Display?
>
> If the Object dialog box displays, you probably clicked the Object *button* instead of the Object *button arrow*. Close the Object dialog box, and then in the Text group, click the Object button arrow, as shown in Figure 1.4. Click *Text from File*, and then continue with Step 5.

Another Way

Open the file, copy the required text, close the file, and then paste the text into the current document.

5 In the **Insert File** dialog box, navigate to the student files that accompany this textbook, locate and select **w01A_Fitness_Flyer**, and then click **Insert**. Compare your screen with Figure 1.4.

A *copy* of the text from the w01A_Fitness_Flyer file displays at the insertion point location; the text is not removed from the original file.

Figure 1.4

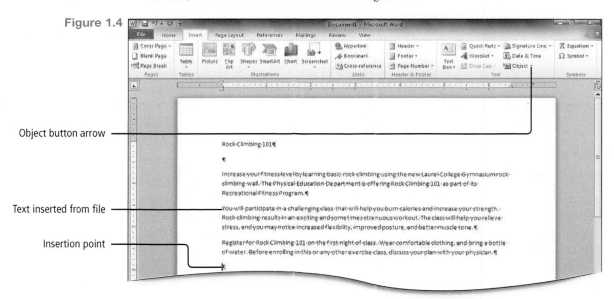

Object button arrow

Text inserted from file

Insertion point

6 On the **Quick Access Toolbar**, click the **Save** button. In the **Save As** dialog box, navigate to the location where you are saving your files for this chapter, and then create and open a new folder named **Word Chapter 1** In the **File name** box, replace the existing text with **Lastname_Firstname_1A_Fitness_Flyer** and then click **Save**.

Word | Creating Documents with Microsoft Word 2010

> **More Knowledge | Word's Default Settings Are Easier to Read Online**
>
> Until just a few years ago, word processing programs used single spacing, an extra blank paragraph to separate paragraphs, and 12 pt Times New Roman as the default formats. Now, studies show that individuals find the Word default formats described in Figure 1.2 to be easier to read online, where many documents are now viewed and read.

Objective 2 | Insert and Format Graphics

To add visual interest to a document, insert *graphics*. Graphics include pictures, clip art, charts, and *drawing objects*—shapes, diagrams, lines, and so on. For additional visual interest, you can convert text to an attractive graphic format; add, resize, move, and format pictures; and add an attractive page border.

Activity 1.02 | Formatting Text Using Text Effects

Text effects are decorative formats, such as shadowed or mirrored text, text glow, 3-D effects, and colors that make text stand out.

1 Including the paragraph mark, select the first paragraph of text—*Rock Climbing 101*. On the **Home tab**, in the **Font group**, click the **Text Effects** button.

2 In the displayed **Text Effects** gallery, in the first row, point to the second effect to display the ScreenTip *Fill - None, Outline - Accent 2* and then click this effect.

3 With the text still selected, in the **Font group**, click in the **Font Size** box to select the existing font size. Type **60** and then press Enter.

> When you want to change the font size of selected text to a size that does not display in the Font Size list, type the number in the Font Size button box and press Enter to confirm the new font size.

4 With the text still selected, in the **Paragraph group**, click the **Center** button to center the text. Compare your screen with Figure 1.5.

Figure 1.5

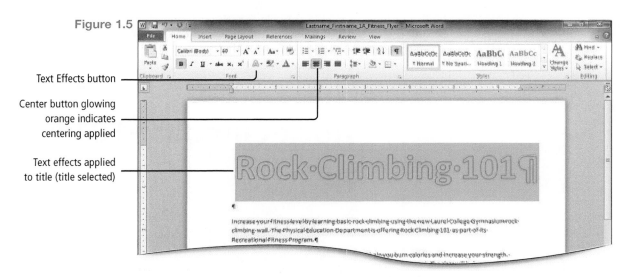

Text Effects button

Center button glowing orange indicates centering applied

Text effects applied to title (title selected)

5 With the text still selected, in the **Font group**, click the **Text Effects** button. Point to **Shadow**, and then under **Outer**, in the second row, click the third style—**Offset Left**.

6 With the text still selected, in the **Font group**, click the **Font Color button arrow**. Under **Theme Colors**, in the fourth column, click the first color—**Dark Blue, Text 2**.

7 Click anywhere in the document to deselect the text, and then compare your screen with Figure 1.6.

Figure 1.6

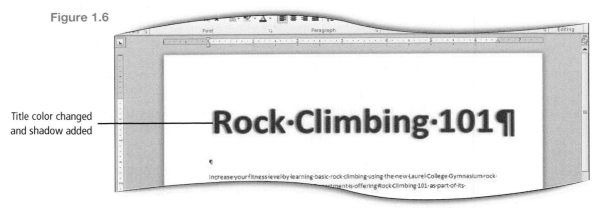

Title color changed and shadow added

8 **Save** 🖫 your document.

Activity 1.03 | Inserting and Resizing Pictures

1 In the paragraph that begins *Increase your fitness*, click to position the insertion point at the beginning of the paragraph.

2 On the **Insert tab**, in the **Illustrations group**, click the **Picture** button. In the **Insert Picture** dialog box, navigate to your student data files, locate and click **w01A_Rock_Climber**, and then click **Insert**.

> Word inserts the picture as an ***inline object***; that is, the picture is positioned directly in the text at the insertion point, just like a character in a sentence. Sizing handles surround the picture indicating it is selected.

3 If necessary, scroll to view the entire picture. Notice the round and square sizing handles around the border of the selected picture, as shown in Figure 1.7.

> The round corner sizing handles resize the graphic proportionally. The square sizing handles resize a graphic vertically or horizontally only; however, sizing with these will distort the graphic. A green rotate handle, with which you can rotate the graphic to any angle, displays above the top center sizing handle.

Figure 1.7

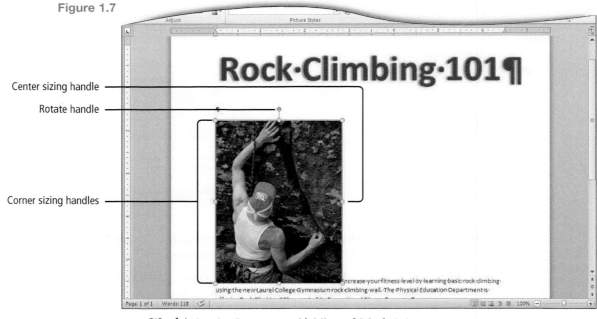

Center sizing handle

Rotate handle

Corner sizing handles

Word | Creating Documents with Microsoft Word 2010

4 At the lower right corner of the picture, point to the round sizing handle until the ⟋ pointer displays. Drag upward and to the left until the bottom of the graphic is aligned at approximately **4 inches on the vertical ruler**. Compare your screen with Figure 1.8. Notice that the graphic is proportionally resized.

Figure 1.8

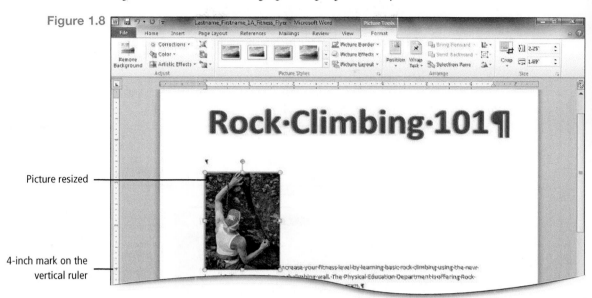

Picture resized ——

4-inch mark on the vertical ruler ——

Another Way

Click the Undo button to undo the change.

5 On the **Format tab**, in the **Adjust group**, click the **Reset Picture button arrow**, and then click **Reset Picture & Size**.

6 In the **Size group**, click the **Shape Height spin box up arrow** as necessary to change the height of the picture to **4.5"**. Scroll down to view the entire picture on your screen, compare your screen with Figure 1.9, and then **Save** your document.

> When you use the Height and Width *spin boxes* to change the size of a graphic, the graphic will always resize proportionally; that is, the width adjusts as you change the height and vice versa.

Figure 1.9

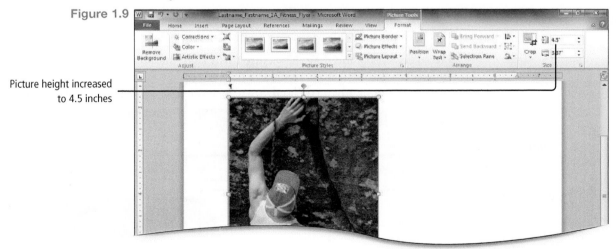

Picture height increased to 4.5 inches ——

Activity 1.04 | Wrapping Text Around a Picture

Graphics inserted as inline objects are treated like characters in a sentence, which can result in unattractive spacing. You can change an inline object to a *floating object*—a graphic that can be moved independently of the surrounding text characters.

1 Be sure the picture is selected—you know it is selected if the sizing handles display.

2 On the **Format tab**, in the **Arrange group**, click the **Wrap Text** button to display a gallery of text wrapping arrangements.

   Text wrapping refers to the manner in which text displays around an object.

3 From the gallery, click **Square** to wrap the text around the graphic, and then notice the *anchor* symbol to the left of the first line of the paragraph. Compare your screen with Figure 1.10.

   Select square text wrapping when you want to wrap the text to the left or right of the image. When you apply text wrapping, the object is always associated with—anchored to—a specific paragraph.

Figure 1.10

Wrap Text button

Anchor symbol

Text wrapped around picture

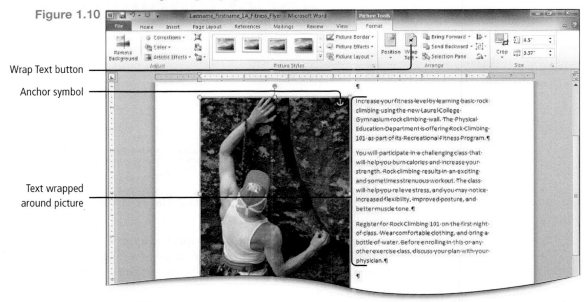

4 **Save** your document.

Activity 1.05 | Moving a Picture

1 Point to the rock climber picture to display the pointer.

2 Hold down Shift and drag the picture to the right until the right edge of the picture aligns at approximately **6.5 inches on the horizontal ruler**. Notice that the picture moves in a straight line when you hold down Shift. Compare your screen with Figure 1.11.

Figure 1.11

Right edge aligned with right margin

Top edge aligned with top of paragraph

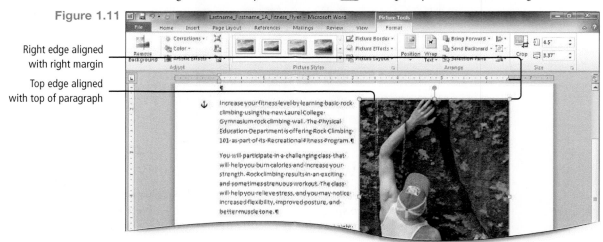

3 If necessary, press any of the arrow keys on your keyboard to *nudge*—move in small increments—the picture in any direction so that the text wraps to match Figure 1.11. **Save** 🖫 your document.

Activity 1.06 | Applying Picture Styles and Artistic Effects

Picture styles include shapes, shadows, frames, borders, and other special effects with which you can stylize an image. *Artistic effects* are formats that make pictures look more like sketches or paintings.

1 Be sure the rock climber picture is selected. On the **Format tab**, in the **Picture Styles group**, click the **Picture Effects** button. Point to **Soft Edges**, and then click **5 Point**.

> The Soft Edges feature fades the edges of the picture. The number of points you choose determines how far the fade goes inward from the edges of the picture.

2 On the **Format tab**, in the **Adjust group**, click the **Artistic Effects** button. In the first row of the gallery, point to, but do not click, the third effect—**Pencil Grayscale**.

> Live Preview displays the picture with the *Pencil Grayscale* effect added.

3 In the second row of the gallery, click the third effect—**Paint Brush**. Notice that the picture looks like a painting, rather than a photograph, as shown in Figure 1.12. **Save** 🖫 your document.

Figure 1.12

Paint Brush artistic effect applied to picture

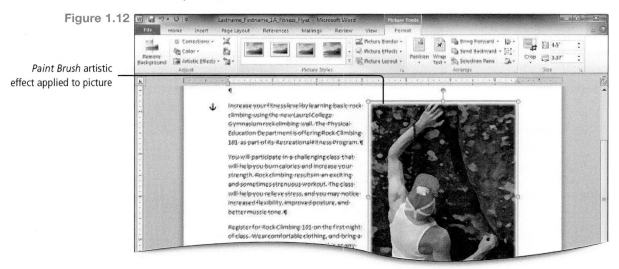

Activity 1.07 | Adding a Page Border

Page borders frame a page and help to focus the information on the page.

1 Click anywhere outside the picture to deselect it. On the **Page Layout tab**, in the **Page Background group**, click the **Page Borders** button.

2 In the **Borders and Shading** dialog box, under **Setting**, click **Box**. Under **Style**, scroll down the list about a third of the way and click the heavy top line with the thin bottom line—check the **Preview** area to be sure the heavier line is the nearest to the edges of the page.

3 Click the **Color arrow**, and then in the fourth column, click the first color—**Dark Blue, Text 2**.

4 Under **Apply to**, be sure *Whole document* is selected, and then compare your screen with Figure 1.13.

Figure 1.13

Page Borders button

Page border preview

Box setting

Border style

Border color

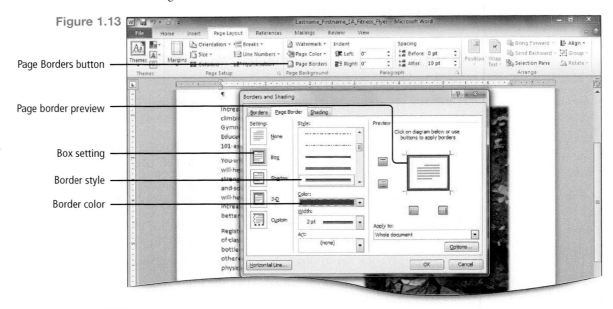

5 At the bottom of the **Borders and Shading** dialog box, click **OK**.

6 Press Ctrl + Home to move to the top of the document, and then compare your page border with Figure 1.14. **Save** your document.

Figure 1.14

Page Border added to document

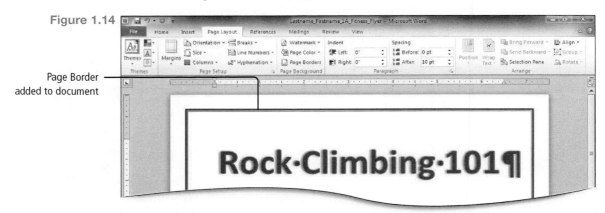

Objective 3 | Insert and Modify Text Boxes and Shapes

Word provides predefined *shapes* and *text boxes* that you can add to your documents. A shape is an object such as a line, arrow, box, callout, or banner. A text box is a movable, resizable container for text or graphics. Use these objects to add visual interest to your document.

Activity 1.08 | Inserting a Shape

1 Press ↓ one time to move to the blank paragraph below the title. Press Enter four times to make space for a text box, and notice that the picture anchored to the paragraph moves with the text.

2 Press Ctrl + End to move to the bottom of the document, and notice that your insertion point is positioned in the empty paragraph at the end of the document.

3 Click the **Insert tab**, and then in the **Illustrations group**, click the **Shapes** button to display the gallery. Compare your screen with Figure 1.15.

Figure 1.15

Shapes button

Rounded Rectangle shape

Shapes gallery

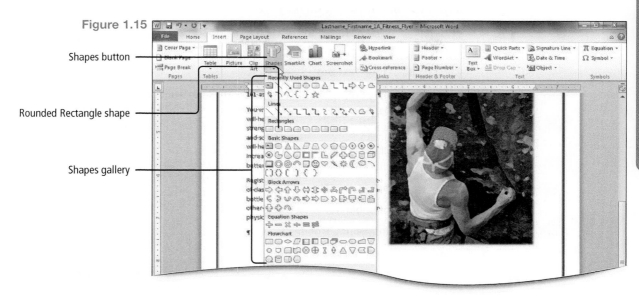

4 Under **Rectangles**, click the second shape—**Rounded Rectangle**, and then move your pointer. Notice that the ⊞ pointer displays.

5 Position the ⊞ pointer just under the lower left corner of the picture, and then drag down approximately **1 inch** and to the right edge of the picture.

6 Point to the shape and right-click, and then from the shortcut menu, click **Add Text**.

7 With the insertion point blinking inside the shape, point inside the shape and right-click, and then on the Mini toolbar, change the **Font Size** to **16**, and be sure **Center** ☰ alignment is selected.

8 Click inside the shape again, and then type **Improve your strength, balance, and coordination** If necessary, use the lower middle sizing handle to enlarge the shape to view your text. Compare your screen with Figure 1.16. **Save** 🖫 your document.

Figure 1.16

Rounded Rectangle
shape inserted and
formatted, text added

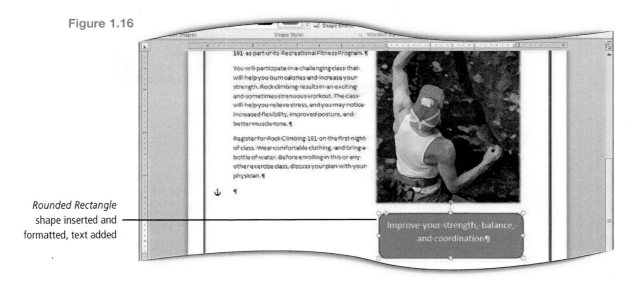

Activity 1.09 | Inserting a Text Box

A text box is useful to differentiate portions of text from other text on the page. You can move a text box anywhere on the page.

1 Press Ctrl + Home to move to the top of the document.

2 On the **Insert tab**, in the **Text group**, click the **Text Box** button. At the bottom of the gallery, click **Draw Text Box**.

3 Position the ⊞ pointer below the letter *k* in *Rock*—at approximately **1.5 inches on the vertical ruler**. Drag down and to the right to create a text box approximately **1.5 inches** high and **3 inches** wide—the exact size and location need not be precise.

4 With the insertion point blinking in the text box, type the following, pressing Enter after each line to create a new paragraph:

Meets Tuesdays and Thursdays, 7-9 p.m.

Begins September 13, ends December 16

College Gymnasium, Room 104

5 Compare your screen with Figure 1.17.

Figure 1.17

Text box with inserted text

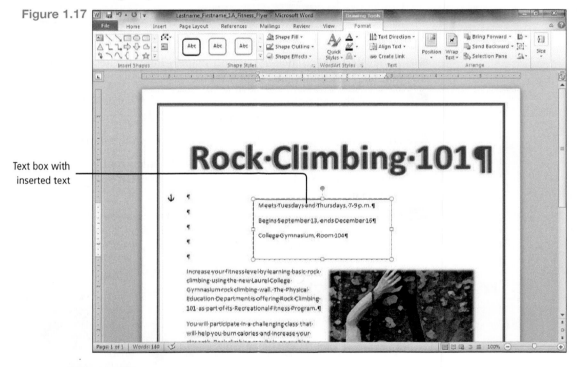

6 **Save** 🖫 your document.

Activity 1.10 | Moving, Resizing, and Formatting Shapes and Text Boxes

1 In the text box you just created in the upper portion of the flyer, select all of the text. From the Mini toolbar, change the **Font Size** to **14**, apply **Bold** B , and then **Center** ☰ the text.

2 On the **Format tab**, in the **Size group**, if necessary, click the **Size** button. Click the **Shape Height spin arrows** as necessary to set the height of the text box to **1.2″**. Click the **Shape Width spin arrows** as necessary to set the width of the text box to **4″**.

3 In the **Shape Styles group**, click the **Shape Effects** button. Point to **Shadow**, and then under **Outer**, in the first row, click the first style—**Offset Diagonal Bottom Right**.

4 In the **Shape Styles group**, click the **Shape Outline button arrow**. In the fourth column, click the first color—**Dark Blue, Text 2** to change the color of the text box border.

5 Click the **Shape Outline button arrow** again, point to **Weight**, and then click **3 pt**.

6 Click anywhere in the document to deselect the text box. Notice that with the text box deselected, you can see all the measurements on the horizontal ruler.

7 Click anywhere in the text box and point to the text box border to display the pointer. By dragging, visually center the text box vertically and horizontally in the space below the *Rock Climbing 101* title. Then, if necessary, press any of the arrow keys on your keyboard to nudge the text box in precise increments to match Figure 1.18.

Figure 1.18

Text formatted and centered in text box, shadow added, border color and weight changed

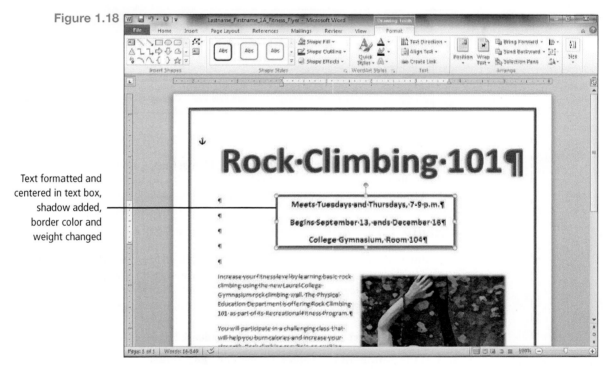

8 Press [Ctrl] + [End] to move to the bottom of the document. Click on the border of the rounded rectangular shape to select it.

9 On the **Format tab**, in the **Size group**, if necessary, click the **Size** button. Click the **Shape Height spin arrows** as necessary to change the height of the shape to **0.8″**.

10 In the **Shape Styles group**, click the **Shape Fill button arrow**, and then at the bottom of the gallery, point to **Gradient**. Under **Dark Variations**, in the third row click the first gradient—**Linear Diagonal - Bottom Left to Top Right**.

11 In the **Shape Styles group**, click the **Shape Outline button arrow**. In the sixth column, click the first color—**Red, Accent 2**.

12 Click the **Shape Outline button arrow** again, point to **Weight**, and then click **1 1/2 pt**. Click anywhere in the document to deselect the shape. Compare your screen with Figure 1.19, and then **Save** 🖫 your document.

Figure 1.19

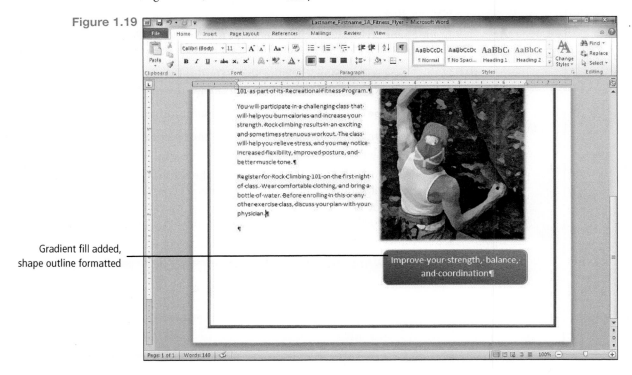

Gradient fill added, shape outline formatted

Objective 4 | Preview and Print a Document

While you are creating your document, it is useful to preview your document periodically to be sure that you are getting the result you want. Then, before printing, make a final preview to be sure the document layout is what you intended.

Activity 1.11 | Adding a File Name to the Footer

Information in headers and footers helps to identify a document when it is printed or displayed electronically. Recall that a header is information that prints at the top of every page; a footer is information that prints at the bottom of every page. In this textbook, you will insert the file name in the footer of every Word document.

Another Way

At the bottom edge of the page, right-click; from the shortcut menu, click Edit Footer.

1 Click the **Insert tab**, and then, in the **Header & Footer group**, click the **Footer** button.

2 At the bottom of the **Footer** gallery, click **Edit Footer**.

The footer area displays with the insertion point blinking at the left edge, and on the Ribbon, the Header & Footer Tools display and add the Design tab.

3 On the **Design tab**, in the **Insert group**, click the **Quick Parts** button, and then click **Field**. In the **Field** dialog box, under **Field names**, use the vertical scroll bar to examine the items that you can insert in a header or footer.

A *field* is a placeholder that displays preset content such as the current date, the file name, a page number, or other stored information.

4 In the **Field names** list, scroll as necessary to locate and then click **FileName**. Compare your screen with Figure 1.20.

Figure 1.20

Quick Parts button

Field dialog box

FileName field

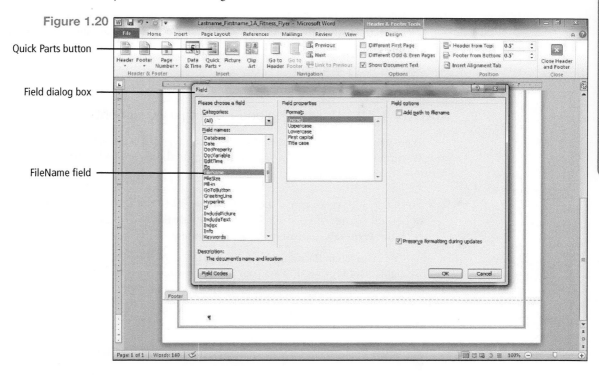

5 In the lower right corner of the **Field** dialog box, click **OK**, and then compare your screen with Figure 1.21.

Figure 1.21

Document text and image dimmed when footer is open

File name in footer

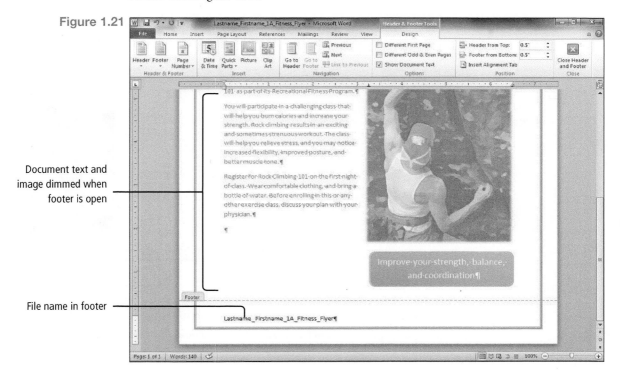

Another Way
Double-click anywhere in the document to close the footer area.

6 On the **Design tab**, at the far right in the **Close group**, click the **Close Header and Footer** button.

> When the body of the document is active, the footer text is dimmed—displays in gray. Conversely, when the footer area is active, the footer text is not dimmed; instead, the document text is dimmed.

7 **Save** 🖫 your document.

Activity 1.12 │ Previewing and Printing a Document

To ensure that you are getting the result you want, it is useful to periodically preview your document. Then, before printing, make a final preview to be sure the document layout is what you intended.

Another Way
Press Ctrl + F2 to display Print Preview.

1 Press Ctrl + Home to move the insertion point to the top of the document. In the upper left corner of your screen, click the **File tab** to display **Backstage** view, and then click the **Print tab** to display the **Print Preview**.

> The Print tab in Backstage view displays the tools you need to select your settings. On the right, Print Preview displays your document exactly as it will print; the formatting marks do not display.

2 In the lower right corner of the **Print Preview**, notice the zoom buttons that display. Compare your screen with Figure 1.22.

Figure 1.22

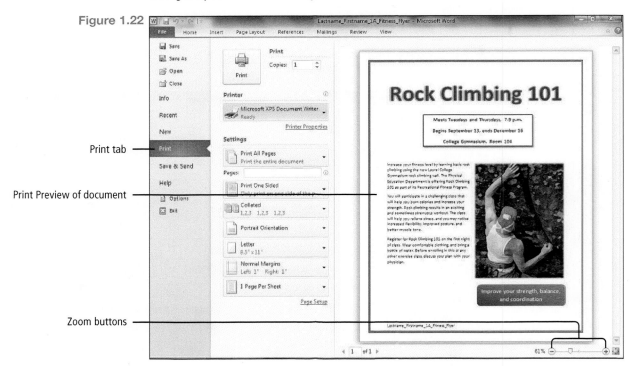

Print tab

Print Preview of document

Zoom buttons

3 Click the **Zoom In** button ⊕ to view the document at full size, and notice that a larger preview is easier to read. Click the **Zoom Out** button ⊖ to view the entire page.

4 Click the **Info tab**. On the right, under the screen thumbnail, click **Properties**, and then click **Show Document Panel**.

Here you can adjust the document properties.

5 In the **Author** box, delete any text and then type your firstname and lastname. In the **Subject** box type your course name and section number, and in the **Keywords** box type **fitness, rock climbing Close** the Document Panel.

6 Save your document. To print, display **Backstage** view, and then on the **navigation bar**, click **Print**. In the **Settings** group, be sure the correct printer is selected, and then in the **Print group**, click the **Print** button. Or, submit your document electronically as directed by your instructor.

7 In **Backstage** view, click **Exit** to close the document and exit Word.

End **You have completed Project 1A** ————————————————

Project 1B Information Handout

myitlab
Project 1B Training

Project Activities

In Activities 1.13 through 1.23, you will format and add lists to an information handout that describes student activities at Laurel College. Your completed document will look similar to Figure 1.23.

Project Files

For Project 1B, you will need the following file:

w01B_Student_Activities

You will save your document as:

Lastname_Firstname_1B_Student_Activities

Project Results

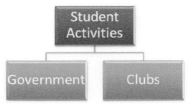

Every spring, students vote for the President, Vice President, Treasurer, Secretary, and Student Trustee for the following year. Executive Officers work with the college administration to manage campus activities and to make changes to policies and procedures. For example, the Student Trustee is a
h consists of elected members from the
college budget, and employee hiring.
the Board to vote for a proposal to
ocations in Laurelton and outlying areas.

:lubs and academic organizations vote for
n information and applications on the
mpus and in the student newspaper.

f interests, including academic, political,
currently in existence at Laurel College. A
in a club, you may enjoy being a member
or you may decide to take a leadership role

fice in the Campus Center, Room CC208, or
d complete the form online. Clubs accept
e following are the first meeting dates and

. October 8, 2:00 p.m., Room CC214
ctober 5, 5:00 p.m., Computer Café
7, 3:00 p.m., Field House, Room 2A
. October 6, 2:00 p.m., Room CC212
6, 4:00 p.m., Math Tutoring Lab, L35
. October 8, 3:00 p.m., Room CC214
4, 5:30 p.m., Photo Lab, Foster Hall
.......October 8, 5:00 p.m., Room L24
. October 7, 4:30 p.m., Room CC214
October 4, 3:00 p.m., Little Theater

listed here, are great, but your goals are
ing a degree or certificate. Maybe you want
u leave Laurel College. Whatever your
ur education, work experience, and
ly ones in which you had a leadership role,

Associated Students of Laurel College

Student Activities

Government

Clubs

Get Involved in Student Activities

Your experience at Laurel College will be richer and more memorable if you get involved in activities that take you beyond the classroom. You will have the opportunity to meet other students, faculty, and staff members and will participate in organizations that make valuable contributions to your college and to the community.

Consider becoming involved in student government or joining a club. You might take part in activities such as these:

- ✓ Volunteering to help with a blood drive
- ✓ Traveling to a foreign country to learn about other cultures
- ✓ Volunteering to assist at graduation
- ✓ Helping to organize a community picnic
- ✓ Planning and implementing advertising for a student event
- ✓ Meeting with members of the state legislature to discuss issues that affect college students—for example, tuition costs and financial aid

Student Government

As a registered student, you are eligible to attend meetings of the Executive Officers of the Associated Students of Laurel College. At the meetings, you will have the opportunity to learn about college issues that affect students. At the conclusion of each meeting, the Officers invite students to voice their opinions. Eventually, you might decide to run for an office yourself. Running for office is a three-step process:

1. Pick up petitions at the Student Government office.
2. Obtain 100 signatures from current students.
3. Turn in petitions and start campaigning.

Lastname_Firstname_1B_Student_Activities

Figure 1.23
Project 1B Student Activities

Objective 5 | Change Document and Paragraph Layout

Document layout includes *margins*—the space between the text and the top, bottom, left, and right edges of the paper. Paragraph layout includes line spacing, indents, and tabs. In Word, the information about paragraph formats is stored in the paragraph mark at the end of a paragraph. When you press the [Enter], the new paragraph mark contains the formatting of the previous paragraph, unless you take steps to change it.

Activity 1.13 | Setting Margins

1 **Start** Word. From **Backstage** view, display the **Open** dialog box. From your student files, locate and open the document **w01B_Student_Activities**. On the **Home tab**, in the **Paragraph group**, be sure the **Show/Hide** button [¶] is active—glows orange—so that you can view the formatting marks.

2 From **Backstage** view, display the **Save As** dialog box. Navigate to your **Word Chapter 1** folder, and then **Save** the document as **Lastname_Firstname_1B_Student_Activities**

3 Click the **Page Layout tab**. In the **Page Setup group**, click the **Margins** button, and then take a moment to study the buttons in the Margins gallery.

> The top button displays the most recent custom margin settings, while the other buttons display commonly used margin settings.

4 At the bottom of the **Margins** gallery, click **Custom Margins**.

5 In the **Page Setup** dialog box, press [Tab] as necessary to select the value in the **Left** box, and then, with *1.25"* selected, type **1**

> This action will change the left margin to 1 inch on all pages of the document. You do not need to type the inch (") mark.

6 Press [Tab] to select the margin in the **Right** box, and then type **1** At the bottom of the dialog box, notice that the new margins will apply to the **Whole document**. Compare your screen with Figure 1.24.

Figure 1.24

Margins button —

Left and Right margins changed —

Changes applied to entire document —

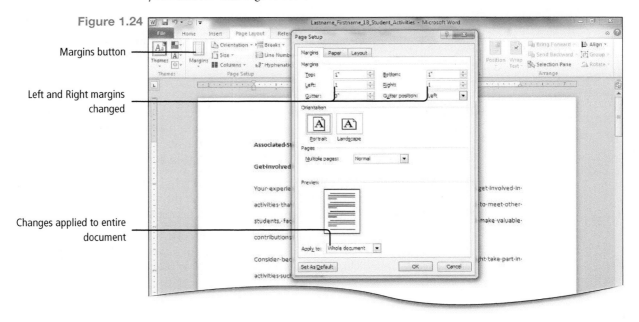

Project 1B: Information Handout | **Word**

Another Way

Click the View tab, and then in the Show group, select the Ruler check box.

7 Click **OK** to apply the new margins and close the dialog box. If the ruler below the Ribbon is not displayed, at the top of the vertical scroll bar, click the View Ruler button 🔲.

8 Scroll to view the bottom of **Page 1** and the top of **Page 2**. Notice that the page edges display, and the page number and total number of pages display on the left side of the status bar.

9 Near the bottom edge of **Page 1**, point anywhere in the margin area, right-click, and then click **Edit Footer** to display the footer area.

10 On the **Design tab**, in the **Insert group**, click the **Quick Parts** button, and then click **Field**. In the **Field** dialog box, under **Field names**, locate and click **FileName**, and then click **OK**.

11 Double-click anywhere in the document to close the footer area, and then **Save** 🔲 your document.

Activity 1.14 | Aligning Text

Alignment refers to the placement of paragraph text relative to the left and right margins. Most paragraph text uses *left alignment*—aligned at the left margin, leaving the right margin uneven. Three other types of paragraph alignment are: *center alignment*—centered between the left and right margins; *right alignment*—aligned at the right margin with an uneven left margin; and *justified alignment*—text aligned evenly at both the left and right margins. See the table in Figure 1.25.

Paragraph Alignment Options		
Alignment	**Button**	**Description and Example**
Align Text Left	🔲	Align Text Left is the default paragraph alignment in Word. Text in the paragraph aligns at the left margin, and the right margin is uneven.
Center	🔲	Center alignment aligns text in the paragraph so that it is centered between the left and right margins.
Align Text Right	🔲	Align Text Right aligns text at the right margin. Using Align Text Right, the left margin, which is normally even, is uneven.
Justify	🔲	The Justify alignment option adds additional space between words so that both the left and right margins are even. Justify is often used when formatting newspaper-style columns.

Figure 1.25

1 Scroll to position the middle of **Page 2** on your screen, look at the left and right margins, and notice that the text is justified—both the right and left margins of multiple-line paragraphs are aligned evenly at the margins. On the **Home tab**, in the **Paragraph group**, notice that the **Justify** button 🔲 is active.

2 In the paragraph that begins *Every spring, students vote*, in the first line, look at the space following the word *Every*, and then compare it with the space following the word *Trustee* in the second line. Notice how some of the spaces between words are larger than others.

> To achieve a justified right margin, Word adjusts the size of spaces between words in this manner, which can result in unattractive spacing in a document that spans the width of a page. Many individuals find such spacing difficult to read.

3 Press Ctrl + A to select all of the text in the document, and then on the **Home tab**, in the **Paragraph group**, click the **Align Text Left** button.

4 Press Ctrl + Home. At the top of the document, in the left margin area, point to the left of the first paragraph—*Associated Students of Laurel College*—until the pointer displays, and then click one time to select the paragraph. On the Mini toolbar, change the **Font Size** to **26**.

> Use this technique to select entire lines of text.

5 Point to the left of the first paragraph—*Associated Students of Laurel College*—to display the pointer again, and then drag down to select the first two paragraphs, which form the title and subtitle of the document.

6 On the Mini toolbar, click the **Center** button to center the title and subtitle between the left and right margins, and then compare your screen with Figure 1.26.

Figure 1.26

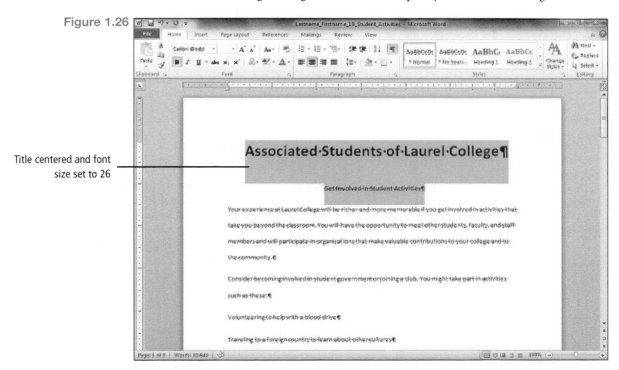

Title centered and font
size set to 26

7 Scroll down to view the bottom of **Page 1**, and then locate the first bold subheading—*Student Government*. Point to the left of the paragraph to display the pointer, and then click one time.

8 With *Student Government* selected, use your mouse wheel or the vertical scroll bar to bring the lower portion of **Page 2** into view. Locate the subheading *Clubs*. Move the pointer to the left of the paragraph to display the pointer, hold down Ctrl, and then click one time.

> Two subheadings are selected; in Windows-based programs, you can hold down Ctrl to select multiple items.

9 On the Mini toolbar, click the **Center** button to center both subheadings, and then click **Save**.

Activity 1.15 | Changing Line Spacing

Line spacing is the distance between lines of text in a paragraph. Three of the most commonly used line spacing options are shown in the table in Figure 1.27.

Line Spacing Options	
Alignment	**Description, Example, and Information**
Single spacing	**This text in this example uses single spacing**. Single spacing was once the most commonly used spacing in business documents. Now, because so many documents are read on a computer screen rather than on paper, single spacing is becoming less popular.
Multiple 1.15 spacing	**This text in this example uses multiple 1.15 spacing**. The default line spacing in Microsoft Word 2010 is 1.15, which is equivalent to single spacing with an extra 1/6 line added between lines to make the text easier to read on a computer screen. Many individuals now prefer this spacing, even on paper, because the lines of text appear less crowded.
Double spacing	**This text in this example uses double spacing**. College research papers and draft documents that need space for notes are commonly double-spaced; there is space for a full line of text between each document line.

Figure 1.27

1 Press Ctrl + Home to move to the beginning of the document. Press Ctrl + A to select all of the text in the document.

2 With all of the text in the document selected, on the **Home tab**, in the **Paragraph group**, click the **Line Spacing** button, and notice that the text in the document is double spaced—**2.0** is checked. Compare your screen with Figure 1.28.

Figure 1.28

Document text double-spaced

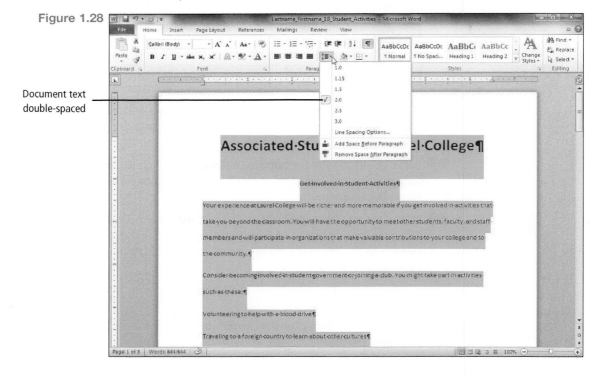

3 On the **Line Spacing** menu, click the *second* setting—**1.15**—and then click anywhere in the document. Compare your screen with Figure 1.29, and then **Save** 🖫 your document.

Double spacing is most commonly used in research papers and rough draft documents. Recall that 1.15 is the default line spacing for new Word documents. Line spacing of 1.15 has slightly more space between the lines than single spacing. On a computer screen, spacing of 1.15 is easier to read than single spacing. Because a large percentage of Word documents are read on a computer screen, 1.15 is the default spacing for a new Word document.

Figure 1.29

Line spacing changed to 1.15

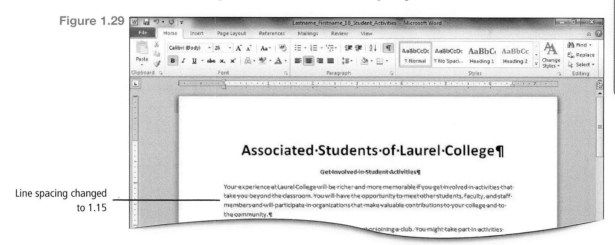

Activity 1.16 | Indenting Text and Adding Space After Paragraphs

Common techniques to distinguish paragraphs include adding space after each paragraph, indenting the first line of each paragraph, or both.

1 Below the title and subtitle of the document, click anywhere in the paragraph that begins *Your experience*.

2 On the **Home tab**, in the **Paragraph group**, click the **Dialog Box Launcher** 🔲.

3 In the **Paragraph** dialog box, on the **Indents and Spacing tab**, under **Indentation**, click the **Special arrow**, and then click **First line** to indent the first line by 0.5″, which is the default indent setting. Compare your screen with Figure 1.30.

Figure 1.30

First line indent applied

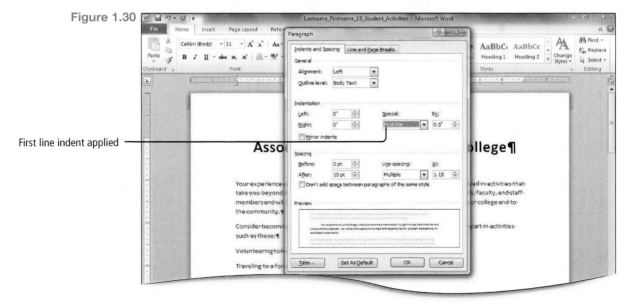

4 Click **OK**, and then click anywhere in the next paragraph, which begins *Consider becoming*. On the ruler under the Ribbon, drag the **First Line Indent** button 🔽 to **0.5 inches on the horizontal ruler**, and then compare your screen with Figure 1.31.

Figure 1.31

First line Indent button

First lines indented

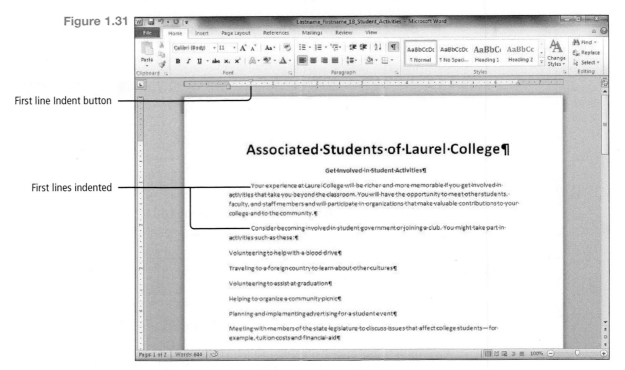

Another Way

On either the Home tab or the Page Layout tab, display the Paragraph dialog box from the Paragraph group, and then under Spacing, click the spin box arrows as necessary.

5 By using either of the techniques you just practiced, or by using the Format Painter, apply a first line indent of **0.5″** in the paragraph that begins *As a registered* to match the indent of the remaining paragraphs in the document.

6 Press Ctrl + A to select all of the text in the document. Click the **Page Layout tab**, and then in the **Paragraph group**, under **Spacing**, click the **After spin box down arrow** one time to change the value to **6 pt**.

To change the value in the box, you can also select the existing number, type a new number, and then press Enter. This document will use 6 pt spacing after paragraphs.

7 Press Ctrl + Home, and then compare your screen with Figure 1.32.

Figure 1.32

Spacing After set to 6 pt

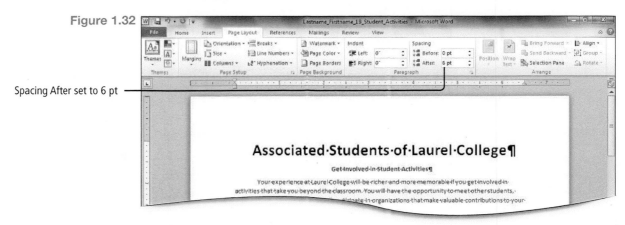

8 Scroll to view the lower portion of **Page 1**. Select the subheading *Student Government*, including the paragraph mark following it, hold down Ctrl, and then select the subheading *Clubs*.

9 With both subheadings selected, in the **Paragraph group**, under **Spacing**, click the **Before up spin box arrow** two times to set the **Spacing Before** to **12 pt**. Compare your screen with Figure 1.33, and then **Save** 💾 your document.

> This action increases the amount of space above each of the two subheadings, which will make them easy to distinguish in the document. The formatting is applied only to the two selected paragraphs.

Figure 1.33
Spacing before set to 12 pt.

12-point spacing before paragraphs

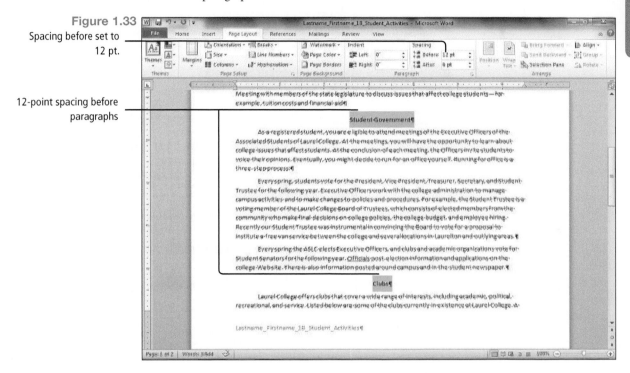

Objective 6 | Create and Modify Lists

To display a list of information, you can choose a ***bulleted list***, which uses ***bullets***— text symbols such as small circles or check marks—to introduce each item in a list. You can also choose a ***numbered list***, which uses consecutive numbers or letters to introduce each item in a list.

Use a bulleted list if the items in the list can be introduced in any order; use a numbered list for items that have definite steps, a sequence of actions, or are in chronological order.

Activity 1.17 | Creating a Bulleted List

1 In the upper portion of **Page 1**, locate the paragraph that begins *Volunteering to help*, and then point to this paragraph from the left margin area to display the 🔏 pointer. Drag down to select this paragraph and the next five paragraphs.

2 On the **Home tab**, in the **Paragraph group**, click the **Bullets** button ⊟˅ to change the selected text to a bulleted list.

> The spacing between each of the bulleted points changes to the spacing between lines in a paragraph—in this instance, 1.15 line spacing. The spacing after the last item in the list is the same as the spacing after each paragraph—in this instance, 6 pt. Each bulleted item is automatically indented.

3 On the ruler, point to the **First Line Indent** button ▽ and read the ScreenTip, and then point to the **Hanging Indent** button ⌂. Compare your screen with Figure 1.34.

> By default, Word formats bulleted items with a first line indent of 0.25″ and adds a Hanging Indent at 0.5″. The hanging indent maintains the alignment of text when a bulleted item is more than one line, for example, the last bulleted item in this list.

Figure 1.34

Hanging Indent button
on ruler

Bulleted list

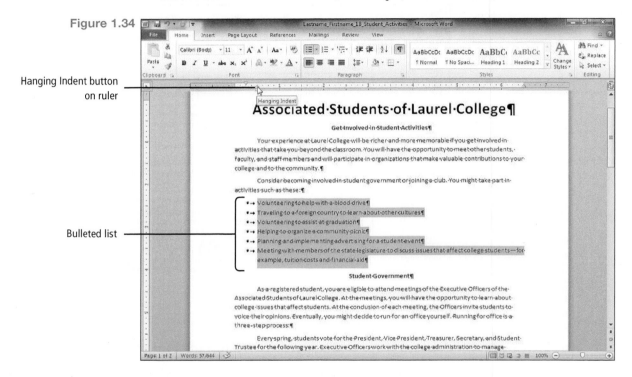

4 Scroll down to view **Page 2**. By using the ⍼ pointer from the left margin area, select all of the paragraphs that indicate the club names and meeting dates, beginning with *Chess Club* and ending with *Theater Club*.

5 In the **Paragraph group**, click the **Bullets** button ⊟˅, and then **Save** 🖫 your document.

Activity 1.18 | Creating a Numbered List

1 Scroll to view **Page 1**, and then under the subheading *Student Government*, in the paragraph that begins *As a registered student*, click to position the insertion point at the *end* of the paragraph following the colon. Press Enter to create a blank paragraph.

2 Notice that the paragraph is indented, because the First Line Indent from the previous paragraph carried over to the new paragraph.

3 To change the indent formatting for this paragraph, on the ruler, drag the **First Line Indent** button ▽ to the left so that it is positioned directly above the lower button. Compare your screen with Figure 1.35.

Figure 1.35

First Line Indent button

Paragraph with no first line indent

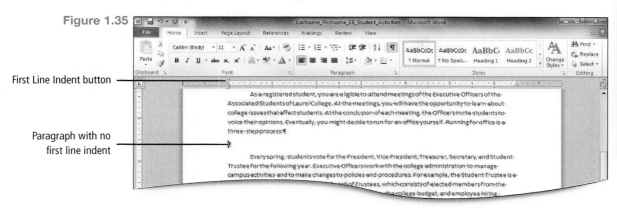

4 Being sure to include the period, type **1.** and press [Spacebar].

Word determines that this paragraph is the first item in a numbered list and formats the new paragraph accordingly, indenting the list in the same manner as the bulleted list. The space after the number changes to a tab, and the AutoCorrect Options button displays to the left of the list item. The tab is indicated by a right arrow formatting mark.

> **Alert! | Activating Automatic Numbered Lists**
>
> If a numbered list does not begin automatically, display Backstage view, and then click the Options tab. On the left side of the Word Options dialog box, click Proofing. Under AutoCorrect options, click the AutoCorrect Options button. In the AutoCorrect dialog box, click the AutoFormat As You Type tab. Under *Apply as you type*, select the *Automatic numbered lists* check box, and then click OK two times to close both dialog boxes.

5 Click the **AutoCorrect Options** button 🕭▾, and then compare your screen with Figure 1.36.

From the displayed list, you can remove the automatic formatting here, or stop using the automatic numbered lists option in this document. You also have the option to open the AutoCorrect dialog box to *Control AutoFormat Options.*

Figure 1.36

AutoCorrect Options button

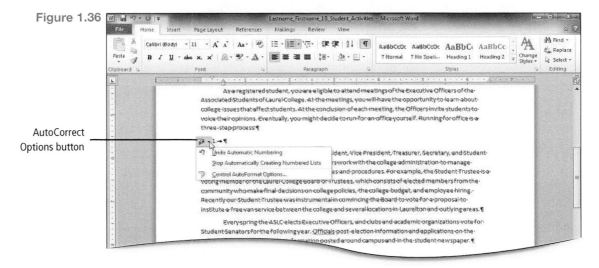

Project 1B: Information Handout | **Word**

6 Click the **AutoCorrect Options** button again to close the menu without selecting any of the commands. Type **Pick up petitions at the Student Government office.** and press Enter. Notice that the second number and a tab are added to the next line.

7 Type **Obtain 100 signatures from current students.** and press Enter. Type **Turn in petitions and start campaigning.** and press Enter. Compare your screen with Figure 1.37.

Figure 1.37

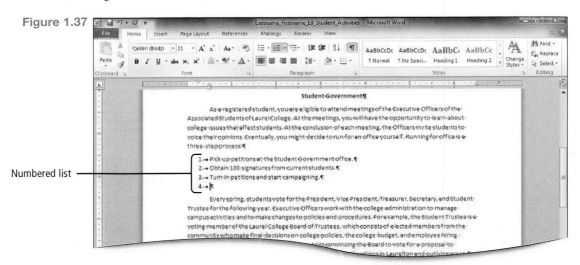

Numbered list

8 Press ←Bksp to turn off the list numbering. Then, press ←Bksp three more times to remove the blank paragraph. Compare your screen with Figure 1.38.

Figure 1.38

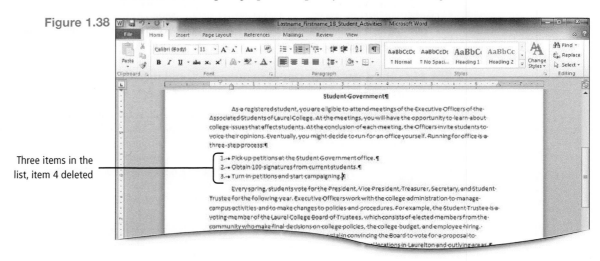

Three items in the
list, item 4 deleted

9 **Save** 💾 your document.

More Knowledge | To End a List

To turn a list off, you can press ←Bksp, click the Numbering or Bullets button, or press Enter a second time. Both list buttons—Numbering and Bullets—act as **toggle buttons**; that is, clicking the button one time turns the feature on, and clicking the button again turns the feature off.

Activity 1.19 | Customizing Bullets

1 Press **Ctrl** + **End** to move to the end of the document, and then scroll up as necessary to display the bulleted list containing the list of clubs.

2 Point to the left of the first list item to display the ▨ pointer, and then drag down to select all the clubs in the list—the bullet symbols are not highlighted.

3 Point to the selected list and right-click. From the shortcut menu, point to **Bullets**, and then compare your screen with Figure 1.39.

Figure 1.39

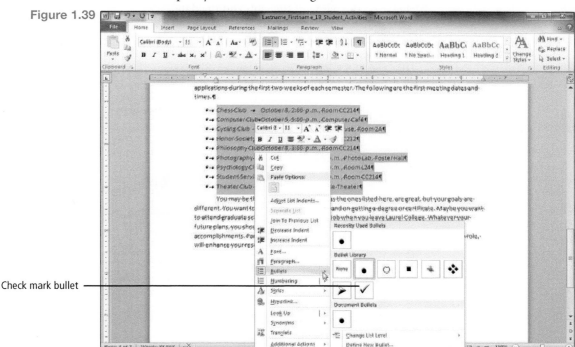

Check mark bullet

4 Under **Bullet Library**, click the **check mark** symbol. If the check mark is not available, choose another bullet symbol.

Another Way

On the Home tab, in the Clipboard group, click the Format Painter button.

5 With the bulleted list still selected, right-click over the list, and then on the Mini toolbar, click the **Format Painter** button ▨.

6 Use the vertical scroll bar or your mouse wheel to scroll to view **Page 1**. Move the pointer to the left of the first item in the bulleted list to display the ▨ pointer, and then drag down to select all of the items in the list and to apply the format of the second bulleted list to this list. Compare your screen with Figure 1.40, and then **Save** ▨ your document.

Figure 1.40

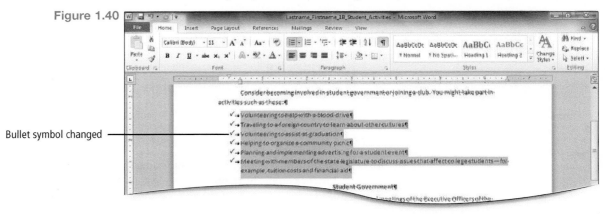

Bullet symbol changed

Project 1B: Information Handout | **Word**

Objective 7 | Set and Modify Tab Stops

Tab stops mark specific locations on a line of text. Use tab stops to indent and align text, and use the Tab key to move to tab stops.

Activity 1.20 | Setting Tab Stops

1 Scroll to view the middle of **Page 2**, and then by using the ▨ pointer at the left of the first item, select all of the items in the bulleted list. Notice that there is a tab mark between the name of the club and the date.

> The arrow that indicates a tab is a nonprinting formatting mark.

2 To the left of the horizontal ruler, point to the **Tab Alignment** button ⬚ to display the *Left Tab* ScreenTip, and then compare your screen with Figure 1.41.

Figure 1.41

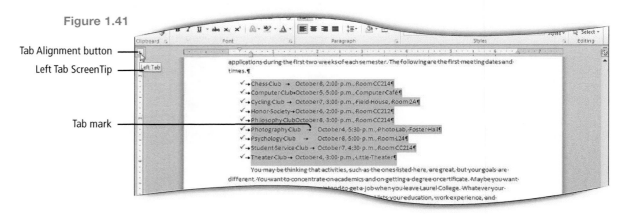

Tab Alignment button

Left Tab ScreenTip

Tab mark

3 Click the **Tab Alignment** button ⬚ several times to view the tab alignment options shown in the table in Figure 1.42.

Tab Alignment Options

Type	Tab Alignment Button Displays This Marker	Description
Left	⬚	Text is left aligned at the tab stop and extends to the right.
Center	⬚	Text is centered around the tab stop.
Right	⬚	Text is right aligned at the tab stop and extends to the left.
Decimal	⬚	The decimal point aligns at the tab stop.
Bar	⬚	A vertical bar displays at the tab stop.
First Line Indent	▽	Text in the first line of a paragraph indents.
Hanging Indent	△	Text in all lines except the first line in the paragraph indents.
Left Indent	⬚	Moves both the First Line Indent and Hanging Indent buttons.

Figure 1.42

4 Display the **Left Tab** button ⬚. Along the lower edge of the horizontal ruler, point to and then click at **3 inches on the horizontal ruler**. Notice that all of the dates left align at the new tab stop location, and the right edge of the column is uneven.

Word | Creating Documents with Microsoft Word 2010

5 Compare your screen with Figure 1.43, and then **Save** 🖫 your document.

Figure 1.43

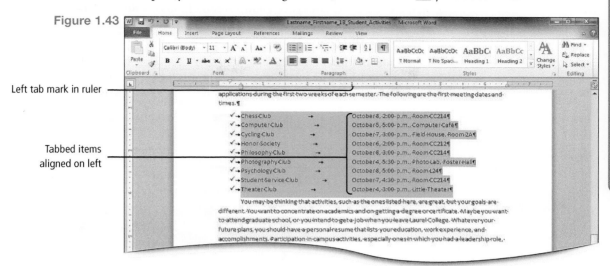

Left tab mark in ruler

Tabbed items aligned on left

Activity 1.21 | Modifying Tab Stops

Tab stops are a form of paragraph formatting, and thus, the information about tab stops is stored in the paragraph mark in the paragraphs to which they were applied.

1 With the bulleted list still selected, on the ruler, point to the new tab marker, and then when the *Left Tab* ScreenTip displays, drag the tab marker to **3.5 inches on the horizontal ruler**.

In all of the selected lines, the text at the tab stop left aligns at 3.5 inches.

> **Another Way**
>
> On the Home tab, in the Paragraph group, click the Dialog Box Launcher. At the bottom of the Paragraph dialog box, click the Tabs button.

2 On the ruler, point to the tab marker to display the ScreenTip, and then double-click to display the **Tabs** dialog box.

3 In the **Tabs** dialog box, under **Tab stop position**, if necessary select *3.5″* and then type **6**

4 Under **Alignment**, click the **Right** option button. Under **Leader**, click the **2** option button. Near the bottom of the **Tabs** dialog box, click **Set**.

Because the Right tab will be used to align the items in the list, the tab stop at 3.5″ is no longer necessary.

5 In the **Tabs** dialog box, in the **Tab stop position** box, click **3.5″** to select this tab stop, and then in the lower portion of the **Tabs** dialog box, click the **Clear** button to delete this tab stop, which is no longer necessary. Compare your screen with Figure 1.44.

Figure 1.44

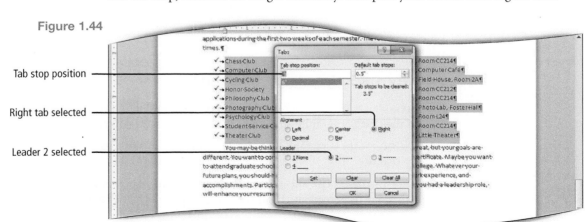

Tab stop position

Right tab selected

Leader 2 selected

Project 1B: Information Handout | **Word**

6 Click **OK**. On the ruler, notice that the left tab marker at *3.5″* no longer displays, a right tab marker displays at *6″*, and a series of dots—a *dot leader*—displays between the columns of the list. Notice also that the right edge of the column is even. Compare your screen with Figure 1.45.

> A *leader character* creates a solid, dotted, or dashed line that fills the space to the left of a tab character and draws the reader's eyes across the page from one item to the next. When the character used for the leader is a dot, it is commonly referred to as a dot leader.

Figure 1.45

Right tab marker

Tabbed items aligned right

Dot leader

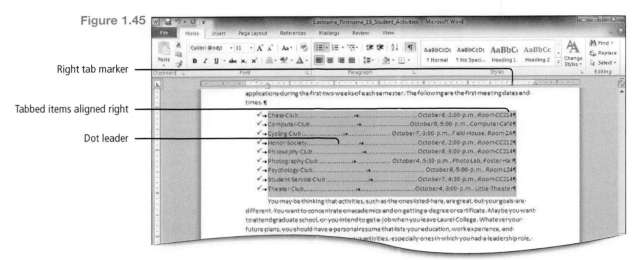

7 In the bulleted list that uses dot leaders, locate the *Honor Society* item, and then click to position the insertion point at the end of that line. Press [Enter] to create a new blank bullet item.

8 Type **Math Club** and press [Tab]. Notice that a dot leader fills the space to the tab marker location.

9 Type **October 6, 4:00 p.m., Math Tutoring Lab, L35** and notice that the text moves to the left to maintain the right alignment of the tab stop.

10 **Save** 💾 your document.

Objective 8 | Insert a SmartArt Graphic

SmartArt graphics are designer-quality visual representations of information, and Word provides many different layouts from which you can choose. A SmartArt graphic can communicate your messages or ideas more effectively than plain text and adds visual interest to a document or Web page.

Activity 1.22 | Inserting a SmartArt Graphic

1 Press [Ctrl] + [Home] to move to the top of the document. Press [End] to move to the end of the first paragraph—the title—and then press [Enter] to create a blank paragraph.

> Because the paragraph above is 26 pt font size, the new paragraph mark displays in that size.

2 Click the **Insert tab**, and then in the **Illustrations group**, point to the **SmartArt** button to display its ScreenTip. Read the ScreenTip, and then click the button.

3 In the center portion of the **Choose a SmartArt Graphic** dialog box, scroll down and examine the numerous types of SmartArt graphics available.

4 On the left, click **Hierarchy**, and then in the first row, click the first graphic—**Organization Chart**.

At the right of the dialog box, a preview and description of the graphic displays.

5 Compare your screen with Figure 1.46.

Figure 1.46

SmartArt button —

Preview of selected SmartArt —

Hierarchy category —

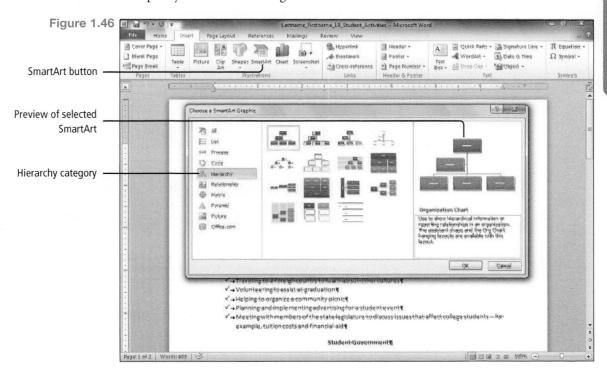

6 Click **OK**. If the pane indicating *Type your text here* does not display on the left side of the graphic, on the Design tab, in the Create Graphic group, click the Text Pane button. **Save** your document.

The SmartArt graphic displays at the insertion point location and consists of two parts—the graphic itself, and the Text Pane. On the Ribbon, the SmartArt Tools add the Design tab and the Format tab. You can type directly into the graphics, or type in the Text Pane. By typing in the Text Pane, you might find it easier to organize your layout.

Activity 1.23 | Modifying a SmartArt Graphic

1 In the SmartArt graphic, in the second row, click the border of the *[Text]* box to display a *solid* border and sizing handles, and then press Del. Repeat this procedure in the bottom row to delete the middle *[Text]* box.

> **Another Way**
>
> Close the Text Pane and type the text directly in the SmartArt boxes.

2 In the **Text Pane**, click in the top bulleted point, and then type **Student Activities** Notice that the first bulleted point aligns further to the left than the other points.

The *top-level points* are the main points in a SmartArt graphic. *Subpoints* are indented second-level bullet points.

3 Press ⬇. Type **Government** and then press ⬇ again. Type **Clubs** and then compare your screen with Figure 1.47.

Figure 1.47

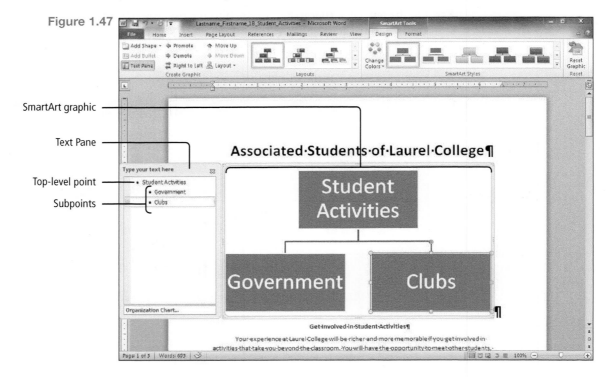

SmartArt graphic

Text Pane

Top-level point

Subpoints

4 In the upper right corner of the **Text Pane**, click the **Close** button.

5 Click the border of the SmartArt graphic—a pale border surrounds it. Click the **Format tab**, and then in the **Size group**, if necessary click the **Size** button to display the **Shape Height** and **Shape Width** boxes.

6 Set the **Height** to **2.5″** and the **Width** to **4.2″**, and then compare your screen with Figure 1.48.

Figure 1.48

Size button

Height and Width set

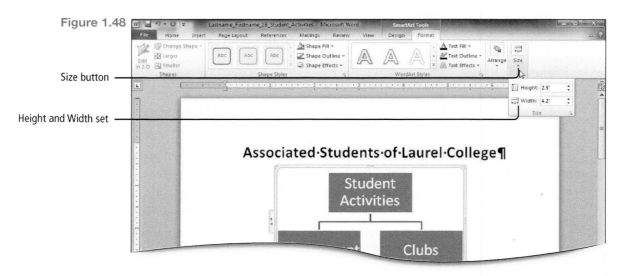

7 With the SmartArt graphic still selected, click the **Design tab**, and then in the **SmartArt Styles group**, click the **Change Colors** button. Under **Colorful**, click the second style—**Colorful Range - Accent Colors 2 to 3**.

8 On the **Design tab**, in the **SmartArt Styles group**, click the **More** button ⏷. Under **3-D**, click the first style—**Polished**. Compare your screen with Figure 1.49.

Figure 1.49

Polished style selected ⎯⎯⎯⎯⎯⎯

SmartArt color and style changed ⎯⎯⎯⎯⎯⎯

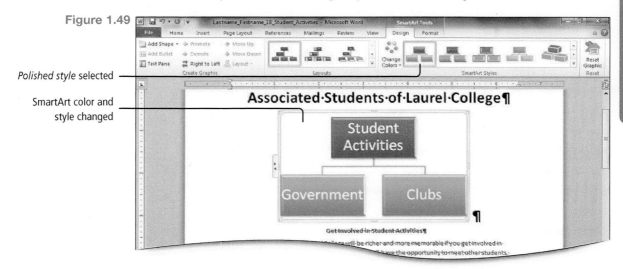

9 Click outside of the graphic to deselect it. Display **Backstage** view. On the right, under the screen thumbnail, click **Properties**, and then click **Show Document Panel**. In the **Author** box, delete any text and then type your firstname and lastname. In the **Subject** box, type your course name and section number, and in the **Keywords** box type **Student Activities, Associated Students Close** ✖ the Document Panel and **Save** 🖫 your document.

10 Display **Backstage** view, and then click **Print** to display **Print Preview**. At the bottom of the preview, click the **Next Page** ▶ and **Previous Page** ◀ buttons to move between pages. If necessary, return to the document and make any necessary changes.

11 As directed by your instructor, print your document or submit it electronically. **Close** ✖ Word.

> More Knowledge | Changing the Bullet Level in a SmartArt Graphic
>
> To increase or decrease the level of an item, on the Design tab, in the Create Graphic group, click either the Promote or the Demote button.

End **You have completed Project 1B** ⎯⎯⎯⎯⎯⎯⎯⎯⎯⎯

Content-Based Assessments

Summary

In this chapter, you created and formatted documents using Microsoft Word 2010. You inserted and formatted graphics, created and formatted bulleted and numbered lists, and created and formatted text boxes. You also created lists using tab stops with dot leaders, and created and modified a SmartArt graphic.

Key Terms

Alignment	Graphics	Right tab stop
Anchor	Inline object	Shapes
Artistic effects	Justified alignment	SmartArt
Bar tab stop	Leader characters	Spin box
Bulleted list	Left alignment	Subpoints
Bullets	Left tab stop	Tab stop
Center alignment	Line spacing	Text box
Center tab stop	Margins	Text effects
Decimal tab stop	Nonprinting	Text wrapping
Dot leader	characters1	Toggle button
Drawing objects	Nudge	Top-level points
Field	Numbered list	Wordwrap
Floating object	Picture styles	
Formatting marks	Right alignment	

Matching

Match each term in the second column with its correct definition in the first column by writing the letter of the term on the blank line in front of the correct definition.

_____ 1. Formats that make pictures look more like sketches or paintings.

_____ 2. A small box with an upward- and downward-pointing arrow that enables you to move rapidly through a set of values by clicking.

_____ 3. Small circles in the corners of a selected graphic with which you can resize the graphic proportionally.

_____ 4. The manner in which text displays around an object.

_____ 5. An object or graphic that can be moved independently of the surrounding text.

_____ 6. The process of using the arrow keys to move an object in small precise increments.

_____ 7. An object or graphic inserted in a document that acts like a character in a sentence.

_____ 8. Frames, shapes, shadows, borders, and other special effects that can be added to an image to create an overall visual style for the image.

_____ 9. Predefined drawing objects, such as stars, banners, arrows, and callouts, included with Microsoft Office, and that can be inserted into documents.

A Artistic effects

B Bullets

C Floating object

D Inline object

E Justified alignment

F Left alignment

G Line spacing

H Nudge

I Picture styles

J Shapes

K Sizing handles

L SmartArt

M Spin box

N Tab stop

O Text wrapping

_____ 10. A commonly used alignment of text in which text is aligned at the left margin, leaving the right margin uneven.

_____ 11. An alignment of text in which the text is evenly aligned on both the left and right margins.

_____ 12. The distance between lines of text in a paragraph.

_____ 13. Text symbols such as small circles or check marks that introduce items in a list.

_____ 14. A mark on the ruler that indicates the location where the insertion point will be placed when you press the Tab key.

_____ 15. A designer-quality graphic used to create a visual representation of information.

Multiple Choice

Circle the correct answer.

1. Characters that display on the screen to show the location of paragraphs, tabs, and spaces, but that do not print, are called:
   A. text effects
   B. bullets
   C. formatting marks

2. The placement of paragraph text relative to the left and right margins is referred to as:
   A. alignment
   B. spacing
   C. indents

3. The symbol that indicates to which paragraph an image is attached is:
   A. a small arrow
   B. an anchor
   C. a paragraph mark

4. A movable, resizable container for text or graphics is a:
   A. text box
   B. dialog box
   C. SmartArt graphic

5. A banner is an example of a predefined:
   A. paragraph
   B. format
   C. shape

6. A placeholder that displays preset content, such as the current date, the file name, a page number, or other stored information is:
   A. a leader
   B. a field
   C. a tab

7. The space between the text and the top, bottom, left, and right edges of the paper are referred to as:
   A. alignment
   B. margins
   C. spacing

8. A group of items in which items are displayed in order to indicate definite steps, a sequence of actions, or chronological order is a:
   A. numbered list
   B. bulleted list
   C. outline list

9. A series of dots following a tab that serve to guide the reader's eye is a:
   A. leader
   B. field
   C. shape

10. Tab stops are a form of:
    A. line formatting
    B. document formatting
    C. paragraph formatting

Apply 1A skills from these Objectives:

- 1 Create a New Document and Insert Text
- 2 Insert and Format Graphics
- 3 Insert and Modify Text Boxes and Shapes
- 4 Preview and Print a Document

Skills Review | Project 1C Welcome Week

In the following Skills Review, you will create and edit a flyer for the Laurel College New Student Welcome Week. Your completed document will look similar to Figure 1.50.

Project Files

For Project 1C, you will need the following files:

New blank Word document
w01C_Welcome_Text
w01C_Welcome_Picture

You will save your document as:

Lastname_Firstname_1C_Welcome_Week

Project Results

Figure 1.50

(Project 1C Welcome Week continues on the next page)

1 **Start** Word and display a new blank document. On the **Home tab**, in the **Paragraph group**, be sure the **Show/Hide ¶** button is active so that you can view formatting marks. In the **Quick Access Toolbar**, click the **Save** button, navigate to your **Word Chapter 1** folder, and then **Save** the document as Lastname_Firstname_1C_Welcome_Week

a. Type **Welcome Week** and then press Enter two times.

b. Type **The Laurel College Student Government Association is sponsoring a week of special activities for new students. This is your opportunity to meet the people and learn about the programs that will help you succeed at Laurel College.**

c. Press Enter one time. Click the **Insert tab**. In the **Text group**, click the **Object button arrow**, and then click **Text from File**. Navigate to your student files, select the file **w01C_Welcome_Text**, and then at the bottom of the **Insert File** dialog box, click **Insert**. **Save** your document.

2 At the top of the document, in the left margin area, point to the left of the first paragraph—*Welcome Week*—until the pointer displays, and then click one time to select the paragraph. On the **Home tab**, in the **Font group**, click the **Text Effects** button. In the displayed **Text Effects** gallery, in the first row, click the fourth effect—**Fill - White, Outline - Accent 1**.

a. With the text still selected, in the **Font group**, click the **Font Size button arrow**, and then click **72**. In the **Paragraph group**, click the **Center** button.

b. With the text still selected, in the **Font group**, click the **Text Effects** button. Point to **Shadow**, and then under **Outer**, in the first row click the third style—**Offset Diagonal Bottom Left**. In the **Font group**, click the **Font Color button arrow**. Under **Theme Colors**, in the fourth column, click the first color—**Dark Blue, Text 2**.

c. In the paragraph that begins *The Laurel College*, click to position the insertion point at the beginning of the paragraph. On the **Insert tab**, in the **Illustrations group**, click the **Picture** button. From your student data files, **Insert** the file **w01C_Welcome_Picture**. On the **Format tab**, in the **Size group**, click the **Shape Height down spin arrow** as necessary to change the height of the picture to **2"**.

d. With the picture still selected, on the **Format tab**, in the **Arrange group**, click the **Wrap Text** button. From the **Wrap Text** gallery, click **Square**.

e. Hold down Shift and point anywhere in the picture to display the pointer. Drag the picture to align the right edge of the picture just to the left of the right margin.

f. On the **Format tab**, in the **Picture Styles group**, click the **Picture Effects** button. Point to **Glow**, and then under **Glow Variations**, in the third row, click the first style—**Blue, 11 pt glow, Accent color 1**. Nudge as necessary to match the picture position shown in Figure 1.50.

g. Click anywhere to deselect the picture. Click the **Page Layout tab**, and then in the **Page Background group**, click the **Page Borders** button. In the **Borders and Shading** dialog box, under **Setting**, click **Box**. Under **Style**, scroll down the list. About two-thirds down the list, click the style with a thin top and bottom line and a slightly thicker middle line.

h. Click the **Color arrow**, and then under **Theme Colors**, in the fourth column, click the first color—**Dark Blue, Text 2**. Click **OK**, and then **Save** your document.

3 Press Ctrl + End to move to the bottom of the document. On the **Insert tab**, in the **Text group**, click the **Text Box** button. At the bottom of the **Text Box** gallery, click **Draw Text Box**.

a. At the bottom of the document, position the pointer in an open area near the left margin, and then drag down and to the right to create a text box approximately **2.5 inches** high and **5.5 inches** wide; you need not be precise.

b. With the insertion point positioned in the text box, type the following:

Welcome Week Highlights

Tuesday: Campus tour and meeting with administrators

Wednesday: Open house in all academic departments

Thursday: Club meetings to recruit members

Friday: Student Government-hosted barbecue

(Project 1C Welcome Week continues on the next page)

c. In the text box, select all of the text. On the Mini toolbar, click the **Font Size button arrow**, and then click **14**. Click the **Bold** button, and then click the **Center** button.

d. On the **Format tab**, in the **Size group**, if necessary click the **Size** button. Click the **Shape Height spin arrows** as necessary to change the height of the text box to **2.5"**. Click the **Shape Width button up spin arrow** as necessary to widen the text box to **5.5"**.

e. In the **Shape Styles group**, click the **Shape Effects** button. Point to **Shadow**, and then under **Outer**, in the second row, click the second style—**Offset Center**. In the **Shape Styles group**, click the **Shape Outline button arrow**. Under **Theme Colors**, in the fourth column, click the first color—**Dark Blue, Text 2**.

f. If necessary, click anywhere inside the text box. Point to the text box border to display the [pointer icon] pointer. Drag the text box to align the left edge at approximately **0.5 inches on the horizontal ruler** and to align the top edge at approximately **5.5 inches on the vertical ruler**. You may have to click outside the text box several times to see the exact location on the rulers.

g. On the **Insert tab**, in the **Illustrations group**, click the **Shapes** button. Under **Basic Shapes**, in the first row, click the seventh shape—**Diamond**.

h. Position the [+] pointer slightly under the text box and at approximately **2 inches on the horizontal ruler**. Drag down approximately **1 inch** and to the right approximately **2 inches**. On the **Format tab**, in the **Size group**, adjust the **Shape Height** to **0.9"** and the **Shape Width** to **2"**.

i. Right-click the new shape, and then click **Add Text**. Type **Enjoy!** and then select the text you typed. On the Mini toolbar, click the **Font Size button arrow**,

and then click **20**. Click the **Bold** button, and then if necessary, click the **Center** button.

j. On the **Format tab**, in the **Shape Styles group**, click the **Shape Fill button arrow**, and then under **Theme Colors**, in the fourth column, click the first color—**Dark Blue, Text 2**.

k. Point to the shape border until the [pointer icon] pointer displays, and then position the shape with its widest points aligned with the lower edge of the text box and approximately centered. As necessary, move the shape in small increments by pressing the arrow keys on your keyboard. Refer to Figure 1.50 for approximate placement. **Save** your document.

4 Click the **Insert tab**, and then, in the **Header & Footer group**, click the **Footer** button. At the bottom of the **Footer** gallery, click **Edit Footer**.

a. On the **Design tab**, in the **Insert group**, click the **Quick Parts** button, and then click **Field**. In the **Field names** list, scroll as necessary to locate and click **FileName**. Click **OK**, and then double-click anywhere in the document.

b. Press [Ctrl] + [Home] to move the insertion point to the beginning of the document. Display **Backstage** view. On the right, under the screen thumbnail, click **Properties**, and then click **Show Document Panel**. In the **Author** box, delete any text and then type your firstname and lastname. In the **Subject** box, type your course name and section number, and in the **Keywords** box type **Welcome Week**

c. **Close** the Document Panel. In **Backstage** view, click the **Print tab** to display the **Print Preview**. If necessary, return to the document to make any corrections or adjustments.

d. **Save** your document, print or submit electronically as directed by your instructor, and then **Close** Word.

End You have completed Project 1C ───────────────

Apply 1B skills from these Objectives:

- 5 Change Document and Paragraph Layout
- 6 Create and Modify Lists
- 7 Set and Modify Tab Stops
- 8 Insert a SmartArt Graphic

Skills Review | Project 1D Constitution

In the following Skills Review, you will edit the constitution of the Associated Students of Laurel College. Your completed document will look similar to Figure 1.51.

Project Files

For Project 1D, you will need the following file:

w01D_Constitution

You will save your document as:

Lastname_Firstname_1D_Constitution

Project Results

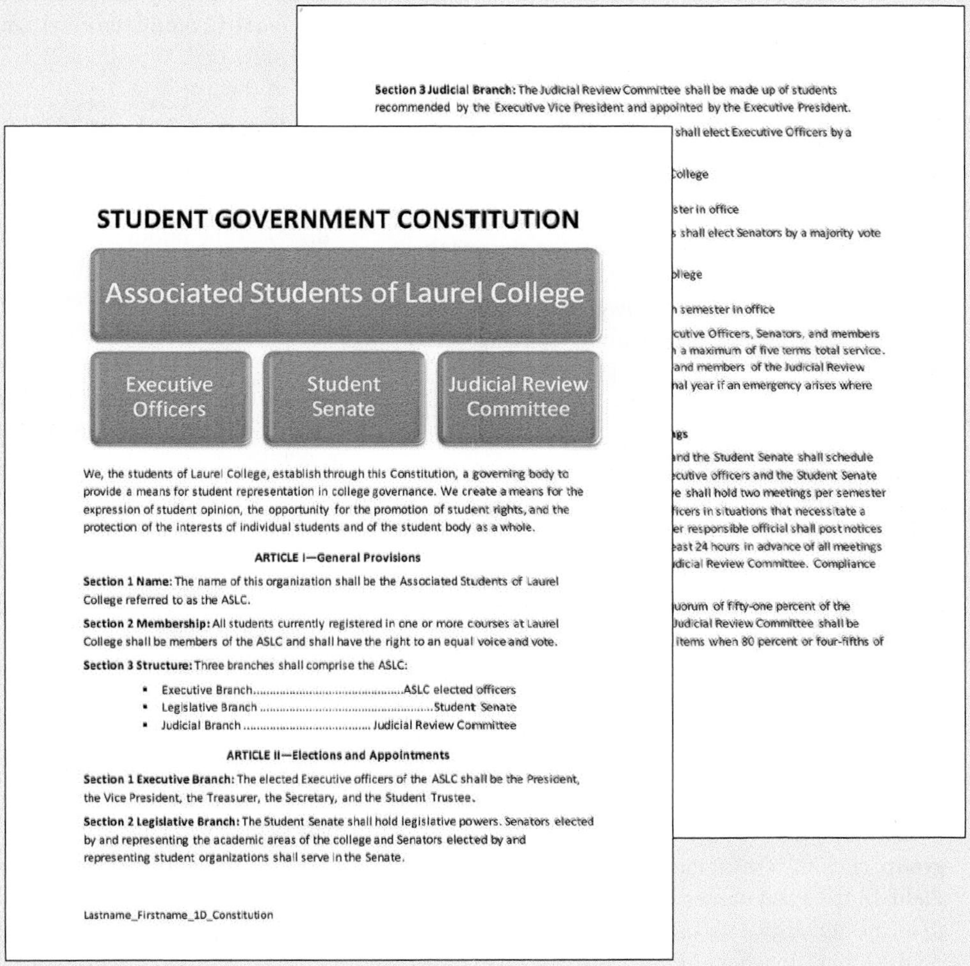

Section 3 Judicial Branch: The Judicial Review Committee shall be made up of students recommended by the Executive Vice President and appointed by the Executive President.

STUDENT GOVERNMENT CONSTITUTION

We, the students of Laurel College, establish through this Constitution, a governing body to provide a means for student representation in college governance. We create a means for the expression of student opinion, the opportunity for the promotion of student rights, and the protection of the interests of individual students and of the student body as a whole.

ARTICLE I—General Provisions

Section 1 Name: The name of this organization shall be the Associated Students of Laurel College referred to as the ASLC.

Section 2 Membership: All students currently registered in one or more courses at Laurel College shall be members of the ASLC and shall have the right to an equal voice and vote.

Section 3 Structure: Three branches shall comprise the ASLC:

- Executive Branch..ASLC elected officers
- Legislative Branch...Student Senate
- Judicial Branch...................................Judicial Review Committee

ARTICLE II—Elections and Appointments

Section 1 Executive Branch: The elected Executive officers of the ASLC shall be the President, the Vice President, the Treasurer, the Secretary, and the Student Trustee.

Section 2 Legislative Branch: The Student Senate shall hold legislative powers. Senators elected by and representing the academic areas of the college and Senators elected by and representing student organizations shall serve in the Senate.

Lastname_Firstname_1D_Constitution

Figure 1.51

(Project 1D Constitution continues on the next page)

Skills Review | Project **1D** Constitution (continued)

1 **Start** Word. From your student files, locate and open the document **w01D_Constitution**. Display **Backstage** view, click **Save As**, and then navigate to your **Word Chapter 1** folder. **Save** the document as **Lastname_Firstname_1D_Constitution**

a. On the **Home tab**, in the **Paragraph group**, be sure the **Show/Hide** button is active so you can view formatting marks. Click the **Page Layout tab**. In the **Page Setup group**, click the **Margins** button, and then at the bottom of the **Margins** gallery, at the bottom of the list, click **Custom Margins**. In the **Page Setup** dialog box, in the **Top** box, type 1 Press (Tab) as necessary to select the values in the **Bottom**, **Left**, and **Right** boxes and change all margins to **1**. Click **OK**.

b. Press (Ctrl) + (A) to select all of the text in the document. On the **Home tab**, in the **Paragraph group**, click the **Align Text Left** button to change the alignment from justified to left aligned.

c. With all of the text still selected, on the **Home tab**, in the **Paragraph group**, click the **Line Spacing** button, and then click **1.15**. Click the **Page Layout tab**, and then in the **Paragraph group**, under **Spacing**, set **After** to **6 pt** spacing after each paragraph.

d. At the top of the document, click anywhere in the title, right-click, and then on the Mini toolbar, click **Center**. Near the top of **Page 1**, locate and select the paragraph that begins *ARTICLE 1*. Hold down (Ctrl), and then use the vertical scroll bar to scroll through the document, and then select the other two paragraphs that begin *ARTICLE*. On the Mini toolbar, click **Center**.

e. With the three subheadings that begin *ARTICLE* still selected, on the **Page Layout tab**, in the **Paragraph group**, under **Spacing**, set **Before** to **12 pt**.

f. Scroll to view the bottom of **Page 1**, point anywhere in the bottom margin area, right-click, and then click **Edit Footer**. On the **Design tab**, in the **Insert group**, click the **Quick Parts** button, and then click **Field**. In the **Field names** list, scroll as necessary to locate and click **FileName**. Click **OK**, and then double-click anywhere in the document to exit the footer area.

2 Near the middle of **Page 1**, *above* the *ARTICLE II* subheading, locate the paragraph that begins *Executive Branch*, and then move the pointer into the left margin

area to display the [⊿] pointer. Drag down to select this paragraph and the next two paragraphs. On the **Home tab**, in the **Paragraph group**, click the **Bullets** button.

a. Scroll to view the bottom of **Page 1**, and then locate the paragraph that begins *Completion of at least*. Select that paragraph and the next two paragraphs. On the **Home tab**, in the **Paragraph group**, click the **Numbering** button.

b. Locate the paragraph that begins *Section 4 Elections*. Click to position the insertion point at the *end* of that paragraph after the colon, and then press (Enter).

c. Type **1.** and press (Spacebar). Type **Completion of at least 12 credit hours at Laurel College** and then press (Enter). Type the following text for items 2 and 3 in the list:

Minimum GPA of 2.75

Enrollment in at least six credit hours each semester in office

d. Near the middle of **Page 1**, select the three items in the bulleted list, right-click the list, and then point to **Bullets**. Under **Bullet Library**, click the **black square** symbol. If the black square is not available, choose another bullet symbol. **Save** your document.

3 Be sure the bulleted list is still selected. Point to the left tab marker at **2″ on the horizontal ruler**. When the *Left Tab* ScreenTip displays, double-click to open the **Tabs** dialog box.

a. Under **Tab stop position**, with *2″* selected, at the bottom of the dialog box, click **Clear** to delete this tab stop. Then, type **5.5** in the **Tab stop position** box.

b. Under **Alignment**, click the **Right** option button. Under **Leader**, click the **2** option button. At the bottom of the **Tabs** dialog box, click the **Set** button, and then click **OK**.

4 Press (Ctrl) + (Home) to move to the top of the document. Click at the end of the title, and then press (Enter) to insert a blank paragraph. Click the **Insert tab**, and then in the **Illustrations group**, click the **SmartArt** button.

a. In the **Choose a SmartArt Graphic** dialog box, on the left, click **Hierarchy**, and in the second row, click the fourth style—**Table Hierarchy**. At the bottom of the **Choose a SmartArt Graphic** dialog box, click **OK**. If necessary, on the Design tab, in the Create Graphic group, activate the Text Pane button.

(Project 1D Constitution continues on the next page)

b. In the SmartArt graphic, in the second row, click the border of the first *[Text]* box, and then press Del. Press Del again to delete a second *[Text]* box. In the **Text Pane**, under **Type your text here** box, click in the last bulleted point. On the **Design tab**, in the **Create Graphic group**, click the **Promote** button to move the list item up one level.

c. In the **Text Pane**, click in the top bulleted point, type **Associated Students of Laurel College** and then press ↓. Type the following in the three remaining boxes:

Executive Officers

Student Senate

Judicial Review Committee

d. In the upper right corner of the **Text Pane**, click the **Close** button. Be sure the graphic is selected—a pale border surrounds the entire graphic, and then click the outside border one time. Click the **Format tab**, and then in the **Size group**, if necessary click the **Size** button. By clicking the spin box arrows, change the **Shape Height** to **2.6″** and the **Shape Width** to **6.5″**.

e. With the SmartArt graphic still selected, on the **Design tab**, in the **SmartArt Styles group**, click the **Change Colors** button. Scroll down, and then under **Accent 5**, click the second style—**Colored Fill - Accent 5**.

f. On the **Design tab**, in the **SmartArt Styles group**, click the **More** button. Under **3-D**, click the second style—**Inset**. Click anywhere in the document to deselect the graphic. Press Ctrl + Home to move the insertion point to the beginning of the document.

g. Display **Backstage** view, on the right, under the screen thumbnail, click **Properties**, and then click **Show Document Panel**. In the **Author** box, type your firstname and lastname. In the **Subject** box type your course name and section number, and in the **Keywords** box type **student constitution**

h. **Close** the Document Panel. Click **Save**. Display **Backstage** view and click the **Print tab**. Examine the **Print Preview**. Print or submit electronically as directed. **Close** Word.

End You have completed Project 1D

Content-Based Assessments

Apply 1A skills from
these Objectives:

▪ Create a New
   Document and
   Insert Text
▪ Insert and Format
   Graphics
▪ Insert and Modify
   Text Boxes and
   Shapes
▪ Preview and Print a
   Document

Mastering Word | Project **1E** Retreat

In the following Mastering Word project, you will create a flyer announcing a retreat for the Associated Students of Laurel College Board. Your completed document will look similar to Figure 1.52.

Project Files

For Project 1E, you will need the following files:

New blank Word document
w01E_Retreat_Text
w01E_Retreat_Picture

You will save your document as:

Lastname_Firstname_1E_Retreat

Project Results

ASLC Board Retreat

College President Diane Gilmore is pleased to announce a retreat for the Board of the Associated Students of Laurel College.

Invitees include the ASLC Board, consisting of the Executive Officers and their appointed directors, Student Senators, Club Presidents, and members of the Judicial Review Committee. The retreat will be held at the Fogelsville campus of Penn State University on Friday, November 12.

The morning session will begin with a continental breakfast at 8:30 a.m., and will include presentations on effective ways to set and achieve goals. Lunch will be served at noon. The afternoon session will begin at 1:30 p.m., and will include small breakout sessions for the sharing and development of goals and a series of exercises to facilitate group interaction.

In addition to goal setting, the retreat is organized to provide a means for Board members to get to know one another. Students are so busy with courses, student government duties, and personal responsibilities that they rarely get to interact with other Board members outside of their immediate circles. The afternoon will be devoted to a series of exercises specially designed for this retreat. It will enable all participants to meet every other person in attendance and to exchange ideas. We have hired the well-known group, Mountain Retreat Planners, to conduct this portion of the program. They have some entertaining activities planned that will help break down barriers to becoming acquainted with other participants.

Prize drawings at lunch include concert tickets, college football jerseys, coffee mugs, and restaurant gift cards.

Lastname_Firstname_1E_Retreat

Figure 1.52

(Project 1E Retreat continues on the next page)

1 **Start** Word and display a new blank document. **Save** the document in your **Word Chapter 1** folder as **Lastname_Firstname_1E_Retreat** and then add the file name to the footer. Be sure the formatting marks and rulers display.

2 Type **ASLC Board Retreat** and press Enter two times. Type **College President Diane Gilmore is pleased to announce a retreat for the Board of the Associated Students of Laurel College.** Press Enter one time. **Insert** the file **w01E_Retreat_Text**.

3 Select the title *ASLC Board Retreat*. On the **Home tab**, in the **Font group**, display the **Text Effects** gallery, and then in the third row, apply the first effect—**Fill - White, Gradient Outline - Accent 1**. Change the **Font Size** to **56** pt. Apply a **Shadow** text effect using the first effect under **Outer—Offset Diagonal Bottom Right**. Change the **Font Color** to **Olive Green, Accent 3, Darker 25%**—in the seventh column, the fifth color.

4 Click to position the insertion point at the beginning of the paragraph that begins *College President*, and then from your student files, **Insert** the picture **w01E_Retreat_Picture**. Change the **Shape Height** of the picture to **2″**, and then set the **Wrap Text** to **Square**. Move the picture so that the right edge aligns with the right margin, and the top edge aligns with the top edge of the text that begins *College President*. Apply a **Film Grain Artistic Effect**—the third effect in the third row. From **Picture Effects**, add a **5 Point Soft Edge**.

5 Scroll to view the lower portion of the page. **Insert** a **Text Box** beginning at the left margin and at approximately **7 inches on the vertical ruler** that is approximately 1″ high and 4.5″ wide. Then, in the **Size group**, make the measurements exact by setting the **Height** to **1″** and the **Width** to **4.6″**. Type the following text in the text box:

> **Prize drawings at lunch include concert tickets, college football jerseys, coffee mugs, and restaurant gift cards.**

6 Select the text in the text box. Change the **Font Size** to **16** pt, apply **Bold**, and **Center** the text. Add a **Shape Fill** to the text box using the theme color **Olive Green, Accent 3, Lighter 40%**. Then apply a **Gradient** fill using the **Linear Right** gradient. Change the **Shape Outline** color to **White, Background 1**. Drag the text box as necessary to center it horizontally between the left and right margins, and vertically between the last line of text and the footer.

7 Display the **Document Panel**. Type your firstname and lastname in the **Author** box, your course name and section number in the **Subject** box, and then in the **Keywords** box type **retreat, ASLC**

8 **Close** the Document Panel. **Save** and preview your document, make any necessary adjustments, and then print your document or submit it electronically as directed. **Close** Word.

End **You have completed Project 1E** ——————————————

Content-Based Assessments

Apply **1B** skills from these Objectives:

- ▣ Change Document and Paragraph Layout
- ▣ Create and Modify Lists
- ▣ Set and Modify Tab Stops
- ▣ Insert a SmartArt Graphic

Mastering Word | Project **1F** Cycling Trip

In the following Mastering Word project, you will create an informational handout about a planned trip by the Laurel College Cycling Club. Your completed document will look similar to Figure 1.53.

Project Files

For Project 1F, you will need the following file:

w01F_Cycling_Trip

You will save your document as:

Lastname_Firstname_1F_Cycling_Trip

Project Results

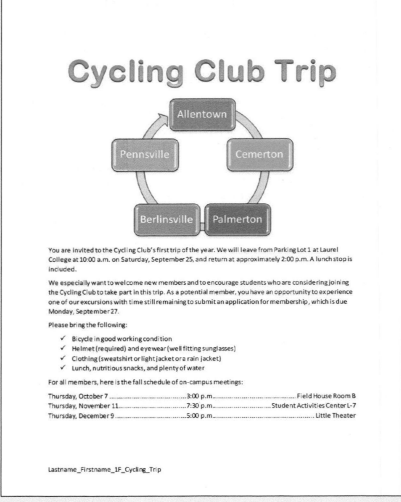

Figure 1.53

(Project 1F Cycling Trip continues on the next page)

Content-Based Assessments

1 **Start** Word. From your student files open the document **w01F_Cycling_Trip**. **Save** the document in your **Word Chapter 1** folder as **Lastname_Firstname_1F_Cycling_Trip** Add the file name to the footer. Display formatting marks.

2 Display the **Page Setup** dialog box. Set the **Top** margin to **1.25″** and the other three margins to **1″**. Select all of the text in the document, including the title. Add **6 pt** spacing after all paragraphs. Change the **Line Spacing** to **1.15**. Change the alignment to **Align Text Left**. **Center** the document title—*Cycling Club Trip*.

3 Locate the paragraph that begins *Bicycle in good*. Select that paragraph and the three paragraphs that follow it. Create a bulleted list from the selected text. Use the shortcut menu to display bullet options, and change the bullet character to a **check mark** or another symbol if the check mark is unavailable.

4 Position the insertion point in the blank paragraph at the end of the document. Add a **Right** tab stop at **3.5″**. Display the **Tabs** dialog box and add a dot leader. **Set** the tab stop, and then add and **Set** another **Right** tab stop with a dot leader at **6.5″**.

5 Type the text shown in **Table 1**, pressing Tab between columns and Enter at the end of each line. Refer to Figure 1.53.

6 Select the first two lines in the tabbed list and change the **Space After** to **0 pt**. Near the top of the document, position the insertion point in the blank line below the title. Display the **Choose a SmartArt Graphic** dialog box, select the **Cycle** category, and then in the second row, select the first style—**Continuous Cycle**.

7 Display the **Text Pane**. Add the following cities in this order: **Allentown** and **Cemerton** and **Palmerton** and **Berlinsville** and **Pennsville**

8 **Close** the Text Pane. Click the SmartArt border. On the **Format tab**, set the **Shape Width** of the SmartArt graphic to **6.5″** and the **Shape Height** to **3″**. On the **Design tab**, from the **SmartArt Styles** gallery, apply the **Cartoon 3-D** style, and change the colors to the first color under **Colorful—Colorful – Accent Colors**.

9 Display the **Document Panel**, type your firstname and lastname in the **Author** box, your course name and section number in the **Subject** box, and then in the **Keywords** box type **cycling, cycling club**

10 **Close** the Document Panel. **Save** your document. Preview your document, check for and make any adjustments, and then print your document or submit it electronically as directed. **Close** Word.

Table 1

Thursday, October 7	3:00 p.m.	Field House Room B
Thursday, November 11	7:30 p.m.	Student Activities Center L-7
Thursday, December 9	5:00 p.m.	Little Theater

- - - ► (Return to Step 6)

End You have completed Project 1F ─────────────────

Apply a combination of
1A and **1B** skills:

■ Create a New
Document and
Insert Text

■ Insert and Format
Graphics

■ Insert and Modify
Text Boxes and
Shapes

■ Preview and Print a
Document

■ Change Document
and Paragraph
Layout

■ Create and Modify
Lists

■ Set and Modify Tab
Stops

■ Insert a SmartArt
Graphic

Mastering Word | Project **1G** Web Sites

In the following Mastering Word project, you will edit guidelines for club Web sites at Laurel
College. Your completed document will look similar to Figure 1.54.

Project Files

For Project 1G, you will need the following files:

New blank Word document
w01G_Chess_Club_Picture
w01G_Web_Sites_Text

You will save your document as:

Lastname_Firstname_1G_Web_Sites

Project Results

Figure 1.54

(Project 1G Web Sites continues on the next page)

1 **Start** Word and display a new blank document. Display formatting marks and rulers. **Save** the document in your **Word Chapter 1** folder as **Lastname_Firstname_ 1G_Web_Sites** Add the file name to the footer.

Type **Club Web Sites** and then press Enter. Select the title you just typed. From the **Text Effects** gallery, in the fourth row, apply the second effect—**Gradient Fill - Orange, Accent 6, Inner Shadow**, change the **Font Size** to **72** pt, and **Center** the title.

2 Click in the blank line below the title. Locate and insert the file **w01G_Web_Sites_Text**. *Except* for the document title, select all of the document text. **Align Text Left**, change the **Line Spacing** to **1.15**, and change the **Spacing After** to **6 pt**. Locate and **Center** the document subtitle that begins *Published by*.

3 In the middle of **Page 1**, under the subheading *Be sure that*, select the six paragraphs down to, but not including, the *General information* subheading. Format the selected text as a bulleted list. Near the bottom of **Page 1** and the top of **Page 2**, under the *Web Site Design Guidelines* subheading, select all of the paragraphs to the end of the document—not including the blank paragraph mark—and create another bulleted list.

4 Under the subheading that begins *General information*, select the six paragraphs and apply **Numbering** to create a numbered list.

Near the top of the document, position the insertion point to the left of the paragraph that begins The Web site. **Insert** the picture **w01G_Chess_Club_Picture**. Set the **Wrap Text** to **Square**. Decrease the picture **Width** to **2.7″**. From the **Picture Effects** gallery, apply the **Soft Edges** effect using **5 Point**.

5 Press Ctrl + End to move to the blank line at the end of the document. Type **For assistance, Student Computing Services hours are:** and then press Enter. Set a **Left** tab stop at **1.5″**. Display the **Tabs** dialog box. At **5″** add a **Right** tab stop with a **dot leader** and click **Set**. Click **OK** to close the dialog box, press Tab to begin, and then type the following information; be sure to press Tab to

begin each line and press Tab between the days and the times and press Enter at the end of each line:

Monday–Thursday	8 a.m. to 10 p.m.
Friday	8 a.m. to 5 p.m.
Saturday	8 a.m. to 12 noon

6 At the top of **Page 2**, position the insertion point to the left of the subheading *Web Site Design Guidelines*. Press Enter one time, and then click in the blank paragraph you just created. **Insert** a **SmartArt** graphic, and then from the **Process** group, select the **Basic Chevron Process**—in the fourth row, the third graphic. Click the border of the graphic, and then on the **Format tab**, set the **Shape Height** of the graphic to **1″** and the **Shape Width** of the graphic to **6.5″**. From the **Design tab**, display the **Text Pane**, and then type **Club** and **Web Site** and **New Members Close** the **Text Pane**. Change style to **3-D Inset** and the colors to **Colored Fill – Accent 6**, which is in the last set of colors.

7 At the bottom of **Page 2**, **Insert** a **Text Box** and set the height to **0.7″** and the width to **5″**. In the text box, type: **The Student Computing Services office is located in the Cedar Building, Room 114, call (215) 555-0932.**

Select the text in the text box. From the Mini toolbar, change the **Font Size** to **16** pt, apply **Bold**, and **Center** the text. Change the **Shape Fill** to **Orange, Accent 6, Darker 25%**. From the **Shape Effects** gallery, apply a **Circle Bevel**. By using the pointer, visually center the text box horizontally between the left and right margins and vertically between the tabbed list and the footer.

8 As the document properties, type your firstname and lastname in the **Author** box, your course name and section number in the **Subject** box, and then in the **Keywords** box type **Web sites, guidelines, Student Computing Services Save** your document, examine the Print Preview, check for and make any adjustments, and then print your document or submit it electronically as directed. **Close** Word.

End You have completed Project 1G

Content-Based Assessments

GO! Fix It | Project **1H** Guidelines

Project Files

For Project 1H, you will need the following file:

w01H_Guidelines

You will save your document as:

Lastname_Firstname_1H_Guidelines

From the student files that accompany this textbook, locate and open the file w01H_More_Guidelines, and then save the file in your Word Chapter 1 folder as **Lastname_Firstname_1H_Guidelines**

This document contains errors that you must find and correct. Read and examine the document, and then edit to correct any errors that you find and to improve the overall document format. Types of errors could include, but are not restricted to:

- Wasted space due to text not wrapping around pictures
- Inconsistent line spacing in paragraphs
- Inconsistent spacing between paragraphs
- Inconsistent paragraph indents
- Inconsistent indenting of lists
- Titles that do not extend across the page
- Text boxes that are too small
- Tabbed lists with wide spaces that do not contain leaders
- Spaces between paragraphs created using empty paragraphs rather than space after paragraphs

Things you should know to complete this project:

- Displaying formatting marks will assist in locating spacing errors.
- There are no errors in the fonts, although the title font size is too small.
- The final flyer should fit on one page.

Save your document and add the file name to the footer. In the Document Panel, type your firstname and lastname in the Author box and your course name and section number in the Subject box. In the Keywords box type **Web site guidelines** and then save your document and submit as directed.

End **You have completed Project 1H** ────────────

Content-Based Assessments

Apply a combination of the **1A** and **1B** skills.

GO! Make It | Project 1I Flyer

Project Files

For Project 1I, you will need the following files:

w01I_Team_Building   w01I_Park_Picture

You will save your document as:

Lastname_Firstname_1I_Team_Building

From the student files that accompany this textbook, locate and open the file w01I_Team_Building, and then save the file in your chapter folder as **Lastname_Firstname_1I_Team_Building**

Use the skills you have practiced, create the document shown in Figure 1.55. The title uses Gradient Fill – Blue, Accent 1, 48 pt. The SmartArt graphic uses the Radial Cycle with an Intense Effect style, is 3″ high and 6.5″ wide, has the Colorful Range – Accent Colors 2 to 3 applied. The w01I_Park_Picture picture has a 2.5 pt soft edge, and is 2.5″ wide. The page border uses Dark Blue, Text 2.

Add the file name to the footer; in the Document Panel, add your name and course information and the Keywords **team building**; save your document; and then submit as directed.

Project Results

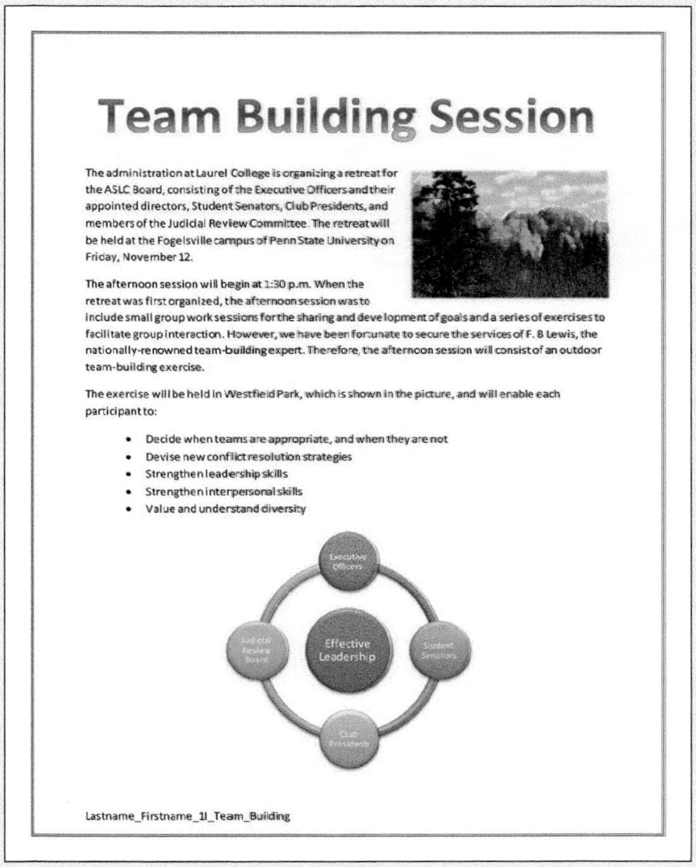

Figure 1.55

End **You have completed Project 1I**

Content-Based Assessments

GO! Solve It | Project **1J** Food Drive

Project Files

For Project 1J, you will need the following file:

New blank Word document
w01J_Food_Drive

You will save your document as:

Lastname_Firstname_1J_Food_Drive

Create a new document and save it in your Word Chapter 1 folder as **Lastname_Firstname_1J_Food_Drive** Use the following information to create a flyer that includes a title that uses Text Effects, introductory text, two lists of an appropriate type, one text box, and a picture with appropriate formatting and text wrapping. Use your own picture or w01J_Food_Drive.

This Thanksgiving, the Associated Students of Laurel College is sponsoring a food drive for the local community. All college clubs are invited to participate. Results will be adjusted for club membership by measuring the results in pounds of food per member. Three kinds of food are acceptable: canned goods, non-perishable dry goods, and boxed or canned dry drink mixes, such as coffee, tea, or lemonade.

To participate, a club must follow this procedure: fill out a competition form, collect the goods, and then turn the food in on November 13. The address and telephone number for the ASLC is the Cedar Building, Room 222, Laurelton, PA 19100, (215) 555-0902.

Add the file name to the footer. To the Properties area, add your name, your course name and section number, and the keywords **food drive, clubs**

		Performance Level	
	Exemplary: You consistently applied the relevant skills	**Proficient:** You sometimes, but not always, applied the relevant skills	**Developing:** You rarely or never applied the relevant skills
Create and format lists	Both lists use the proper list type and are formatted correctly.	One of the lists is formatted correctly.	Neither of the lists are formatted correctly.
Insert and format a picture	The picture is inserted and positioned correctly, and text is wrapped around the picture.	The picture is inserted but not formatted properly.	No picture is inserted.
Insert a text box	A text box with appropriate information is inserted and formatted.	A text box is adequately formatted but is difficult to read or unattractive.	No text box is inserted.
Insert introductory text	Introductory text explains the reason for the flyer, with no spelling or grammar errors.	Some introductory text is included, but does not contain sufficient information and/or includes spelling or grammar errors.	No introductory text, or insufficient introductory text.
Insert title using Text Effects	Text Effects title inserted and centered on the page.	Text Effects title is inserted, but not centered or formatted attractively on the page.	No Text Effects title is included.

Performance Criteria

End **You have completed Project 1J**

Content-Based Assessments

Apply a combination of the **1A** and **1B** skills..

GO! Solve It | Project **1K** Fitness Services

Project Files

For Project 1K, you will need the following files:

New blank Word document
w01K_Volleyball

You will save your document as:

Lastname_Firstname_1K_Fitness_Services

Create a new file and save it as **Lastname_Firstname_1K_Fitness Services** Use the following information to create a flyer that includes introductory text, a SmartArt graphic, a title that uses Text Effects, and a picture that has an artistic effect applied and uses text wrapping. Use your own picture or w01K_Volleyball.

The Associated Students of Laurel College sponsors fitness activities. These take place both on campus and off campus. The activities fall into two categories: Fitness Services and Intramural Sports. Fitness Services are noncompetitive activities, with the most popular being Kickboxing, Jogging, and Aerobics. The most popular Intramural Sports activities—which include competitive team and club sports—are Field Hockey, Volleyball, and Basketball.

Add the file name to the footer, and add your name, your course name and section number, and the keywords **fitness, sports** to the Properties area.

	Performance Level		
	Exemplary: You consistently applied the relevant skills	**Proficient:** You sometimes, but not always, applied the relevant skills	**Developing:** You rarely or never applied the relevant skills
Insert title using Text Effects	Text Effects title inserted and centered on the page.	Text Effects title is inserted, but not centered on the page.	No Text Effects title is included.
Insert introductory text	Introductory text explains the reason for the flyer, with no spelling or grammar errors.	Some introductory text is included, but does not sufficiently explain the topic and/or includes spelling or grammar errors.	No or insufficient introductory text is included.
Insert and format a picture	The picture is inserted and positioned correctly, an artistic effect is applied, and text is wrapped around the picture.	The picture is inserted but not formatted properly.	No picture is inserted in the document.
Insert and format SmartArt	The SmartArt graphic displays both categories of fitness activities and examples of each type.	The SmartArt graphic does not display fitness activities by category.	No SmartArt graphic inserted.

(left side vertical label: Performance Criteria)

End You have completed Project 1K

Outcomes-Based Assessments

Rubric

The following outcomes-based assessments are *open-ended assessments*. That is, there is no specific correct result; your result will depend on your approach to the information provided. Make *Professional Quality* your goal. Use the following scoring rubric to guide you in *how* to approach the problem and then to evaluate *how well* your approach solves the problem.

The *criteria*—Software Mastery, Content, Format and Layout, and Process—represent the knowledge and skills you have gained that you can apply to solving the problem. The *levels of performance*—Professional Quality, Approaching Professional Quality, or Needs Quality Improvements—help you and your instructor evaluate your result.

	Your completed project is of Professional Quality if you:	Your completed project is Approaching Professional Quality if you:	Your completed project Needs Quality Improvements if you:
1-Software Mastery	Choose and apply the most appropriate skills, tools, and features and identify efficient methods to solve the problem.	Choose and apply some appropriate skills, tools, and features, but not in the most efficient manner.	Choose inappropriate skills, tools, or features, or are inefficient in solving the problem.
2-Content	Construct a solution that is clear and well organized, contains content that is accurate, appropriate to the audience and purpose, and is complete. Provide a solution that contains no errors in spelling, grammar, or style.	Construct a solution in which some components are unclear, poorly organized, inconsistent, or incomplete. Misjudge the needs of the audience. Have some errors in spelling, grammar, or style, but the errors do not detract from comprehension.	Construct a solution that is unclear, incomplete, or poorly organized; contains some inaccurate or inappropriate content; and contains many errors in spelling, grammar, or style. Do not solve the problem.
3-Format and Layout	Format and arrange all elements to communicate information and ideas, clarify function, illustrate relationships, and indicate relative importance.	Apply appropriate format and layout features to some elements, but not others. Overuses features, causing minor distraction.	Apply format and layout that does not communicate information or ideas clearly. Do not use format and layout features to clarify function, illustrate relationships, or indicate relative importance. Use available features excessively, causing distraction.
4-Process	Use an organized approach that integrates planning, development, self-assessment, revision, and reflection.	Demonstrate an organized approach in some areas, but not others; or, uses an insufficient process of organization throughout.	Do not use an organized approach to solve the problem.

Apply a combination of the **1A** and **1B** skills..

GO! Think | Project **1L** Academic Services

Project Files

For Project 1L, you will need the following file:

New blank Word document

You will save your document as:

Lastname_Firstname_1L_Academic_Services

The Services Coordinator of the Associated Students of Laurel College needs to create a flyer to inform students of academic services available at the ASLC office. Referrals are available for medical, legal, and counseling services, as well as tutoring and volunteer organizations. Among the services offered at the ASLC office are free printing (up to 250 pages per semester), help with minor legal issues, housing information, bicycle repair, minor computer repair, and help placing students with volunteer organizations.

Create a flyer with basic information about the services provided. Be sure the flyer is easy to read and understand and has an attractive design. If you need more information about student services available at other colleges, search the Web for **student government** and add whatever services you think might be (or should be) available at your college. Add appropriate information to the Document Panel. Save the document as **Lastname_Firstname_1L_Academic_Services** and submit it as directed.

 End **You have completed Project 1L** ───────────

Apply a combination of the **1A** and **1B** skills.

GO! Think | Project **1M** Campus Bookstore

Project Files

For Project 1M, you will need the following files:

New blank Word document
w01L_Campus_Bookstore

You will save your document as:

Lastname_Firstname_1M_Campus_Bookstore

The manager of the Laurel College Bookstore needs to create a flyer that can be handed out by the ASLC to students during Welcome Week. The bookstore gives students attending Welcome Week a discount of 20% on special items such as sweatshirts and other college-related clothing, coffee mugs, calendars, and similar items. Door prizes will also be awarded. The bookstore is open Monday and Thursday from 8 a.m. to 10 p.m., Tuesday and Wednesday from 8 a.m. to 8 p.m., and Friday from 8 a.m. to 5 p.m.

Using your own campus bookstore as an example, create a flyer that gives general information about the bookstore, provides one or more lists of items that are on sale, displays the picture w01M_ Campus_Bookstore, and has a highlighted area that gives the store hours.

Add appropriate information to the Document Panel. Save the document as **Lastname_Firstname_1M_Campus_Bookstore** and submit it as directed.

End **You have completed Project 1M** ───────────

Outcomes-Based Assessments

You and GO! | Project **1N** Family Flyer

Project Files

For Project 1N, you will need the following file:

New blank Word document

You will save your document as

Lastname_Firstname_1N_Family_Flyer

In this project, you will create a one-page flyer that you can send to your family. Include any information that may interest your family members, such as work-related news, school events, vacation plans, and the activities and accomplishments of you, your spouse, your friends, or other family members. Choose any writing style that suits you—chatty, newsy, entertaining, or humorous.

To complete the assignment, be sure to include a title, at least one list, a picture, and either a SmartArt graphic or a text box or shape. Before you submit the flyer, be sure to check it for grammar and spelling errors, and also be sure to format the document in an attractive manner, using the skills you practiced in this chapter.

Save the file as **Lastname_Firstname_1N_Family_Flyer** Add the file name to the footer, and add your name, your course name and section number, and the keywords **flyer** and **family** to the Properties area. Submit your file as directed.

End **You have completed Project 1N** —————————————

Using Tables and Templates to Create Resumes and Cover Letters

OUTCOMES

At the end of this chapter you will be able to:

OBJECTIVES

Mastering these objectives will enable you to:

PROJECT 2A
Create a resume by using a Word table.

1. Create a Table
2. Add Text to a Table
3. Format a Table

PROJECT 2B
Create a cover letter and resume by using a template.

4. Create a New Document from an Existing Document
5. Change and Reorganize Text
6. Use the Proofing Options
7. Create a Document Using a Template

James Thew/Shutterstock

In This Chapter

Tables are useful for organizing and presenting data. Because a table is so easy to use, many individuals prefer to arrange tabular information in a Word table rather than setting a series of tabs. Use a table when you want to present rows and columns of information or to create a structure for a document such as a resume.

When using Word to write business or personal letters, use a commonly approved letter format. You will make a good impression on prospective employers if you use a standard business letter style when you are writing a cover letter for a resume. You can create a resume using one of the Microsoft resume templates included with Microsoft Office or available online.

The projects in this chapter relate to **Madison Staffing Services**. Many companies prefer to hire employees through a staffing service, so that both the employer and the employee can determine if the match is a good fit. Madison Staffing Services takes care of the details of recruiting, testing, hiring, and paying the employee. At the end of the employment assignment, neither the employer nor the employee is required to make a permanent commitment. Many individuals find full-time jobs with an employer for whom they initially worked through a staffing agency.

Project 2A Resume

Project Activities

In Activities 2.01 through 2.09, you will create a table to use as the structure for a resume for one of Madison Staffing Services' clients. Your completed document will look similar to Figure 2.1.

Project Files

For Project 2A, you will need the following file:

w02A_Experience

You will save your document as:

Lastname_Firstname_2A_Resume

Project Results

Figure 2.1
Project 2A Resume

Objective 1 | Create a Table

A ***table*** is an arrangement of information organized into rows and columns. The intersection of a row and a column in a table creates a box called a ***cell*** into which you can type. Tables are useful to present information in a logical and orderly manner.

Activity 2.01 | Creating a Table

1 Start **Word**, and in the new blank document, display formatting marks and rulers.

2 Click the **File tab**, and then in **Backstage** view, click **Save As**. In the **Save As** dialog box, navigate to the location where you are storing your projects for this chapter. Create a new folder named **Word Chapter 2**

3 **Save** the file in the **Word Chapter 2** folder as **Lastname_Firstname_2A_Resume**

4 Scroll to the end of the document, right-click near the bottom of the page, and then click **Edit Footer**. On the **Design tab**, in the **Insert group**, click the **Quick Parts** button, and then click **Field**.

5 Under **Field names**, scroll down, click **FileName**, and then click **OK**. **Close** the footer area.

6 On the **Insert tab**, in the **Tables group**, click the **Table** button. In the **Table** grid, in the fourth row, point to the second square, and notice that the cells display in orange and *2 × 4 Table* displays at the top of the grid. Compare your screen with Figure 2.2.

Figure 2.2

Table button
Table size
Pointer indicates table size
Preview of table

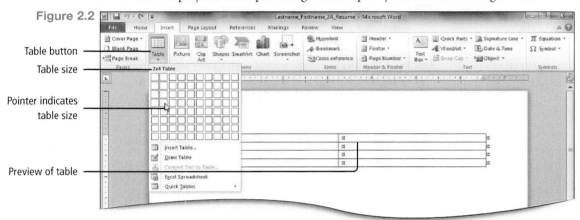

7 Click one time to create the table. Notice that formatting marks in each cell indicate the end of the contents of each cell and the mark to the right of each *row* indicates the row end. **Save** your document, and then compare your screen with Figure 2.3.

A table with four rows and two columns displays at the insertion point location, and the insertion point displays in the upper left cell. The table fills the width of the page, from the left margin to the right margin. On the Ribbon, Table Tools display and add two tabs—*Design* and *Layout*. Borders display around each cell in the table.

Figure 2.3

Table Tools
Indicates the end of a row
Indicates the end of cell contents

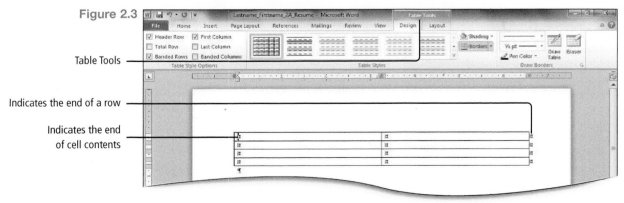

Project 2A: Resume | **Word**

Objective 2 | Add Text to a Table

In a Word table, each cell behaves similarly to a document. For example, as you type in a cell, when you reach the right border of the cell, wordwrap moves the text to the next line. When you press Enter, the insertion point moves down to a new paragraph in the same cell. You can also insert text from another document into a table cell.

Activity 2.02 | Adding Text to a Table

There are numerous acceptable formats for resumes, many of which can be found in Business Communications textbooks. The layout used in this project is suitable for a recent college graduate and places topics in the left column and details in the right column.

1 Scroll up to view the top of the document. With the insertion point blinking in the first cell in the first row, type **OBJECTIVE** and then press Tab.

> Pressing Tab moves the insertion point to the next cell in the row, or, if the insertion point is already in the last cell in the row, pressing Tab moves the insertion point to the first cell in the following row.

2 Type **Retail sales manager position in the cellular phone industry, using good communication and negotiating skills.** Notice that the text wraps in the cell and the height of the row adjusts to fit the text.

3 Press Tab to move to the first cell in the second row. Type **SUMMARY OF QUALIFICATIONS** and then press Tab. Type the following, pressing Enter at the end of each line *except* the last line:

> **Five years' experience in retail sales**
>
> **Excellent interpersonal and communication skills**
>
> **Proficiency using Microsoft Office**
>
> **Fluency in spoken and written Spanish**
>
> The default font and font size in a table are the same as for a document—Calibri 11 pt. The default line spacing in a table is single spacing with no space before or after paragraphs, which differs from the defaults for a document.

4 **Save** 🖫 your document, and then compare your screen with Figure 2.4.

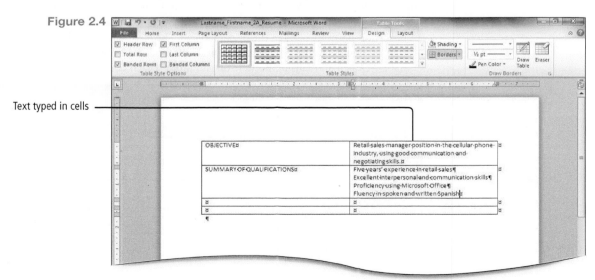

Figure 2.4

Text typed in cells

Word | Using Tables and Templates to Create Resumes and Cover Letters

Activity 2.03 | Inserting Existing Text into a Table Cell

1 Press (Tab) to move to the first cell in the third row. Type **EXPERIENCE** and then press (Tab).

2 Type the following, pressing (Enter) after each line:

> **Retail Sales Representative, Universe Retail Stores, Deerfield, WI October 2010 to October 2011**
>
> **Exceeded monthly sales goals for 8 months out of 12**
>
> **Provided technical training on products and services to new sales reps**

3 Be sure your insertion point is positioned in the second column to the left of the cell marker below *sales reps*. Compare your screen with Figure 2.5.

Figure 2.5

Insertion point in blank line at bottom of cell

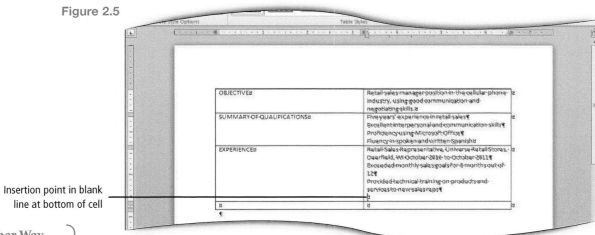

Another Way

Open the second document and select the text you want. Copy the text, and then paste at the desired location.

4 On the **Insert tab**, in the **Text group**, click the **Object button arrow**, and then click **Text from File**. Navigate to your student files, select **w02A_Experience**, and then click **Insert**.

5 Press (Backspace) one time to remove the blank line at the end of the inserted text, and then compare your screen with Figure 2.6.

Figure 2.6

Text inserted from file

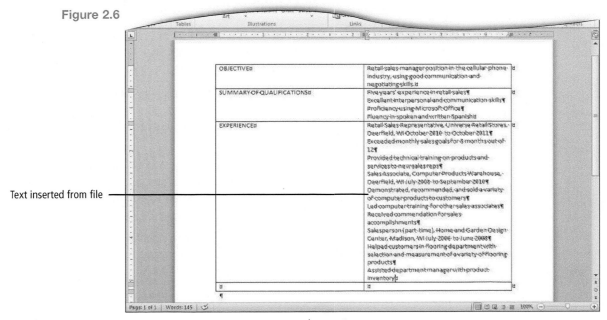

6 Press ⌑Tab⌑ to move to the first cell in the fourth row. Type **EDUCATION** and then press ⌑Tab⌑.

7 Type the following, pressing ⌑Enter⌑ at the end of each item *except* the last one:

> **University of Wisconsin, Madison, WI**
>
> **Bachelor's in Business Administration, June 2011**
>
> **Madison Area Technical College, Madison, WI**
>
> **Associate's in Information Systems, June 2009**

8 Compare your screen with Figure 2.7.

Figure 2.7

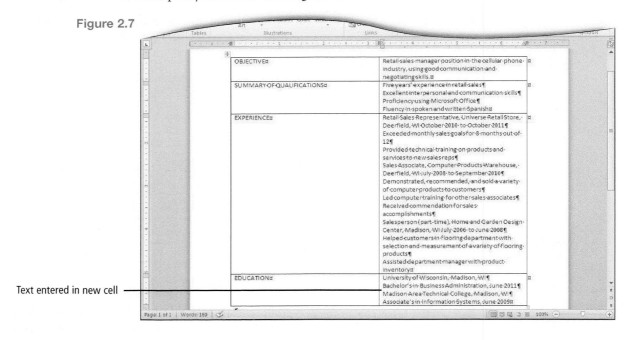

Text entered in new cell

9 **Save** 💾 your document.

Activity 2.04 | Creating Bulleted Lists in a Table

1 Scroll to view the top of your document, and then in the cell to the right of *SUMMARY OF QUALIFICATIONS*, select all of the text.

2 On the **Home tab**, in the **Paragraph group**, click the **Bullets** button ⌑≣ ▾⌑.

> The selected text displays as a bulleted list. Using a bulleted list in this manner makes each qualification more distinctive.

3 In the **Paragraph group**, click the **Decrease Indent** button ⌑≣⌑ one time to align the bullets at the left edge of the cell.

4 In the **Clipboard group**, double-click the **Format Painter** button. In the cell to the right of *EXPERIENCE*, select the second and third paragraphs—beginning *Exceeded* and *Provided*—to create the same style of bulleted list as you did in the previous step.

> When you double-click the Format Painter button, it remains active until you turn it off.

5 In the same cell, under *Sales Associate*, select the three paragraphs that begin *Demonstrated* and *Led* and *Received* to create another bulleted list aligned at the left edge of the cell.

Another Way

Click the Format Painter again.

6 With the Format Painter pointer still active, in the same cell, select the paragraphs that begin *Helped* and *Assisted* to create the same type of bulleted list.

7 Press Esc to turn off the Format Painter. Click anywhere in the table to deselect the text, and then compare your screen with Figure 2.8.

Figure 2.8

Bullets added to text

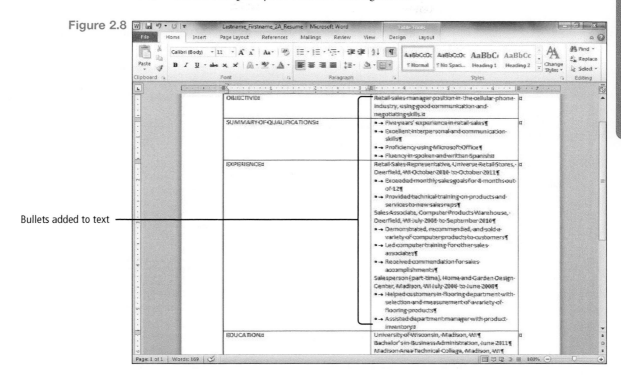

8 **Save** your document.

Objective 3 | Format a Table

Use Word's formatting tools to make your tables attractive and easy to read. Types of formatting you can add to a table include changing the row height and the column width, removing or adding borders, increasing or decreasing the paragraph or line spacing, or enhancing the text.

Activity 2.05 | Changing the Width of Table Columns

When you create a table, all of the columns are of equal width. In this activity, you will change the width of the columns.

1 In any row, point to the vertical border between the two columns to display the ⊹⊹ pointer.

2 Drag the column border to the left to approximately **1.25 inches on the horizontal ruler**.

3 Scroll to the top of the document. Notice that in the second row, the text *SUMMARY OF QUALIFICATIONS* wraps to two lines to accommodate the new column width.

4 If necessary, in the left column, click in any cell. On the Ribbon, under **Table Tools**, click the **Layout tab**.

5 In the **Cell Size group**, click the **Table Column Width button spin arrows** as necessary to change the width of the first column to **1.4″**. Compare your screen with Figure 2.9.

> After dragging a border with your mouse, use the Width button to set a precise measurement if necessary.

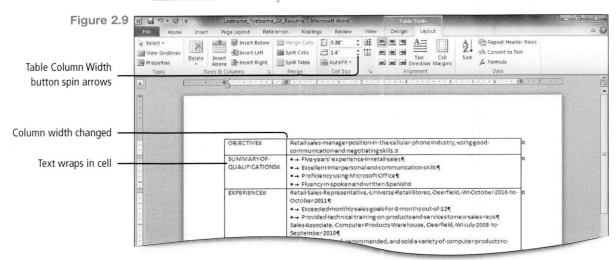

Figure 2.9

Table Column Width button spin arrows

Column width changed

Text wraps in cell

6 **Save** your document.

More Knowledge | Changing Column Widths

You will typically get the best results if you change the column widths starting at the left side of the table, especially in tables with three or more columns. Word can also calculate the best column widths for you. To do this, select the table. Then, on the Layout tab, in the Cell Size group, click the AutoFit button and click AutoFit Contents.

Activity 2.06 | Adding Rows to a Table

You can add rows or columns anywhere in a table.

1 Scroll to view the lower portion of the table. In the last row of the table, click anywhere in the *second* cell that contains the educational information, and then press Tab.

> A new row displays at the bottom of the table. When the insertion point is in the last cell in the bottom row of a table, you can add a row by pressing the Tab key; the insertion point will display in the first cell of the new row.

2 Type **HONORS AND ACTIVITIES** and then press Tab.

3 Type the following, pressing Enter after the first item but not the second item:

Elected to Beta Gamma Sigma, international honor society for business students

Qualified for Dean's List, six academic periods

4 Select the text you typed in the last cell of the bottom row. On the **Home tab**, in the **Paragraph group**, click the **Bullets** button, and then click the **Decrease Indent** button one time to align the bullets at the left edge of the cell.

5 Scroll up to view the entire table, click anywhere in the table to deselect the text, and then compare your screen with Figure 2.10.

Figure 2.10

Row added to table ————

Bullets added to text ————

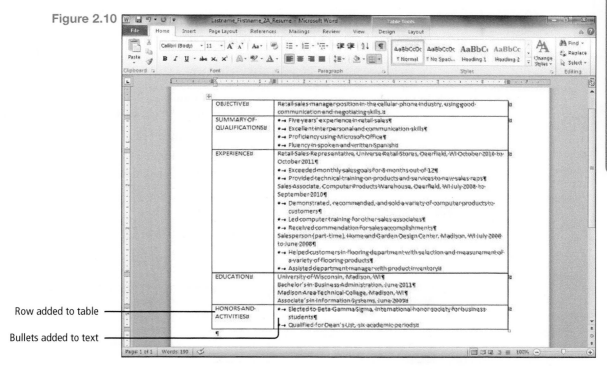

Another Way

Right-click in the top row, point to Insert, and then click Insert Rows Above.

6 Click anywhere in the top row of the table.

7 On the **Layout tab**, in the **Rows & Columns group**, click the **Insert Above** button. Compare your screen with Figure 2.11.

A new row displays above the row that contained the insertion point, and the new row is selected.

Figure 2.11

Row inserted at top of table ————

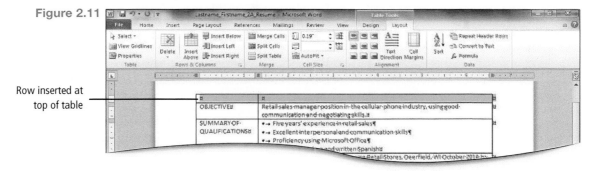

8 **Save** 💾 your document.

Activity 2.07 | Merging Cells

The title of a table typically spans all of the columns. In this activity, you will merge cells so that you can position the personal information across both columns.

1 Be sure the two cells in the top row are selected; if necessary, drag across both cells to select them.

Another Way

Right-click the selected row and click Merge Cells on the shortcut menu.

2 On the **Layout tab**, in the **Merge group**, click the **Merge Cells** button.

> The cell border between the two cells no longer displays.

3 With the merged cell still selected, on the **Home tab**, in the **Paragraph group**, click the **Dialog Box Launcher** to display the **Paragraph** dialog box.

4 In the **Paragraph** dialog box, on the **Indents and Spacing tab**, in the lower left corner, click the **Tabs** button to display the **Tabs** dialog box.

5 In the **Tabs** dialog box, under **Tab stop position**, type **6.5** and then under **Alignment**, click the **Right** option button. Click **Set**, and then click **OK** to close the dialog box.

6 Type **Daniela Johnstone** Hold down Ctrl and then press Tab. Notice that the insertion point moves to the right-aligned tab stop at 6.5″.

> In a Word table, you must use Ctrl + Tab to move to a tab stop, because pressing Tab is reserved for moving the insertion point from cell to cell.

7 Type **(608) 555-0588** and then press Enter.

8 Type **1343 Siena Lane, Deerfield, WI 53531** Hold down Ctrl and then press Tab.

9 Type **djohnstone@alcona.net** and then compare your screen with Figure 2.12.

Figure 2.12

Right tab stop added to ruler

Cells merged in top row

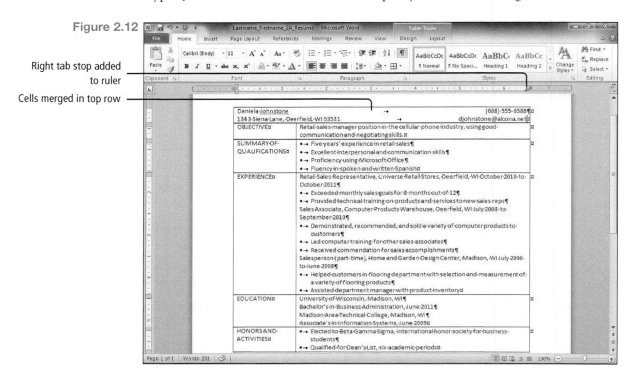

10 **Save** your document.

Activity 2.08 | Formatting Text in Cells

1 In the first row of the table, select the name *Daniela Johnstone*, and then on the Mini toolbar, apply **Bold** and change the **Font Size** to **16**.

2 Under *Daniela Johnstone*, click anywhere in the second line of text, which contains the address and e-mail address.

3 On the **Page Layout tab**, in the **Paragraph group**, click the **Spacing After up spin arrow** three times to add **18 pt** spacing between the first row of the table and the second row. Compare your screen with Figure 2.13.

> These actions separate the personal information from the body of the resume and adds focus to the applicant's name.

Figure 2.13

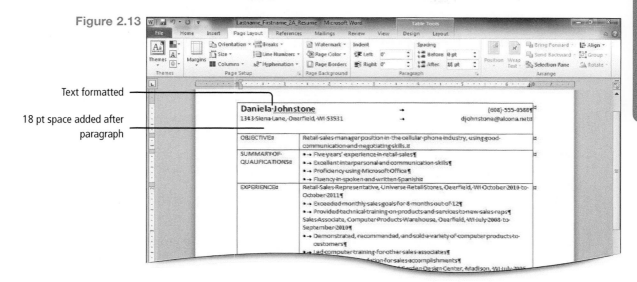

Text formatted

18 pt space added after paragraph

4 Using the technique you just practiced, in the second column, click in the last paragraph of every cell and add **18 pt Spacing After** the last paragraph of all rows including the last row; a border will be added to the bottom of the table, and spacing will be needed between the last row and the border.

5 In the second row, point to the word *OBJECTIVE*, hold down the left mouse button, and then drag downward in the first column only to select all the headings in uppercase letters. On the Mini toolbar, click the **Bold** button 📄.

> **Note** | Selecting Only One Column
>
> When you drag downward to select the first column, a fast mouse might also begin to select the second column when you reach the bottom. If this happens, drag upward slightly to deselect the second column and select only the first column.

6 In the cell to the right of *EXPERIENCE*, without selecting the following comma, select *Retail Sales Representative* and then on the Mini toolbar, click the **Bold** button 📄.

7 In the same cell, apply **Bold** 📄 to the other job titles—*Sales Associate* and *Salesperson*—but do not bold *(part time)*.

8 In the cell to the right of *EDUCATION*, apply **Bold** 📄 to *University of Wisconsin, Madison, WI* and *Madison Area Technical College, Madison, WI*.

9 In the same cell, click anywhere in the line beginning *Bachelor's*. On the **Page Layout tab**, in the **Paragraph group**, click the **Spacing After up spin arrow** two times to add **12 pt** spacing after the paragraph.

10 In the cell to the right of *EXPERIENCE*, under *Retail Sales Representative*, click anywhere in the second bulleted item, and then add **12 pt Spacing After** the item.

Project 2A: Resume | **Word**

11 In the same cell, repeat this process for the last bulleted item under *Sales Associate*.

12 Scroll to the top of the screen, and then compare your screen with Figure 2.14.

Figure 2.14

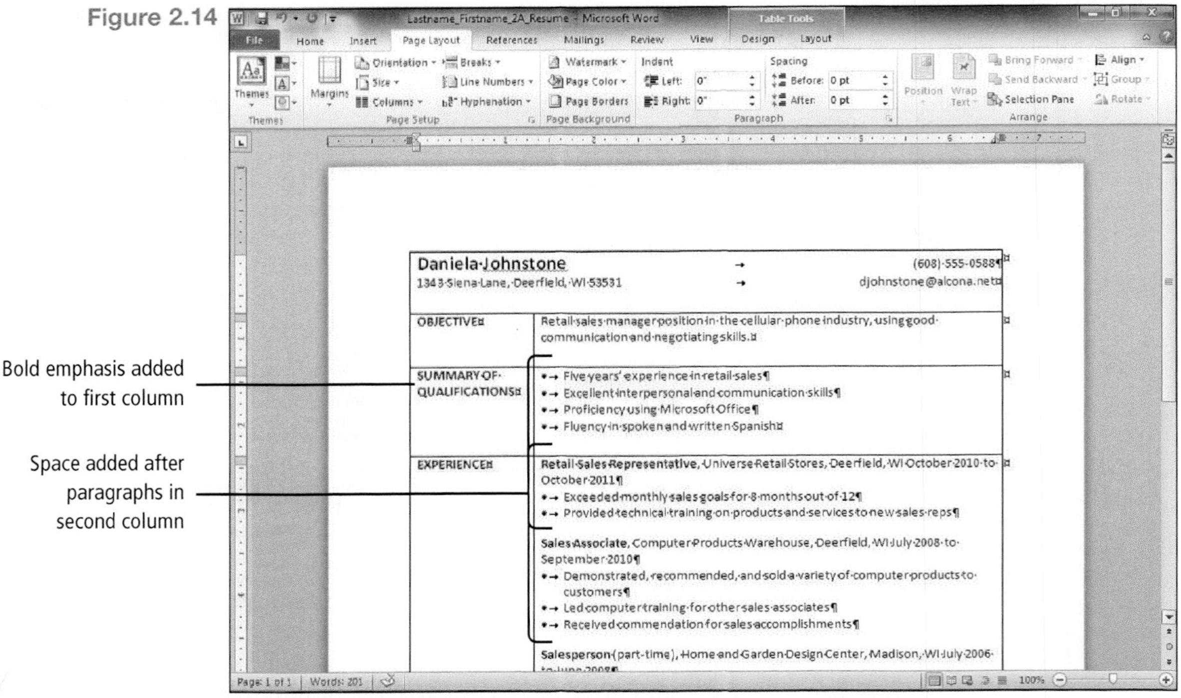

Bold emphasis added to first column

Space added after paragraphs in second column

13 Save [icon] your document.

Activity 2.09 | Changing the Table Borders

When you create a table, all of the cells have black borders. Most resumes do not display any cell borders. A border at the top and bottom of the resume, however, is attractive and adds a professional look to the document.

1 If necessary, press [Ctrl] + [Home] to move the insertion point to the top of the table, and then point slightly outside of the upper left corner of the table to display the **table move handle** [icon].

2 With the [icon] pointer, click one time to select the entire table, and notice that the row markers at the end of each row are also selected.

Shaded row markers indicate that the entire row is selected.

3 Click the **Design tab**. In the **Table Styles group**, click the **Borders button arrow**, and then click **No Border**.

The black borders no longer display; instead, depending on your setup, either no borders—the default setting—or nonprinting blue dashed borders display.

4 Click the **File tab** to display **Backstage** view, and then click the **Print tab** to preview the table. Notice that no borders display in the preview, as shown in Figure 2.15.

Figure 2.15

Document preview

All table borders removed

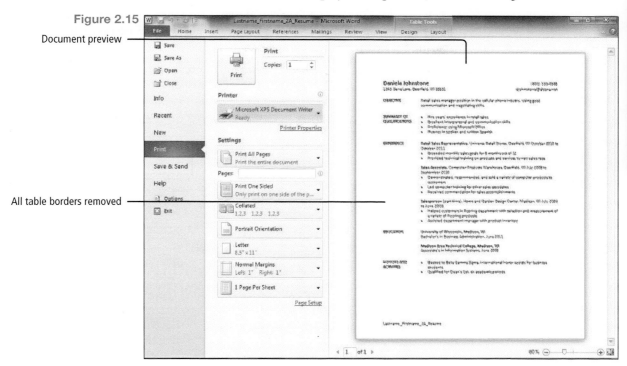

5 Click the **Design tab**; be sure the table is still selected. In the **Table Styles group**, click the **Borders button arrow**, and then at the bottom of the **Borders** gallery, click **Borders and Shading**.

6 Under **Setting**, click the **Custom** button. Under **Style**, scroll down about a third of the way and click the style with the thick upper line and the thin lower line.

7 In the **Preview** box at the right, point to the *top* border of the small preview and click one time.

8 Under **Style**, click the style with the thin upper line and the thick lower line, and then in the **Preview** box, click the *bottom* border of the preview. Compare your screen with Figure 2.16.

Figure 2.16

Borders applied to table

Borders display in Preview

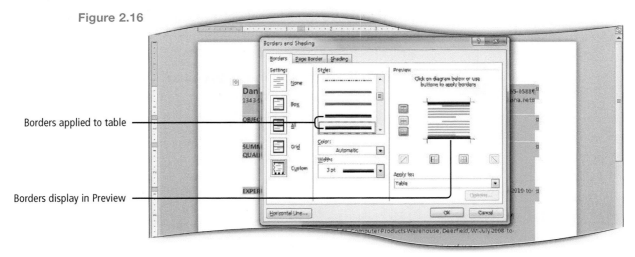

Project 2A: Resume | **Word**

69

9 Click **OK**, click anywhere to cancel the selection, and then notice that there is only a small amount of space between the upper border and the first line of text.

10 Click anywhere in the text *Daniela Johnstone*, and then on the **Page Layout tab**, in the **Paragraph group**, click the **Spacing Before up spin arrow** as necessary to add **18 pt** spacing before the first paragraph.

11 Display **Backstage** view. Click the **Print tab** to preview the table. Compare your screen with Figure 2.17.

Figure 2.17

Top border

Spacing added above first paragraph

Bottom border

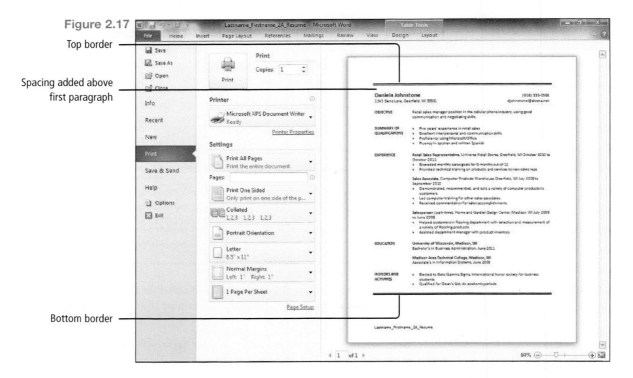

12 In **Backstage** view, click the **Info tab**. On the right, under the document thumbnail, click **Properties**, and then click **Show Document Panel**. In the **Author** box, delete any text and then type your firstname and lastname. In the **Subject** box, type your course name and section number, and in the **Keywords** box type **resume, Word table**

13 **Close** ☒ the **Document Panel**. **Save** 🖫 and then print your document, or submit it electronically, as directed by your instructor. **Exit** Word.

End You have completed Project 2A ———————————————

Word | Using Tables and Templates to Create Resumes and Cover Letters

Project 2B Cover Letter and Resume

myitlab
Project 2B Training

Project Activities

In Activities 2.10 through 2.22, you will create a letterhead, and then use the letterhead to create a cover letter. You will also create a short resume using a Microsoft template and save it as a Web page. Your completed documents will look similar to Figure 2.18.

Project Files

For Project 2B, you will need the following file:

w02B_Cover_Letter_Text

You will save your documents as:

Lastname_Firstname_2B_Letterhead
Lastname_Firstname_2B_Cover_Letter
Lastname_Firstname_2B_Brief_Resume
Lastname_Firstname_2B_HTML_Resume

Project Results

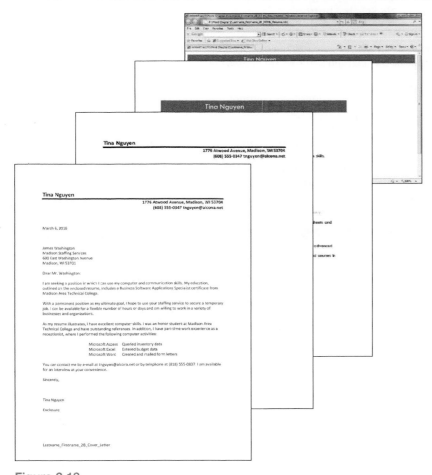

Figure 2.18
Project 2B Cover Letter and Resume

Objective 4 | Create a New Document from an Existing Document

A *template* is an *existing* document that you use as a starting point for a *new* document. The template document opens a copy of itself, unnamed, and then you use the structure—and possibly some content, such as headings—as the starting point for a new document.

All documents are based on a template. When you create a new blank document, it is based on Word's *Normal template*, which serves as the starting point for all new Word documents.

Activity 2.10 | Creating a Letterhead

A *letterhead* is the personal or company information that displays at the top of a letter, and which commonly includes a name, address, and contact information. The term also refers to a piece of paper imprinted with such information at the top.

1 **Start** Word, and in the new blank document, be sure that formatting marks and rulers display.

2 On the **Home tab**, in the **Styles group**, click the **More** button ⊡. In the displayed gallery, click the **No Spacing** button.

> Recall that the default spacing for a new Word document is 10 points of blank space following a paragraph and line spacing of 1.15. The *No Spacing style* inserts *no* extra space following a paragraph and uses single spacing.
>
> By using the No Spacing style, you will be able to follow the prescribed format of a letter, which Business Communications texts commonly describe in terms of single spacing.

3 Type **Tina Nguyen** and then press Enter.

4 Type **1776 Atwood Avenue, Madison, WI 53704** and then press Enter.

5 Type **(608) 555-0347 tnguyen@alcona.net** and then press Enter. If the e-mail address changes to blue text, right-click the e-mail address, and then from the shortcut menu, click **Remove Hyperlink**. Compare your screen with Figure 2.19.

Figure 2.19

No Spacing style button

No Spacing style applied

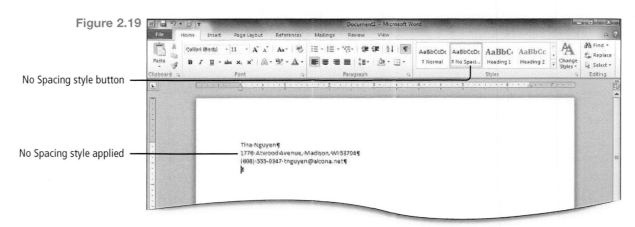

6 Select the first paragraph—*Tina Nguyen*—and then on the Mini toolbar, apply **Bold** B and change the **Font Size** to **16**.

7 Select the second and third paragraphs. On the Mini toolbar, apply **Bold** **B** and change the **Font Size** to **12**.

Another Way
Press Ctrl + R to align text to the right.

8 With the two paragraphs still selected, on the **Home tab**, in the **Paragraph group**, click the **Align Text Right** button **≡**.

9 Click anywhere in the first paragraph—*Tina Nguyen*. In the **Paragraph group**, click the **Borders button arrow** **⊞ ▾**, and then at the bottom, click **Borders and Shading**.

10 In the **Borders and Shading** dialog box, under **Style**, be sure the first style—a single solid line—is selected.

Another Way
Alternatively, click the bottom border button **⊞**.

11 Click the **Width arrow**, and then click **3 pt**. To the right, under **Preview**, click the bottom border of the diagram. Under **Apply to**, be sure *Paragraph* displays. Compare your screen with Figure 2.20.

Figure 2.20

Borders button arrow

3 pt line applied to bottom border

Width arrow

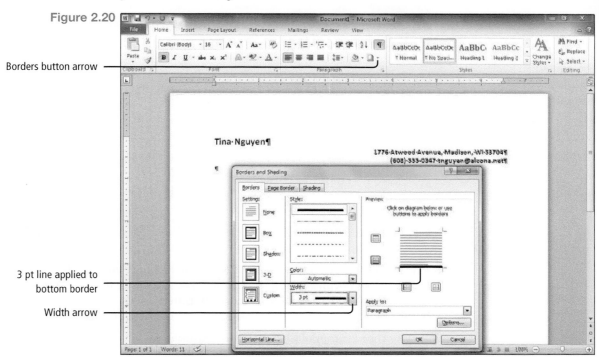

12 Click **OK** to display a 3 pt line below *Tina Nguyen*, which extends from the left margin to the right margin.

13 Display **Save As** dialog box, **Save** the document in your **Word Chapter 2** folder as **Lastname_Firstname_2B_Letterhead** and then add the file name to the footer.

14 Display **Backstage** view, click the **Info tab**, and then on the right, under the document thumbnail, click **Properties**. Click **Show Document Panel**. In the **Author** box, delete any text and then type your firstname and lastname. In the **Subject** box, type your course name and section number, and in the **Keywords** box type **personal letterhead**

15 **Close** **×** the **Document Panel**.

16 **Save** **⊟** your document. Display **Backstage** view, and then click **Close** to close the document but leave Word open. Hold this file until you complete this project.

Activity 2.11 | Creating a Document from an Existing Document

To use an existing document as the starting point for a new document, Word provides the *New from existing* command.

1 Click the **File tab** to display **Backstage** view, and then click **New** to display the new document options. Compare your screen with Figure 2.21.

> Here you can create a new document in a variety of ways, including from an existing document.

Figure 2.21

New from Existing template

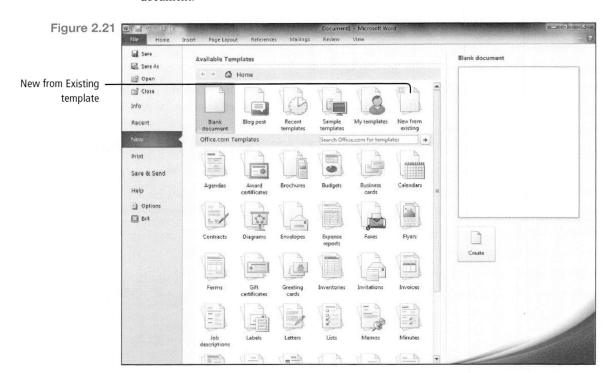

2 Under **Available Templates**, click the **New from existing** button. In the displayed **New from Existing Document** dialog box, if necessary, navigate to your **Word Chapter 2** folder, click your **Lastname_Firstname_2B_Letterhead** document to select it, and then in the lower right corner, click **Create New**. Compare your screen with Figure 2.22.

> Word opens a copy of your 2B_Letterhead document in the form of a new Word document—the title bar indicates *Document* followed by a number. You are not opening the original document, and changes that you make to this new document will not affect the contents of your 2B_Letterhead document.

Figure 2.22

Document opens unnamed

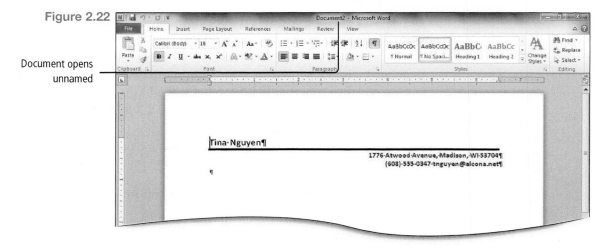

Word | Using Tables and Templates to Create Resumes and Cover Letters

3 Display the **Save As** dialog box, and then navigate to your **Word Chapter 2** folder. **Save** the file as **Lastname_Firstname_2B_Cover_Letter**

> The personal information that you typed in the 2B_Letterhead Document Panel remains in the new document.

4 Scroll down to view the footer area, and notice that a footer displays.

> The footer displays because it was included in the document that you saved as a template. The *FileName* field does not automatically update to the new file name.

5 Point to the footer and right-click, and then click **Edit Footer**. Point to the highlighted footer text, right-click, and then from the shortcut menu, click **Update Field**. At the far right end of the Ribbon, click the **Close Header and Footer** button.

6 **Save** your document.

> **More Knowledge** | **Creating a Template File**
>
> You can also identify an original document so that your Windows operating system always knows that you want to create a new unnamed copy. To do so, save your document as a template file instead of a document. Word will then attach the dotx extension to the file, instead of the docx extension that is applied for a document, and will store the template file in a special location with other templates. Then, you can open the template from the New Document dialog box by clicking *My templates*.

Objective 5 | Change and Reorganize Text

Business letters follow a standard format and contain the following parts: the current date, referred to as the **date line**; the name and address of the person receiving the letter, referred to as the **inside address**; a greeting, referred to as the **salutation**; the text of the letter, usually referred to as the **body** of the letter; a closing line, referred to as the **complimentary closing**; and the **writer's identification**, which includes the name or job title (or both) of the writer, and which is also referred to as the **writer's signature block**.

Some letters also include the initials of the person who prepared the letter, an optional **subject line** that describes the purpose of the letter, or a list of **enclosures**—documents included with the letter.

Activity 2.12 | Recording AutoCorrect Entries

You can correct commonly misspelled words automatically by using Word's **AutoCorrect** feature. Commonly misspelled words—such as *teh* instead of *the*—are corrected using a built-in list that is installed with Office. If you have words that you frequently misspell, you can add them to the list for automatic correction.

1 Click the **File tab** to display **Backstage** view. On the **Help tab**, click **Options** to display the **Word Options** dialog box.

2 On the left side of the **Word Options** dialog box, click **Proofing**, and then under **AutoCorrect options**, click the **AutoCorrect Options** button.

3 In the **AutoCorrect** dialog box, click the **AutoCorrect tab**. Under **Replace**, type **resumee** and under **With**, type **resume**

> If another student has already added this AutoCorrect entry, a Replace button will display.

4 Click **Add**. If the entry already exists, click Replace instead, and then click Yes.

5 In the **AutoCorrect** dialog box, under **Replace**, type **computr** and under **With**, type **computer** and then compare your screen with Figure 2.23.

Figure 2.23

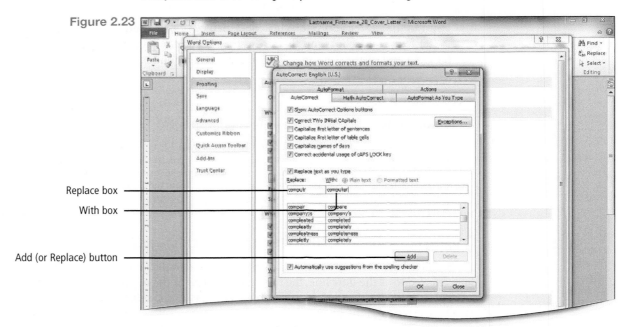

Replace box ⎯⎯⎯

With box ⎯⎯⎯

Add (or Replace) button ⎯⎯⎯

6 Click **Add** (or Replace) and then click **OK** two times to close the dialog boxes.

Activity 2.13 | Creating a Cover Letter

There are a variety of accepted letter formats that you will see in reference manuals and Business Communication texts. The one used in this chapter is a block style cover letter taken from *Business Communication Today*.

1 Press Ctrl + End to move the insertion point to the blank line below the letterhead. Press Enter three times, and then type **March 16, 2016** to create the dateline.

> Most Business Communication texts recommend that the dateline be positioned at least 0.5 inch (3 blank lines) below the letterhead; or, position the dateline approximately 2 inches from the top edge of the paper.

2 Press Enter four times, which leaves three blank lines. Type the following inside address on four lines, but do not press Enter following the last line:

James Washington

Madison Staffing Services

600 East Washington Avenue

Madison, WI 53701

> The recommended space between the dateline and inside address varies slightly among Business Communication texts and office reference manuals. However, all indicate that the space can be from one to 10 blank lines depending on the length of your letter.

3 Press [Enter] two times to leave one blank line. Compare your screen with Figure 2.24.

Figure 2.24

Three blank lines between letterhead and dateline ——

Dateline ——

Three blank lines between dateline and inside address ——

Inside address ——

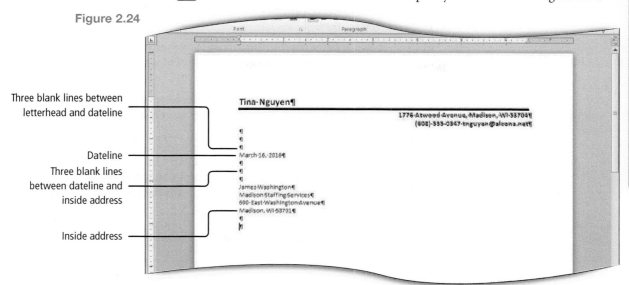

4 Type the salutation **Dear Mr. Washington:** and then press [Enter] two times.

Always leave one blank line above and below the salutation.

5 Type, exactly as shown, the following opening paragraph that includes an intentional word usage error: **I am seeking a position in witch I can use my** and press [Spacebar]. Type, exactly as shown, **computr** and then watch *computr* as you press [Spacebar].

The AutoCorrect feature recognizes the misspelled word, and then changes *computr* to *computer* when you press [Spacebar], [Enter], or a punctuation mark.

6 Type the following, including the misspelled last word: **and communication skills. My education, outlined on the enclosed resumee** and then type **,** (a comma). Notice that when you type the comma, AutoCorrect replaces *resumee* with *resume*.

7 Press [Spacebar]. Complete the paragraph by typing **includes a Business Software Applications Specialist certificate from MATC.** Compare your screen with Figure 2.25.

Figure 2.25

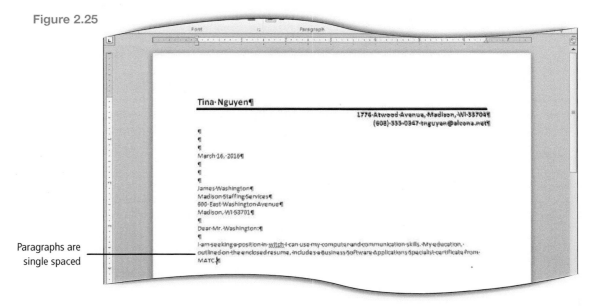

Paragraphs are single spaced ——

Project 2B: Cover Letter and Resume | **Word**

8 Press [Enter] two times. On the **Insert tab**, in the **Text group**, click the **Object button arrow**, and then click **Text from File**. From your student files, locate and **Insert** the file **w02B_Cover_Letter_Text**.

> Some of the words in the cover letter text display red, green, or blue wavy underlines. These indicate potential spelling, grammar, or word usage errors, and you will correct them before the end of this project.

9 Scroll as necessary to display the lower half of the letter on your screen, and be sure your insertion point is positioned in the blank paragraph at the end of the document.

10 Press [Enter] one time to leave one blank line between the last paragraph of the letter and the complimentary closing.

11 Type **Sincerely,** as the complimentary closing, and then press [Enter] four times to leave three blank lines between the complimentary closing and the writer's identification.

12 Type **Tina Nguyen** as the writer's identification, and then press [Enter] two times.

13 Type **Enclosure** to indicate that a document is included with the letter. **Save** 🖫 your document, and then compare your screen with Figure 2.26.

Figure 2.26

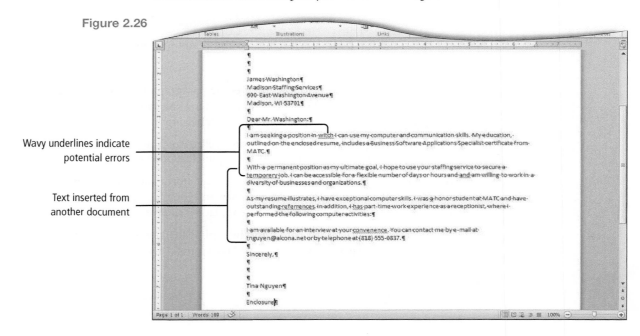

Wavy underlines indicate potential errors

Text inserted from another document

Activity 2.14 | Finding and Replacing Text

Use the Find command to locate text in a document quickly. Use the Find and Replace command to make the same change, or to make more than one change at a time, in a document.

1 Press [Ctrl] + [Home] to position the insertion point at the beginning of the document.

> Because a find operation—or a find and replace operation—begins from the location of the insertion point and proceeds to the end of the document, it is good practice to position the insertion point at the beginning of the document before initiating the command.

Another Way
Hold down [Ctrl] and press [F].

2 On the **Home tab**, in the **Editing group**, click the **Find** button.

> The Navigation Pane displays on the left side of the screen, with a search box at the top of the pane.

3 In the search box, type **ac** If necessary, scroll down slightly in your document to view the entire body text of the letter, and then compare your screen with Figure 2.27.

In the document, the search letters *ac* are selected and highlighted in yellow for all three words that contain the letters *ac* together. In the Navigation Pane, the three instances are shown in context—*ac* displays in bold.

Figure 2.27

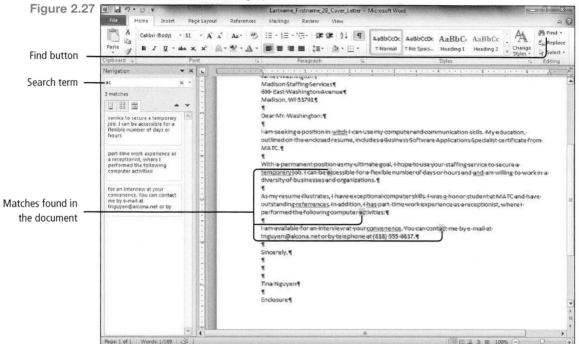

Find button

Search term

Matches found in the document

4 In the search box, complete the word **accessible**.

One match for the search term displays in context in the Navigation Pane and is highlighted in the document.

5 In the document, point to the yellow highlighted word *accessible*, double-click, and then type **available** to replace the word. Notice that the list of results is now empty.

6 **Close** ☒ the **Navigation Pane**, and then on the **Home tab**, in the **Editing group**, click the **Replace** button.

7 In the **Find and Replace** dialog box, in the **Find what** box, replace the existing text by typing **MATC** In the **Replace with** box, type **Madison Area Technical College** and then compare your screen with Figure 2.28

Figure 2.28

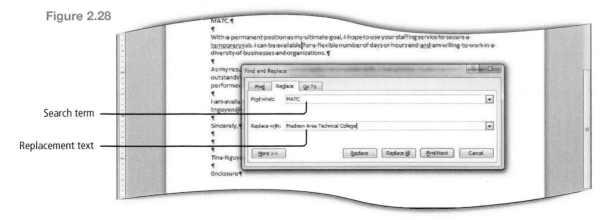

Search term

Replacement text

Project 2B: Cover Letter and Resume | **Word**

8 In the lower left corner of the dialog box, click the **More** button to expand the dialog box, and then under **Search Options**, select the **Match case** check box.

> The acronym *MATC* appears in the document two times. In a formal letter, the reader may not know what the acronym means, so you should include the full text instead of an acronym. In this instance, you must select the *Match case* check box so that the replaced text will match the case you typed in the Replace with box, and *not* display in all uppercase letters in the manner of *MATC*.

9 In the **Find and Replace** dialog box, click the **Replace All** button to replace both instances of *MATC*. Click **OK** to close the message box.

10 In the **Find and Replace** dialog box, clear the **Match case** check box, click the **Less** button, and then **Close** the dialog box.

> The Find and Replace dialog box opens with the settings used the last time it was open. Thus, it is good practice to reset this dialog box to its default settings each time you use it.

11 **Save** 🖫 your document.

Activity 2.15 | Selecting and Moving Text to a New Location

By using Word's ***drag-and-drop*** feature, you can use the mouse to drag selected text from one location to another. Drag-and-drop is most effective when the text to be moved and the destination are on the same screen.

1 Take a moment to study the table in Figure 2.29 to become familiar with the techniques you can use to select text in a document quickly.

Selecting Text in a Document

To Select	Do This
A portion of text	Click to position the insertion point at the beginning of the text you want to select, hold down Shift, and then click at the end of the text you want to select. Alternatively, hold down the left mouse button and drag from the beginning to the end of the text you want to select.
A word	Double-click the word.
A sentence	Hold down Ctrl and click anywhere in the sentence.
A paragraph	Triple-click anywhere in the paragraph; or, move the pointer to the left of the line, into the margin area. When the ◩ pointer displays, double-click.
A line	Move the pointer to the left of the line. When the ◩ pointer displays, click one time.
One character at a time	Position the insertion point to the left of the first character, hold down Shift, and press ← or → as many times as desired.
A string of words	Position the insertion point to the left of the first word, hold down Shift and Ctrl, and then press ← or → as many times as desired.
Consecutive lines	Position the insertion point to the left of the first word, hold down Shift and press ↑ or ↓.
Consecutive paragraphs	Position the insertion point to the left of the first word, hold down Shift and Ctrl and press ↑ or ↓.
The entire document	Hold down Ctrl and press A. Alternatively, move the pointer to the left of any line in the document. When the ◩ pointer displays, triple-click.

Figure 2.29

Word | Using Tables and Templates to Create Resumes and Cover Letters

2 Be sure you can view the entire body of the letter on your screen. In the paragraph that begins *With a permanent position*, in the second line, locate and double-click *days*.

3 Point to the selected word to display the 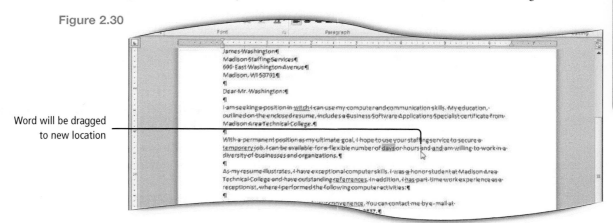 pointer.

4 Drag to the right until the dotted vertical line that floats next to the pointer is positioned to the right of the word *hours* in the same line, as shown in Figure 2.30.

Figure 2.30

Word will be dragged to new location

5 Release the mouse button to move the text. Select the word *hours* and drag it to the left of the word *or*—the previous location of the word *days*. Click anywhere in the document to deselect the text.

6 Examine the text that you moved, and add or remove spaces as necessary.

7 Hold down Ctrl, and then in the paragraph that begins *I am available*, click anywhere in the first sentence to select the entire sentence.

8 Drag the selected sentence to the end of the paragraph by positioning the small vertical line that floats with the pointer to the left of the paragraph mark. Compare your screen with Figure 2.31.

Figure 2.31

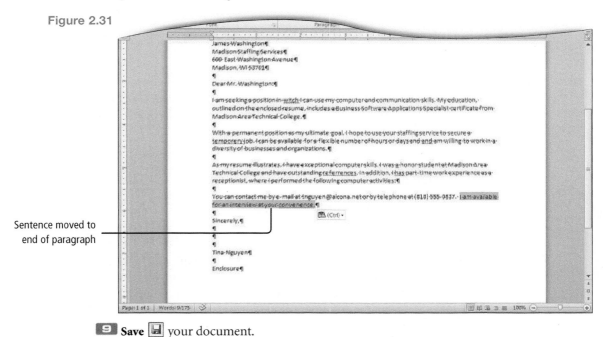

Sentence moved to end of paragraph

9 **Save** your document.

Project 2B: Cover Letter and Resume | **Word**

Activity 2.16 | Inserting and Formatting a Table in a Document

1 Locate the paragraph that begins *As my resume*, and then click to position the insertion point in the blank line below that paragraph. Press Enter one time.

2 On the **Insert tab**, in the **Tables group**, click the **Table** button. In the **Table** grid, in the third row, click the second square to insert a 2 × 3 table.

3 In the first cell of the table, type **Microsoft Access** and then press Tab. Type **Queried inventory data** and then press Tab. Complete the table using the following information:

Microsoft Excel	**Entered budget data**
Microsoft Word	**Created and mailed form letters**

4 Point slightly outside of the upper left corner of the table to display the **table move handle** button ⊞. With the pointer, click one time to select the entire table.

5 On the **Layout tab**, in the **Cell Size group**, click the **AutoFit** button, and then click **AutoFit Contents** to have Word choose the best column widths for the two columns based on the text you entered.

6 On the **Home tab**, in the **Paragraph group**, click the **Center** button ≡ to center the table between the left and right margins.

7 On the **Design tab**, in the **Table Styles group**, click the **Borders button arrow**, and then click **No Border**. Click anywhere to cancel the selection of the table, and then compare your screen with Figure 2.32.

> A light dashed line may display in place of the original table borders if your default settings have been changed.

Figure 2.32

Table inserted in letter

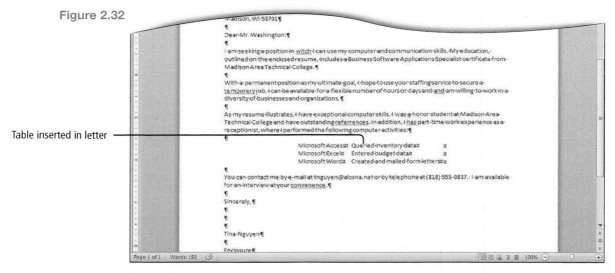

8 Save 🖫 your document.

Objective 6 | Use the Proofing Options

Word compares your typing to words in the Office dictionary and compares your phrases and punctuation to a list of grammar rules. This automatic proofing is set by default. Words that are not in the dictionary are marked with a wavy red underline. Phrases and punctuation that differ from the grammar rules are marked with a wavy green underline.

Word also compares commonly misused words with a set of word usage rules, and marks misused words with a wavy blue underline; for example the misuse of *their*, *there*, and *they're*. However, Word will not flag the word *sign* as misspelled even though you intended to type *sing a song* rather than *sign a song*, because both are words contained within Word's dictionary. Your own knowledge and proofreading skills are still required, even when using a sophisticated Word processing program like Word.

Activity 2.17 | Checking Spelling and Grammar Errors

There are two ways to respond to spelling and grammar errors flagged by Word. You can right-click a flagged word or phrase, and then from the shortcut menu choose a correction or action. Or, you can initiate the Spelling and Grammar command to display the Spelling and Grammar dialog box, which provides more options than the shortcut menus.

Alert! | Spelling and Grammar Checking

If you do not see any wavy red, green, or blue lines under words, the automatic spelling and/or grammar checking has been turned off on your system. To activate the spelling and grammar checking, display Backstage view, on the Help tab, click Options, click Proofing, and then under *When correcting spelling in Microsoft Office programs*, select the first four check boxes. Under *When correcting spelling and grammar in Word*, select the first four check boxes, and then click the Writing Style arrow and click Grammar Only. Under *Exceptions for*, clear both check boxes. To display the flagged spelling and grammar errors, click the Recheck Document button, and then close the dialog box.

---

1 Position the body of the letter on your screen, and then examine the text to locate green, red, and blue wavy underlines. Compare your screen with Figure 2.33.

A list of grammar rules applied by a computer program like Word can never be exact, and a computer dictionary cannot contain all known words and proper names. Thus, you will need to check any words flagged by Word with wavy underlines, and you will also need to proofread for content errors.

Figure 2.33

Blue wavy underline indicates potential word usage problem

Red wavy underline indicates potential spelling problem

Green wavy underline indicates potential grammar problem

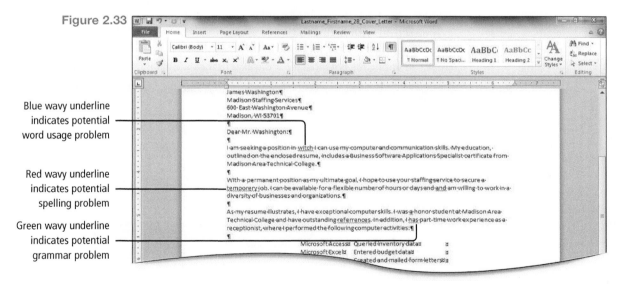

2 In the lower left corner of your screen, in the status bar, locate and point to the icon to display the ScreenTip *Proofing errors were found. Click to correct.*

If this button displays, you know there are potential errors identified in the document.

3 In the paragraph that begins *With a permanent*, locate the word *temporery* with the wavy red underline. Point to the word and right-click to display the shortcut menu, and then compare your screen with Figure 2.34.

Figure 2.34

Suggested spelling correction
Misspelled word
Shortcut menu

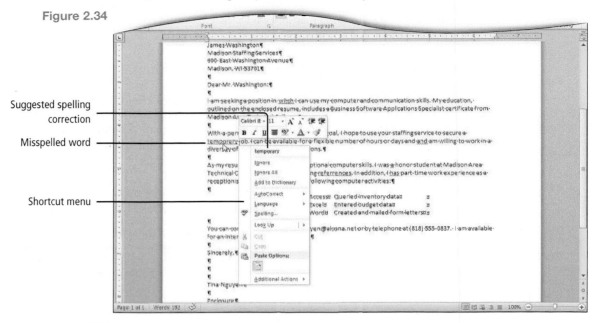

4 On the shortcut menu, click **temporary** to correct the spelling error.

5 In the next line, locate the word *and* that displays with a wavy red underline, point to word and right-click, and then from the shortcut menu, click **Delete Repeated Word** to delete the duplicate word.

> **Another Way**
> Press F7 to start the Spelling & Grammar command.

6 Press Ctrl + Home to move the insertion point to the beginning of the document. Click the **Review tab**, and then in the **Proofing group**, click the **Spelling & Grammar** button to check the spelling and grammar of the text in the document. Compare your screen with Figure 2.35.

The word *witch* is highlighted—a *Possible Word Choice Error*—and the sentence containing the potential error displays in the dialog box. A suggested change also displays.

Figure 2.35

Word usage error
Suggested correction

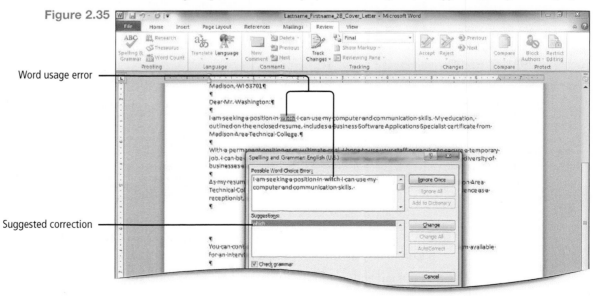

Word | Using Tables and Templates to Create Resumes and Cover Letters

7 In the **Spelling and Grammar** dialog box, click the **Change** button to change to the correct usage *which*.

The next marked word—a possible spelling error—displays.

8 Click the **Change** button to change *referrences* to *references*. Notice that the next error is a possible grammar error.

9 Click the **Change** button to change *a* to *an*. Continue the spelling and grammar check and change *has* to *have* and correct the spelling of *convenence*.

10 When Word indicates *The spelling and grammar check is complete*, click **OK**.

11 Save 🖫 your document.

Activity 2.18 | Using the Thesaurus

A *thesaurus* is a research tool that lists *synonyms*—words that have the same or similar meaning to the word you selected.

1 Scroll so that you can view the body of the letter. In the paragraph that begins *With a permanent*, at the end of the second line, locate and right-click the word *diversity*.

2 On the shortcut menu, point to **Synonyms**, and then compare your screen with Figure 2.36.

A list of synonyms displays; the list will vary in length depending on the selected word.

Figure 2.36

List of synonyms

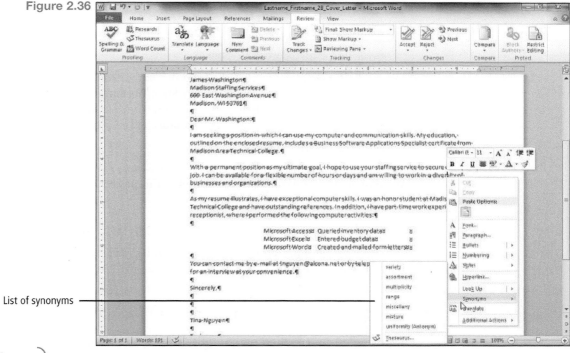

Another Way

Click the word, and then on the Review tab, in the Proofing group, click the Thesaurus button.

3 From the list of synonyms, click **variety** to replace *diversity* with *variety*.

4 In the paragraph that begins *As my resume*, point to the word *exceptional*, right-click, point to **Synonyms**, and then at the bottom of the shortcut menu, click **Thesaurus** to display the **Research** task pane.

5 In the **Research** task pane, under **Thesaurus**, point to the non-bold word *excellent*, and then click the **arrow**. Compare your screen with Figure 2.37.

Figure 2.37

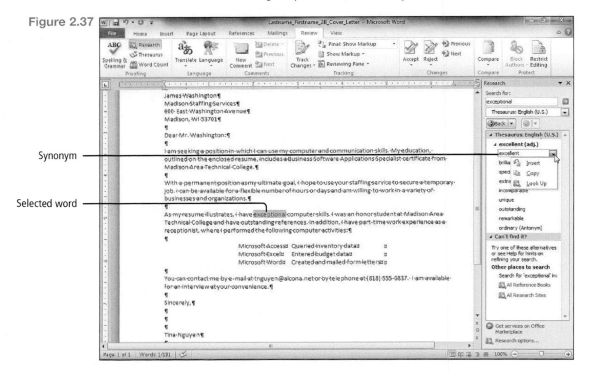

Synonym

Selected word

6 On the menu, click **Insert**, and then **Close** ☒ the **Research** task pane.

    excellent replaces the word *exceptional*.

7 Display **Backstage** view and click the **Info tab**. On the right, under the document thumbnail, click **Properties**, and then click **Show Document Panel**. In the **Author** box, type your firstname and lastname. Be sure your course name and section number display in the **Subject** box, and as the **Keywords**, replace any existing text with **cover letter**

8 Close ☒ the **Document Panel**.

9 Save 🖫, and then display **Backstage** view. Click **Close** to close the document but leave Word open. Hold this file until you complete this project.

Objective 7 | Create a Document Using a Template

Microsoft provides pre-designed templates for letters, resumes, invoices, and other types of documents. Recall that when you open a template, it opens unnamed so that you can reuse it as often as you need to do so.

Activity 2.19 | Locating and Opening a Template

If you need to create a short resume quickly, or if you need ideas about how to format your resume, Microsoft Word provides pre-designed resume templates. Some templates are available on your computer; many more are available online. After opening a template, you can add text as indicated, modify the layout and design, and add or remove resume elements.

1 Close any open documents, and then from **Backstage** view, click **New**.

2 Under **Available Templates**, click **Sample templates**.

Word | Using Tables and Templates to Create Resumes and Cover Letters

3 Under **Available Templates**, scroll toward the bottom of the window, and then click **Median Resume**. Notice that a preview of the *Median Resume* template displays on the right. Compare your screen with Figure 2.38.

Figure 2.38

Preview of template

Selected template

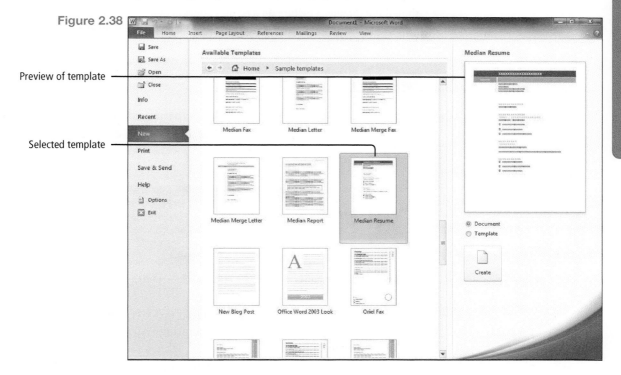

4 In the lower right corner, click the **Create** button.

> The template opens a copy of itself in the form of a new Word document—the title bar indicates *Document* followed by a number. Recall that you are not opening the template itself, and that changes you make to this new document will not affect the contents of the template file.

5 Display the **Save As** dialog box. **Save** the document in your **Word Chapter 2** folder as **Lastname_Firstname_2B_Brief_Resume** and then add the file name to the footer— called the *First Page Footer* in this template.

6 **Save** 🖫 your document.

Activity 2.20 | Replacing Template Placeholder Text

After you save the template file as a Word document, you can begin to substitute your own information in the indicated locations. You can also remove unneeded resume elements that are included with the template.

1 Click on the picture, and notice that a Picture Tool tab is added to the Ribbon.

2 Click the **Layout tab**, and then in the **Table group**, click the **View Gridlines** button to display non-printing table borders.

> This template consists of two Word tables, and the name in the first row of the upper table displays either the user name or the text *[Type your name]* in square brackets.

3 At the top of the upper table, click the **Resume Name tab arrow**, and then compare your screen with Figure 2.39.

> There are two styles available with the Median template—with or without a photo. You should not include a picture on a resume unless physical appearance is directly related to the job for which you are applying—for example, for a job as an actor or a model.

Figure 2.39

Resume Name tab arrow —

Two styles available —

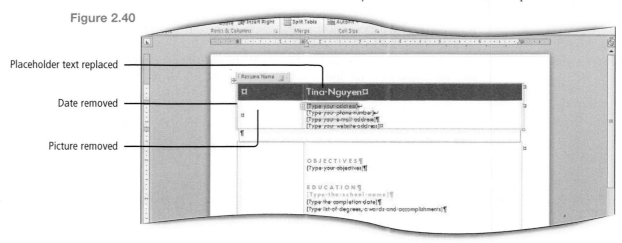

4 In the **Resume Name** gallery, click the first style—**Name**—to switch to the style with no picture.

5 In the first row of the table, select the displayed text—typically the name of your computer as indicated in your Windows operating system—and replace the text by typing **Tina Nguyen**

Another Way
Select the entire row, right-click, and then from the shortcut menu, click Delete Rows.

6 In the second row, click anywhere in the date control *[Select the Date]*. On the Ribbon, click the **Layout tab**. In the **Rows & Columns group**, click the **Delete** button, and then click **Delete Rows**.

> Text surrounded by brackets is called a ***content control***. There are several different types of content controls, including date, picture, and ***text controls***. Most of the controls in this template are text controls. Because resumes do not typically include a date, you can delete this row.

7 Click anywhere in the content control *[Type your address]*. Compare your screen with Figure 2.40.

> For the name and address at the top of the document, all of the text controls are grouped together. Each control has ***placeholder text***, text that indicates the type of information to be entered. The name in the first row may also be a content control with placeholder text.

Figure 2.40

Placeholder text replaced —

Date removed —

Picture removed —

Word | Using Tables and Templates to Create Resumes and Cover Letters

8 Complete the personal information by using the following information:

[Type your address]	**1776 Atwood Avenue, Madison, WI 53704**
[Type your phone number]	**(608) 555-0347**
[Type your e-mail address]	**tnguyen@alcona.net**
[Type your website address]	(leave this blank)

9 In the lower table, click in the *[Type your objectives]* control, and then type **To obtain a position using my computer and communications skills.**

10 Complete the **Education** section by using the following information:

[Type the school name]	**Madison Area Technical College**
[Type the completion date]	**June 2015**
[Type list of degrees, awards and accomplishments] *(type three separate lines)*	**Business Computing Specialist certificate** **Dean's List, four semesters** **President, Community Service Club**

11 Complete the **Experience** section by using the following information:

[Type the job title]	**Office Assistant (part-time)**
[Type the company name]	**The Robinson Company**
[Type the start date]	**September 2014**
[Type the end date]	**present**
[Type list of job responsibilities]	**Data entry and report generation using company spreadsheets and databases.**

12 Click in the *[Type list of skills]* control, type **Proficiency using Word, Excel, and Access (completed advanced courses in Microsoft Office programs)** and then press Enter.

13 As the second bulleted point, type **Excellent written and verbal communications (completed courses in Business Communications, PowerPoint, and Speech)** and then compare your screen with Figure 2.41. **Save** your document.

Figure 2.41

Placeholder text replaced ——

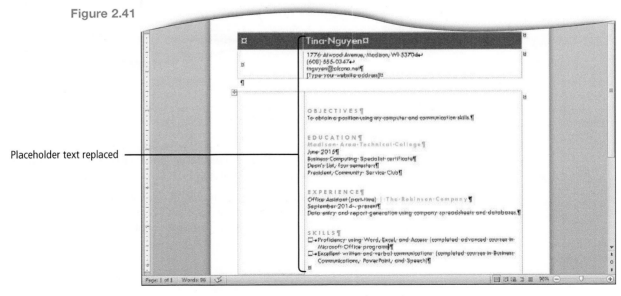

Project 2B: Cover Letter and Resume | **Word**

Activity 2.21 | Removing Template Controls and Formatting the Resume

1 Near the top of the document, point to the text control that you did not use—*[Type your website address]*. Right-click the control, and then from the shortcut menu, click **Remove Content Control**. Press ⌨Backspace as necessary to position the insertion point at the end of the e-mail address. Select the three lines with the address, phone, and e-mail information. On the Mini toolbar, notice that the text size is *11.5*. Click the **Font Size button arrow**, and then click **12**.

2 Click anywhere in lower table—the table with the *Objectives* row at the top—and then point to the upper left corner of the active table to display the **move table handle**. Click one time to select the lower table.

3 On the Mini toolbar, change the **Font Size** to **12** to match the table above.

4 Click anywhere to cancel the selection. On the **Page Layout tab**, in the **Page Setup group**, click the **Margins** button, and then click **Custom Margins**. Change the **Top** margin to **1.5** and the **Left** and **Right** margins to **1** to make this short resume better fill the page. Compare your screen with Figure 2.42.

Figure 2.42

New margins

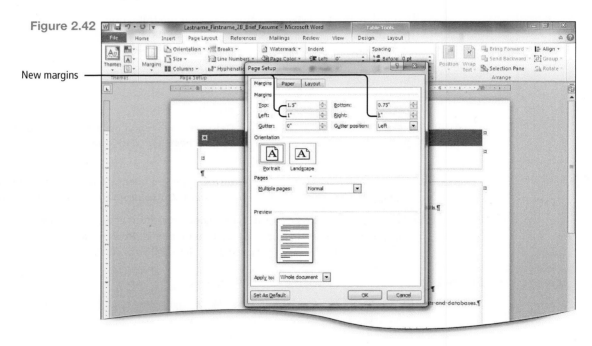

5 Click **OK** to close the **Page Setup** dialog box and apply the new margins. If the name at the top of the document changes back to a placeholder, click the control and type **Tina Nguyen**

6 Right-click the name at the top of the document—*Tina Nguyen*—and then from the shortcut menu, click **Remove Content Control**.

> This action will leave the name but remove the control. Remove the control if the Document Properties will have an author other than the name in this control. If you do *not* remove the content control, when you add document properties, the name will change to the name you type in the Author box.

7 Press `Ctrl` + `F2` to display the Print Preview in **Backstage** view. Click the **Info tab**. On the right, under the document thumbnail, click **Properties**, and then click **Show Document Panel**. In the **Author** box, delete any text and then type your firstname and lastname. In the **Subject** box, type your course name and section number, and in the **Keywords** box, type **short resume, template**

8 **Close** ✕ the **Document Panel. Save** 🔲 your document, and then hold this file until you complete this project. Leave the resume displayed on your screen.

Activity 2.22 | Saving a Resume as a Web Page

You can save your resume as a Web page. This enables you to post the Web page on your own Web site or on Web space provided by your college. It also enables you to send the resume as an e-mail attachment that can be opened using any Web browser.

1 With your **2B_Brief_Resume** still open on your screen, click **Save** 🔲 to be sure the current version of the document is saved.

2 Display the **Save As** dialog box. In the lower portion of the **Save As** dialog box, click the **Save as type arrow**, and then click **Single File Web Page**.

A *Single File Web Page* is a document saved using the *Hypertext Markup Language (HTML)*. HTML is the language used to format documents that can be opened using a Web browser such as Internet Explorer.

3 In the **Save As** dialog box, in the **File name** box, type **Lastname_Firstname_2B_HTML_Resume** Click **Save**, and then click **Yes** if a message box displays. Notice that the Web page displays in Word.

4 Display **Backstage** view. On the right, click **Properties**, and then click **Advanced Properties**. In the **Properties** dialog box, on the **Summary tab**, in the **Subject** box, be sure your course name and section number display. In the **Author** box, be sure your first and last names display. In the **Keywords** box, replace the existing text with **HTML** Click **OK**, and then click the **Home tab**. **Save** 🔲 the document; print or submit electronically as directed.

5 **Exit** Word. From the **Start** menu 🪟, click **Computer**. Navigate to your **Word Chapter 2** folder, and then double-click your **Lastname_Firstname_2B_HTML_Resume** file to open the resume in your Web browser. Compare your screen with Figure 2.43.

Figure 2.43

Resume displayed in a Web browser

6 **Close** ✕ your Web browser. As directed by your instructor, print or submit electronically the four files from this project—2B_Letterhead, 2B_Cover_Letter, 2B_Brief_Resume, and 2B_HTML_Resume.

End **You have completed Project 2B** ————————

Project 2B: Cover Letter and Resume | **Word**

Content-Based Assessments

Summary

In this chapter, you created a table, and then used the table to create a resume. You created a letterhead template, and then created a document using a copy of the letterhead template. You created a cover letter for the resume, moved text, corrected spelling and grammar, and used the built-in thesaurus. Finally, you created a short resume using a template, and also saved the resume as a Web page.

Key Terms

AutoCorrect	Hypertext Markup Language (HTML)	Subject line
Body		Synonyms
Cell	Inside address	Table
Complimentary closing	Letterhead	Template
	New from existing	Text control
Content control	No Spacing style	Thesaurus
Date line	Normal template	Writer's identification
Drag and drop	Placeholder text	Writer's signature block
Enclosures	Salutation	
HTML	Single File Web Page	

Matching

Match each term in the second column with its correct definition in the first column by writing the letter of the term on the blank line in front of the correct definition.

_____ 1. An arrangement of information organized into rows and columns.

_____ 2. The box at the intersection of a row and column in a table.

_____ 3. A document structure that opens a copy of itself, opens unnamed, and is used as the starting point for another document.

_____ 4. The template that serves as a basis for all new Word documents.

_____ 5. The personal or company information that displays at the top of a letter.

_____ 6. The Word style that inserts no extra space following a paragraph and uses single spacing.

_____ 7. The first line in a business letter that contains the current date and that is positioned just below the letterhead if a letterhead is used.

_____ 8. The name and address of the person receiving a letter and positioned below the date line.

_____ 9. The greeting line of a letter.

_____ 10. A parting farewell in a letter.

_____ 11. The name and title of the author of a letter, placed near the bottom of the letter under the complimentary closing.

_____ 12. The optional line following the inside address in a business letter that states the purpose of the letter.

A AutoCorrect

B Cell

C Complimentary closing

D Date line

E Drag and drop

F Enclosures

G Inside address

H Letterhead

I No Spacing

J Normal template

K Salutation

L Subject line

M Table

N Template

O Writer's identification

_____ 13. Additional documents included with a business letter.

_____ 14. A Word feature that corrects common spelling errors as you type, for example changing *teh* to *the*.

_____ 15. A technique by which you can move, by dragging, selected text from one location in a document to another.

Multiple Choice

Circle the correct answer.

1. When you create a table, the width of all of cells in the table is:
   A. equal   B. proportional   C. 1 inch

2. To indicate words that might be misspelled because they are not in Word's dictionary, Word flags text with:
   A. blue wavy underlines   B. green wavy underlines   C. red wavy underlines

3. To indicate possible grammar errors, Word flags text with:
   A. blue wavy underlines   B. green wavy underlines   C. red wavy underlines

4. To indicate possible errors in word usage, Word flags text with:
   A. blue wavy underlines   B. green wavy underlines   C. red wavy underlines

5. A research tool that provides a list of words with similar meanings is:
   A. a thesaurus   B. a dictionary   C. an encyclopedia

6. A word with the same or similar meaning as another word is:
   A. an acronym   B. a search term   C. a synonym

7. In a template, an area indicated by placeholder text into which you can add text, pictures, dates, or lists is a:
   A. text control   B. content control   C. quick control

8. A document saved in HTML, which can be opened using a Web browser, is a:
   A. Web page   B. template   C. resume

9. Using drag-and-drop to move text is most useful when both the text and the destination are on the same:
   A. document   B. section   C. screen

10. To locate specific text in a document quickly, use the:
    A. Find command   B. Replace command   C. Locate command

Content-Based Assessments

Skills Review | Project **2C** Student Resume

In the following Skills Review, you will use a table to create a resume for Joshua Green. Your completed resume will look similar to Figure 2.44.

Project Files

For Project 2C, you will need the following files:

New blank Word document
w02C_Skills
w02C_Experience

You will save your document as:

Lastname_Firstname_2C_Student_Resume

Project Results

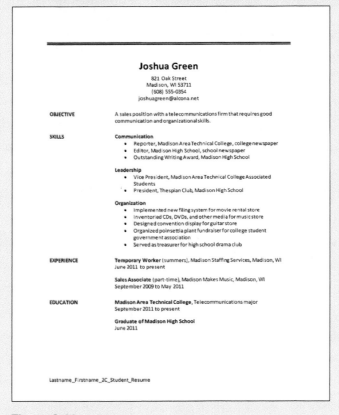

Figure 2.44

(Project 2C Student Resume continues on the next page)

Word | Using Tables and Templates to Create Resumes and Cover Letters

1 **Start** Word. In the new blank document, be sure that formatting marks and rulers display. **Save** the document in your **Word Chapter 2** folder as **Lastname_Firstname_ 2C_Student_Resume**

a. Add the file name to the footer, and then close the footer area. Click the **Insert tab**, and then in the **Tables group**, click the **Table** button. In the **Table** grid, in the fourth row, click the second square to insert a **2 × 4** table.

b. In the first cell of the table, type **Joshua Green** and then press Enter. Type the following text, pressing Enter after each line *except* the last line:

821 Oak Street

Madison, WI 53711

(608) 555-0354

joshuagreen@alcona.net

c. Press ↓ to move to the first cell in the second row. Type **SKILLS** and then press ↓ to move to the first cell in the third row.

d. Type **EXPERIENCE** and then press ↓. Type **EDUCATION**

e. In the first cell, if the e-mail address displays in blue, right-click the e-mail address, and then from the shortcut menu, click **Remove Hyperlink**. **Save** your document

2 Click in the cell to the right of *SKILLS*, and then type the following, pressing Enter after each item:

Communication
Reporter, Madison Area Technical College, college newspaper
Editor, Madison High School, school newspaper
Outstanding Writing Award, Madison High School

a. With the insertion point in the new line at the end of the cell, click the **Insert tab**. In the **Text group**, click the **Object button arrow**, and then click **Text from File**.

b. Navigate to your student files, select **w02C_Skills**, and then click **Insert**. Press Backspace one time to remove the blank line.

c. Click in the cell to the right of *EXPERIENCE*, and then insert the file **w02C_Experience**. Press Backspace one time to remove the blank line.

d. Click in the cell to the right of *EDUCATION*, and then type the following, pressing Enter after all *except* the last item:

Madison Area Technical College, Telecommunications major

September 2011 to present

Graduate of Madison High School

June 2011

3 Click anywhere in the top row of the table. Click the **Layout tab**, and then in the **Rows & Columns group**, click the **Insert Below** button. Type **OBJECTIVE** and then press Tab.

a. Type **A sales position with a telecommunications firm that requires good communication and organizational skills.**

b. In any row, point to the vertical border between the two columns to display the |↔| pointer. Drag the column border to the left to approximately **1.75 inches on the horizontal ruler**.

c. Click anywhere in the left column. Click the **Layout tab**. In the **Cell Size group**, in the **Table Column Width** box, if necessary, type **1.75** and press Enter.

d. In the first row of the document, drag across both cells to select them. On the **Layout tab**, in the **Merge group**, click the **Merge Cells** button. Right-click the selected cell, and then from the Mini toolbar, click the **Center** button.

e. In the top row, select the first paragraph of text— *Joshua Green*. From the Mini toolbar, increase the **Font Size** to **20** and apply **Bold**.

f. In the second row, point to the word *OBJECTIVE*, hold down the left mouse button, and then drag down to select the row headings in uppercase letters. On the Mini toolbar, click the **Bold** button. **Save** your document.

4 Click in the cell to the right of *OBJECTIVE*. On the **Page Layout tab**, in the **Paragraph group**, click the **Spacing After up spin arrow** three times to change the spacing to **18 pt**.

a. In the cell to the right of *SKILLS*, apply **Bold** to the words *Communication, Leadership,* and *Organization*. Then, under each bold heading in the cell, select the lines of text, and create a bulleted list.

b. In the first two bulleted lists, click in the last bullet item, and then on the **Page Layout tab**, in the **Paragraph group**, set the **Spacing After** to **12 pt**.

(Project 2C Student Resume continues on the next page)

Skills Review | Project 2C Student Resume (continued)

c. In the last bulleted list, click in the last bullet item, and then set the **Spacing After** to **18 pt**.

d. In the cell to the right of *EXPERIENCE*, apply **Bold** to *Temporary Worker* and *Sales Associate*. Click in the line *June 2011 to present* and apply **Spacing After** of **12 pt**. Click in the line *September 2009 to May 2011* and apply **Spacing After** of **18 pt**.

e. In the cell to the right of *EDUCATION*, apply **Bold** to *Madison Area Technical College* and *Graduate of Madison High School*.

f. In the same cell, click in the line *September 2011 to present* and apply **Spacing After** of **12 pt**.

g. In the first row, click in the last line—*joshuagreen@alcona.net*—and then change the **Spacing After** to **18 pt**. Click in the first line—*Joshua Green*—and set the **Spacing Before** to **30 pt** and the **Spacing After** to **6 pt**.

5 Point to the upper left corner of the table, and then click the displayed **table move handle** button ⊞ to select the entire table. On the **Design tab**, in the **Table Styles group**, click the **Borders button arrow**, and then click **No Border**.

a. On the **Design tab**, in the **Table Styles group**, click the **Borders button arrow** again, and then at the bottom of the gallery, click **Borders and Shading**. In the **Borders and Shading** dialog box, under **Setting**, click **Custom**. Under **Style**, scroll down slightly, and then click the style with two equal lines.

b. Click the **Width arrow**, and then click **1 1/2 pt**. Under **Preview**, click the top border of the preview box, and then click **OK**.

c. Click the **File tab** to display **Backstage** view, and then click the **Print tab** to display the Print Preview.

d. Click the **Info tab**. On the right side, under the document thumbnail, click **Properties**, and then click **Show Document Panel**.

e. In the **Author** box, delete any text and then type your firstname and lastname. In the **Subject** box, type your course name and section number, and in the **Keywords** box type **resume, table**

f. **Close** the **Document Panel**. **Save** 🖫 and then, as directed by your instructor, print your document or submit it electronically. **Exit** Word.

End **You have completed Project 2C** ────────────

Content-Based Assessments

Skills Review | Project **2D** Ross Letter

In the following Skills Review, you will create a letterhead, and then create a new document from the letterhead to create a resume cover letter. You will also create a short resume using a Microsoft template and save it as a Web page. Your completed documents will look similar to Figure 2.45.

Project Files

For Project 2D, you will need the following files:

New blank Word document
w02D_Letter_Text
Equity Resume Template from Word's installed templates

You will save your documents as:

Lastname_Firstname_2D_Ross_Letterhead
Lastname_Firstname_2D_Ross_Letter
Lastname_Firstname_2D_Resume
Lastname_Firstname_2D_Web_Resume

Project Results

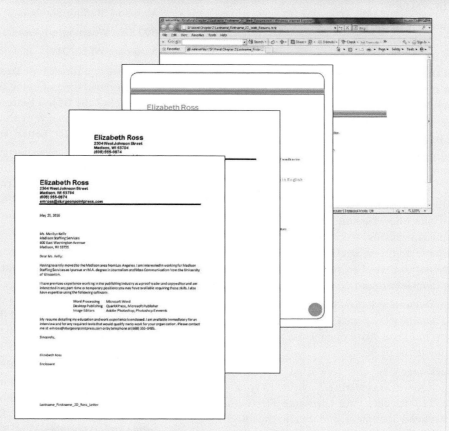

Figure 2.45

(Project 2D Ross Letter continues on the next page)

Content-Based Assessments

Skills Review | Project **2D** Ross Letter (continued)

1 **Start** Word. In the new blank document, be sure that formatting marks and rulers display. On the **Home tab**, in the **Styles group**, click the **No Spacing** button.

a. Type **Elizabeth Ross** and then press Enter. Type **2304 West Johnson Street** and press Enter. Type **Madison, WI 53704** and then press Enter.

b. Type **(608) 555-0874** and then press Enter. Type **emross@sturgeonpointpress.com** and then press Enter three times. If the e-mail address changes to blue text, right-click the e-mail address, and then click Remove Hyperlink.

c. Select all five lines of the personal information, but do not select the blank paragraphs. From the Mini toolbar, change the **Font** to **Arial Rounded MT Bold**. Select the first paragraph—*Elizabeth Ross*—and then on the Mini toolbar, apply **Bold** and change the **Font Size** to **20**.

d. Click anywhere in the fifth line of text—the e-mail address. On the **Home tab**, in the **Paragraph group**, click the **Borders button arrow**, and then click **Borders and Shading**. Under **Style**, click the first style—a single solid line. Click the **Width arrow**, and then click **3 pt**. In the **Preview** area, click the bottom border, and then click **OK**.

e. Display **Backstage** view, and then click **Save As**. Save the document in your **Word Chapter 2** folder as **Lastname_Firstname_2D_Ross_Letterhead**

f. Add the file name to the footer, and then close the footer area. Display **Backstage** view, click **Properties**, and then click **Show Document Panel**. In the **Author** box, delete any text and then type your firstname and lastname. In the **Subject** box, type your course name and section number, and in the **Keywords** box, type **personal letterhead**

g. **Close** the **Document Panel**. **Save** your document. From **Backstage** view, click **Close** to close the document but leave Word open. Hold this file until you complete the project.

2 From **Backstage** view, click **New**. Under **Available Templates**, click **New from existing**. Navigate to your **Word Chapter 2** folder, click your **Lastname_Firstname_2D_Ross_Letterhead** document, and then in the lower right corner, click **Create New**. From **Backstage** view, click **Save As**. Navigate to your **Word Chapter 2** folder, and Save the file as **Lastname_Firstname_2D_Ross_Letter**

Double-click the footer, right-click the file name, and then click **Update Field**. Close the footer area.

a. From **Backstage** view, display the **Word Options** dialog box. In the **Word Options** list, click **Proofing**, and then under **AutoCorrect options**, click the **AutoCorrect Options** button.

b. In the **AutoCorrect** dialog box, click the **AutoCorrect tab**. Under **Replace**, type **expereince** and under **With**, type **experience** Click **Add**. If the entry already exists, click Replace instead, and then click Yes. Click **OK** two times to close the dialog boxes.

c. Press Ctrl + End, type **May 25, 2016** and then press Enter four times. Type the following inside address using four lines:

Ms. Marilyn Kelly

Madison Staffing Services

600 East Washington Avenue

Madison, WI 53701

d. Press Enter two times, type **Dear Ms. Kelly:** and then press Enter two times. On the **Insert tab**, in the **Text group**, click the **Object button arrow**, and then click **Text from File**. From your student files, locate and insert the file **w02D_Letter_Text**.

e. Scroll to view the lower portion of the page, and be sure your insertion point is in the empty paragraph mark at the end. Press Enter, type **Sincerely,** and then press Enter four times. Type **Elizabeth Ross** and press Enter two times. Type **Enclosure** and then **Save** your document.

f. Near the bottom of the document, locate the paragraph that begins *I am available* and click to position the insertion point at the beginning of the paragraph. Type **My resume detailing my education and work** Press Spacebar and then type the misspelled word **expereince** Press Spacebar and notice that AutoCorrect corrects the misspelling. Type **is enclosed.** and then press Spacebar.

g. Press Ctrl + Home. On the **Home tab**, in the **Editing group**, click the **Replace** button. In the **Find what** box, type **association** In the **Replace with** box, type **organization** and then click **Replace All**. Click **OK** to close the message box, and then **Close** the **Find and Replace** dialog box.

(Project 2D Ross Letter continues on the next page)

Content-Based Assessments

h. In the paragraph that begins *I have previous*, double-click *experience*. Point to the selected word to display the ⬚ pointer, and then drag the word to the left of *working*. Adjust spacing as necessary.

i. Below the paragraph that begins *I have previous*, position the insertion point in the second blank line. On the **Insert tab**, in the **Tables group**, click the **Table** button. In the **Table** grid, in the third row, click the second square to insert a 2 × 3 table. Type the following information in the table:

Word Processing	Microsoft Word
Desktop Publishing	QuarkXPress, Microsoft Publisher
Image Editors	Adobe Photoshop, Photoshop Elements

j. Point outside of the upper left corner and click the **table move handle** button to select the entire table. On the **Layout tab**, in the **Cell Size group**, click the **AutoFit** button, and then click **AutoFit Contents**. On the **Home tab**, in the **Paragraph group**, click the **Center** button. On the **Design tab**, in the **Table Styles group**, click the **Borders button arrow**, and then click **No Border**. **Save** your document.

3 If you do not see any wavy red and green lines under words, refer to the Alert in Activity 2.17 to enable the default settings for automatic proofing.

a. In the paragraph that begins *Having lately*, in the second line, locate and right-click the phrase *an M.A. degrees*, and then from the shortcut menu, click *an M.A. degree*. In the same paragraph, locate and right-click *Journlism*. From the shortcut menu, click *Journalism*.

b. Press Ctrl + Home. On the **Review tab**, in the **Proofing group**, click the **Spelling & Grammar** button. In the **Spelling and Grammar** dialog box, click the **Change** button to change *are* to *am*. For the misspelled word *expertis*, under **Suggestions**, be sure *expertise* is selected, and then click **Change**.

c. **Change** *qualifie* to *qualify*, and then click **OK** to close the message box.

d. Near the top of the document, in the paragraph that begins *Having lately*, right-click *lately*. In the shortcut menu, point to **Synonyms**, and then click *recently*. In the same line, right-click *region*, and replace it with the synonym *area*.

e. Display **Backstage** view, click **Properties**, and then click **Show Document Panel**. Type your firstname and lastname as the **Author** and your course number and section as the **Subject**. In the **Keywords** box, replace any existing text with **cover letter Close** the **Document Panel**. **Save** your document. From **Backstage** view, **Close** the document but leave Word open. Hold this file until you complete the project.

4 Display **Backstage** view, and then click **New**. Under **Available Templates**, click **Sample templates**. Locate and click **Equity Resume**. In the lower right corner, click **Create**.

a. **Save** the document in your **Word Chapter 2** folder as **Lastname_Firstname_2D_Resume** and then add the file name to the footer—called *First Page Footer* in this template. At the top of the resume, select the text in the first control, which displays the name of the computer at which you are working. Replace this text by typing **Elizabeth Ross** Right-click the name, and then from the shortcut menu, click **Remove Content Control**.

b. Click the *[Type your phone number]* control, and then type **(608) 555-0874** Click the *[Type your address]* control, type **2304 West Johnson Street** and press Enter. Type **Madison, WI 53703**

c. Click the *[Type your e-mail address]* control, and then type **emross@sturgeonpointpress.com** Right-click the *[Type your website]* control, and then from the shortcut menu, click **Remove Content Control**. Press Backspace to remove the *website* line.

d. Click the *[Type the objectives]* control, and then type **A copy editing or proofreading position where my editing and advanced computer skills will be of benefit to the organization.**

e. Under *Education*, click the *[Type the completion date]* control, and then type **University of Wisconsin-Milwaukee, May 2015** Click the *[Type the degree]* control, and then type **Bachelor of Arts in English** For the *[Type list of accomplishments]* bulleted list, type:

Dean's list, six terms

Harriet McArthur Creative Writing Award

(Project 2D Ross Letter continues on the next page)

Assistant Editor of college newspaper

3.8 GPA

f. Under *Experience*, enter the text shown in **Table 1** below.

g. Click the *[Type list of skills]* control and type **Word** Press Enter, and then type two additional bullet points with **QuarkXPress** and **Adobe Photoshop**

h. Display **Backstage** view, click **Properties**, and then click **Show Document Panel**. Type your firstname and lastname as the **Author**. In the **Subject** box, type your course and section number. In the **Keywords** box, **resume, template Close** the **Document Panel**.

i. **Save** your document.

j. Display **Backstage** view, click **Save As**, and then in the **Save as type** box, click **Single File Web Page**. Navigate to your **Word Chapter 2** folder. In the **File name** box,

type **Lastname_Firstname_2D_Web_Resume** Click **Save**.

k. Display **Backstage** view, click **Properties**, and then click **Advanced Properties**. In the **Properties** dialog box, be sure your name displays in the *Author* box, and then in the **Keywords** box, add **HTML** to the list of keywords. Click **OK** and **Save** your document.

l. **Exit** Word. From the **Start** menu, click **Computer** (or My Computer). Navigate to your **Word Chapter 2** folder, and then double-click your **2D_Web_Resume** file to open the resume in your Web browser. **Close** the Web browser. As directed by your instructor, print or submit electronically the four files that are the results of this project—2D_Ross_Letterhead, 2D_Ross_Letter, 2D_Resume, and 2D_Web_Resume.

Table 1

[Type the start date]	**May 2012**
[Type the end date]	**Present-**
[Type the job title]	**Senior Copy Editor**
[Type the company name]	**Sturgeon Point Press**
[Type the company address]	**Milwaukee, WI**
[Type job responsibilities]	**Produced final edited copy of books, technical manuals, and pamphlets; supervised three copy editors.**

(Return to Step 4-g)

End **You have completed Project 2D**

Content-Based Assessments

Apply **2A** skills from these Objectives:

1. Create a Table
2. Add Text to a Table
3. Format a Table

Mastering Word | Project **2E** Job Listings

In the following Mastering Word project, you will create an announcement for new job postings at Madison Staffing Services. Your completed document will look similar to Figure 2.46.

Project Files

For Project 2E, you will need the following files:

New blank Word document
w02E_New_Jobs

You will save your document as:

Lastname_Firstname_2E_Job_Listings

Project Results

Madison Staffing Services

Job Alert! New Health Care Listings Just Added!

January 7

Madison Staffing Services has just added several new jobs in the Health Care Industry for the week of January 7. These listings are just in, so apply now to be one of the first candidates considered!

For further information about any of these new jobs, or a complete listing of jobs that are available through Madison Staffing Services, please call Marilyn Kelly at (608) 555-0386 or visit our Web site at www.madisonstaffing.com.

New Health Care Listings for the Week of January 7

Job Title	Type	Location
Computer Developer	Radiology Office	Dane County
Executive Assistant	Medical Records	Deerfield
Insurance Biller	Dental Office	Madison
Office Assistant	Health Clinic	Madison

To help prepare yourself before applying for these jobs, we recommend that you review the following articles on our Web site at www.madisonstaffing.com.

Topic	Article Title
Research	Working in Health Care
Interviewing	Interviewing in Health Care

Lastname_Firstname_2E_Job_Listings

Figure 2.46

(Project 2E Job Listings continues on the next page)

Content-Based Assessments

1 **Start** Word and display a new blank document; display formatting marks and rulers. **Save** the document in your **Word Chapter 2** folder as **Lastname_Firstname_2E_Job_Listings** and then add the file name to the footer.

2 Type **Madison Staffing Services** and press Enter. Type **Job Alert! New Health Care Listings Just Added!** and press Enter. Type **January 7** and press Enter two times. **Insert** the file **w02E_New_Jobs**.

3 At the top of the document, select and **Center** the three title lines. Select the title *Madison Staffing Services* and change the **Font Size** to **20** pt and apply **Bold**. Apply **Bold** to the second and third title lines. Locate the paragraph that begins *For further information*, and then below that paragraph, click to position the insertion point in the second blank paragraph. **Insert** a **3 × 4** table. Enter the following:

Job Title	Type	Location
Executive Assistant	Medical Records	Deerfield
Insurance Biller	Dental Office	Madison
Office Assistant	Health Clinic	Madison

4 In the table, click anywhere in the second row, and then insert a row above. Add the following information so that the job titles remain in alphabetic order:

Computer Developer	Radiology Office	Dane County

5 Select the entire table. On the **Layout tab**, in the **Cell Size group**, use the **AutoFit** button to **AutoFit**

Contents. With the table still selected, **Center** the table. With the table still selected, on the **Page Layout tab**, add **6 pt Spacing Before** and **6 pt Spacing After**.

6 With the table still selected, remove all table borders, and then add a **Custom 1 pt** solid line top border and bottom border. Select all three cells in the first row, apply **Bold**, and then **Center** the text. Click anywhere in the first row, and then insert a new row above. Merge the three cells in the new top row, and then type **New Health Care Listings for the Week of January 7** Notice that the new row keeps the formatting of the row from which it was created.

7 At the bottom of the document, **Insert** a **2 × 3** table. Enter the following:

Topic	Article Title
Research	Working in Health Care
Interviewing	Interviewing in Health Care

8 Select the entire table. On the **Layout tab**, in the **Cell Size group**, use the **AutoFit** button to **AutoFit Contents**. On the **Home tab**, **Center** the table. On the **Page Layout tab**, add **6 pt Spacing Before** and **6 pt Spacing After**.

9 With the table still selected, remove all table borders, and then add a **Custom 1 pt** solid line top border and bottom border. Select the cells in the first row, apply **Bold**, and then **Center** the text.

10 In the **Document Panel**, add your name and course information and the **Keywords new listings, health care Save** and then print or submit the document electronically as directed. **Exit** Word.

End **You have completed Project 2E** ————————————

Content-Based Assessments

Apply **2B** skills from these Objectives:

4 Create a New Document from an Existing Document

5 Change and Reorganize Text

6 Use the Proofing Options

7 Create a Document Using a Template

Mastering Word | Project **2F** Job Tips

In the following Mastering Word project, you will create a fax and a memo that includes job tips for Madison Staffing Services employees. Your completed documents will look similar to Figure 2.47.

Project Files

For Project 2F, you will need the following files:

w02F_Memo_Heading
w02F_Memo_Text
Origin Fax template from Word's installed templates

You will save your documents as:

Lastname_Firstname_2F_Job_Tips
Lastname_Firstname_2F_Fax

Project Results

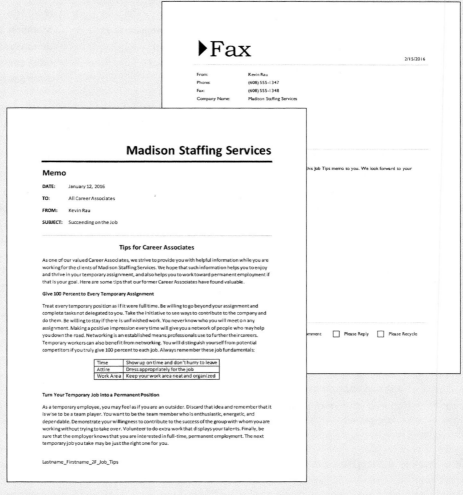

Figure 2.47

(Project 2F Job Tips continues on the next page)

Content-Based Assessments

Mastering Word | Project 2F Job Tips (continued)

1 **Start** Word; display rulers and formatting marks. In **Backstage** view, create a **New** document using the **New from existing** template. In the **New from Existing Document** dialog box, navigate to your student files, click **w02F_Memo_Heading**, and then click **Create New**.

2 Display the **Document Panel**, add your name and course information and the **Keywords memo, associates**

3 **Save** the document in your **Word Chapter 2** folder as **Lastname_Firstname_2F_Job_Tips** Add the file name to the footer.

4 At the top of your document, in the *DATE* paragraph, click to the right of the tab formatting mark, and then type **January 12, 2016** Use a similar technique to add the following information:

TO:	**All Career Associates**
FROM:	**Kevin Rau**
SUBJECT:	**Succeeding on the Job**

5 Position the insertion point in the blank paragraph below the memo heading. **Insert** the file **w02F_Memo_Text** and press Backspace to remove the blank line at the end of the selected text.

6 Select and **Center** the title *Tips for Career Associates*. By using either the **Spelling and Grammar** dialog box, or by right-clicking selected words, correct all spelling, grammar, and word usage errors.

7 In the first line of the paragraph that begins *Treat every*, locate and right-click *provisional*. Use the shortcut menu to change the word to the synonym *temporary*. In the second line of the same paragraph, change *donate* to the synonym *contribute*.

8 At the end of the paragraph that begins *Treat every temporary*, create a blank paragraph. **Insert** at **2 × 3** table, and then type the following information:

Time	Show up on time and don't hurry to leave
Attire	Dress appropriately for the job
Work Area	Keep your work area neat and organized

9 Select the entire table. **AutoFit Contents**, **Center** the table, and remove the table borders. Display **Backstage** view and preview the document. **Save** and **Close** the document but leave Word open. Hold this file until you complete this project.

10 From **Sample templates**, create a document based on the **Origin Fax** template. Save the document in your **Word Chapter 2** folder as **Lastname_Firstname_2F_Fax** and then add the file name to the footer—called the *First Page Footer* in this template.

11 Click the *Pick a date* placeholder, type **2/15/2016** and then type the following for the remaining controls:

From:	**Kevin Rau**
Phone:	**(608) 555-1347**
Fax:	**(608) 555-1348**
Company Name:	**Madison Staffing Services**
To:	**Jane Westerfield**
Phone:	**(608) 555-0034**
Fax:	**(608) 555-0035**

12 Locate and right-click *Kevin Rau*; remove the content control. Delete the lower *Company Name* text and remove the control to its right. In the *Type comments* control, type **Jane: I know you are on leave, so I thought I would fax this Job Tips memo to you. We look forward to your return.**

13 In the **Document Panel**, add your name and course information and the **Keywords job tips, fax Save** the document.

14 As directed by your instructor, print or submit electronically the two files that are the results of this project. **Exit** Word.

End **You have completed Project 2F**

Content-Based Assessments

Apply **2A** and **2B** skills from these Objectives:

1 Create a Table

2 Add Text to a Table

3 Format a Table

4 Create a New Document from an Existing Document

5 Change and Reorganize Text

6 Use the Proofing Options

7 Create a Document Using a Template

Mastering Word | Project **2G** Job Letter

In the following Mastering Word project, you will create a new document from an existing document, format a table, and then create a fax cover using a template. Your completed documents will look similar to Figure 2.48.

Project Files

For Project 2G, you will need the following files:

    w02G_Letter_Text
    w02G_Letterhead
    w02G_Resume
    Equity Fax template from Word's installed templates

You will save your documents as:

    Lastname_Firstname_2G_Job_Letter
    Lastname_Firstname_2G_Resume
    Lastname_Firstname_2G_Fax

Project Results

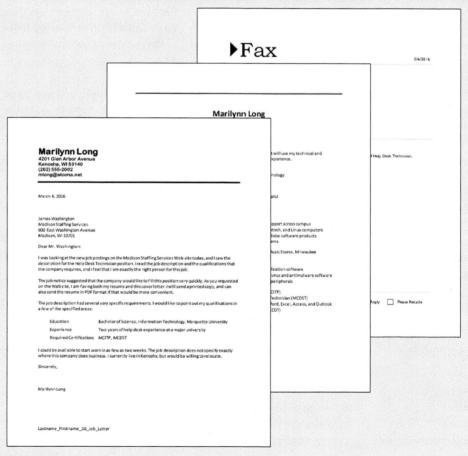

Figure 2.48

(Project 2G Job Letter continues on the next page)

Mastering Word | Project **2G** Job Letter (continued)

1 **Start** Word and display rulers and formatting marks. By using the **New from existing** template, create a document from the file **w02G_Letterhead**. **Save** the document in your **Word Chapter 2** folder as **Lastname_Firstname_2G_Job_Letter** Add the file name to the footer. Move to the end of the document, and then on the **Home tab**, apply the **No Spacing** style. Type **March 6, 2016** and then press Enter four times. Type the following:

> **James Washington**
> **Madison Staffing Services**
> **600 East Washington Avenue**
> **Madison, WI 53701**

2 Press Enter two times, type **Dear Mr. Washington:** and press Enter two times. **Insert** the text from the file **w02G_Letter_Text** and remove the blank line at the bottom of the selected text.

3 Move to the top of the document, and then by using either the **Spelling and Grammar** dialog box, or by right-clicking selected words, correct spelling, grammar, and word usage errors. In the paragraph that begins *I was looking*, in the third line, locate and right-click *corporation*. Use the shortcut menu to open the **Thesaurus** and change the word to the synonym *company*. In the same line, change *correct* to the synonym *right*.

4 In the paragraph that begins *I currently*, select the first sentence of the paragraph and drag it to the end of the same paragraph. In the second blank line below the paragraph that begins *The job description*, **Insert** a **2 × 3** table, and then type the text shown in **Table 1** below.

5 Select the entire table. **AutoFit Contents**, **Center** the table, remove the table borders, and then add **3 pt** spacing before and after by typing **3** in the **Spacing** boxes and pressing Enter.

6 In the **Document Panel**, add your name and course information and the **Keywords job letter** Preview the document. **Save** and **Close** the document but leave Word open. Hold the file until you complete this project.

7 From your student files, open **w02G_Resume**. **Save** the document in your **Word Chapter 2** folder as **Lastname_Firstname_2G_Resume** Add the file name to the footer.

8 **Insert** a new second row in the table. In the first cell of the new row, type **OBJECTIVE** and then press Tab. Type **To obtain a Help Desk Technician position that will use my technical and communication skills and computer support experience.** In the same cell, add **12 pt Spacing After**.

9 Select the entire table. On the **Layout tab**, **AutoFit Contents**. Remove the table borders, and then display the **Borders and Shading** dialog box. With the table selected, create a **Custom** single solid line **1 1/2 pt** top border.

10 In the first row of the table, select both cells and then **Merge Cells. Center** the five lines and apply **Bold**. In the first row, select *Marilynn Long* and change the **Font Size** to **20 pt** and add **36 pt Spacing Before**. In the e-mail address at the bottom of the first row, add **24 pt Spacing After**.

11 In the first column, apply **Bold** to the four headings. In the cell to the right of *EDUCATION*, **Bold** the names of the two schools, and add **12 pt Spacing After** the two lines that begin *September*. In the cell to the right of *RELEVANT EXPERIENCE*, bold the names of the two jobs—*IT Help Desk Specialist* and *Computer Technician*. In the same cell, below the line that begins *January 2014*, apply bullets to the four lines that comprise the job duties. Create a similar bulleted list for the duties as a Computer Technician. Add **12 pt Spacing After** to the last line of each of the bulleted lists.

12 In the cell to the right of *CERTIFICATIONS*, select all four lines and create a bulleted list. In the **Document Panel**, add your name and course information and the **Keywords help desk resume** and then submit your document as directed. **Save** and **Close** the document but leave Word open.

13 From **Sample templates**, create a document based on the **Origin Fax** template. **Save** the document in your **Word**

Table 1

Education	Bachelor of Science, Information Technology, Marquette University
Experience	Two years of help desk experience at a major university
Required Certifications	MCITP, MCDST

(Return to Step 5)

(Project 2G Job Letter continues on the next page)

Mastering Word | Project **2G** Job Letter (continued)

Chapter 2 folder as **Lastname_Firstname_2G_Fax** and then add the file name to the footer—called a *First Page Footer* in this template.

14 Type the text shown in **Table 2** for the content controls.

15 Locate and right-click *Marilynn Long*; remove the content control. In the **Document Panel**, add your name and course information and the **Keywords fax cover page** As directed by your instructor, print or submit electronically the three files from this project. **Exit** Word.

Table 2

Pick a date	3/6/2016
From:	**Marilynn Long**
Phone:	**(608) 555-0967**
Fax:	**(608) 555-0966**
Company Name:	Remove this content control and row heading
To:	**James Washington, Recruiter**
Phone:	**(608) 555-0034**
Fax:	**(608) 555-0035**
Company Name	**Madison Staffing Services**
Comments:	**Two pages to follow that include my resume and a cover letter for the position of Help Desk Technician.**

(Return to Step 15)

End You have completed Project 2G

Content-Based Assessments

GO! Fix It | Project 2H New Jobs

In this project, you will construct a solution by applying any combination of the skills you practiced from the Objectives in Projects 2A and 2B.

Project Files

For Project 2H, you will need the following file:

w02H_New_Jobs

You will save your document as:

Lastname_Firstname_2H_New_Jobs

From the student files that accompany this textbook, locate and open the file w02H_New_Jobs, and then save the file in your Word Chapter 2 folder as **Lastname_Firstname_2H_New_Jobs**

This document contains errors that you must find and correct. Read and examine the document, and then edit to correct the errors that you find and to improve the overall document format. Types of errors could include, but are not restricted to:

- Spelling errors
- Grammar errors
- Word choice errors
- Duplicate words
- Unattractive table column widths
- Title not merged across the top row of the table
- Inconsistent spacing before and after paragraphs in the table

Things you should know to complete this project:

- Viewing the document in Print Preview will help identify some of the problems
- The Spelling and Grammar checker will be useful
- Adjust the column widths *before* merging the title

Save your document and add the file name to the footer. In the Document Panel, type your firstname and lastname in the Author box and your course name and section number in the Subject box. In the Keywords box type **job listings** and then save your document and submit as directed.

 You have completed Project 2H _____

Apply a combination of the **2A** and **2B** skills.

GO! Make It | Project 2I Training

Project Files

For Project 2I, you will need the following file:

New blank Word document

You will save your document as:

Lastname_Firstname_2I_Training

Start Word, and then save the file in your Word Chapter 2 folder as **Lastname_Firstname_2I_Training**

Use the skills you practiced in this chapter to create the table shown in Figure 2.49. The first row font is Cambria 16 pt, the remainder is Cambria 14 pt. The spacing after the first row is 36 pt, the spacing at the bottom of the rows is 12 pt.

Add the file name to the footer; in the Document Panel, add your name and course information and the Keywords **online training** Save your document, and then submit as directed.

Project Results

Selected Training Programs Available Online

Software	Program Title
Microsoft Word	• Create your first Word document I • Getting started with Word 2010 • Use the Navigation Pane to search and move around in your document • Create your first Word document II
Microsoft Excel	• Get to know Excel 2010: Create your first workbook • Charts I: How to create a chart in Excel • Get to know Excel 2010: Enter formulas • Sort data in a range or table

Lastname_Firstname_2I_Training

Figure 2.49

End **You have completed Project 2I**

Content-Based Assessments

Apply a combination of the **2A** and **2B** skills.

GO! Solve It | Project **2J** Job Postings

Project Files

For Project 2J, you will need the following files:

New blank Word document
w02J_Job_Postings

You will save your documents as:

Lastname_Firstname_2J_Letterhead
Lastname_Firstname_2J_Job_Postings

Print the w02J_Job_Postings document, and use the information to complete this project. Create a new company letterhead and save it in your Word Chapter 2 folder as **Lastname_Firstname_2J_Letterhead** Add the file name to the footer. Add your name, your course name and section number, and the keyword **letterhead** to the Properties area.

Create a new document based on the existing document you just created. The new document will be a list of new jobs posted by Madison Staffing Services. The job posting should include the letterhead, introductory text, and a table that includes the information about the new jobs that are currently available. The job list should be in table format. Use either two or three columns, and label the columns appropriately. Format the table, the table borders, and the text in an attractive, readable manner.

Save the document as **Lastname_Firstname_2J_Job_Postings** Add the file name to the footer, and add your name, your course name and section number, and the keywords **new jobs** to the Properties area. Submit your two files as directed.

	Performance Level		
Performance Element	**Exemplary:** You consistently applied the relevant skills	**Proficient:** You sometimes, but not always, applied the relevant skills	**Developing:** You rarely or never applied the relevant skills
Create and format a letterhead template	The text in the letterhead is appropriately formatted, the company name stands out, and the spacing between paragraphs is attractive.	The letterhead is complete, but the line spacing or text formatting is not appropriate for a letterhead.	The spacing and formatting is not appropriate for a letterhead.
Insert a table	The inserted table has the appropriate number of columns and rows to display the information.	The table is not structured to effectively display the information.	No table is inserted in the document.
Format the table structure	Table column widths fit the information, extra space is added between the rows, and borders are attractively formatted.	The column widths do not reflect the amount of information in the column, and the spacing between the cells is insufficient.	Table displays only default column widths and spacing.
Format the text in the table	Important text is highlighted and formatted appropriately, making the text easy to read and interpret.	Some text formatting is added, but the formatting does not highlight the important information.	No text formatting is included.

End You have completed Project 2J ——————

Content-Based Assessments

Apply a combination of the 2A and 2B skills.

GO! Solve It | Project 2K Agenda

Project Files

For Project 2K, you will need the following file:

Agenda template from Word's Online templates

You will save your document as:

Lastname_Firstname_2K_Agenda

Create a new document based on an agenda template—such as the *Formal meeting agenda* template—from the Agenda templates at Microsoft Office Online. Save the agenda as **Lastname_ Firstname_2K_Agenda** Use the following information to prepare an agenda for a Madison Staffing Services meeting.

The meeting will be chaired by Marilyn Kelly and will be the monthly meeting of the company administrators—Kevin Rau, Marilyn Kelly, Andre Randolph, Susan Nguyen, and Charles James. The meeting will be held on March 15, 2016, at 3:00 p.m. The old business (open issues) include 1) expanding services into the printing and food service industries; 2) recruitment at the UW-Madison and MATC campuses; and 3) the addition of a part-time trainer. The new business will include 1) recruitment at the University of Wisconsin, Milwaukee; 2) rental of office space in or around Milwaukee; 3) purchase of new computers for the training room; and 4) renewal of snow removal service contract.

Add the file name to the footer, and add your name, your course name and section number, and the keywords **agenda, monthly administrative meeting** to the Properties area. Submit as directed.

	Performance Level		
	Exemplary: You consistently applied the relevant skills	**Proficient:** You sometimes, but not always, applied the relevant skills	**Developing:** You rarely or never applied the relevant skills
Select an agenda template	Agenda template is appropriate for the information provided for the meeting.	Agenda template is used, but does not fit the information provided.	No template is used for the agenda.
Add appropriate information to the template	All information is inserted in the appropriate places. All unused controls are removed.	All information is included, but not in the appropriate places, and not all of the unused controls are removed.	Information is missing and unused placeholders are not removed.
Format template information	All text in the template is properly aligned and formatted.	All text is included, but alignment or formatting is inconsistent.	No additional formatting has been added.

Performance Element (vertical label)

End **You have completed Project 2K** ———————————————

Outcomes-Based Assessments

Rubric

The following outcomes-based assessments are *open-ended assessments*. That is, there is no specific correct result; your result will depend on your approach to the information provided. Make *Professional Quality* your goal. Use the following scoring rubric to guide you in *how* to approach the problem and then to evaluate *how well* your approach solves the problem.

The *criteria*—Software Mastery, Content, Format and Layout, and Process—represent the knowledge and skills you have gained that you can apply to solving the problem. The *levels of performance*—Professional Quality, Approaching Professional Quality, or Needs Quality Improvements—help you and your instructor evaluate your result.

	Your completed project is of Professional Quality if you:	Your completed project is Approaching Professional Quality if you:	Your completed project Needs Quality Improvements if you:
1-Software Mastery	Choose and apply the most appropriate skills, tools, and features and identify efficient methods to solve the problem.	Choose and apply some appropriate skills, tools, and features, but not in the most efficient manner.	Choose inappropriate skills, tools, or features, or are inefficient in solving the problem.
2-Content	Construct a solution that is clear and well organized, contains content that is accurate, appropriate to the audience and purpose, and is complete. Provide a solution that contains no errors in spelling, grammar, or style.	Construct a solution in which some components are unclear, poorly organized, inconsistent, or incomplete. Misjudge the needs of the audience. Have some errors in spelling, grammar, or style, but the errors do not detract from comprehension.	Construct a solution that is unclear, incomplete, or poorly organized; contains some inaccurate or inappropriate content; and contains many errors in spelling, grammar, or style. Do not solve the problem.
3-Format and Layout	Format and arrange all elements to communicate information and ideas, clarify function, illustrate relationships, and indicate relative importance.	Apply appropriate format and layout features to some elements, but not others. Overuse features, causing minor distraction.	Apply format and layout that does not communicate information or ideas clearly. Do not use format and layout features to clarify function, illustrate relationships, or indicate relative importance. Use available features excessively, causing distraction.
4-Process	Use an organized approach that integrates planning, development, self-assessment, revision, and reflection.	Demonstrate an organized approach in some areas, but not others; or, use an insufficient process of organization throughout.	Do not use an organized approach to solve the problem.

Outcomes-Based Assessments

Apply a combination of the **2A** and **2B** skills.

GO! Think | Project **2L** Workshops

Project Files

For Project 2L, you will need the following files:

New blank Word document
w02L_Workshop_Information

You will save your document as:

Lastname_Firstname_2L_Workshops

Madison Staffing Services offers a series of workshops for its employee-clients. Any temporary employee who is available during the workshop hours can attend the workshops and there is no fee. Currently, the company offers three-session workshops covering Excel and Word, a two-session workshop covering Business Communication, and a one-session workshop covering *Creating a Resume*.

Print the w02L_Workshop_Information file and use the information to complete this project. Create an announcement with a title, an introductory paragraph, and a table listing the workshops and the topics covered in each workshop. Use the file w02L_Workshop_Information for help with the topics covered in each workshop. Format the table cells appropriately. Add an appropriate footer and information to the Document Panel. Save the document as **Lastname_Firstname_2L_ Workshops** and submit it as directed.

 You have completed Project 2L ————————————————

Apply a combination of the **2A** and **2B** skills.

GO! Think | Project **2M** Planner

Project Files

For Project 2M, you will need the following files:

Weekly appointment sheet template from Word's Online templates
w02M_Workshop_Information

You will save your document as:

Lastname_Firstname_2M_Planner

To keep track of workshops provided to employees, the trainer fills out a weekly schedule. Each workshop lasts two hours. Print the w02M_Workshop_Information file and use part or all of the information to complete this project.

Create a new document using a template, for example the *Weekly appointment sheet* template found in the Planners category in the online template list. Create a template for a week, and include the first part of each workshop series, along with the Creating a Resume workshop. Customize the template as necessary to include *Room* and *Workshop* titles for each day of the week. The computer skills workshops are held in the Lab, the others are held in Room 104. The trainer always schedules the hour before each workshop for preparation. Fill out the workshop schedule and use your choice of formatting to indicate that the workshops cover a two-hour period. Add appropriate information to the Document Panel. Save the document as **Lastname_Firstname_2M_Planner** and submit it as directed.

 You have completed Project 2M ————————————————

Outcomes-Based Assessments

Apply a combination of the 2A and 2B skills.

You and GO! | Project **2N** Personal Resume

Project Files

For Project 2N, you will need the following file:

New blank Word document

You will save your documents as

Lastname_Firstname_2N_Personal_Resume
Lastname_Firstname_2N_Cover_Letter

Locate and print the information for a job for which you would like to apply, and then create your own personal resume using a table and a cover letter. Include any information that is appropriate, including your objective for a specific job, your experience, skills, education, honors, or awards. Create your own letterhead and cover letter, using the cover letter you created in Project 2B as a guide.

To complete the assignment, be sure to format the text appropriately, resize the table columns in the resume to best display the information, and check both documents for spelling and grammar errors.

Save the resume as **Lastname_Firstname_2N_Personal_Resume** and the cover letter as **Lastname_Firstname_2N_Personal_Cover_Letter** Add the file name to the footer, and add your name, your course name and section number, and the keywords **my resume** and **cover letter** to the Properties area. Submit your file as directed.

 You have completed Project 2N ——————————————————

Creating Research Papers, Newsletters, and Merged Mailing Labels

OUTCOMES

At the end of this chapter you will be able to:

OBJECTIVES

Mastering these objectives will enable you to:

PROJECT 3A
Create a research paper that includes citations and a bibliography.

1. Create a Research Paper
2. Insert Footnotes in a Research Paper
3. Create Citations and a Bibliography in a Research Paper

PROJECT 3B
Create a multiple-column newsletter and merged mailing labels.

4. Format a Multiple-Column Newsletter
5. Use Special Character and Paragraph Formatting
6. Create Mailing Labels Using Mail Merge

prism68/Shutterstock

In This Chapter

Microsoft Word provides many tools for creating complex documents. For example, Word has tools that enable you to create a research paper that includes citations, footnotes, and a bibliography. You can also create multiple-column newsletters, format the nameplate at the top of the newsletter, use special character formatting to create distinctive title text, and add borders and shading to paragraphs to highlight important information.

In this chapter, you will edit and format a research paper, create a two-column newsletter, and then create a set of mailing labels to mail the newsletter to multiple recipients.

The projects in this chapter relate to **Memphis Primary Materials** located in the Memphis area. In addition to collecting common recyclable materials, the company collects and recycles computers, monitors, copiers and fax machines, cell phones, wood pallets, and compostable materials. The company's name comes from the process of capturing the "primary materials" of used items for reuse. Memphis Primary Materials ensures that its clients comply with all state and local regulations. They also provide training to clients on the process and benefits of recycling.

From Word Chapter 3 of *GO! with Microsoft® Office 2010 Volume 1*, First Edition, Shelley Gaskin, Robert L. Ferrett, Alicia Vargas, Carolyn McClennan. Copyright © 2011 by Pearson Education, Inc. Published by Pearson Prentice Hall. All rights reserved.

Project 3A Research Paper

Project Activities

In Activities 3.01 through 3.07, you will edit and format a research paper that contains an overview of recycling activities in which businesses can engage. This paper was created by Elizabeth Freeman, a student intern working for Memphis Primary Metals, and will be included in a customer information packet. Your completed document will look similar to Figure 3.1.

Project Files

For Project 3A, you will need the following file:

w03A_Green_Business

You will save your document as:

Lastname_Firstname_3A_Green_Business

Project Results

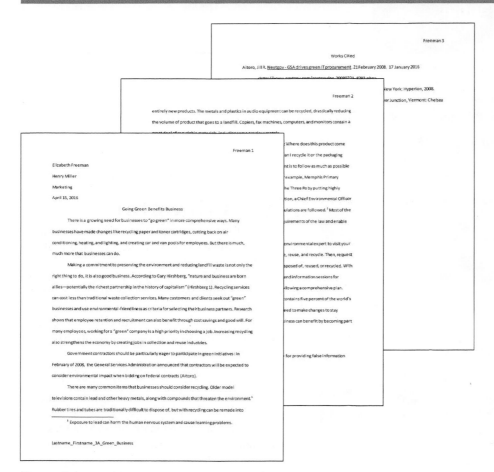

Figure 3.1
Project 3A Green Business

Objective 1 | Create a Research Paper

When you write a research paper or a report for college or business, follow a format prescribed by one of the standard *style guides*—a manual that contains standards for the design and writing of documents. The two most commonly used styles for research papers are those created by the *Modern Language Association (MLA)* and the *American Psychological Association (APA)*; there are several others.

Activity 3.01 | Formatting Text and Page Numbers in a Research Paper

When formatting the text for your research paper, refer to the standards for the style guide that you have chosen. In this activity, you will create a research paper using the MLA style. The MLA style uses 1-inch margins, a 0.5″ first line indent, and double spacing throughout the body of the document, with no extra space above or below paragraphs.

1 **Start** Word. From your student files, locate and open the document **w03A_Green_Business**. If necessary, display the formatting marks and rulers. In the location where you are storing your projects for this chapter, create a new folder named **Word Chapter 3** and then save the file in the folder as **Lastname_Firstname_3A_Green_Business**

2 Press Ctrl + A to select the entire document. On the **Home tab**, in the **Paragraph group**, click the **Line and Paragraph Spacing** button, and then change the line spacing to **2.0**. On the **Page Layout tab**, in the **Paragraph group**, change the **Spacing After** to **0 pt**.

3 Press Ctrl + Home to deselect and move to the top of the document. Press Enter one time to create a blank line at the top of the document, and then click to position the insertion point in the blank line. Type **Elizabeth Freeman** and press Enter.

4 Type **Henry Miller** and press Enter. Type **Marketing** and press Enter. Type **April 15, 2016** and press Enter. Type **Going Green Benefits Business** Right-click anywhere in the line you just typed, and then on the Mini toolbar, click the **Center** button. Compare your screen with Figure 3.2.

Figure 3.2

Title centered

Text double-spaced

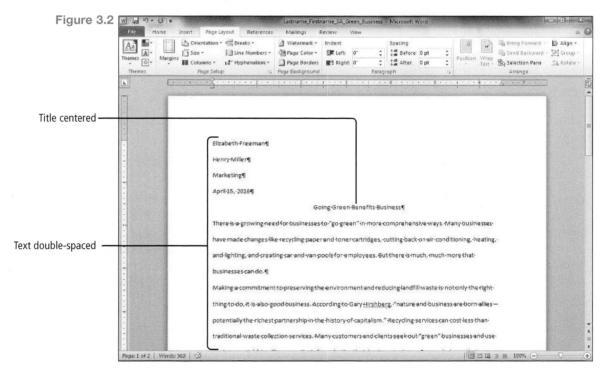

More Knowledge | Creating a Document Heading for a Research Paper

On the first page of an MLA-style research paper, on the first line, type the report author. On the second line, type the person for whom the report is prepared—for example, your professor or supervisor. On the third line, type the name of the class or department or organization. On the fourth line, type the date. On the fifth line type the report title and center it.

5 At the top of the **Page 1**, point anywhere in the white top margin area, right-click, and then click **Edit Header**. In the header area, type **Freeman** and then press Spacebar.

Recall that the text you insert into a header or footer displays on every page of a document. Within a header or footer, you can insert many different types of information; for example, automatic page numbers, the date, the time, the file name, or pictures.

6 On the **Design tab**, in the **Header & Footer group**, click the **Page Number** button, and then point to **Current Position**. In the displayed gallery, under **Simple**, click **Plain Number**. Compare your screen with Figure 3.3.

Word will automatically number the pages using this number format.

Figure 3.3

Page number field added to header

Last name in header

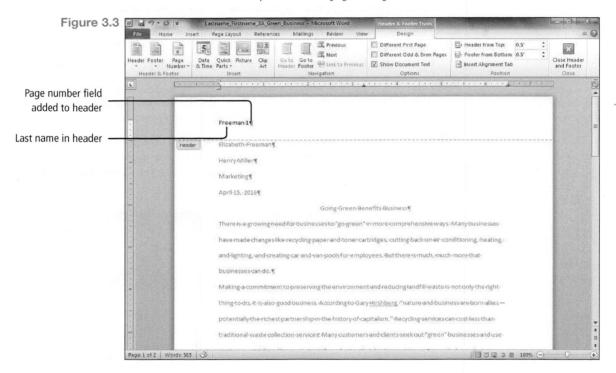

7 On the **Home tab**, in the **Paragraph group**, click the **Align Text Right** button. Double-click anywhere in the document to close the header area.

8 Near the top of **Page 1**, locate the paragraph beginning *There is a growing*, and then click to position the insertion point at the beginning of the paragraph. By moving the vertical scroll bar, scroll to the end of the document, hold down Shift, and then click to right of the last paragraph mark to select all of the text from the insertion point to the end of the document. Release Shift.

9 With the text selected, on the ruler, point to the **First Line Indent** button ▽, and then drag the button to **0.5" on the horizontal ruler**. Compare your screen with Figure 3.4.

> The MLA style uses 0.5-inch indents at the beginning of the first line of every paragraph. Indenting—moving the beginning of the first line of a paragraph to the right or left of the rest of the paragraph—provides visual cues to the reader to help divide the document text and make it easier to read.

Figure 3.4

First Line Indent button moved to 0.5" on the ruler

First line indented 0.5 inch

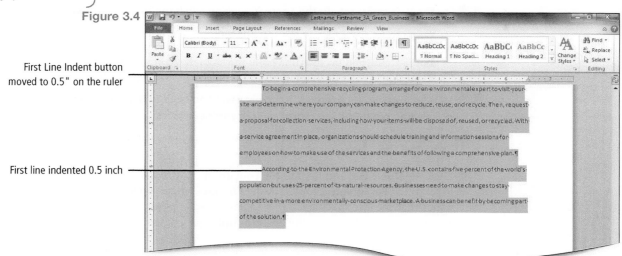

10 Click anywhere to deselect the text. Scroll to view the bottom of **Page 1**, point anywhere in the bottom white margin area, right-click, and then click **Edit Footer**. On the **Design tab**, in the **Insert group**, click the **Quick Parts** button, and then click **Field**. In the **Field** dialog box, under **Field names**, locate and click **FileName**, and then click **OK**.

> The file name in the footer is *not* part of the research report format, but it is included in projects in this textbook so that you and your instructor can identify your work.

11 Double-click anywhere in the document to close the Footer area, and then **Save** 🖫 your document.

More Knowledge | **Suppressing the Page Number on the First Page**

Some style guidelines require that the page number and other header and footer information on the first page be hidden from view—*suppressed*. To hide the information contained in the header and footer areas on Page 1 of a document, double-click in the header or footer area. Then, on the Design tab, in the Options group, select the Different First Page check box.

Objective 2 | Insert Footnotes in a Research Paper

Reports and research papers typically include information that you find in other sources, and these must be credited. Within report text, numbers mark the location of *notes*—information that expands on the topic being discussed but that does not fit well in the document text. The numbers refer to *footnotes*—notes placed at the bottom of the page containing the note, or to *endnotes*—notes placed at the end of a document or chapter.

Activity 3.02 | Inserting Footnotes

Footnotes can be added as you type the document or after the document is complete. Word renumbers the footnotes automatically, so footnotes do not need to be entered in order, and if one footnote is removed, the remaining footnotes renumber automatically.

1 Scroll to view the top of **Page 2**. Locate the paragraph that begins *Consumers and businesses*. In the seventh line of text, toward the end of the line, click to position the insertion point to the right of the period after *followed*.

2 On the **References tab**, in the **Footnotes group**, click the **Insert Footnote** button.

Word creates space for a footnote in the footnote area at the bottom of the page and adds a footnote number to the text at the insertion point location. Footnote *1* displays in the footnote area, and the insertion point moves to the right of the number. A short black line is added just above the footnote area. You do not need to type the footnote number.

3 Type **Tennessee, for example, imposes penalties of up to $10,000 for providing false information regarding the recycling of hazardous waste.**

This is an explanatory footnote; the footnote provides additional information that does not fit well in the body of the report.

4 Click the **Home tab**, and then in the **Font group**, notice that the font size of the footer is *10 pt*. In the **Paragraph group**, click the **Line and Paragraph Spacing** button, and notice that the line spacing is *1.0*—single-spaced—even though the font size of the document text is 11 pt and the text is double-spaced, as shown in Figure 3.5.

Figure 3.5

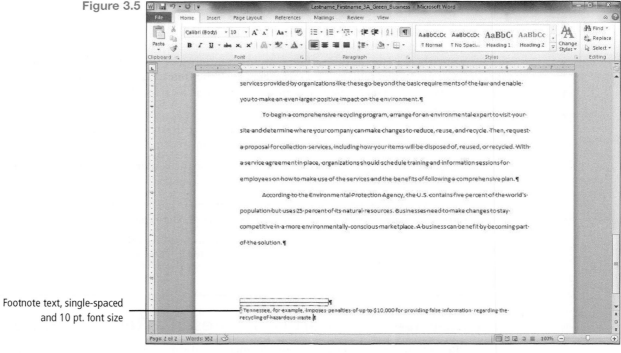

Footnote text, single-spaced and 10 pt. font size

5 Scroll to view the bottom of **Page 1**, and then locate the paragraph that begins *There are many common*. At the end of the second line of text, click to position the insertion point to the right of the period following *environment*.

6 On the **References tab**, in the **Footnotes group**, click the **Insert Footnote** button. Type **Exposure to lead can harm the human nervous system and cause learning problems.** Notice that the footnote you just added becomes the new footnote *1*, as shown in Figure 3.6.

> The first footnote is renumbered as footnote *2*.

Figure 3.6

Footnote number in text —

New footnote —

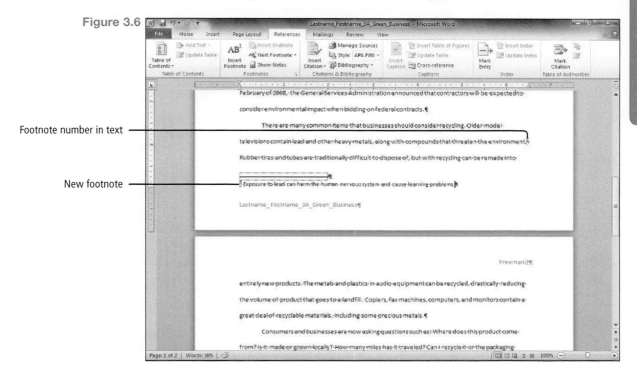

7 **Save** your document.

More Knowledge | **Using Symbols Rather Than Numbers for Notes**

Instead of using numbers to designate footnotes, you can use standard footnote symbols. The seven traditional symbols, available from the Footnote and Endnote dialog box, in order, are * (asterisk), † (dagger), ‡ (double dagger), § (section mark), ‖ (parallels), ¶ (paragraph mark), and # (number or pound sign). This sequence can be continuous (this is the default setting), or can begin anew with each page.

Activity 3.03 | Modifying a Footnote Style

Microsoft Word contains built-in paragraph formats called ***styles***—groups of formatting commands, such as font, font size, font color, paragraph alignment, and line spacing—which can be applied to a paragraph with one command.

The default style for footnote text is a single-spaced paragraph that uses a 10-point Calibri font and no paragraph indents. MLA style specifies double-spaced text in all areas of a research paper—including footnotes. According to the MLA style, first lines of footnotes must also be indented 0.5 inch and use the same font size as the report text.

1 Scroll to view the bottom of **Page 2**. Point anywhere in the footnote text and right-click, and then from the shortcut menu, click **Style**. Compare your screen with Figure 3.7.

> The Style dialog box displays, listing the styles currently in use in the document, in addition to some of the word processing elements that come with special built-in styles. Because you right-clicked on the footnote text, the selected style is the Footnote Text style.

Style dialog box ———

Footnote Text style ———

Insertion point
in footnote ———

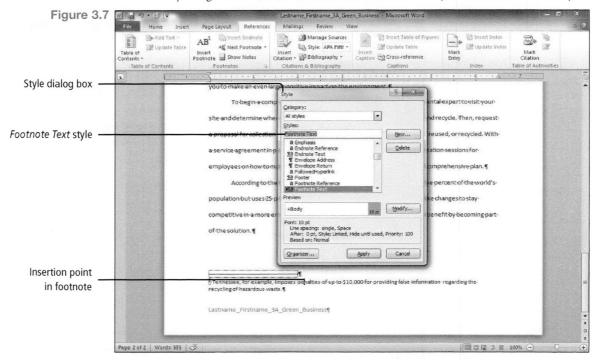

2 In the **Style** dialog box, click the **Modify** button to display the **Modify Style** dialog box.

3 In the **Modify Style** dialog box, locate the small **Formatting** toolbar in the center of the dialog box, click the **Font Size button arrow**, click **11**, and then compare your screen with Figure 3.8.

Figure 3.8

Style name ———

Font Size button ———

Formatting toolbar ———

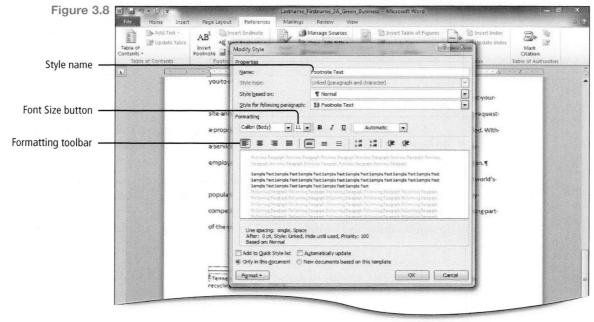

Word | Creating Research Papers, Newsletters, and Merged Mailing Labels

4 In the lower left corner of the dialog box, click the **Format** button, and then click **Paragraph**. In the **Paragraph** dialog box, under **Indentation**, click the **Special arrow**, and then click **First line**.

5 Under **Spacing**, click the **Line spacing** button arrow, and then click **Double**. Compare your dialog box with Figure 3.9.

Figure 3.9

First line indent selected ——

Line spacing set to *Double* ——

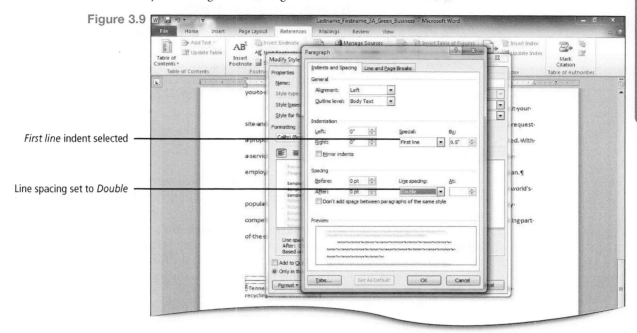

6 Click **OK** to close the **Paragraph** dialog box, click **OK** to close the **Modify Style** dialog box, and then click **Apply** to apply the new style. Notice that when you click Apply, the Style dialog box closes. Compare your screen with Figure 3.10.

Your inserted footnotes are formatted with the new Footnote Text paragraph style; any new footnotes that you insert will also use this format.

Figure 3.10

First line indented ——

Footnote text double-spaced ——

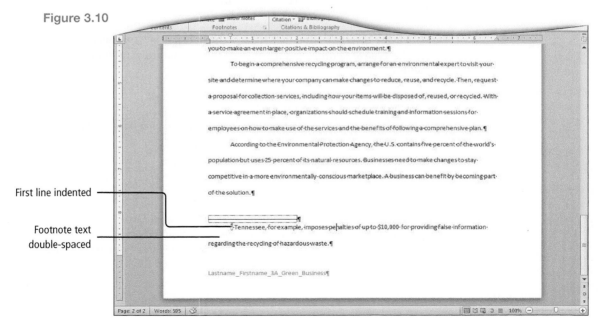

Project 3A: Research Paper | **Word**

7 Scroll to view the bottom of **Page 1** to confirm that the new format was also applied to the first footnote, and then **Save** ⬚ your document.

Objective 3 | Create Citations and a Bibliography in a Research Paper

When you use quotations from, or detailed summaries of, other people's work, you must specify the source of the information. A *citation* is a note inserted into the text of a report or research paper that refers the reader to a source in the bibliography. Create a *bibliography* at the end of a document to list the sources referred to in the document. Such a list is typically titled *Works Cited* (in MLA style), *Bibliography*, *Sources*, or *References*.

Activity 3.04 | Adding Citations

When writing a long research paper, you will likely reference numerous books, articles, and Web sites. Some of your research sources may be referenced many times, others only one time. References to sources within the text of your research paper are indicated in an *abbreviated* manner. However, as you enter a citation for the first time, you can also enter the *complete* information about the source. Then, when you have finished your paper, you will be able to automatically generate the list of sources that must be included at the end of your research paper.

1 Press [Ctrl] + [Home], and then locate the paragraph that begins *Making a commitment.* In the third line, following the word *capitalism*, click to position the insertion point to the right of the quotation mark.

> The citation in the document points to the full source information in the bibliography, which typically includes the name of the author, the full title of the work, the year of publication, and other publication information.

2 On the **References tab**, in the **Citations & Bibliography group**, click the **Style button arrow**, and then click **MLA Sixth Edition** (or the latest edition) to insert a reference using MLA style.

3 Click the **Insert Citation** button, and then click **Add New Source**. Be sure *Book* is selected as the **Type of Source**. Add the following information, and then compare your screen with Figure 3.11:

Author:	**Hirshberg, Gary**
Title:	**Stirring it Up: How to Make Money and Save the World**
Year:	**2008**
City:	**New York**
Publisher:	**Hyperion**

In the MLA style, citations that refer to items on the *Works Cited* page are placed in parentheses and are referred to as *parenthetical references*—references that include the last name of the author or authors and the page number in the referenced source, which you add to the reference. No year is indicated, and there is no comma between the name and the page number.

Figure 3.11

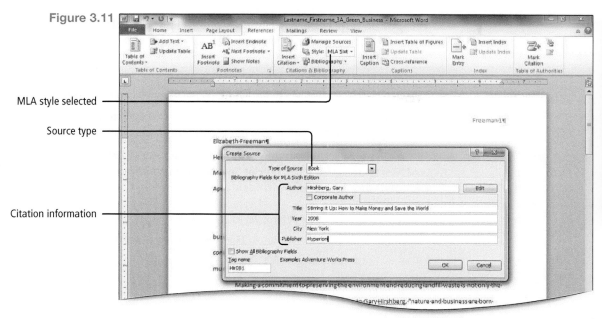

MLA style selected

Source type

Citation information

Note | Citing Corporate Authors

If the author of a document is identified as the name of an organization only, select the Corporate Author check box and type the name of the organization in the Corporate Author box.

---

4 Click **OK** to insert the citation. In the paragraph, point to *(Hirshberg)* and click one time to select the citation.

5 In the lower right corner of the box that surrounds the reference, point to the small arrow to display the ScreenTip *Citation Options*. Click this **Citation Options arrow**, and then from the list of options, click **Edit Citation**.

6 In the **Edit Citation** dialog box, under **Add**, in the **Pages** box, type **1** to indicate that you are citing from page 1 of this source. Compare your screen with Figure 3.12.

Figure 3.12

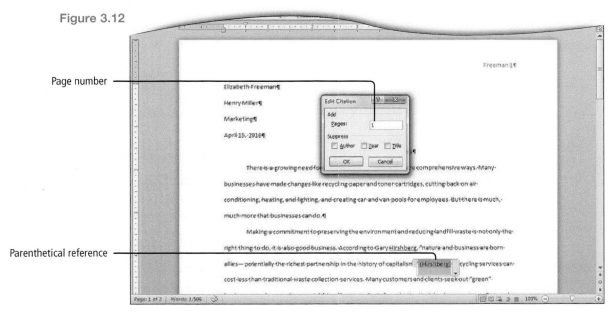

Page number

Parenthetical reference

7 Click **OK** to display the page number of the citation. Click outside of the citation box to deselect it. Then type a period to the right of the citation, and delete the period to the left of the quotation mark.

> In the MLA style, if the reference occurs at the end of a sentence, the parenthetical reference always displays to the left of the punctuation mark that ends the sentence.

8 In the next paragraph, which begins *Government contractors*, click to position the insertion point at the end of the paragraph, but before the period.

9 In the **Citations & Bibliography group**, click the **Insert Citation** button, and then click **Add New Source**. Click the **Type of Source arrow**, scroll down as necessary, and then click **Web site**. Add the following information:

Author:	**Aitoro, Jill R.**
Name of Web Page:	**Nextgov - GSA drives green IT procurement**
Year:	**2008**
Month:	**February**
Day:	**21**
Year Accessed:	**2016**
Month Accessed:	**January**
Day Accessed:	**17**
URL:	**http://www.nextgov.com/nextgov/ng_20080221_8792.php**

10 Compare your screen with Figure 3.13, and then click **OK** to close the **Create Source** dialog box and add the citation.

> A parenthetical reference is added. Because the cited Web page has no page numbers, only the author name is used in the parenthetical reference.

Figure 3.13

Web site citation —

Insertion point indicates location of parenthetical reference

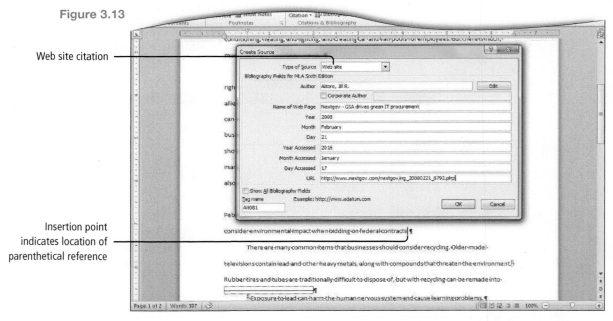

11 Near the top of **Page 2**, in the paragraph that begins *Consumers and businesses*, in the third line, click to position the insertion point following the word *toxic* to the left of the question mark.

Word | Creating Research Papers, Newsletters, and Merged Mailing Labels

12 In the **Citations & Bibliography group**, click the **Insert Citation** button, and then click **Add New Source**. Click the **Type of Source arrow**, if necessary scroll to the top of the list, click **Book**, and then add the following information:

Author:	**Scott, Nicky**
Title:	**Reduce, Reuse, Recycle: An Easy Household Guide**
Year:	**2007**
City:	**White River Junction, Vermont**
Publisher:	**Chelsea Green Publishing**

13 Click **OK**. Click the inserted citation to select it, click the **Citation Options arrow**, and then click **Edit Citation**.

14 In the **Edit Citation** dialog box, under **Add**, in the **Pages** box, type **7** to indicate that you are citing from page 7 of this source. Click **OK**.

15 On the **References tab**, in the **Citations & Bibliography group**, click the **Manage Sources** button. In the **Source Manager** dialog box, under **Current List**, click the third source and then compare your screen with Figure 3.14.

> The Source Manager dialog box displays. Other citations on your computer display in the Master List box. The citations for the current document display in the Current List box. Word maintains the Master List so that if you use the same sources regularly, you can copy sources from your Master List to the current document. A preview of the selected bibliography entry also displays at the bottom of the dialog box.

Figure 3.14

Sources used in this document

Other available sources (yours will vary)

Preview of selected citation

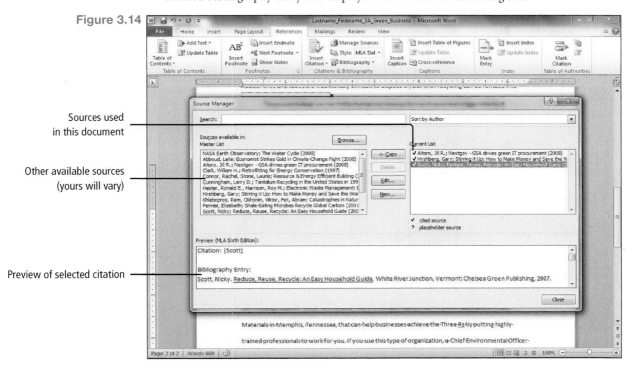

16 At the bottom of the **Source Manager** dialog box, click **Close**. Click anywhere in the document to deselect the parenthetical reference, and then **Save** your document.

Activity 3.05 | Inserting Page Breaks

In this activity you will insert a manual page break so that you can begin your bibliography on a new page.

1 Press `Ctrl` + `End` to move the insertion point to the end of the document. Notice that the insertion point displays at the end of the final paragraph, but above the footnote—the footnote is always associated with the page that contains the citation.

2 Press `Ctrl` + `Enter` to insert a manual page break.

> A ***manual page break*** forces a page to end at the insertion point location, and then places any subsequent text at the top of the next page. Recall that the new paragraph retains the formatting of the previous paragraph, so the first line is indented.

3 On the ruler, point to the **First Line Indent** button ⌂, and then drag the **First Line Indent** button to the left to **0 inches on the horizontal ruler**.

4 Scroll as necessary to position the bottom of **Page 2** and the top of **Page 3** on your screen.

5 Compare your screen with Figure 3.15, and then **Save** 💾 your document.

> A ***page break indicator***, which shows where a manual page break was inserted, displays at the bottom of the Page 2, and the footnote remains on the page that contains the citation, even though it displays below the page break indicator.

Figure 3.15

First Line Indent button at 0 inches

Page Break indicator shows manual page break inserted

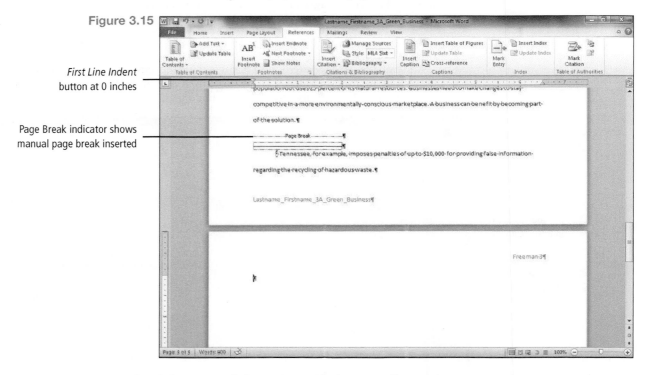

Activity 3.06 | Creating a Reference Page

At the end of a report or research paper, include a list of each source referenced. *Works Cited* is the reference page heading used in the MLA style guidelines. Other styles may refer to this page as a *Bibliography* (Business Style) or *References* (APA Style). This information is always displayed on a separate page.

1 With the insertion point blinking in the first line of **Page 3**, type **Works Cited** and then press `Enter`. On the **References tab**, in the **Citations & Bibliography group**, in the **Style** box, be sure *MLA* displays.

2 In the **Citations & Bibliography group**, click the **Bibliography** button, and then near the bottom of the list, click **Insert Bibliography**.

3 Scroll as necessary to view the entire list of three references, and then click anywhere in the inserted text.

> The bibliography entries that you created display as a field, which is indicated by the gray shading when you click in the text. The field links to the Source Manager for the citations. The references display alphabetically by the author's last name.

4 In the bibliography, point to the left of the first entry—beginning *Aitoro, Jill*—to display the ⌐ pointer. Drag down to select all three references.

Another Way

Display the Paragraph dialog box. Under Spacing, click the Line spacing arrow, and then click Double. Under Spacing, in the After box, type 0.

5 On the **Home tab**, in the **Paragraph group**, change the **Line spacing** to **2.0**, and then on the **Page Layout tab**, in the **Paragraph group**, change the **Spacing After** to **0 pt**.

> The entries display according to MLA guidelines; the text is double-spaced, the extra space between paragraphs is removed, and each entry uses a *hanging indent*—the first line of each entry extends 0.5 inch to the left of the remaining lines of the entry.

6 At the top of **Page 3**, right-click the *Works Cited* title, and then click the **Center** button ☰. Compare your screen with Figure 3.16, and then **Save** 🖫 your document.

> In MLA style, the *Works Cited* title is centered.

Figure 3.16

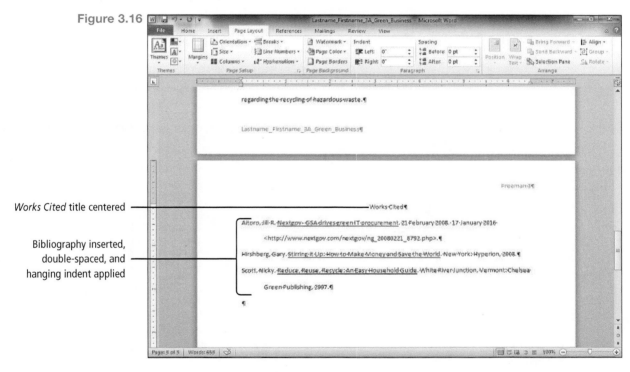

Works Cited title centered

Bibliography inserted, double-spaced, and hanging indent applied

Activity 3.07 | Managing Document Properties

Recall that document property information is stored in the Document Panel. An additional group of property categories is also available.

1 Display **Backstage** view. On the right, under the document thumbnail, click **Properties**, and then click **Show Document Panel** to display the **Document Panel**.

2 Type your name and course information, and then add the keywords **green business, research paper**

3 In the upper left corner of the **Document Panel**, click the **Document Properties** button, and then compare your screen with Figure 3.17.

Figure 3.17

Document Panel

Document Properties button

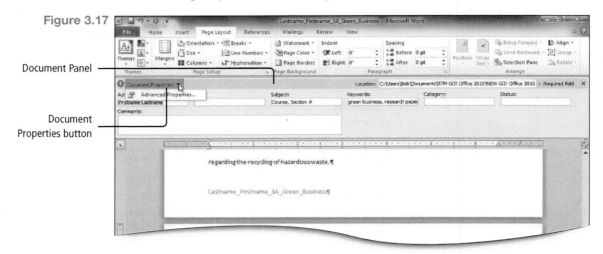

4 Click **Advanced Properties**. In the **Properties** dialog box, click the **Statistics tab**, and then compare your screen with Figure 3.18.

> The document statistics show the number of revisions made to the document, the last time the document was edited, and the number of paragraphs, lines, words, and characters in the document.

Figure 3.18

Statistics tab

Document statistics (yours may vary)

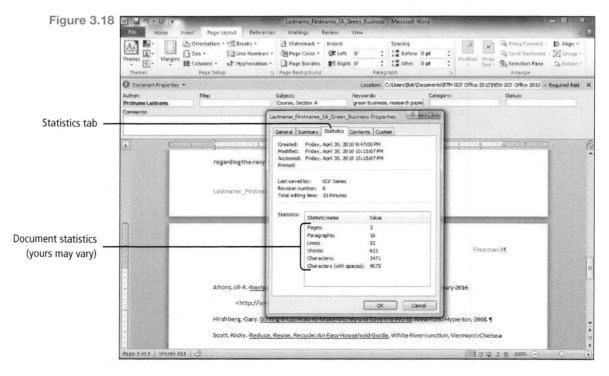

5 In the **Properties** dialog box, click the **Summary tab**. Notice that not all of the categories are filled in, and also notice that there are categories on this tab that are not found in the Document Panel.

> Some of the boxes may contain information from your computer system.

Word | Creating Research Papers, Newsletters, and Merged Mailing Labels

6 In the **Properties** dialog box, click in the **Title** box and type **Going Green Benefits Business**

7 Click in the **Manager** box and type **Henry Miller**

8 In the **Company** box, select and delete any existing text, and then type **Memphis Primary Materials**

9 Click in the **Category** box and type **Marketing Documents**

10 Click in the **Comments** box and type **Draft copy of a research report that will be included in the marketing materials packet**

Additional information categories are available by clicking the Custom tab.

11 Compare your screen with Figure 3.19, and then at the bottom of the **Properties** dialog box, click **OK**.

Figure 3.19

Summary tab

Properties not available on Document Information Panel

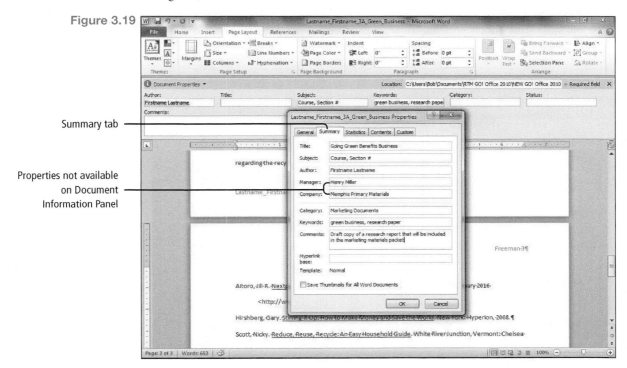

12 **Close** ✕ the **Document Panel**. Press Ctrl + F2, and then examine the three pages of your document in **Print Preview**. Redisplay your document.
If necessary, make any corrections or adjustments.

13 **Save** 🖫 your document, and then print or submit electronically as directed by your instructor. **Exit** Word.

End You have completed Project 3A ————————————

Project 3B Newsletter with Mailing Labels

Project Activities

In Activities 3.08 through 3.17, you will edit a newsletter that Memphis Primary Materials sends to its list of customers and subscribers. Your completed documents will look similar to Figure 3.20.

Project Files

For Project 3B, you will need the following files:

New blank Word document
w03B_Memphis_Newsletter
w03B_Addresses

You will save your documents as:

Lastname_Firstname_3B_Memphis_Newsletter
Lastname_Firstname_3B_Mailing_Labels
Lastname_Firstname_3B_Addresses

Project Results

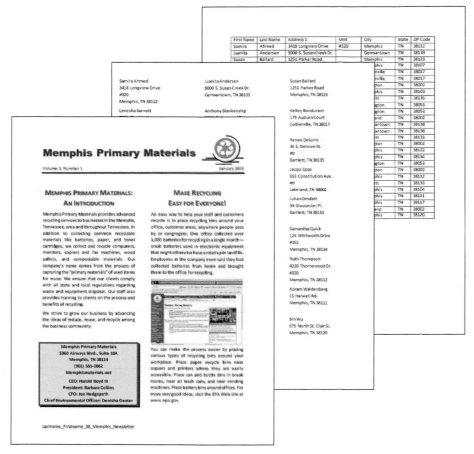

Figure 3.20
Project 3B Memphis Newsletter

Objective 4 | Format a Multiple-Column Newsletter

All newspapers and most magazines and newsletters use multiple columns for articles because text in narrower columns is easier to read than text that stretches across a page. Word has a tool with which you can change a single column of text into two or more columns, and then format the columns. If a column does not end where you want it to, you can end the column at a location of your choice by inserting a *manual column break*.

Activity 3.08 | Changing One Column of Text to Two Columns

Newsletters are usually two or three columns wide. When using 8.5 × 11-inch paper in portrait orientation, avoid creating four or more columns because they are so narrow that word spacing looks awkward, often resulting in one long word on a line by itself.

1 **Start** Word. From your student files, locate and open the document **w03B_Memphis_Newsletter**. If necessary, display the formatting marks and rulers. **Save** the file in your **Word Chapter 3** folder as **Lastname_Firstname_3B_Memphis_Newsletter** and then add the file name to the footer.

2 Select the first paragraph of text—*Memphis Primary Materials*. From the Mini toolbar, change the **Font** to **Arial Black** and the **Font Size** to **24**.

3 Select the first two paragraphs—the title and the Volume information and date. From the Mini toolbar, click the **Font Color button arrow** , and then under **Theme Colors**, in the fifth column, click the last color—**Blue, Accent 1, Darker 50%**.

4 With the text still selected, on the **Home tab**, in the **Paragraph group**, click the **Borders button arrow**, and then at the bottom, click **Borders and Shading**.

5 In the **Borders and Shading** dialog box, on the **Borders tab**, click the **Color arrow**, and then under **Theme Colors**, in the fifth column, click the last color—**Blue, Accent 1, Darker 50%**.

> **Another Way**
>
> In the Preview area, click the Bottom Border button.

6 Click the **Width arrow**, and then click **3 pt**. In the **Preview** box at the right, point to the *bottom* border of the small preview and click one time. Compare your screen with Figure 3.21.

Figure 3.21

Preview of border

Color set to *Blue, Accent 1, Darker 50%*

Line width set to 3 pt

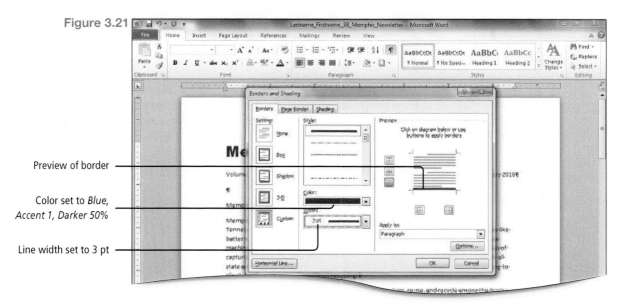

7 In the **Borders and Shading** dialog box, click **OK**.

> The line visually defines the newsletter *nameplate*—the banner on the front page of a newsletter that identifies the publication.

8 Below the nameplate, beginning with the paragraph *Memphis Primary Materials: An Introduction*, select all of the text to the end of the document, which extends to two pages.

9 On the **Page Layout tab**, in the **Page Setup group**, click the **Columns** button. From the **Columns** gallery, click **Two**.

10 Scroll up to view the top of **Page 1**, and then compare your screen with Figure 3.22, and then **Save** 🖫 the document.

> Word divides the text into two columns, and inserts a *section break* below the nameplate, dividing the one-column section of the document from the two-column section of the document. A *section* is a portion of a document that can be formatted differently from the rest of the document. A section break marks the end of one section and the beginning of another section. Do not be concerned if your columns do not break at the same line as shown in the figure.

Figure 3.22

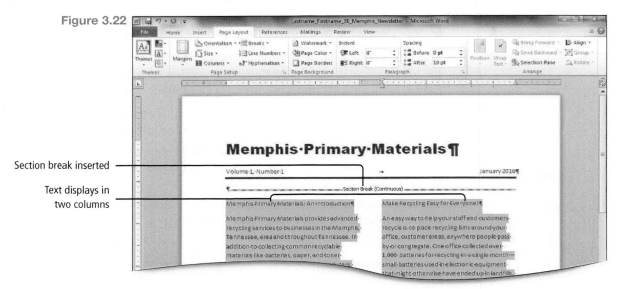

Section break inserted

Text displays in two columns

Activity 3.09 | Formatting Multiple Columns

The uneven right margin of a single page-width column is easy to read. When you create narrow columns, justified text is sometimes preferable. Depending on the design and layout of your newsletter, you might decide to reduce extra space between paragraphs and between columns to improve the readability of the document.

1 With the two columns of text still selected, on the **Page Layout tab**, in the **Paragraph group**, click the **Spacing After down spin arrow** one time to change the spacing after to **6 pt**.

2 On the **Home tab**, in the **Paragraph group**, click the **Justify** button 🔳.

3 Click anywhere in the document to deselect the text, and then compare your screen with Figure 3.23. **Save** 🖫 the document.

Figure 3.23

Column text justified ————

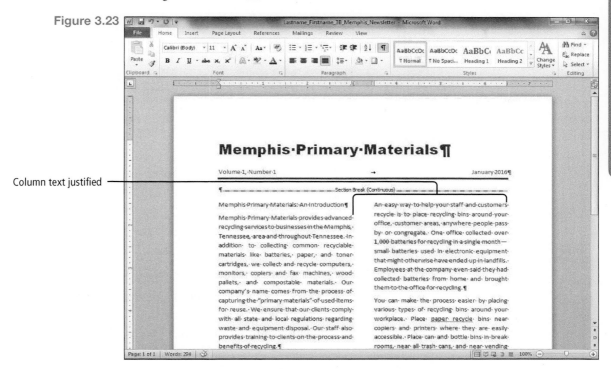

Activity 3.10 | Inserting a Column Break

1 Scroll down to view the lower portion of the page. In the first column, locate the company address that begins with the paragraph *Memphis Primary Materials*, and then select that paragraph and the three following paragraphs, ending with the telephone number.

2 On the **Page Layout tab**, in the **Paragraph group**, click the **Spacing After down spin arrow** one time to change the spacing after to **0 pt**.

3 Select the three paragraphs that begin with *CEO* and end with *CFO*, and then in the **Paragraph group**, change the **Spacing After** to **0 pt**.

4 Near the bottom of the first column, click to position the insertion point at the beginning of the line that begins *Make Recycling*.

5 On the **Page Layout tab**, in the **Page Setup group**, click the **Breaks** button to display the gallery of Page Breaks and Section Breaks. Compare your screen with Figure 3.24.

Figure 3.24

Column break command

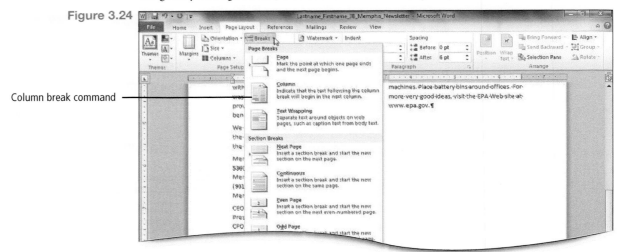

6 Under **Page Breaks**, click **Column**. Scroll to view the bottom of the first column.

A column break displays at the insertion point; text to the right of the insertion point moves to the top of the next column.

7 Compare your screen with Figure 3.25, and then **Save** 🖫 the document.

A *column break indicator*—a dotted line containing the words *Column Break*—displays at the bottom of the column.

Figure 3.25

Manual column break inserted

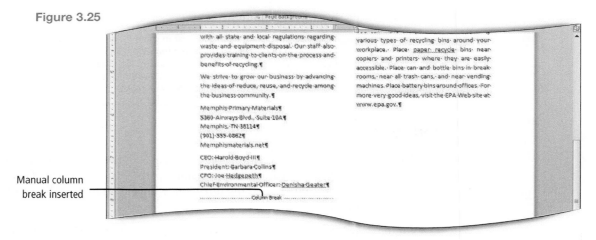

Activity 3.11 | Inserting a ClipArt Image

Clip art images—predefined graphics included with Microsoft Office or downloaded from the Web—can make your document visually appealing and more interesting.

1 Press [Ctrl] + [Home]. On the **Insert tab**, in the **Illustrations group**, click the **Clip Art** button to display the **Clip Art** task pane on the right of your screen.

2 In the **Clip Art** task pane, click in the **Search for** box, and then replace any existing text with **environmental awareness** so that Word can search for images that contain the keywords *environmental* and *awareness*.

3 In the **Clip Art** task pane, click the **Results should be arrow**. Be sure the **Illustrations** check box is selected, and then click as necessary to clear the *Photographs*, *Videos*, and *Audio* check boxes. Click the **Results should be** arrow again to collapse the list. Be sure the **Include Office.com content** check box is selected.

4 In the **Clip Art** task pane, click the **Go b**utton. Locate the image of the three white arrows in a blue circle. Click on the image to insert it, and then compare your screen with Figure 3.26.

> Recall that when you insert a graphic, it is inserted as an inline object; that is, it is treated as a character in a line of text. Here, the inserted clip art becomes the first character in the nameplate.

Figure 3.26

Clip Art task pane —

Search term —

Selected image —

Image inserted in document —

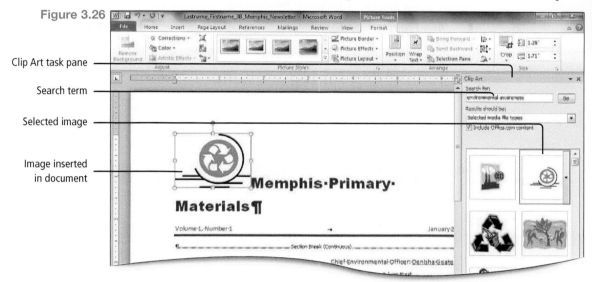

5 **Close** ☒ the **Clip Art** task pane. With the image still selected, on the **Format tab**, in the **Size group**, click in the **Shape Height** box, type **1** and then press Enter. In the **Arrange group**, click the **Wrap Text** button, and then click **Square**.

6 Point to the image to display the ⬚ pointer, and then drag the image to the right so that the bottom edge aligns slightly above *January 2016*, and the right side aligns with the right margin. Recall that you can press the arrow keys as necessary to move the image in small, precise increments.

7 Compare your screen with Figure 3.27, and then **Save** 🖫 the document.

Figure 3.27

Image resized —

Text wrapping applied to image —

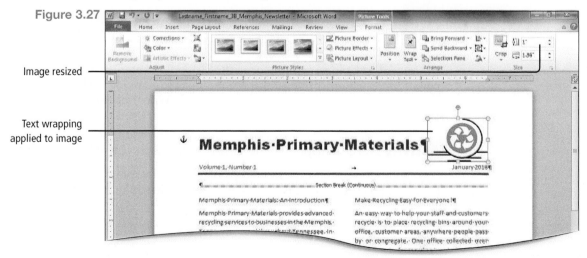

Project 3B: Newsletter with Mailing Labels | **Word**

Activity 3.12 | Inserting a Screenshot

A *screenshot* is an image of an active window on your computer that you can paste into a document. Screenshots are especially useful when you want to insert an image of a Web site into a document you are creating in Word. You can insert a screenshot of any open window on your computer.

1 In the second column, click to position the insertion point at the beginning of the paragraph that begins *You can make*. Open your Internet browser, and then in the address bar type **www.epa.gov/osw/conserve/rrr** and press Enter. Maximize 🗖 the browser window, if necessary.

2 From the taskbar, redisplay your **3B_Memphis_Newletter** document.

3 On the **Insert tab**, in the **Illustrations group**, click the **Screenshot** button.

> All of your open windows display in the Available Windows gallery and are available to paste into the document.

4 In the **Screenshot** gallery, click the browser window that contains the EPA site to insert the screenshot at the insertion point, and notice that the image resizes to fit between the column margins. Compare your screen with Figure 3.28. **Save** 🖫 the document.

Figure 3.28

Screenshot inserted in document

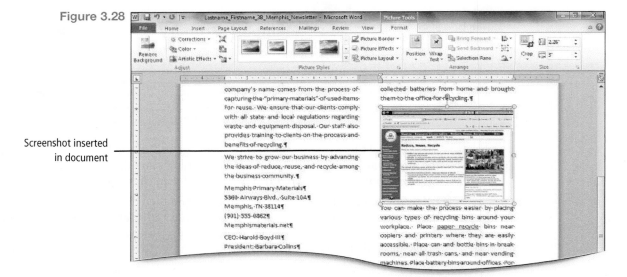

Objective 5 | Use Special Character and Paragraph Formatting

Special text and paragraph formatting is useful to emphasize text, and it makes your newsletter look more professional. For example, you can place a border around one or more paragraphs or add shading to a paragraph. When adding shading, use light colors; dark shading can make the text difficult to read.

Activity 3.13 | Applying the Small Caps Font Effect

For headlines and titles, *small caps* is an attractive font effect. The effect changes lowercase letters to uppercase letters, but with the height of lowercase letters.

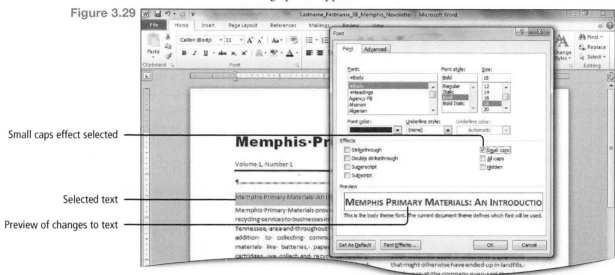

1 At the top of the first column, select the paragraph *Memphis Primary Materials: An Introduction* including the paragraph mark.

2 Right-click the selected text, and then from the shortcut menu, click **Font**. In the **Font** dialog box, click the **Font color arrow**, and then under **Theme Colors**, in the fifth column, click the last color—**Blue, Accent 1, Darker 50%**.

3 Under **Font style**, click **Bold**. Under **Size**, click **18**. Under **Effects**, select the **Small caps** check box. Compare your screen with Figure 3.29.

> The Font dialog box provides more options than are available on the Ribbon and enables you to make several changes at the same time. In the Preview box, the text displays with the selected formatting options applied.

Figure 3.29

Small caps effect selected

Selected text

Preview of changes to text

4 Click **OK**. Right-click the selected text, and then on the Mini toolbar, click **Center**.

5 With the text still selected, right-click, and then on the Mini toolbar, click the **Format Painter** button. Then, with the pointer, at the top of the second column, select the paragraph *Make Recycling Easy for Everyone!* to apply the same formats. Notice that the column title wraps placing a single word on the second line.

6 Position the insertion point to the right of the word *Recycling*, and then press [Del] to remove the space. Hold down [Shift] and then press [Enter].

> Holding down [Shift] while pressing [Enter] inserts a ***manual line break***, which moves the text to the right of the insertion point to a new line while keeping the text in the same paragraph. A ***line break indicator***, in the shape of a bent arrow, indicates that a manual line break was inserted.

7 Compare your screen with Figure 3.30, and then **Save** the document.

Figure 3.30

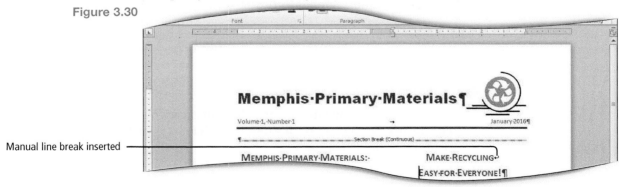

Manual line break inserted

Project 3B: Newsletter with Mailing Labels | **Word**

Activity 3.14 | Adding a Border and Shading to a Paragraph

Paragraph borders provide strong visual cues to the reader. Paragraph shading can be used with or without borders. When used with a border, light shading can be very effective in drawing the reader's eye to the text.

1 In the first column, in the paragraph that begins *We strive to grow*, click to position the insertion point at the end of the paragraph, and then press Enter one time.

2 At the bottom of the column, select the nine lines of company information, beginning with *Memphis Primary Materials* and ending with the paragraph that begins *Chief Environmental*. On the Mini toolbar, apply **Bold** **B** and **Center** **≡**.

3 With the text still selected, on the **Home tab**, in the **Paragraph group**, click the **Borders button arrow** **⊞▾**, and then click **Borders and Shading**.

4 In the **Borders and Shading** dialog box, be sure the **Borders tab** is selected. Under **Setting**, click **Shadow**. If necessary, click the **Color arrow**, and then in the fifth column, click the last color—**Blue, Accent 1, Darker 50%**. Click the **Width arrow**, and then click **3 pt**. Compare your screen with Figure 3.31.

In the lower right portion of the Borders and Shading dialog box, the *Apply to* box displays *Paragraph*. The *Apply to* box directs where the border will be applied—in this instance, the border will be applied only to the selected paragraphs.

Figure 3.31

Preview of paragraph border

Shadow border selected

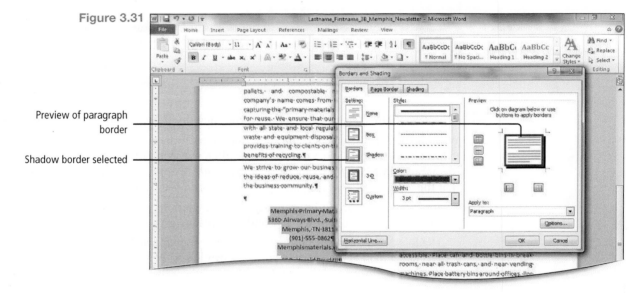

Note | Adding Simple Borders to Text

You can add simple borders from the Borders button gallery, located in the Paragraph group. This button offers less control over the border appearance, however, because the line thickness and color applied will match whatever was last used on this computer. The Borders and Shading dialog box enables you to make your own custom selections.

---

5 At the top of the **Borders and Shading** dialog box, click the **Shading tab**.

6 Click the **Fill arrow**, and then in the fifth column, click the second color—**Blue, Accent 1, Lighter 80%**. Notice that the shading change is reflected in the Preview area on the right side of the dialog box.

7 At the bottom of the **Borders and Shading** dialog box, click **OK**. Click anywhere in the document to deselect the text, and then compare your screen with Figure 3.32.

Figure 3.32

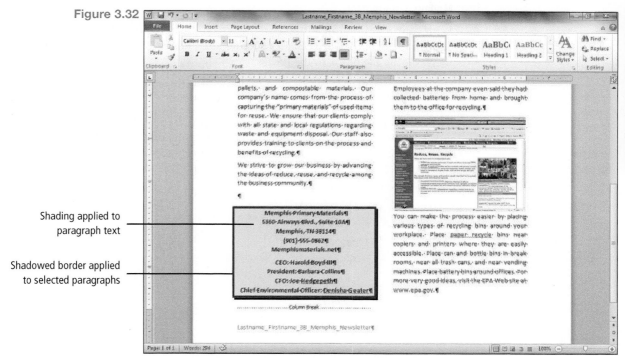

Shading applied to paragraph text

Shadowed border applied to selected paragraphs

8 From **Backstage** view, display the **Document Panel**.

9 In the **Author** box, delete any text and then type your firstname and lastname. In the **Subject** box, type your course name and section number, and in the **Keywords** box, type **newsletter, January Close** ⊠ the **Document Panel**.

10 Press `Ctrl` + `F2` to view the **Print Preview**. **Close** the preview, make any necessary corrections, and then click **Save** 🖫. **Exit** Word; hold this file until you complete this Project.

Objective 6 | Create Mailing Labels Using Mail Merge

Word's *mail merge* feature joins a *main document* and a *data source* to create customized letters or labels. The main document contains the text or formatting that remains constant. For labels, the main document contains the formatting for a specific label size. The data source contains information including the names and addresses of the individuals for whom the labels are being created. Names and addresses in a data source might come from a Word table, an Excel spreadsheet, or an Access database.

The easiest way to perform a mail merge is to use the Mail Merge Wizard, which asks you questions and, based on your answers, walks you step by step through the mail merge process.

Activity 3.15 | Opening the Mail Merge Wizard Template

In this activity, you will open the data source for the mail merge, which is a Word table containing names and addresses.

1 **Start** Word and display a new blank document. Display formatting marks and rulers. **Save** the document in your **Word Chapter 3** folder as **Lastname_Firstname_3B_Mailing_Labels**

2 With your new document open on the screen, **Open** the file **w03B_Addresses**. **Save** the address file in your **Word Chapter 3** folder as **Lastname_Firstname_3B_Addresses** and then add the file name to the footer.

> This document contains a table of addresses. The first row contains the column names. The remaining rows contain the names and addresses.

3 Click to position the insertion point in the last cell in the table, and then press Tab to create a new row. Enter the following information, and then compare your table with Figure 3.33:

First Name	**John**
Last Name	**Wisniewski**
Address 1	**1226 Snow Road**
Address 2	**#234**
City	**Lakeland**
State	**TN**
ZIP Code	**38002**

Figure 3.33

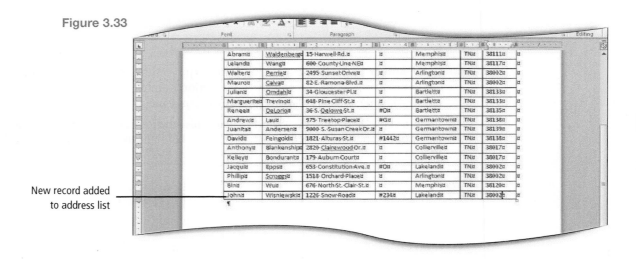

New record added to address list

4 **Save**, and then **Close** the table of addresses. Be sure your blank **Lastname_Firstname_3B_Mailing_Labels** document displays.

5 Click the **Mailings tab**. In the **Start Mail Merge group**, click the **Start Mail Merge** button, and then click **Step by Step Mail Merge Wizard** to display the **Mail Merge** task pane.

6 Under **Select document type**, click the **Labels** option button. At the bottom of the task pane, click **Next: Starting document** to display Step 2 of 6 of the Mail Merge Wizard.

7 Under **Select starting document**, be sure **Change document layout** is selected, and then under **Change document layout**, click **Label options**.

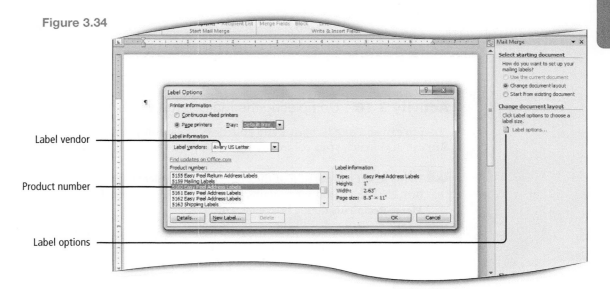

8 In the **Label Options** dialog box, under **Printer information**, click the **Tray arrow**, and then click **Default tray (Automatically Select)**—the exact wording may vary depending on your printer, but select the *Default* or *Automatic* option—to print the labels on regular paper rather than manually inserting labels in the printer.

9 Under **Label information**, click the **Label vendors arrow**, and then click **Avery US Letter**. Under **Product number**, scroll about halfway down the list, and then click **5160 Easy Peel Address Labels**. Compare your screen with Figure 3.34.

> The Avery 5160 address label is a commonly used label. The precut sheets contain three columns of 10 labels each—for a total of 30 labels per sheet.

Figure 3.34

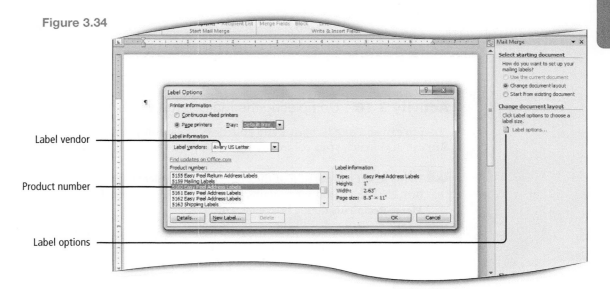

Label vendor

Product number

Label options

10 At the bottom of the **Label Options** dialog box, click **OK**. If a message box displays, click OK to set up the labels. At the bottom of the task pane, click **Next: Select recipients**.

> The label page is set up with three columns and ten rows. The label borders may or may not display on your screen, depending on your settings. Here in Step 3 of the Mail Merge Wizard, you must identify the recipients—the data source. For your recipient data source, you can choose to use an existing list—for example, a list of names and addresses that you have in an Access database, an Excel worksheet, a Word table, or your Outlook contacts list. If you do not have an existing data source, you can type a new list at this point in the wizard.

11 If gridlines do not display, click the **Layout tab**. In the **Table group**, click the **View Gridlines** button, and then notice that each label is outlined with a dashed line. If you cannot see the right and left edges of the page, in the status bar, click the **Zoom Out** button as necessary to see the right and left edges of the label sheet on your screen.

12 Under **Select recipients**, be sure the **Use an existing list** option button is selected. Under **Use an existing list**, click **Browse**.

13 Navigate to your **Word Chapter 3** folder, select your **Lastname_Firstname_3B_Addresses** file, and then click **Open** to display the **Mail Merge Recipients** dialog box.

> In the Mail Merge Recipients dialog box, the column headings are formed from the text in the first row of your Word table of addresses. Each row of information that contains data for one person is referred to as a *record*. The column headings—for example, *Last_Name* and *First_Name*—are referred to as *fields*. An underscore replaces the spaces between words in the field name headings.

14 Compare your screen with Figure 3.35.

Figure 3.35

Mail Merge Recipients dialog box

Gridlines indicate label borders

Path containing your file name

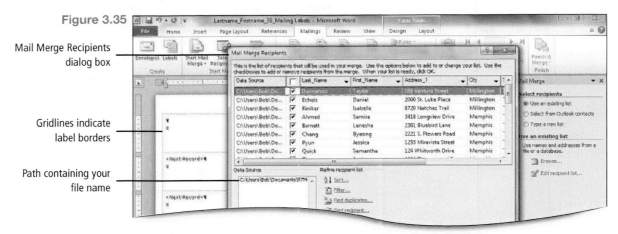

Activity 3.16 | Completing the Mail Merge Wizard

You can add or edit names and addresses while completing the Mail Merge Wizard. You can also match your column names with preset names used in Mail Merge.

1 In the lower left portion of the **Mail Merge Recipients** dialog box, in the **Data Source** box, click the path that contains your file name. Then, at the bottom of the **Mail Merge Recipients** dialog box, click **Edit**.

2 In the upper right corner of the **Data Form** dialog box, click **Add New**. In the blank record, type the following, pressing Tab to move from field to field, and then compare your **Data Form** dialog box with Figure 3.36.

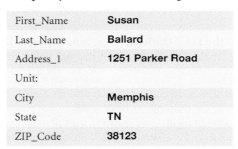

First_Name	Susan
Last_Name	Ballard
Address_1	1251 Parker Road
Unit:	
City	Memphis
State	TN
ZIP_Code	38123

Figure 3.36

New record

Edit button

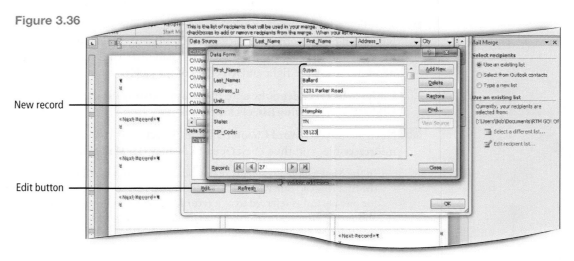

Word | Creating Research Papers, Newsletters, and Merged Mailing Labels

3 In the lower right corner of the **Data Form** dialog box, click **Close**. Scroll to the end of the recipient list to confirm that the record for *Susan Ballard* that you just added is in the list. At the bottom of the **Mail Merge Recipients** dialog box, click **OK**.

4 At the bottom of the **Mail Merge** task pane, click **Next: Arrange your labels**.

5 Under **Arrange your labels**, click **Address block**. In the **Insert Address Block** dialog box, under **Specify address elements**, examine the various formats for names. If necessary, under *Insert recipient's name in this format*, select the *Joshua Randall Jr.* format. Compare your dialog box with Figure 3.37.

Figure 3.37

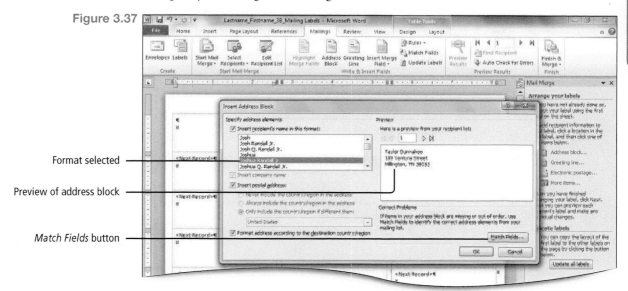

Format selected
Preview of address block
Match Fields button

6 In the lower right corner of the **Insert Address Block** dialog box, click **Match Fields**.

If your field names are descriptive, the Mail Merge program will identify them correctly, as is the case with most of the information in the *Required for Address Block* section. However, the Address 2 field is unmatched—in the source file, this column is named *Unit*.

7 Scroll down and examine the dialog box, and then compare your screen with Figure 3.38.

Figure 3.38

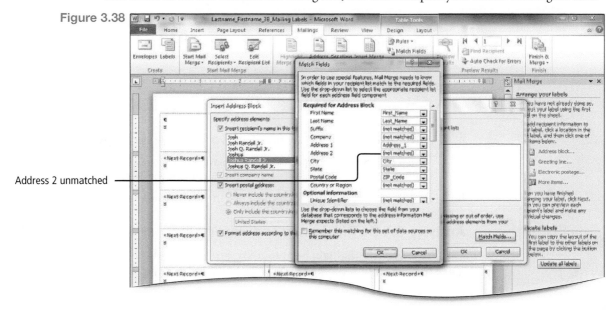

Address 2 unmatched

8 Click the **Address 2 arrow**, and then from the list of available fields, click **Unit** to match the Mail Merge field with the field in your data source.

9 At the bottom of the **Match Fields** dialog box, click **OK**. At the bottom of the **Insert Address Block** dialog box, click **OK**.

Word inserts the Address block in the first label space surrounded by double angle brackets. The *AddressBlock* field name displays, which represents the address block you saw in the Preview area of the Insert Address Block dialog box.

10 In the task pane, under **Replicate labels**, click **Update all labels** to insert an address block in each label space for each subsequent record.

11 At the bottom of the task pane, click **Next: Preview your labels**. Notice that for addresses with four lines, the last line of the address is cut off.

12 Press [Ctrl] + [A] to select all of the label text, click the **Page Layout tab**, and then in the **Paragraph group**, click in the **Spacing Before** box. Type **3** and press [Enter].

13 Click in any label to deselect, and notice that 4-line addresses are no longer cut off. Compare your screen with Figure 3.39.

Figure 3.39

Preview of mailing labels

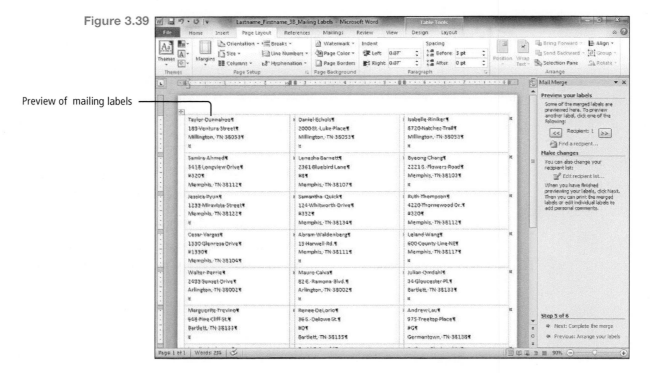

14 At the bottom of the task pane, click **Next: Complete the merge**.

Step 6 of the Mail Merge task pane displays. At this point you can print or edit your labels, although this is done more easily in the document window.

15 Save 🖫 your labels, and then **Close** ✕ the **Mail Merge** task pane.

Activity 3.17 | Previewing and Printing the Mail Merge Document

If you discover that you need to make further changes to your labels, you can still make them even though the Mail Merge task pane is closed.

1 Add the file name to the footer, close the footer area, and then move to the top of Page 2. Click anywhere in the empty table row, click the **Layout tab**, in the **Rows & Columns group**, click the **Delete** button, and then click **Delete Rows**.

> Adding footer text to a label sheet replaces the last row of labels on a page with the footer text, and moves the last row of labels to the top of the next page. In this instance, a blank second page is created, which you can delete by deleting the blank row.

2 Press Ctrl + F2 to display the **Print Preview**. Notice that the labels do not display in alphabetical order.

3 Click the **Mailings tab**, and then in the **Start Mail Merge group**, click the **Edit Recipient List** button to display the list of names and addresses.

4 In the **Mail Merge Recipients** dialog box, click the **Last_Name** field heading, and notice that the names are sorted alphabetically by the recipient's last name.

> Mailing labels are often sorted by either last name or by ZIP Code.

5 Click the **Last_Name** field heading again, and notice that the last names are sorted in descending order. Click the **Last_Name** field one more time to return to ascending order, and then click **OK**. Press Ctrl + Home, and then compare your screen with Figure 3.40.

Figure 3.40

Labels in alphabetical order

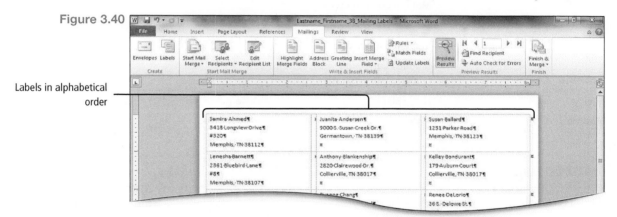

6 From **Backstage** view, display the **Document Panel**. In the **Author** box, delete any text and then type your firstname and lastname. In the **Subject** box, type your course name and section number, and in the **Keywords** box type **newsletter mailing labels** **Close** ☒ the **Document Panel**.

7 Click **Save** 🖫. Display **Backstage** view, and then click the **Print tab**. Examine the **Print Preview** on the right side of the window.

8 As directed by your instructor, print or submit electronically.

> If you print, the labels will print on whatever paper is in the printer; unless you have preformatted labels available, the labels will print on a sheet of paper. Printing the labels on plain paper enables you to proofread the labels before you print them on more expensive label sheets.

9 **Close** the document, click **Yes** to save the data source, and then if necessary, click **Save** to save the labels.

10 In addition to your labels and address document, print or submit your **3B_Memphis_ Newsletter** document as directed. **Exit** Word.

End **You have completed Project 3B**

Content-Based Assessments

Summary

In this chapter, you created a research paper using the MLA style. You added a header, footnotes, citations, and a bibliography, and changed the footnote style. You created a newsletter that used multiple columns. You added a column break, a page break, and a manual line break. You added special font effects, and added a border and shading to a paragraph. Finally, you used the Mail Merge Wizard to create a set of mailing labels for the newsletter.

Key Terms

American Psychological
   Association (APA)

Bibliography

Citation

Clip Art

Column break
   indicator

Data source

Endnote

Fields

Footnote

Hanging indent

Line break indicator

Mail merge

Main document

Manual column break

Manual line break

Manual page break

Modern Language
   Association (MLA)

Nameplate

Note

Page break indicator

Parenthetical
   reference

Record

Screenshot

Section

Section break

Small caps

Style

Style guide

Works Cited

Matching

Match each term in the second column with its correct definition in the first column by writing the letter of the term on the blank line in front of the correct definition.

_____ 1. A manual that contains standards for the design and writing of documents.

_____ 2. One of two commonly used style guides for formatting research papers.

_____ 3. An image of an active window on your computer that you can paste into a document.

_____ 4. In a research paper, information that expands on the topic, but that does not fit well in the document text.

_____ 5. In a research paper, a note placed at the bottom of the page.

_____ 6. In a research paper, a note placed at the end of a document or chapter.

_____ 7. A list of cited works in a report or research paper, also referred to as *Works Cited*, *Sources*, or *References*, depending upon the report style.

_____ 8. In the MLA style, a list of cited works placed at the end of a research paper or report.

_____ 9. A group of formatting commands, such as font, font size, font color, paragraph alignment, and line spacing that can be applied to a paragraph with one command.

_____ 10. A note, inserted into the text of a research paper that refers the reader to a source in the bibliography.

_____ 11. In the MLA style, a citation that refers to items on the *Works Cited* page, and which is placed in parentheses; the citation includes the last name of the author or authors, and the page number in the referenced source.

A American
Psychological
Association (APA)

B Bibliography

C Citation

D Endnote

E Footnote

F Hanging indent

G Manual column
break

H Manual page break

I Note

J Page break indicator

K Parenthetical
reference

L Screenshot

M Style

N Style guide

O Works Cited

Word | Creating Research Papers, Newsletters, and Merged Mailing Labels

_____ 12. The action of forcing a page to end and placing subsequent text at the top of the next page.

_____ 13. A dotted line with the text *Page Break* that indicates where a manual page break was inserted.

_____ 14. An indent style in which the first line of a paragraph extends to the left of the remaining lines, and that is commonly used for bibliographic entries.

_____ 15. An artificial end to a column to balance columns or to provide space for the insertion of other objects.

Multiple Choice

Circle the correct answer.

1. Column text that is aligned to both the left and right margins is referred to as:
   A. centered   **B.** justified   **C.** indented

2. The banner on the front page of a newsletter that identifies the publication is the:
   A. heading   **B.** nameplate   **C.** title

3. A portion of a document that can be formatted differently from the rest of the document is a:
   A. tabbed list   **B.** paragraph   **C.** section

4. A font effect, commonly used in titles, that changes lowercase text into uppercase letters using a reduced font size is:
   A. Small Caps   **B.** Level 2 Head   **C.** Bevel

5. To end a line before the normal end of the line, without creating a new paragraph, hold down the Shift key while pressing the:
   A. Enter key   **B.** Ctrl key   **C.** Alt key

6. The nonprinting symbol that displays where a manual line break is inserted is the:
   A. short arrow   **B.** bent arrow   **C.** anchor

7. In mail merge, the document that contains the text or formatting that remains constant is the:
   A. data source   **B.** mailing list   **C.** main document

8. In mail merge, the list of variable information, such as names and addresses, that is merged with a main document to create customized form letters or labels is the:
   A. data source   **B.** mailing list   **C.** main document

9. In mail merge, a row of information that contains data for one person is a:
   A. record   **B.** field   **C.** label

10. To perform a mail merge using Word's step-by-step guided process, use the:
   A. Mail Merge Template   **B.** Mail Merge Management Source   **C.** Mail Merge Wizard

Content-Based Assessments

Apply **3A** skills from these Objectives:

1 Create a Research Paper

2 Insert Footnotes in a Research Paper

3 Create Citations and a Bibliography in a Research Paper

Skills Review | Project **3C** Recycling Report

In the following Skills Review, you will format and edit a research paper for Memphis Primary Materials. The research topic is recycling in the natural environment. Your completed document will look similar to Figure 3.41.

Project Files

For Project 3C, you will need the following file:

w03C_Recycling_Report

You will save your document as:

Lastname_Firstname_3C_Recycling_Report

Project Results

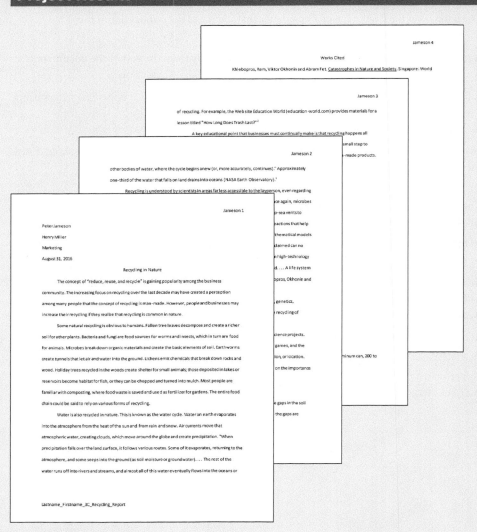

Figure 3.41

(Project 3C Recycling Report continues on the next page)

Content-Based Assessments

1 **Start** Word. From your student files, locate and open the document **w03C_Recycling_Report**. Display the formatting marks and rulers. **Save** the file in your **Word Chapter 3** folder as **Lastname_Firstname_3C_Recycling_Report**

 a. Press Ctrl + A. On the **Home tab**, in the **Paragraph group**, click the **Line spacing** button, and then change the line spacing to **2.0**. On the **Page Layout tab**, in the **Paragraph group**, change the **Spacing After** to **0 pt**.

 b. Press Ctrl + Home, press Enter to create a blank line at the top of the document, and then click to position the insertion point in the blank line. Type **Peter Jameson** and then press Enter. Type **Henry Miller** and then press Enter. Type **Marketing** and then press Enter. Type **August 31, 2016** and then press Enter.

 c. Type **Recycling in Nature** and then right-click anywhere in the title you just typed. From the Mini toolbar, **Center** the title.

 d. Near the top of **Page 1**, locate the paragraph beginning *The concept of*, and then click to position the insertion point at the beginning of the paragraph. Scroll to the end of the document, hold down Shift, and then click to the right of the last paragraph mark to select all of the text from the insertion point to the end of the document. On the horizontal ruler, drag the **First Line Indent** button to **0.5″**.

 e. On **Page 1**, point to the top margin area and right-click. Click **Edit Header**. In the header area, type **Jameson** and then press Spacebar.

 f. On the **Design tab**, in the **Header & Footer group**, click the **Page Number** button, and then point to **Current Position**. In the displayed gallery, under **Simple**, click **Plain Number**. On the **Home tab**, in the **Paragraph group**, click the **Align Text Right** button.

 g. Click the **Design tab**, and then in the **Navigation group**, click the **Go to Footer** button. In the **Insert group**, click the **Quick Parts** button, and then click **Field**. In the **Field** dialog box, under **Field names**, locate and click **FileName**, and then click **OK**.

 h. Double-click anywhere outside the footer area. **Save** your document.

2 Scroll to view the top of **Page 2**, locate the paragraph that ends *drains into oceans*, and then click to position the insertion point to the right of the period following *oceans*. On the **References tab**, in the **Footnotes group**, click the **Insert Footnote** button.

 a. Type **Groundwater is found in two layers of the soil, the "zone of aeration," where gaps in the soil are filled with both air and water, and, further down, the "zone of saturation," where the gaps are completely filled with water.**

 b. In the lower half of **Page 2**, locate the paragraph that begins *School students*. Click to position the insertion point at the end of the paragraph and insert a footnote.

 c. As the footnote text, type **A wool sock will last one year in a landfill; a soup can, 80 to 100 years; an aluminum can, 200 to 500 years; and plastic rings from a six–pack of cans, 450 years. Save** your document.

 d. At the bottom of **Page 2**, right-click anywhere in either footnote. From the shortcut menu, click **Style**. In the **Style** dialog box, click the **Modify** button. In the **Modify Style** dialog box, locate the small Formatting toolbar in the center of the dialog box, click the **Font Size button arrow**, and then click **11**.

 e. In the lower left corner of the dialog box, click the **Format** button, and then click **Paragraph**. In the **Paragraph** dialog box, under **Indentation**, click the **Special arrow**, and then click **First line**. Under **Spacing**, click the **Line spacing button arrow**, and then click **Double**.

 f. Click **OK** to close the **Paragraph** dialog box, click **OK** to close the **Modify Style** dialog box, and then click **Apply** to apply the new style. Notice that the second footnote moves to **Page 3**. **Save** your document.

3 Scroll to view the top of **Page 2**, and then locate the footnote marker at the end of the second line of text. Click to position the insertion point to the left of the period at the end of the paragraph.

 a. On the **References tab**, in the **Citations & Bibliography group**, click the **Style button arrow**, and then click **MLA** to insert a reference using MLA style. Click the **Insert Citation** button, and then click **Add New Source**. Click the **Type of Source arrow**,

(Project 3C Recycling Report continues on the next page)

and then click **Web site**. Select the **Corporate Author** check box, and then add the following information (type the URL on one line):

Corporate Author:	**NASA Earth Observatory**
Name of Web Page:	**The Water Cycle**
Year:	**2009**
Month:	**March**
Day:	**3**
Year Accessed:	**2016**
Month Accessed:	**May**
Day Accessed:	**24**
URL:	**http://earthobservatory.nasa.gov/ Features/Water/water_2.php**

b. Click **OK** to insert the citation. In the next paragraph, which begins *Recycling is understood,* in the fifth line, click to position the insertion point to the right of the quotation mark. In the **Citations & Bibliography group**, click the **Insert Citation** button, and then click **Add New Source**. Click the **Type of Source arrow**, click **Journal Article**, and then add the following information (type the Title on one line):

Author:	**Pennisi, Elizabeth**
Title:	**Shale-Eating Microbes Recycle Global Carbon**
Journal Name:	**Science**
Year:	**2001**
Pages:	**1043**

c. Click **OK**. In the text, click to select the citation, click the **Citation Options arrow**, and then click **Edit Citation**. In the **Edit Citation** dialog box, under **Add**, in the **Pages** box, type **1043** and then click **OK**. Add a period to the right of the citation and delete the period to the left of the quotation mark.

d. In the same paragraph, position the insertion point at the end of the paragraph. In the **Citations & Bibliography group**, click the **Insert Citation** button, and then click **Add New Source**. Click the **Type of**

Source arrow, click **Book**, and then add the following information (type the Author information on one line):

Author:	**Khlebopros, Rem; Okhonin, Viktor; Fet, Abram**
Title:	**Catastrophes in Nature and Society**
Year:	**2007**
City:	**Singapore**
Publisher:	**World Scientific Publishing Company**

e. Click **OK**. Click to select the citation, click the **Citation Options arrow**, and then click **Edit Citation**. In the **Edit Citation** dialog box, under **Add**, in the **Pages** box, type **111** Click **OK**. Add a period to the right of the citation and delete the period to the left of the quotation mark.

f. Press Ctrl + End to move the insertion point to the end of the document. Press Ctrl + Enter to insert a manual page break. On the ruler, drag the **First Line Indent** button to the left to **0 inches on the horizontal ruler**.

g. Type **Works Cited** and then press Enter. On the **References tab**, in the **Citations & Bibliography group**, be sure **MLA** displays in the **Style** box. In the **Citations & Bibliography group**, click the **Bibliography** button, and then click **Insert Bibliography**.

h. In the bibliography, move the pointer to the left of the first entry—beginning *Khlebopros*—to display the pointer. Drag down to select all three references. On the **Home tab**, in the **Paragraph group**, set the **Line spacing** to **2.0**. On the **Page Layout tab**, set the **Spacing After** to **0 pt**.

i. Right-click the *Works Cited* title, and then from the Mini toolbar, click the **Center** button. **Save** your document.

4 From **Backstage** view, display the **Document Panel**, type your name and course information, and then add the keywords **recycling, nature, research paper** In the upper left corner of the panel, click the **Document Properties** button, and then click **Advanced Properties**.

(Project 3C Recycling Report continues on the next page)

Skills Review | Project **3C** Recycling Report (continued)

a. In the **Properties** dialog box, click the **Summary tab**. In the **Properties** dialog box, fill in the following information:

Title:	**Recycling in Nature**
Manager:	**Henry Miller**
Company:	**Memphis Primary Materials**
Comments:	**Draft of a new white paper research report on recycling**

b. At the bottom of the **Properties** dialog box, click **OK. Close** the **Document Panel**. **Save** your document. View the Print Preview, and then print or submit electronically as directed by your instructor. **Exit** Word.

 You have completed Project 3C ⎯⎯⎯⎯⎯⎯⎯⎯⎯⎯⎯⎯⎯⎯⎯

Skills Review | Project **3D** Company Newsletter

In the following Skills Review, you will format a newsletter for Memphis Primary Materials, and then create a set of mailing labels for the newsletter. Your completed documents will look similar to Figure 3.42.

Project Files

For Project 3D, you will need the following files:

New blank Word document
w03D_Company_Newsletter
w03D_Addresses

You will save your documents as:

Lastname_Firstname_3D_Company_Newsletter
Lastname_Firstname_3D_Addresses
Lastname_Firstname_3D_Labels

Project Results

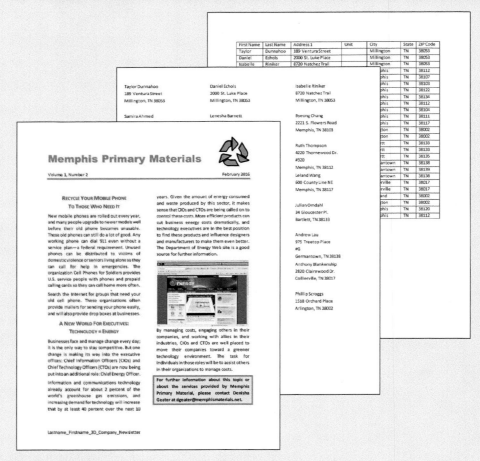

Figure 3.42

(Project 3D Company Newsletter continues on the next page)

Skills Review | Project **3D** Company Newsletter (continued)

1 **Start** Word. From your student files, open the document **w03D_Company_Newsletter**. **Save** the file in your **Word Chapter 3** folder as **Lastname_Firstname_3D_Company_Newsletter** and then add the file name to the footer.

a. Select the first paragraph of text—*Memphis Primary Materials*. From the Mini toolbar, change the **Font** to **Arial Black** and the **Font Size** to **24**. Select the title you just formatted. Click the **Font Color button arrow**, and then under **Theme Colors**, in the seventh column, click the fifth color—**Olive Green, Accent 3, Darker 25%**.

b. Select the second paragraph. On the **Home tab**, in the **Paragraph group**, click the **Borders button arrow**, and then click **Borders and Shading**. In the **Borders and Shading** dialog box, click the **Color arrow**, and then under **Theme Colors**, in the seventh column, click the fifth color—**Olive Green, Accent 3, Darker 25%**. Click the **Width arrow**, and then click **3 pt**. In the **Preview** area, click the *bottom* border of the Preview and then click **OK**.

c. Below the nameplate, locate the paragraph that begins *Recycle Your Mobile*, and then select all of the text from that point to the end of the document. On the **Page Layout tab**, in the **Page Setup group**, click the **Columns** button, and then click **Two**.

d. With the text still selected, in the **Paragraph group**, set **Spacing After** to **6 pt**. On the **Home tab**, in the **Paragraph group**, click the **Justify** button. Click anywhere in the document to deselect the text, and then **Save** the newsletter.

e. Press **Ctrl** + **Home**. On the **Insert tab**, in the **Illustrations group**, click the **Clip Art** button. In the **Clip Art** task pane, click in the **Search for** box, and then type **conservation**

f. In the **Clip Art** task pane, click the **Results should be arrow**, and be sure that only the **Illustrations** check box is selected. Be sure the **Include Office.com content** check box is selected, and then click **Go**. Locate the image of three green arrows, as shown in Figure 3.42, and then click on the image.

g. On the **Format tab**, in the **Size group**, click in the **Shape Height** box, type **1** and then press **Enter**. In the **Arrange group**, click the **Wrap Text** button, and then click **Square**. **Close** the Clip Art task pane, and then drag the image to the location shown in Figure 3.42.

h. In the second column, position the insertion point at the beginning of the paragraph that begins *By managing costs*. Open your Web browser. In the address bar, type **www.energy.gov** and then press **Enter**. Maximize the browser window. Use the taskbar to return to your Word document.

i. On the **Insert tab**, in the **Illustrations group**, click the **Screenshot** button. In the gallery, click the DOE screenshot to insert it. **Close** your Web browser, and then **Save** your document.

2 At the top of the first column, select the paragraph that begins *Recycle Your Mobile*. Be sure to include the paragraph mark. Right-click the selected text, and then click **Font**. In the **Font** dialog box, click the **Font color arrow**, and then under **Theme Colors**, in the seventh column, click the last color—**Olive Green, Accent 3, Darker 50%**. Under **Font style**, click **Bold**. Under **Size**, click **14**. Under **Effects**, select the **Small caps** check box.

a. In the **Font** dialog box, click **OK**. Right-click the selected text, and then click the **Center** button. In the title you just formatted, click to position the insertion point to the right of *Phone*, and then press **Del** to remove the space. Hold down **Shift**, and then press **Enter** to insert a manual line break.

b. Select and right-click the title you just formatted, and then on the Mini toolbar, click the **Format Painter** button. Near the middle of the first column, select the paragraph that begins *A New World* to apply the same formatting.

c. At the bottom of the second column, in the paragraph that begins *For further*, select the entire paragraph. On the Mini toolbar, apply **Bold**.

d. With the text still selected, on the **Home tab**, in the **Paragraph group**, click the **Borders button arrow**, and then click **Borders and Shading**. In the **Borders and Shading** dialog box, be sure the **Borders tab** is selected. Under **Setting**, click **Box**. Click the **Width arrow**, and then click **3 pt**. If necessary, click the **Color arrow**, and then in the seventh column, click the fifth color—**Olive Green, Accent 3, Darker 25%**.

e. At the top of the **Borders and Shading** dialog box, click the **Shading tab**. Click the **Fill arrow**, and then in the seventh column, click the second color—**Olive Green, Accent 3, Lighter 80%**. At the bottom of the **Borders and Shading** dialog box, click **OK**. Click anywhere in the document to deselect the text.

(Project 3D Company Newsletter continues on the next page)

f. Near the bottom of the first column, in the paragraph that begins *Information and communications*, click to position the insertion point at the beginning of the sixth line. On the **Page Layout tab**, in the **Page Setup group**, click the **Breaks** button. Under **Page Breaks**, click **Column**.

g. From **Backstage** view, display the **Document Panel**, type your name and course information. Add the keywords **newsletter, energy** and then **Close** the **Document Panel**. **Save** the document, view the Print Preview, and then **Exit** Word. Hold this file until you complete this project.

3 **Start** Word and display a new blank document. Display formatting marks and rulers. **Save** the document in your **Word Chapter 3** folder as **Lastname_Firstname_3D_Labels Open** the file **w03D_Addresses Save** the address file in your **Word Chapter 3** folder as **Lastname_Firstname_3D_Addresses** and then add the file name to the footer.

a. Click to position the insertion point in the last cell in the table, and then press ⌷Tab⌷ to create a new row. Enter the following new record:

First Name	**Eldon**
Last Name	**Aarons**
Address 1	**5354 Thornewood Dr.**
Unit	**#2B**
City	**Memphis**
State	**TN**
ZIP Code	**38112**

b. **Save**, and then **Close** the table of addresses; be sure your blank **Lastname_Firstname_3D_Labels** document displays. Click the **Mailings tab**. In the **Start Mail Merge group**, click the **Start Mail Merge** button, and then click **Step by Step Mail Merge Wizard**. Under **Select document type**, click the **Labels** option button.

c. At the bottom of the task pane, click **Next: Starting document**. Under **Select starting document**, be sure **Change document layout** is selected, and then under **Change document layout**, click **Label options**.

d. In the **Label Options** dialog box, under **Printer information**, click the **Tray arrow**, and then click **Default tray (Automatically Select)**.

e. Under **Label information**, click the **Label vendors arrow**, and then click **Avery US Letter**. Under **Product number**, scroll about halfway down the list, and then click **5160**. At the bottom of the **Label Options** dialog box, click **OK**. At the bottom of the task pane, click **Next: Select recipients**.

f. Under **Select recipients**, be sure the **Use an existing list** option button is selected. Under **Use an existing list**, click **Browse**. Navigate to your **Word Chapter 3** folder, select your **Lastname_Firstname_3D_Addresses** file, and then click **Open**. At the bottom of the **Mail Merge Recipients** dialog box, click **OK**, and then in the **Mail Merge** task pane, click **Next: Arrange your labels**.

g. Under **Arrange your labels**, click **Address block**. If necessary, in the **Insert Address Block** dialog box, under **Insert recipient's name in this format**, select the **Joshua Randall Jr.** format.

h. Click **Match Fields**. Click the **Address 2 arrow**, and then click **Unit**. Click **OK** two times.

i. In the task pane, under **Replicate labels**, click **Update all labels**. Click **Next: Preview your labels**. Press ⌷Ctrl⌷ + ⌷A⌷ to select all of the label text, and then on the **Page Layout tab**, click in the **Spacing Before** box, type **4** and press ⌷Enter⌷ to ensure that the four-line addresses will fit on the labels. **Save** your labels, and then **Close** the **Mail Merge** task pane.

4 Add the file name to the footer, and then close the footer area. Click in the bottom empty row of the table, click the **Layout tab**, in the **Rows & Columns group**, click **Delete**, and then click **Delete Rows**. From **Backstage** view, display the **Document Panel**, type your name and course information, and then add the keywords **newsletter mailing labels Close** the **Document Panel**.

a. Print or submit electronically your 3D_Company_Newsletter, 3D_Addresses, and 3D_Labels documents.

b. **Close** the document, click **Save** to save the labels, and then **Exit** Word.

End **You have completed Project 3D** _____

Content-Based Assessments

Apply **3A** skills from these Objectives:

1. Create a Research Paper
2. Insert Footnotes in a Research Paper
3. Create Citations and a Bibliography in a Research Paper

Mastering Word | Project **3E** Hazards

In the following Mastering Word project, you will edit and format a research paper for Memphis Primary Materials, the topic of which is hazardous materials in electronic waste. Your completed document will look similar to Figure 3.43.

Project Files

For Project 3E, you will need the following file:

w03E_Hazards

You will save your document as:

Lastname_Firstname_3E_Hazards

Project Results

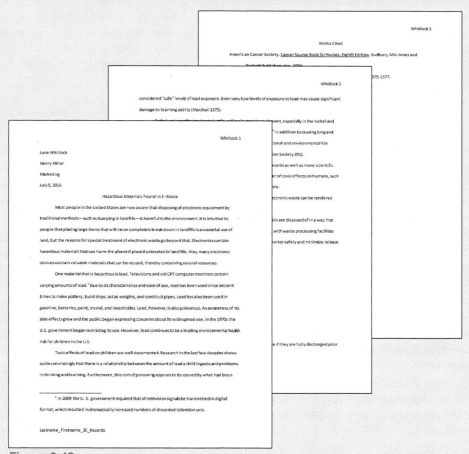

Figure 3.43

(Project 3E Hazards continues on the next page)

Mastering Word | Project **3E** Hazards (continued)

1 **Start** Word. From your student files open the document **w03E_Hazards**. **Save** the document in your **Word Chapter 3** folder as **Lastname_Firstname_3E_Hazards** Display the header area, type **Whitlock** and then press Spacebar. Display the **Page Number gallery**, and then in the **Current Position**, add the **Plain Number** style. Apply **Align Text Right** formatting to the header. Add the file name to the footer.

2 Return to the beginning of the document, press Enter to insert a blank line, click in the blank line, type **June Whitlock** and then press Enter. Type **Henry Miller** and press Enter. Type **Marketing** and press Enter. Type **July 5, 2016**

3 Select all of the text in the document. Change the **Line Spacing** to **2.0**, and change the **Spacing After** to **0 pt**. Deselect the text, right-click anywhere in the title *Hazardous Materials Found in E-Waste*, and then **Center** the title.

Starting with the paragraph that begins *Most people*, select the text from that point to the end of the document, and then set the **First Line Indent** to **0.5"**.

4 Near the middle of **Page 1**, in the paragraph that begins *One material*, in the second line, click to position the insertion point to the right of the period following *lead*, and then add the following footnote:

> **In 2009 the U.S. government required that all television signals be transmitted in digital format, which resulted in dramatically increased numbers of discarded television sets.**

On **Page 2**, in the paragraph that begins *Cadmium is another*, in the second line, click to position the insertion point to the right of the period following *devices*, and then add the following footnote:

> **Newer lithium batteries are not considered hazardous waste if they are fully discharged prior to disposal.**

5 Right-click anywhere in the footnote, modify the **Style** to set the **Font Size** to **11**, and then change the **Format** of paragraphs to add a **First line** indent and use double-spacing.

Near the bottom of **Page 1**, locate the paragraph that begins *Toxic effects*, and then click position the insertion

point to the left of the period at the end of the paragraph, which displays at the top of **Page 2**. In the **MLA** format, add the following **Journal Article** citation (type the Title on one line):

Author:	**Marshall, Eliot**
Title:	**EPA May Allow More Lead in Gasoline**
Journal Name:	**Science**
Year:	**1982**
Pages:	**1375–1377**

6 Near the top of **Page 2**, locate the paragraph that begins *Cadmium*, and then click to position the insertion point to the left of the period at the end of the paragraph. Add the following **Book** citation, using a **Corporate Author** (type the Title on one line):

Corporate Author:	**American Cancer Society**
Title:	**Cancer Source Book for Nurses, Eighth Edition**
Year:	**2004**
City:	**Sudbury, MA**
Publisher:	**Jones and Bartlett Publishers, Inc.**

Select the *Marshall* citation and add the page number **1375** At the end of the next paragraph, select the *American Cancer Society* citation and add the page number **291**

7 Move to the end of the document, and then insert a manual page break to create a new page. Change the **First Line Indent** to **0″**. Add a **Works Cited** title, and then **Insert Bibliography**. Select the two references, apply **Double** line spacing, and then remove spacing after the paragraphs. **Center** the *Works Cited* title.

Display the **Document Panel** and add your name and course information and the keywords **hazardous materials Save** your document. Display the Print Preview, make any necessary adjustments, and then print or submit electronically as directed. **Exit** Word.

 You have completed Project 3E ————————

Content-Based Assessments

Apply 3B skills from these Objectives:

4 Format a Multiple-Column Newsletter

5 Use Special Character and Paragraph Formatting

6 Create Mailing Labels Using Mail Merge

Mastering Word | Project 3F Spring Newsletter

In the following Mastering Word project, you will format a newsletter for Memphis Primary Materials, and then create a set of mailing labels for the newsletter. Your completed documents will look similar to Figure 3.44.

Project Files

For Project 3F, you will need the following files:

New blank Word document
w03F_Spring_Newsletter
w03F_Addresses

You will save your documents as:

Lastname_Firstname_3F_Spring_Newsletter
Lastname_Firstname_3F_Labels

Project Results

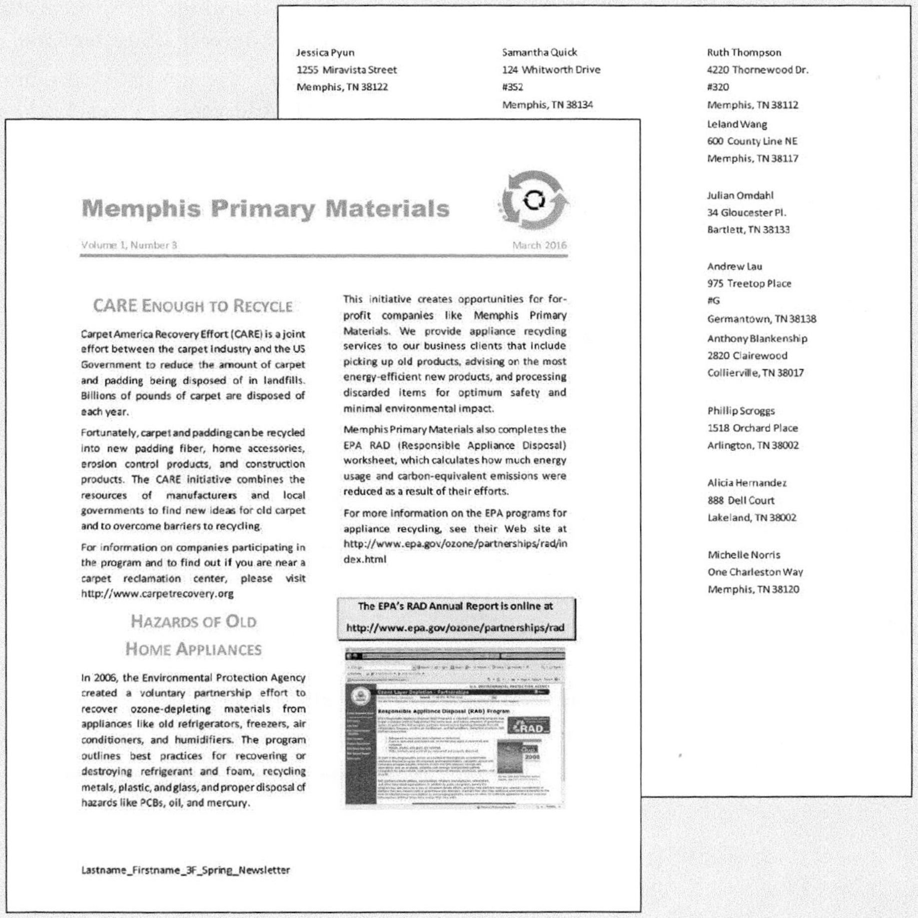

Jessica Pyun
1255 Miravista Street
Memphis, TN 38122

Samantha Quick
124 Whitworth Drive
#352
Memphis, TN 38134

Ruth Thompson
4220 Thornewood Dr.
#320
Memphis, TN 38112

Leland Wang
600 County Line NE
Memphis, TN 38117

Julian Omdahl
34 Gloucester Pl.
Bartlett, TN 38133

Andrew Lau
975 Treetop Place
#G
Germantown, TN 38138

Anthony Blankenship
2820 Clairewood
Collierville, TN 38017

Phillip Scroggs
1518 Orchard Place
Arlington, TN 38002

Alicia Hernandez
888 Dell Court
Lakeland, TN 38002

Michelle Norris
One Charleston Way
Memphis, TN 38120

Memphis Primary Materials

Volume 1, Number 3

March 2016

CARE ENOUGH TO RECYCLE

Carpet America Recovery Effort (CARE) is a joint effort between the carpet industry and the US Government to reduce the amount of carpet and padding being disposed of in landfills. Billions of pounds of carpet are disposed of each year.

Fortunately, carpet and padding can be recycled into new padding fiber, home accessories, erosion control products, and construction products. The CARE initiative combines the resources of manufacturers and local governments to find new ideas for old carpet and to overcome barriers to recycling.

For information on companies participating in the program and to find out if you are near a carpet reclamation center, please visit http://www.carpetrecovery.org

HAZARDS OF OLD HOME APPLIANCES

In 2006, the Environmental Protection Agency created a voluntary partnership effort to recover ozone-depleting materials from appliances like old refrigerators, freezers, air conditioners, and humidifiers. The program outlines best practices for recovering or destroying refrigerant and foam, recycling metals, plastic, and glass, and proper disposal of hazards like PCBs, oil, and mercury.

This initiative creates opportunities for for-profit companies like Memphis Primary Materials. We provide appliance recycling services to our business clients that include picking up old products, advising on the most energy-efficient new products, and processing discarded items for optimum safety and minimal environmental impact.

Memphis Primary Materials also completes the EPA RAD (Responsible Appliance Disposal) worksheet, which calculates how much energy usage and carbon-equivalent emissions were reduced as a result of their efforts.

For more information on the EPA programs for appliance recycling, see their Web site at http://www.epa.gov/ozone/partnerships/rad/index.html

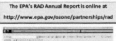

The EPA's RAD Annual Report is online at http://www.epa.gov/ozone/partnerships/rad

Lastname_Firstname_3F_Spring_Newsletter

Figure 3.44

(Project 3F Spring Newsletter continues on the next page)

Content-Based Assessments

Mastering Word | Project 3F Spring Newsletter (continued)

1 **Start** Word. Open **w03F_Spring_Newsletter**, and then save it in your **Word Chapter 3** folder as **Lastname_Firstname_3F_Spring_Newsletter** Add the file name to the footer. Display the rulers and formatting marks.

Select the first line of text—*Memphis Primary Materials*. Change the **Font** to **Arial Black**, the **Font Size** to **24**, and the **Font Color** to **Orange, Accent 6, Darker 25%**.

Select the second line of text—the date and volume. Change the **Font Color** to **Orange, Accent 6, Darker 25%**. Display the **Borders and Shading** dialog box, and then add an **Orange, Accent 6, Darker 25%, 3 pt** line below the selected text.

2 Click at the beginning of the newsletter title. Display the **Clip Art** task pane, search for **recycle earth** and then insert the image of the orange and tan recycle arrows. Change the **Height** to **1** and then apply **Square** text wrapping. Close the **Clip Art** task pane. Drag the image to the location shown in Figure 3.44.

Starting with the paragraph that begins *CARE enough*, select all of the text from that point to the end of the document. Change the **Spacing After** to **6 pt**, format the text in two columns, and apply the **Justify** alignment.

3 At the top of the first column, select the paragraph *CARE Enough to Recycle*. From the **Font** dialog box, change the **Font Size** to **20**, apply **Bold**, add the **Small caps** effect, and change the **Font color** to **Orange, Accent 6, Darker 25%**. **Center** the paragraph. Near the bottom of the same column, apply the same formatting to the paragraph that begins *Hazards of Old*. Add a manual line break between *Old* and *Home*.

Move to the blank line at the bottom of the second column. Open your Web browser and open the **www.epa.gov/ozone/partnerships/rad/** Web site. Maximize the browser window and return to your Word document. Insert a **Screenshot** of the EPA Web page. **Close** your Web browser.

4 Select the two lines of text above the inserted screenshot. **Center** the text and apply **Bold**. Add a **Shadow** border, change the **Color** to **Tan, Background 2, Darker 25%**, the **Width** to **1 1/2 pt**, and then on the **Shading tab** of the dialog box, apply a **Fill** of **Tan, Background 2** shading—in the third column, the first color.

Display the **Document Panel** and add your name, course information, and the **Keywords Spring newsletter** Display the **Print Preview**, return to your document and make any necessary corrections, and then **Save** and **Close** the document. Hold this document until you complete the project.

5 Display a **New** blank document. **Save** the document in your **Word Chapter 3** folder as **Lastname_Firstname_3F_Labels** On the **Mailings tab**, start the **Step by Step Mail Merge Wizard.**

In **Step 1**, select **Labels** as the document type. In **Step 2**, set **Label options** to use the **Auto default** tray (yours may vary) and **Avery US Letter 5160**.

In **Step 3**, use an existing list, browse to select **w03F_Addresses**. In **Step 4**, add an **Address block** to the labels, use the *Joshua Randall Jr.* format, and then **Match Fields** by matching *Address 2* to *Unit*.

Update all labels and **Preview**. Select all of the label text, and then on the **Page Layout tab**, click in the **Spacing Before** box, type **4** and press Enter to ensure that the four-line addresses will fit on the labels. On the **Layout tab**, in the **Table group**, if necessary click **View Gridlines** to check the alignment of the labels.

Complete the merge, and then **Close** the **Mail Merge** task pane. Delete the last two empty rows of the table, and then add the file name to the footer.

6 Display the **Document Panel**, and then add your name and course information and the keywords **mailing labels** Display the **Print Preview**, return to your document and make any necessary corrections, and then **Save**. Print or submit electronically your two files that are the results of this project—3F_Spring_Newsletter and 3F_Labels. **Exit** Word.

End **You have completed Project 3F**

Content-Based Assessments

Apply **3A** and **3B** skills from these Objectives:

1. Create a Research Paper
2. Insert Footnotes in a Research Paper
3. Create Citations and a Bibliography in a Research Paper
4. Format a Multiple-Column Newsletter
5. Use Special Character and Paragraph Formatting
6. Create Mailing Labels Using Mail Merge

Mastering Word | Project **3G** Economics

In the following Mastering Word project, you will edit and format a newsletter and a research paper for Memphis Primary Materials on the topic of environmental economics. Your completed documents will look similar to Figure 3.45.

Project Files

For Project 3G, you will need the following files:

New blank Word document
w03G_Economics
w03G_Addresses
w03G_April_Newsletter

You will save your documents as:

Lastname_Firstname_3G_Economics
Lastname_Firstname_3G_April_Newsletter
Lastname_Firstname_3G_Labels

Project Results

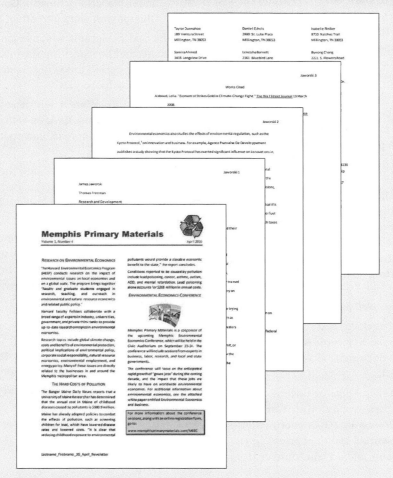

Figure 3.45

(Project 3G Economics continues on the next page)

Mastering Word | Project **3G** Economics (continued)

1 **Start** Word. Open the document **w03G_April_ Newsletter**, and then save the document in your **Word Chapter 3** folder as **Lastname_Firstname_3G_April_ Newsletter** Add the file name to the footer. Starting with the paragraph that begins *Research on Environmental Economics*, select all of the text from that point to the end of the document—the document text extends to two pages. Set the **Spacing After** to **6 pt**, format the selected text as two columns, and set the alignment to **Justify**.

2 Near the bottom of the first column, in the paragraph that begins *Maine has already*, click to position the insertion point to the left of the sixth line, which begins *pollutants would*. Insert a column break. At the top of the first column, select the paragraph *Research on Environmental Economics*.

Display the **Font** dialog box, set the **Font Size** to **14**, apply **Bold**, set the **Font color** to **Dark Blue, Text 2**, and then add the **Small caps** effect. **Center** the paragraph. Use the Format Painter to copy the formatting and then apply the same formatting to the paragraph *The Hard Costs of Pollution* located near the bottom of the first column and to *Environmental Economics Conference* in the second column.

3 At the bottom of the second column, select the last two paragraphs of text. From the **Borders and Shading** dialog box, apply a **1 1/2 pt**, **Shadow** border using the **Dark Blue, Text 2** color, and then on the **Shading tab**, apply a **Fill** of **Dark Blue, Text 2, Lighter 80%**.

In the second column, click to position the insertion point at the beginning of the paragraph that begins *Memphis Primary Materials is a cosponsor*. Display the **Clip Art** task pane. Search for **conference** and limit your search to **Illustrations**. **Insert** the image shown in Figure 3.45, apply **Top and Bottom** text wrapping, decrease the **Height** of the image to **1″**, and position the image as shown. **Close** the Clip Art task pane.

Display the **Document Panel** and add your name and course information and the **Keywords April newsletter Save** and then **Close** the document. Hold this file until you complete this project.

4 From your student files, open the document **w03G_Economics**, and then save it in your **Word Chapter 3** folder as **Lastname_Firstname_3G_Economics** Display the header area, type **Jaworski** and then press (Spacebar). In the **Header & Footer group**, add a **Plain Number** from the

Current Position gallery. Apply **Align Text Right** formatting to the header. Move to the footer area and add the file name to the footer.

Select all of the text in the document. Change the **Line Spacing** to **2.0**, and change the **Spacing After** to **0**. Near the top of the document, **Center** the title *Environmental Economics and Business*. Beginning with the text below the centered title, select the text from that point to the end of the document, and then set a **First Line Indent** at **0.5″**.

5 At the bottom of **Page 1**, in the paragraph that begins *Environmental economics also*, in the second line, click to position the insertion point to the right of the comma following *Protocol*, and then insert the following footnote:

> **The Kyoto Protocol is an international agreement under the UN Framework Convention on Climate Change that went into effect in 2005.**

In the next paragraph, which begins *In the United States*, in the second line, position the insertion point to the right of the period following *Economics*, and then insert the following footnote:

> **The NCEE offers a centralized source of technical expertise to the EPA, as well as other federal agencies, Congress, universities, and other organizations.**

Right-click in the footnote, and then modify the style to set the **Font Size** to **11** and the format of the paragraph to include a **First line** indent and double-spacing. **Save** your document.

6 Near the bottom of **Page 1**, in the paragraph that begins *Environmental economists*, position the insertion point to the left of the period at the end of the paragraph. Using **MLA** format, add the following **Article in a Periodical** citation (type the Title on one line):

Author:	**Abboud, Leila**
Title:	**Economist Strikes Gold in Climate-Change Fight**
Periodical Title:	**The Wall Street Journal**
Year:	**2008**
Month:	**March**
Day:	**13**

(Project 3G Economics continues on the next page)

Select the *Abboud* citation and add the page number **A1** Near the middle of **Page 2**, in the paragraph that begins *In the United States*, click to position the insertion point to the left of the period at the end of the paragraph. Add the following **Book** citation in **MLA** format (type the Title on one line):

Author:	**Tietenberg, Tom; Folmer, Henk, Editors**
Title:	**The International Yearbook of Environmental Resource Economics, 2006/2007**
Year:	**2006**
City:	**Northampton, MA**
Publisher:	**Edward Elgar Publishers**

7 Select the *Tietenberg* citation and add the page number **1** Insert a manual page break at the end of the document. On the new **Page 3**, on the ruler, set the **First Line Indent** to **0"**. Type **Works Cited** and then press Enter.

On the **References tab**, in the **Citations & Bibliography group**, be sure *MLA* displays in the **Style** box. Insert the bibliography. Select the inserted references, set the **Line Spacing** to **2.0**, and then set **Spacing After** to **0 pt**. Center the *Works Cited* title.

Display the **Document Panel** and add your name and course information and the **Keywords environmental**

economics Display the **Print Preview** to check your document, make any necessary adjustments, **Save**, and then **Close** the document. Hold this file until you complete this project.

8 Display a **New** blank document. **Save** the document in your **Word Chapter 3** folder as **Lastname_Firstname_ 3G_Labels** On the **Mailings tab**, start the **Step by Step Mail Merge Wizard**. In **Step 1**, select **Labels** as the document type. In **Step 2**, set **Label options** to use the **Auto default** tray (yours may vary) and **Avery US Letter 5160**. If you cannot see the gridlines, on the **Layout tab**, in the **Table group**, click **View Gridlines**. In **Step 3**, use an existing list, browse to select **w03G_Addresses**, and then click **OK**.

In **Step 4**, add an **Address block** to the labels, use the *Joshua Randall Jr.* format, and then **Match Fields** by matching *Address 2* to *Unit*. **Update all labels** and then **Preview**. Select all of the label text, and then on the **Page Layout tab**, click in the **Spacing Before** box, type **4** and press Enter. Complete the merge, and then **Close** the **Mail Merge** task pane. Delete the last two empty rows of the table, and then add the file name to the footer, which adds an additional page.

Display the **Document Panel**, and then add your name, course information, and the keywords **mailing labels** Click **Save**. Print or submit electronically your three files that are the results of this project—3G_Economics, 3G_April_Newsletter, and 3G_Labels. **Exit** Word.

End **You have completed Project 3G** ─────────

Content-Based Assessments

GO! Fix It | Project **3H** Metals Report

Project Files

For Project 3H, you will need the following file:

w03H_Metals_Report

You will save your document as:

Lastname_Firstname_3H_Metals_Report

From the student files that accompany this textbook, locate and open the file w03H_Metals_Report, and then save the file in your Word Chapter 3 folder as **Lastname_Firstname_3H_Metals_Report**

This document contains errors that you must find and correct. Read and examine the document, and then edit to correct any errors that you find and to improve the overall document format. Types of errors could include, but are not restricted to:

- Formatting does not match MLA style guidelines that you practiced in the chapter
- Incorrect header format
- Incorrect spacing between paragraphs
- Incorrect paragraph indents
- Incorrect line spacing
- Incorrect footnote format
- Incorrectly formatted reference page

Things you should know to complete this project:

- Displaying formatting marks will assist in locating spacing errors.
- There are no errors in the parenthetical references in the document.
- There are no errors in the information in the footnotes or bibliographical references.

Save your document and add the file name to the footer. In the Document Panel, add your name, course information, and the keywords **valuable metals, recycling** Save your document and submit as directed.

End **You have completed Project 3H** ⎯⎯⎯⎯⎯⎯⎯⎯⎯⎯⎯⎯⎯⎯⎯⎯

Content-Based Assessments

Apply a combination of the **3A** and **3B** skills.

GO! Make It | Project **3I** Green Newsletter

Project Files

For Project 3I, you will need the following files:

New blank Word document   w03I_Kids
w03I_Competition

You will save your document as:

Lastname_Firstname_3I_Green_Newsletter

Start with a new Word document, and then save the file in your chapter folder as **Lastname_Firstname_3I_Green_Newsletter** Create the document shown in Figure 3.46. Create a nameplate, and then insert the files w03I_Competition and w03I_Kids. The title is Arial Black, 24 pt, Dark Blue, Text 2. Other titles and borders are Dark Blue, Text 2. The two titles in the columns are Calibri, 16 pt. The clip art image can be found by using the search term **recycle** and the screenshot can be found at the Web address in the last line of the newsletter.

Add the file name to the footer; in the Document Panel, add your name and course information and the Keywords **green, campuses, kids** Save your document and submit as directed.

Project Results

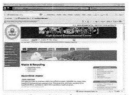

Figure 3.46

End You have completed Project 3I

Content-Based Assessments

GO! Solve It | Project **3J** Municipal Newsletter

Project Files

For Project 3J, you will need the following file:

New blank Word document

You will save your document as:

Lastname_Firstname_3J_Municipal_Newsletter

Memphis Primary Materials writes an informational newsletter for customers. Create a new document and save it in your Word Chapter 3 folder as **Lastname_Firstname_3J_Municipal_ Newsletter** Use the following information to create a newsletter that includes a nameplate, multiple columns, at least two articles with article titles formatted so that they stand out, at least one clip art image, one screenshot, and one paragraph that includes a border and shading.

This issue (Volume 1, Number 6—June 2016) will focus on municipal solid waste—the waste generated by householders and small businesses. This category of waste does not include hazardous, industrial, or construction waste. The articles you write can be on any topic regarding municipal waste, and might include an introduction to the topic and a discussion of recycling in the U.S. or in the Memphis community. You will need to research this topic on the Web. A good place to start is www.epa.gov, which has many articles on solid municipal waste, and also provides links to further articles on the topic. You might also consider doing a Web search for the term **municipal solid waste recycling**

Add the file name to the footer. To the Document Panel, add your name, your course name and section number, and the keywords **municipal solid waste recycling**

	Performance Level		
	Exemplary: You consistently applied the relevant skills	**Proficient:** You sometimes, but not always, applied the relevant skills	**Developing:** You rarely or never applied the relevant skills
Create and format nameplate	The nameplate includes both the company name and the date and volume information, and is formatted attractively.	One or more of the nameplate elements are done correctly, but other items are either omitted or not formatted properly.	The newsletter does not include a nameplate.
Insert at least two articles in multiple-column format	The newsletter contains at least two articles, displayed in multiple columns that are well written and are free of grammar and spelling errors.	The newsletter contains only one article, or the text is not divided into two columns, or there are spelling and grammar errors in the text.	The newsletter contains only one article, the article is not divided into multiple columns, and there are spelling and grammar errors.
Insert and format at least one clip art image	An appropriate clip art image is included. The image is sized and positioned appropriately.	A clip art image is inserted, but is either inappropriate, or is formatted or positioned poorly.	No clip art image is included.
Border and shading added to a paragraph	One or more paragraphs display an attractive border with shading that enables the reader to read the text.	A border or shading is displayed, but not both; or, the shading is too dark to enable the reader to easily read the text.	No border or shading is added to a paragraph.
Insert a screenshot	A screenshot is inserted in one of the columns; the screenshot is related to the content of the article.	A screenshot is inserted in the document, but does not relate to the content of the article.	No screenshot is inserted.

Performance Element

End You have completed Project 3J

Content-Based Assessments

Apply a combination of the **3A** and **3B** skills.

GO! Solve It | Project **3K** Paper Report

Project Files

For Project 3K, you will need the following file:

New blank Word document

You will save your document as:

Lastname_Firstname_3K_Paper_Report

Create a new file and save it as **Lastname_Firstname_3K_Paper_Report** Use the following information to create a report written in the MLA format. The report should include at least two footnotes, at least two citations, and should include a *Works Cited* page.

Memphis Primary Materials writes and distributes informational reports on topics of interest to the people of Memphis. This report will be written by Sarah Stanger for the head of Marketing, Henry Miller. Information reports are provided as a public service of the company, and are distributed free of charge.

The topic of the report is recycling and reuse of paper and paper products. The report should contain an introduction, and then details about how much paper is used, what it is used for, the increase of paper recycling over time, and how paper products can be recycled or reused. A good place to start is www.epa.gov, which has many articles on paper use and recycling, and also provides links to further articles on the topic. You might also consider doing a Web search for the terms **paper recycling**

Add the file name to the footer, and add your name, your course name and section number, and the keywords **paper products, recycling** to the Document Panel.

Performance Element	Performance Level		
	Exemplary: You consistently applied the relevant skills	**Proficient:** You sometimes, but not always, applied the relevant skills	**Developing:** You rarely or never applied the relevant skills
Format the header and heading	The last name and page number are right-aligned in the header, and the report has a four-line heading and a centered title.	The header and heading are included, but are not formatted according to MLA style guidelines.	The header or heading is missing or incomplete.
Format the body of the report	The report is double-spaced, with no space after paragraphs. The first lines of paragraphs are indented 0.5".	Some, but not all, of the report formatting is correct.	The majority of the formatting does not follow MLA guidelines.
Footnotes are included and formatted correctly	Two or more footnotes are included, and the footnote text is 11 pt, double-spaced, and the first line of each footnote is indented.	The correct number of footnotes is included, but the footnotes are not formatted properly.	No footnotes are included.
Citations and bibliography are included and formatted according to MLA guidelines	At least two citations are included in parenthetical references, with page numbers where appropriate, and the sources are included in a properly formatted Works Cited page.	Only one citation is included, or the citations and sources are not formatted correctly.	No citations or Works Cited page are included.

End You have completed Project 3K

Rubric

The following outcomes-based assessments are *open-ended assessments*. That is, there is no specific correct result; your result will depend on your approach to the information provided. Make *Professional Quality* your goal. Use the following scoring rubric to guide you in *how* to approach the problem, and then to evaluate *how well* your approach solves the problem.

The *criteria*—Software Mastery, Content, Format and Layout, and Process—represent the knowledge and skills you have gained that you can apply to solving the problem. The *levels of performance*—Professional Quality, Approaching Professional Quality, or Needs Quality Improvements—help you and your instructor evaluate your result.

	Your completed project is of Professional Quality if you:	Your completed project is Approaching Professional Quality if you:	Your completed project Needs Quality Improvements if you:
1-Software Mastery	Choose and apply the most appropriate skills, tools, and features and identify efficient methods to solve the problem.	Choose and apply some appropriate skills, tools, and features, but not in the most efficient manner.	Choose inappropriate skills, tools, or features, or are inefficient in solving the problem.
2-Content	Construct a solution that is clear and well organized, contains content that is accurate, appropriate to the audience and purpose, and is complete. Provide a solution that contains no errors in spelling, grammar, or style.	Construct a solution in which some components are unclear, poorly organized, inconsistent, or incomplete. Misjudge the needs of the audience. Have some errors in spelling, grammar, or style, but the errors do not detract from comprehension.	Construct a solution that is unclear, incomplete, or poorly organized; contains some inaccurate or inappropriate content; and contains many errors in spelling, grammar, or style. Do not solve the problem.
3-Format and Layout	Format and arrange all elements to communicate information and ideas, clarify function, illustrate relationships, and indicate relative importance.	Apply appropriate format and layout features to some elements, but not others. Overuse features, causing minor distraction.	Apply format and layout that does not communicate information or ideas clearly. Do not use format and layout features to clarify function, illustrate relationships, or indicate relative importance. Use available features excessively, causing distraction.
4-Process	Use an organized approach that integrates planning, development, self-assessment, revision, and reflection.	Demonstrate an organized approach in some areas, but not others; or, use an insufficient process of organization throughout.	Do not use an organized approach to solve the problem.

Outcomes-Based Assessments

Apply a combination of the 3A and 3B skills.

GO! Think | Project 3L Jobs Newsletter

Project Files

For Project 3L, you will need the following file:

New blank Word document

You will save your document as:

Lastname_Firstname_3L_Jobs_Newsletter

The marketing manager of Memphis Primary Materials needs to create the next issue of the company's monthly newsletter (Volume 1, Number 7—July 2016), which will focus on "green jobs." Green jobs are jobs associated with environmentally friendly companies or are positions with firms that manufacture, sell, or install energy-saving or resource-saving products.

Use the following information to create a newsletter that includes a nameplate, multiple columns, at least two articles with article titles formatted so that they stand out, at least one clip art image, one screenshot, and one paragraph that includes a border and shading.

The articles you write can be on any topic regarding green jobs, and might include an introduction to the topic, information about a recent (or future) green job conference, and a discussion of green jobs in the United States. You will need to research this topic on the Web. A good place to start is www.epa.gov. You might also consider doing a Web search for the terms **green jobs** or **green jobs conference**

Add the file name to the footer. Add appropriate information to the Document Panel. Save the document as **Lastname_Firstname_3L_Jobs_Newsletter** and submit it as directed.

 You have completed Project 3L ———————————

Apply a combination of the 3A and 3B skills.

GO! Think | Project 3M Construction Report

Project Files

For Project 3M, you will need the following file:

New blank Word document

You will save your document as:

Lastname_Firstname_3M_Construction_Report

As part of the ongoing research provided on environment topics by the staff of Memphis Primary Materials, the Marketing Director, Henry Miller, has asked a summer intern, James Bodine, to create a report on recycling and reuse in the construction and demolition of buildings.

Create a new file and save it as **Lastname_Firstname_3M_Construction_Report** Use the following information to create a report written in the MLA format. The report should include at least two footnotes, at least two citations, and should include a *Works Cited* page.

The report should contain an introduction, and then details about, for example, how much construction material can be salvaged from existing buildings, how these materials can be reused in future buildings, and how materials can be saved and recycled on new building projects. A good place to start is www.epa.gov, which has a number of articles on recycling and reuse of materials during construction and demolition. You might also consider doing a Web search for the terms **construction recycling** or **demolition recycling** or **construction and demolition**

Add the file name to the footer. Add appropriate information to the Document Panel and submit it as directed.

 You have completed Project 3M ———————————

Apply a combination of the **3B** skills.

You and GO! | Project **3N** College Newsletter

Project Files

For Project 3N, you will need the following file:

New blank Word document

You will save your document as

Lastname_Firstname_3N_College_Newsletter

In this project, you will create a one-page newsletter. The newsletter should include at least one article describing your college and one article about an academic or athletic program at your college.

Be sure to include a nameplate, at least two articles, at least one clip art or screenshot image, and a bordered paragraph or paragraphs. Before you submit the newsletter, be sure to check it for grammar and spelling errors, and also be sure to format the newsletter in an attractive manner by using the skills you practiced in this chapter.

Save the file as **Lastname_Firstname_3N_College_Newsletter** Add the file name to the footer, and add your name, your course name and section number, and the keywords **newsletter** and **college** to the Document Panel. Save and submit your file as directed.

End You have completed Project 3N ——————————————

Getting Started with Windows 7

PROJECT 1A
Familiarize Yourself with Windows 7.

1. Get Started with Windows 7
2. Use the Start Menu and Manage Windows
3. Resize, Move, and Scroll Windows

PROJECT 1B
Manage Files and Folders.

4. Create, Move, and Rename Folders
5. Copy, Move, Rename, and Delete Files
6. Find Files and Folders

Dmitriy Shironosov/Shutterstock

In This Chapter

Windows 7 is the software that coordinates the activities of your computer's hardware. Windows 7 controls how your screen is displayed, how you open and close programs, and the start-up, shut-down, and navigation procedures for your computer. It is useful to become familiar with the basic features of the Microsoft Windows operating system, especially working with the Start button and the taskbar; opening, closing, moving, and resizing windows; and finding, saving, and managing files and folders.

From Chapter 1 of *Go! with Microsoft® Windows 7 Getting Started*, First Edition, Shelley Gaskin, Robert L. Ferrett. Copyright © 2011 by Pearson Education, Inc. Published by Pearson Prentice Hall. All rights reserved.

Project 1A Familiarize Yourself with Windows 7

Project Activities

In Activities 1.01 through 1.09, you will explore the Windows 7 screen and practice navigating Windows 7. You will open, close, resize, and move windows, and you will open several windows at one time. The screens that you will be working with will look similar to those in Figure 1.1.

Project Files

For Project 1A, you will need the following files:

No files are needed for this project

You will save your documents as

Lastname_Firstname_1A_Taskbar (not submitted)
Lastname_Firstname_1A_Windows (not submitted)
Lastname_Firstname_1A_WordPad

Project Results

Figure 1.1

Objective 1 | Get Started with Windows 7

Windows 7 is an ***operating system***—software that controls the ***hardware*** attached to your computer, including its memory, disk drive space, attached devices such as printers and scanners, and the central processing unit. Windows 7 and earlier versions of Windows are similar; they use a ***graphical user interface (GUI)***. A GUI uses graphics or pictures to represent commands and actions and lets you see document formatting on the screen as it will look when printed on paper. ***Windows***, when spelled with a capital *W*, refers to the operating system that runs your computer.

Starting Windows is an automatic procedure; you turn on your computer, and after a few moments, the version of Windows installed on your computer displays. Some computers require that you log in, and some do not. Windows 7 is available in several versions: Starter, Home Premium, Professional, and Ultimate. For large institutions, there is also an Enterprise edition. For most tasks, the Home Premium, Professional, and Ultimate editions work the same. The Starter edition is typically used only on small notebook computers.

Alert! | **Does your screen differ?**

This chapter uses Windows 7 Ultimate edition, and there may be some differences in the look of this edition and the other editions. More importantly, the look of the screen will depend largely on the setting options that have been selected for your computer, the shape of your monitor, and on the type of hardware installed in your computer—especially the video card and memory.

Activity 1.01 | Exploring the Windows 7 Desktop

In this activity, you will examine the different components of the Windows 7 desktop.

1 Turn on your computer and wait for the Windows program to display, or follow the log-on instructions required for the computer you are using. For example, you might have to click a name on a Welcome screen, or enter a user ID or password. If this is your home computer and you are the only user, it is likely that you need do nothing except wait for a few moments.

The Windows *desktop*, which is the working area of the Windows 7 screen, displays. The screen look will vary, depending on which version of Windows you are using and what you have on your own desktop.

2 Compare your Windows desktop with Figure 1.2 and then take a moment to study the Windows elements identified in the table in Figure 1.3. Your icons may vary.

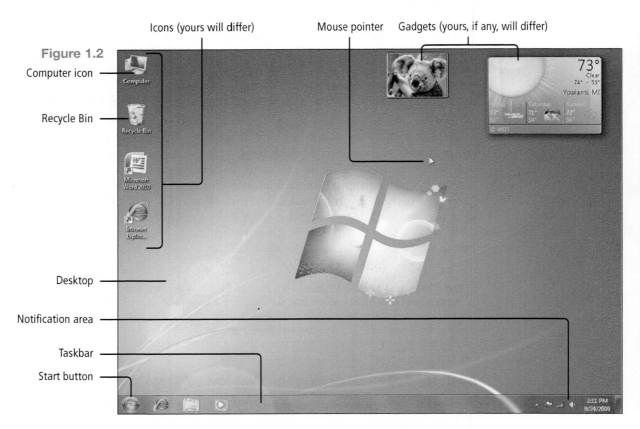

Figure 1.2

Windows Screen Elements

Screen Element	Description
Command bar	A toolbar that offers easy access to settings or features.
Computer icon	An icon that represents the computer on which you are working, and that provides access to the drives, folders, and files on your computer.
Desktop	The working area of the Windows 7 screen, consisting of program icons, a taskbar, gadgets (optional), and a Start button.
Gadgets	Small dynamic programs that run on the desktop, such as a clock, a stock market ticker, or a weather forecast.
Icon	A graphic representation of an object that you can select and open, such as a drive, a disk, a folder, a document, or a program.
Mouse pointer	The arrow, I-beam, or other symbol that moves when you move the mouse or other pointing device, and that indicates a location or position on your screen—also called the *pointer*.
Notification area	The area on the right side of the taskbar, formerly called the *system tray* or *status area*, where the clock and system notifications display. These notifications keep you informed about active processes.
Recycle Bin	A temporary storage area for files that you have deleted from hard drives. Files can be either recovered or permanently removed from the Recycle Bin.
Start button	The button on the left side of the taskbar that is used to start programs, change system settings, find Windows help, search for programs or documents, or shut down the computer.
Taskbar	Displays the Start button and icons for any open programs. The taskbar also displays shortcut buttons for other programs.

Figure 1.3

3 On the left side of the taskbar, *click*—press the left mouse button one time—the **Windows Explorer** button 📁. Compare your screen with Figure 1.4, and then take a moment to study the *Windows Explorer* window elements in the table in Figure 1.5. **Windows Explorer** is a program used to create and manage folders, and to copy, move, sort, and delete files. If the Windows Explorer button does not display on your taskbar, click the Start button, click All Programs, click Accessories, and then click Windows Explorer. If the Menu bar does not display, on the Toolbar, click the Organize button, point to Layout, and then click Menu bar.

The Windows Explorer window displays. When you click the Windows Explorer button, the window opens with *Libraries* selected in the Navigation pane and displayed in the file list. A *window*—spelled with a lowercase *w*—is a rectangular box that displays information or a program. When a window is open, the name of the window is sometimes displayed in the title bar.

Alert! | **Does your screen differ?**

Because the configuration of your Windows Explorer window depends on how it was last used, your window may not display all of the elements shown in Figure 1.4, in particular the Menu bar, Details pane, Navigation pane, and Search pane. A Preview pane may display on the right side of the window, and the window may cover the entire screen.

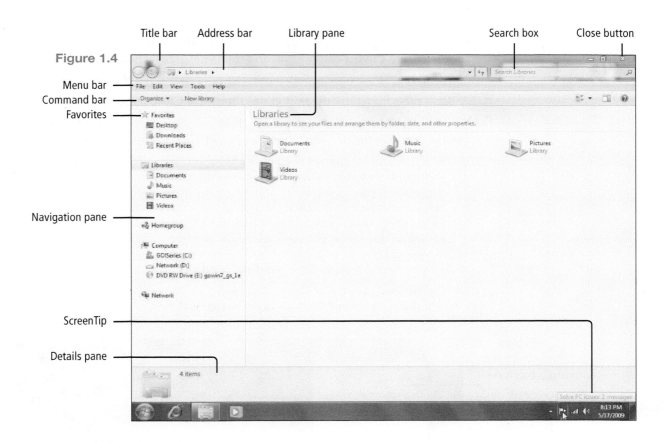

Figure 1.4

Title bar   Address bar   Library pane   Search box   Close button

Menu bar
Command bar
Favorites
Navigation pane
ScreenTip
Details pane

Parts of a Window

Screen Element	Description
Address bar	A toolbar that displays the organizational path to the active file, folder, or window.
Close button	A button in a title bar that closes a window or a Program
Details pane	Displays details about the drive, folder, or file selected in the file list.
Favorites	The upper part of the Navigation pane that displays favorite destinations associated with the current user.
File list	Displays the contents of the current folder or library.
Library pane	Displays above the file list when a Library is selected in the Navigation pane.
Menu bar	The bar near the top of a window that lists the names of menu categories.
Navigation pane	The pane on the left side of the Windows Explorer window that contains personal Favorites, Libraries, access to personal files and folders, and other items.
ScreenTip	A small box, activated by pointing to a button or other screen object, that displays the name of or further information about the screen element.
Search box	A box in which you type a search word or phrase.
Title bar	The area at the top of a window that includes the Minimize, Maximize, and Close buttons. The title bar also often contains the name of the program and the name of the open document.
Toolbar	A row of buttons that activates commands with a single click of the left mouse button.

Figure 1.5

4 In the upper right corner of the **Windows Explorer** window title bar, point to, but do not click, the **Close** button ▣, and then notice that the ScreenTip *Close* displays.

A *ScreenTip* is a small note that provides information about or describes a screen element.

5 Click—press the left mouse button one time—the **Close** button ▣ to close the window.

6 Point to the **Computer** icon in the upper left corner of the desktop and click the right mouse button—this action is known as a *right-click*. Compare your screen with Figure 1.6.

A shortcut menu displays. A *menu* is a list of commands within a category. *Shortcut menus* list *context-sensitive commands*—commands commonly used when working with the selected object. On this shortcut menu, the Open command is displayed in bold because it is the default action that occurs when you double-click this icon. To *double-click* an icon, point to the icon and then press the left mouse button quickly two times in succession, taking care not to move the mouse between clicks.

> **Alert! | Does the Computer icon not display on your desktop?**
>
> If the Computer icon does not display on the desktop, click the Start button 🪟. On the right side of the Start menu, right-click Computer, and then from the shortcut menu, click *Show on Desktop*.

Figure 1.6

Command in bold is the
default action

Shortcut menu

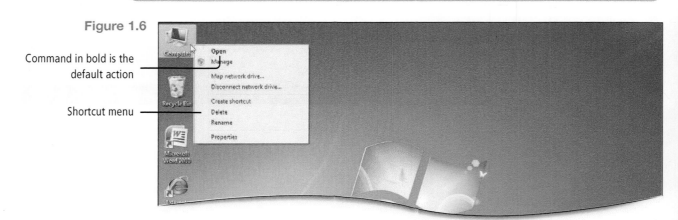

7 From the displayed shortcut menu, point to **Open** to select the command, and then click one time. Compare your screen with Figure 1.7.

> The Windows Explorer window displays, but this time the pane on the right is a file list, not a Libraries pane. The *file list* displays the contents of the item selected in the Navigation pane; in this case, the fixed and removable drives attached to the computer. A *drive* is an area of storage that is formatted with the Windows file system, and that has a drive letter such as C, D, E, and so on. The main drive inside your computer is referred to as the *hard drive*—there may be more than one hard drive in a computer. Also, network drives may display here.

Figure 1.7

Fixed local drives

Removable drives

File list

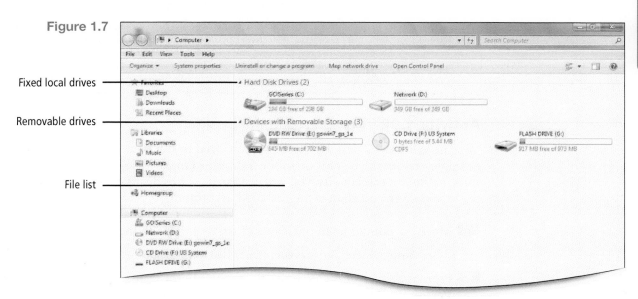

8 Near the top of the **file list**, point to and then click the disk drive labeled **(C:)**, and then notice the **Details** pane. Compare your screen with Figure 1.8.

Figure 1.8

Drive C: selected

Details of drive C: (your drive name may vary)

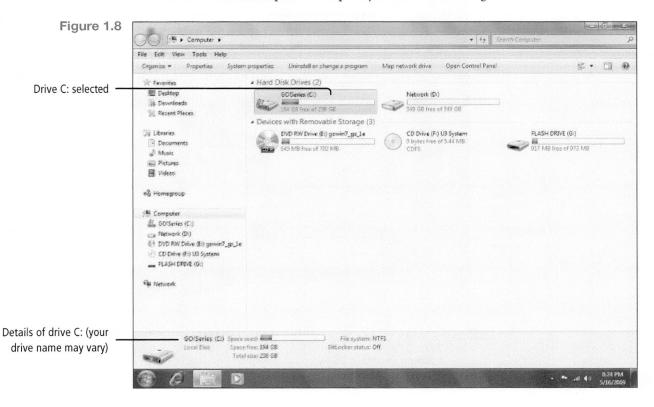

9 In the **Windows Explorer** window title bar, click the **Close** button 🗙.

More Knowledge | The Windows Aero User Interface

The screen you see in the figures in this chapter uses the Windows Aero user interface. *Windows Aero*—which is an acronym for *A*uthentic, *E*nergetic, *R*eflective, *O*pen—features a three-dimensional look, with transparent window frames, live previews of open windows, and multiple color schemes. This user interface is available with all but the most basic versions of Windows 7, but requires extra memory and a good video card. If your screen does not have the same look, your computer may not be capable of displaying the Aero interface.

Activity 1.02 | Personalizing the Desktop

The Windows 7 desktop can be personalized to suit your needs and tastes. You can, for example, change the resolution of the monitor to make it easier to read or display more information. In this activity, you will change the icons displayed on the desktop, change the screen saver, and change the desktop background.

1 Move the pointer to an open area of the desktop, and then right-click.

A shortcut menu displays commands that are available for your desktop.

2 From the shortcut menu, move the pointer to the bottom of the list, and then click **Personalize**. Notice that the Personalization window displays, as shown in Figure 1.9.

Figure 1.9
Personalization window —

Desktop background options —

Current background picture —

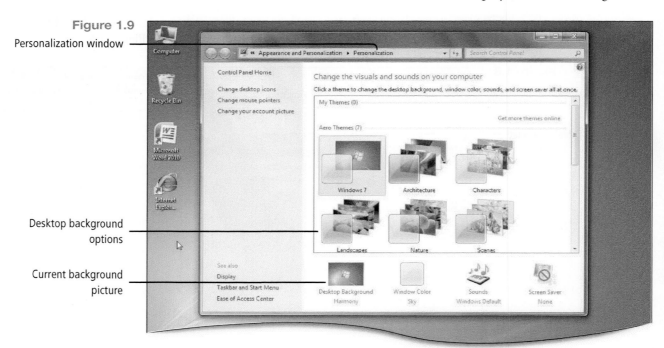

3 In the lower right corner of the **Personalization** window, click **Screen Saver**.

A *screen saver* is a picture or animation that displays on your screen after a preset period of computer inactivity.

4 In the **Screen Saver Settings** dialog box, click the **Screen saver box arrow**. From the displayed list, click **Ribbons**, and then compare your screen with Figure 1.10.

A *dialog box* is a box that asks you to make a decision about an individual object or topic. The Ribbons screen saver is selected, and a preview displays near the top of the dialog box. The default length of inactivity to trigger the screen saver is 1 minute.

Figure 1.10

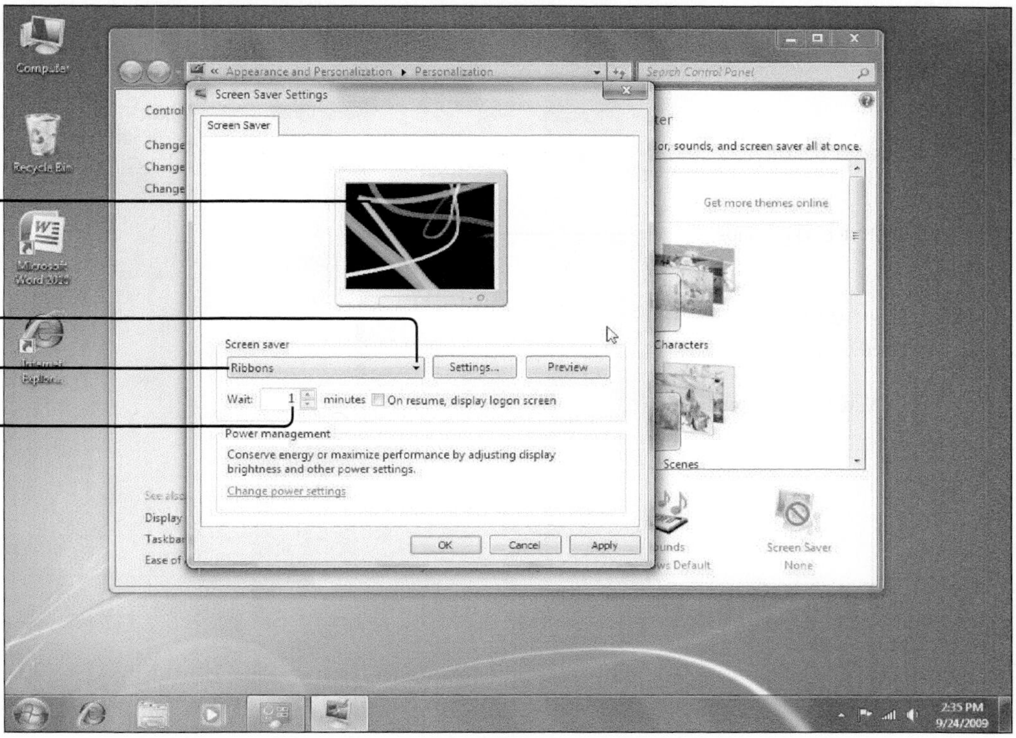

Preview of Ribbons screen saver

Screen saver box arrow

Selected screen saver

Period of inactivity before screen saver displays

5 In the **Screen Saver Settings** dialog box, click the **Preview** button to preview a full-screen version of the screen saver. When you are through, move the mouse to turn off the full-screen screen saver preview. If you want to turn on the screen saver, click **OK**; otherwise, click **Cancel**.

6 In the left panel of the **Personalization** window, click **Change desktop icons**.

7 At the top of the **Desktop Icon Settings** dialog box, select—click to add a check mark to—the **Control Panel** check box. Click **OK** to save your changes and close the Desktop Icon Settings dialog box. Notice that a Control Panel icon is added to the left side of the desktop.

8 At the bottom of the **Personalization** window, click **Desktop Background**. Click the **up arrow** 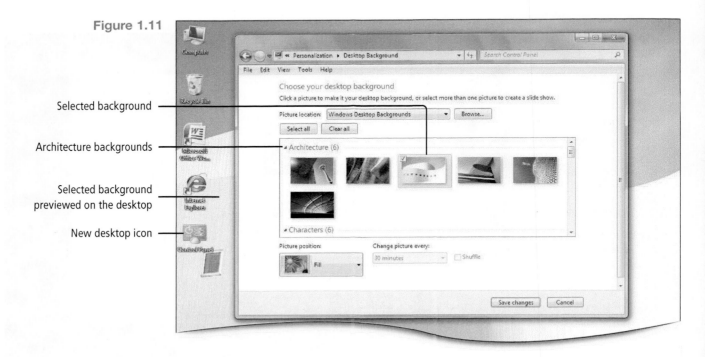 at the top of the scroll bar several times to move to the top of the backgrounds list. Under **Architecture**, click the third picture—the picture of the white building. The new background previews on the screen, as shown in Figure 1.11.

The *desktop background* is the picture, pattern, or color that displays on the desktop.

Figure 1.11

Selected background

Architecture backgrounds

Selected background
previewed on the desktop

New desktop icon

9 At the bottom of the **Personalization** window, click **Save changes**.

10 In the upper right corner of the **Personalization** window, click the **Close** button , and then compare your screen with Figure 1.12.

Figure 1.12

New background applied
to desktop

Activity 1.03 | Adding and Removing Gadgets

Gadgets are used to display dynamic programs such as a currency converter, a calendar, a stock market ticker, or a clock. You can move the gadgets anywhere on the screen, and you can modify or resize most of them.

1 In an open area of the desktop, right-click to display a shortcut menu. On the shortcut menu, click **Gadgets**. Compare your screen with Figure 1.13.

Figure 1.13

Gadgets available on your computer

Online link to other gadgets

2 In the **Gadgets** window, double-click the **Weather** gadget. In the upper right corner of the **Gadgets** dialog box, click the **Close** button.

Alert! | Are there already gadgets on your desktop?

Your desktop may contain one or more gadgets, including a Weather gadget. In fact, you can have more than one of the same gadgets on the desktop at a time. For example, if you are interested in the weather in two different locations, you can add two weather gadgets to the desktop and keep an eye on two locations at one time.

3 Point to the **Weather** gadget. Notice that a four-button tool set, called the *gadget controls*, displays on the right, as shown in Figure 1.14. Take a moment to study the functions of the buttons, as shown in the table in Figure 1.15.

Figure 1.14

Weather gadget ——

Gadget controls ——

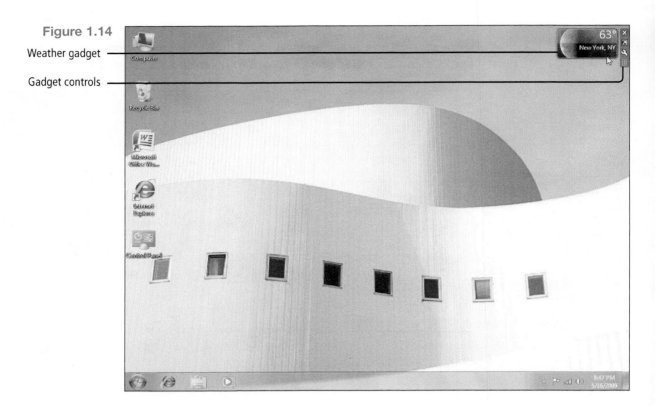

Gadget Controls

Button Name	Button	Description
Close	☒	Closes the gadget.
Larger size	▣	Increases the size of the gadget; occupies the same position as the Smaller size button.
Smaller size	▣	Decreases the size of the gadget; occupies the same position as the Larger size button.
Options	🔧	Displays different settings for each gadget.
Drag gadget	▦	Used to move the gadget anywhere on the desktop.

Figure 1.15

4 Point to the **Weather** gadget, click the **Larger size** button ▣, and then click the **Options** button 🔍. In the **Select current location** box, type **Madison, Wisconsin** and then press Enter. Click **OK**, and then compare your screen with Figure 1.16.

Figure 1.16

Weather gadget enlarged

Selected city

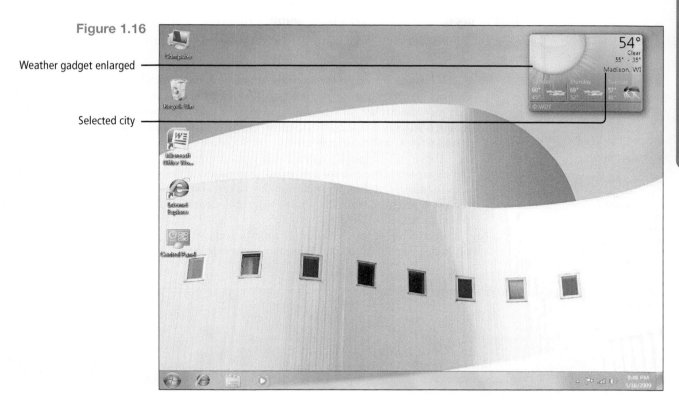

5 In an open area of the desktop, right-click to display a shortcut menu. On the shortcut menu, click **Gadgets**. In the **Gadgets** window, double-click the **Slide Show** gadget, and then double-click the **Slide Show** gadget again. In the upper right corner of the **Gadgets** dialog box, click the **Close** button ▣.

Two additional gadgets are added to the desktop.

6 Point to either of the **Slide Show** gadgets, and then in the gadget controls, click the **Close** button ⊠ to remove the gadget from the desktop.

7 Point to the remaining **Slide Show** gadget, point to the **Drag gadget** button ▦, and then drag the gadget near the upper edge of the desktop. Notice that as you move near the top of the desktop, the gadget snaps into position, slightly below the top of the desktop.

Objective 2 | Use the Start Menu and Manage Windows

Some programs and documents are available from the desktop. For most things, however, you will turn to the Start menu. The *Start menu* gives you access to all of the programs on your computer, and also enables you to change the way Windows operates, to access and configure your network, and to get help and support when it is needed. After you have opened several programs, you can rearrange and resize the program windows to fit your needs.

Activity 1.04 | Using the Start Menu

In this activity, you will use the Start menu to open a program, and also to open the Windows Explorer window.

Another Way

Press the Start button on your keyboard—a key with the Windows logo, often found to the left of the spacebar.

1 In the lower left corner of the screen, on the left end of the taskbar, point to and then click the **Start** button 🌐. Compare your screen with Figure 1.17.

The left side of the Start menu contains four areas. At the bottom is the Search box, which enables you to search for files or programs. Above the Search box is the **All Programs** command, which takes you to a list of all of the programs you can access on the computer. *All Programs* displays an arrow, which indicates that a submenu is available for a command. A **submenu** is a second-level menu; the arrow indicates that more items can be found related to the menu command.

Above *All Programs* is an area that contains the most recently opened programs. On the upper left is the **pinned programs area**—an area reserved for programs that you want to display permanently, although you can also remove programs from this area. To remove a program from the pinned list, right-click the program, and then click *Remove from this list*.

On the top of the right side are links to your personal folders, while the bottom sections give you access to computer management features.

Figure 1.17

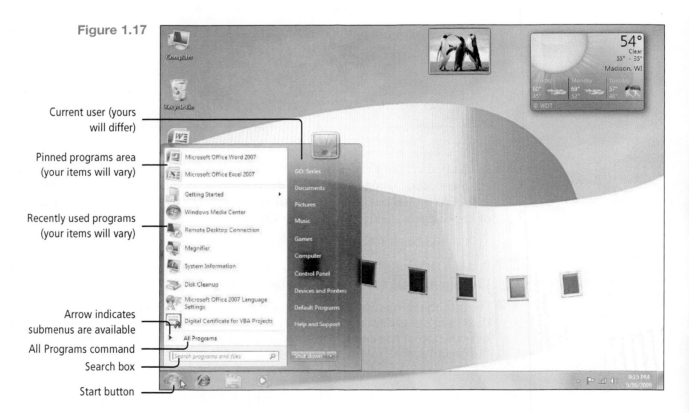

Current user (yours will differ)

Pinned programs area (your items will vary)

Recently used programs (your items will vary)

Arrow indicates submenus are available

All Programs command

Search box

Start button

Alert! | **Is your taskbar hidden?**

Some computers are set up to hide the taskbar when it is not in use. This adds more workspace to the desktop, and is particularly useful on portable computers with small screens. When the taskbar is hidden, move the pointer to the bottom of the screen, and it will display. However, in this chapter, it is assumed that the taskbar is displayed at all times.

To keep the taskbar displayed on your screen, find an open area on the taskbar, right-click, and then from the shortcut menu, click Properties. In the Taskbar and Start Menu Properties dialog box, on the Taskbar tab, locate the *Auto-hide the taskbar* check box. If the taskbar is hidden, there will be a check mark in the check box. To remove the Auto-hide feature, click the check box one time to clear—remove—the check mark.

2 From the **Start** menu, point to, but do not click, the **All Programs** command. Compare your screen with Figure 1.18.

The All Programs submenu displays—displaying a portion of the contents found within All Programs—and the *All Programs* command changes to a *Back* command. Your menu will differ from the one shown in Figure 1.18 because your computer will have different programs installed. Folders in the menu contain more programs or more folders or some of each.

Figure 1.18

Programs

Accessories folder

Back command

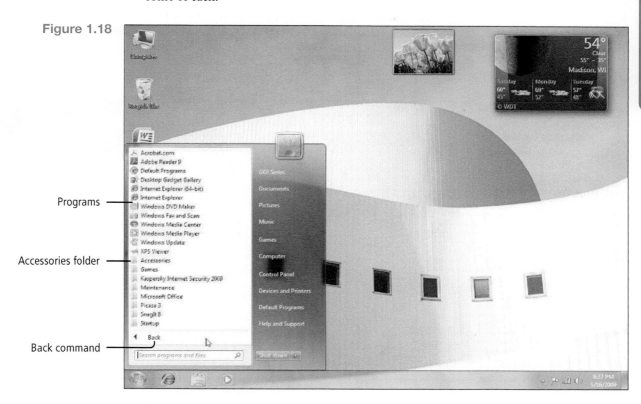

3 Click the **Accessories** folder, and then from the displayed list, click **Calculator**. Notice that the *window name*—*Calculator*—displays in the title bar.

The Calculator window opens, and the Start menu closes. You can access the Accessories programs from the Start menu and use them while you are using other programs. For example, you might want to make a quick calculation while you are typing a document in Microsoft Word. You can open the calculator, make the calculation, and then place the result in your Word document without closing Word.

4 Click the **Start** button ⊕ again, and near the middle of the right side of the **Start menu**, click **Computer**. If the Windows Explorer window fills the entire screen, near the right side of the title bar, click the Restore Down button 🗗 . Compare your screen with Figure 1.19.

The Windows Explorer window opens, but the Calculator window is either partially or completely hidden, as shown in Figure 1.19. The buttons in the taskbar, however, indicate that two programs are open. The buttons that are outlined indicate the programs that have one or more windows open. The *active window*—the window in which the pointer movements, commands, or text entry occur when two or more windows are open—displays a darker title bar.

Figure 1.19

Darker title bar indicates the active window

Window name in title bar

Computer window hides most of the Calculator window

Calculator window button

Computer window button

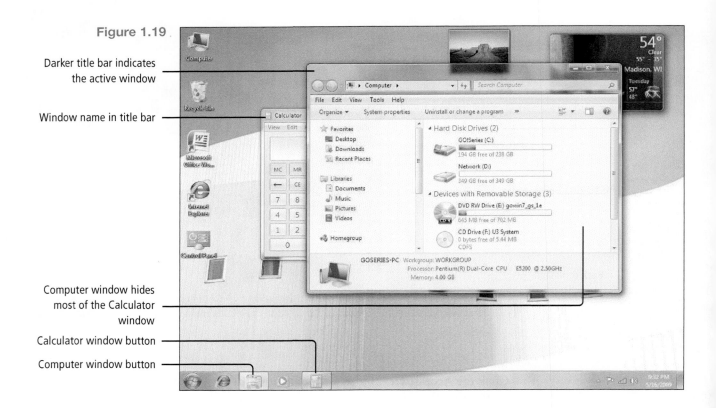

5 Click the **Start** button ⊕ , and then click in the **Search programs and files** box. Type **wordpad** and press ⏎. If the WordPad window fills the entire screen, near the right side of the title bar, click the Restore Down button 🗗 .

If you type a program name into the Start menu Search box, the program will open, which enables you to quickly open programs rather than try to find them. *WordPad* is a simple word processing program that comes with Windows 7.

Activity 1.05 │ Adding Shortcuts to the Start Menu, Desktop, and Taskbar

There are programs that you will seldom use, and there are programs that you will use all the time. To make frequently used programs easily and quickly available, you can pin a shortcut to the program in the Start menu *pinned programs area*, or you can add a shortcut icon to the desktop or pin the program to the taskbar.

1 Click the **Start** button ⊕ , point to **All Programs**, click **Accessories**, and then right-click **Calculator**.

2 From the displayed shortcut menu, click **Pin to Start Menu**. At the bottom of the **Start menu**, click the **Back** button, and notice that *Calculator* has been added to the pinned programs area, as shown in Figure 1.20.

Figure 1.20

Calculator program
pinned to Start menu

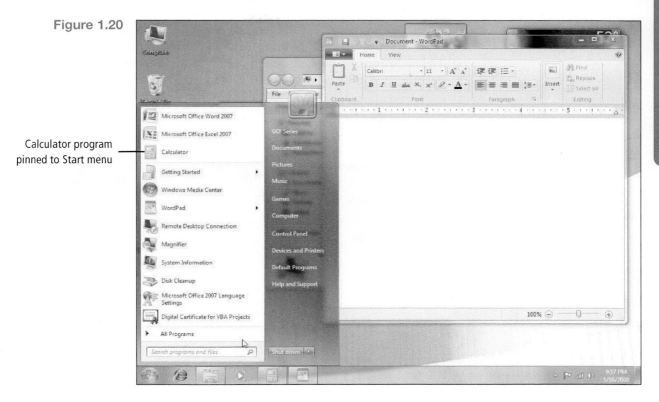

3 Click the **Start** button 🌐, point to **All Programs**, if necessary click **Accessories**, right-click **Calculator**, and then point to—but do not click—**Send to**. Notice the available commands on the *Send to* list, as shown in Figure 1.21.

Figure 1.21

Shortcut menu

Send to command

Desktop (create shortcut)
command

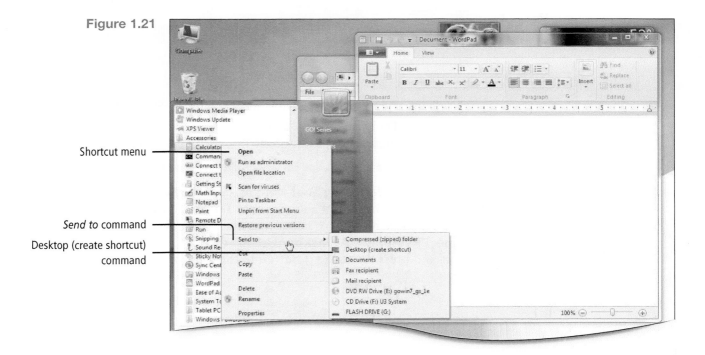

4 From the displayed shortcut menu, click **Desktop (create shortcut)**, and then click in any open area of the desktop.

A Calculator icon is placed on the desktop. The shortcut icon has a small blue arrow in the lower left corner. Depending on the windows you have open, and the number of icons on your desktop, your Calculator shortcut icon may be hidden.

5 Click the **Start** button 🌐, point to **All Programs**, if necessary click **Accessories**, right-click **Snipping Tool**, and then click **Pin to Taskbar**. Click in an open area on the desktop, and then compare your screen with Figure 1.22.

You can use *Snipping Tool* to capture a screen shot, or *snip*, of the entire screen or of any object on your screen, and then make notes on, save, or share the image. You will use this tool throughout this chapter.

Figure 1.22

Calculator shortcut icon added to the desktop

Snipping Tool added to taskbar

6 On the taskbar, click the **Snipping Tool** button ✂.

The Snipping Tool window displays, and the rest of the screen appears faded.

7 In the **Snipping Tool** window, click the arrow to the right of the **New** button to display a list of potential snips. From the list, click **Full-screen Snip**.

The entire screen is captured, and displays in the Snipping Tool window.

8 Near the top of the **Snipping Tool** window, click the **Save Snip** button 💾. In the **Save As** dialog box, in the left column, click **Desktop** to save the snip to the desktop. In the **File name** box, using your own last and first names, type **Lastname_Firstname_1A_Taskbar** Use the underscore between words—hold down Shift and press the dash (-) button to the right of the numbers near the top of the keyboard. Click in the **Save as type** box, and then from the menu, click **JPEG file**. Compare your screen with Figure 1.23.

Figure 1.23

File will be saved on the desktop

File name

File saved in JPEG format

Save button

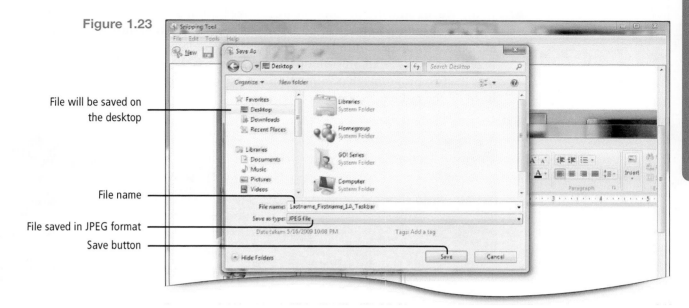

9 At the bottom of the **Save As** dialog box, click **Save** to save the snip on the desktop.

10 In the upper right corner of the **Snipping Tool** window, click the **Close** button. Notice that your file displays as an icon on the desktop.

Activity 1.06 | Minimizing, Maximizing, and Restoring a Window

You can *maximize* a window, which enlarges the window to occupy the entire screen, and you can *restore* a window, which reduces the window to the size it was before being maximized. You can also *minimize* a window, which reduces the window to a button on the taskbar, removing it from the screen entirely without actually closing it. When you need to view the window again, you can click the taskbar button to bring it back into view.

1 Click anywhere in the **WordPad** window to make it the active window, and then examine the three buttons in the upper right corner of the window. The left button is the **Minimize** button, the middle button is the **Maximize** button, and the right button is the **Close** button.

> **Another Way**
> Double-click in the bar at the top of the window.

2 In the **WordPad** window, click the **Maximize** button. Notice that the window expands to cover the entire screen, and the Maximize button changes to a Restore Down button, as shown in Figure 1.24.

Figure 1.24

Maximize button changes to Restore Down button

Another Way

Double-click in the title bar at the top of the window.

3 In the **WordPad** window, click the **Restore Down** button 🗗. Notice that the window resumes its former shape, size, and location.

4 In the **WordPad** window, click the **Minimize** button 🗕. In the taskbar, click the **Calculator** button to make it the active window, and then in the **Calculator** window, click the **Minimize** button 🗕 to display the Windows Explorer window. Notice that the Windows Explorer window now displays as the active window. Notice also that the two programs that you minimized are not closed—their buttons are still outlined on the taskbar, as shown in Figure 1.25.

Figure 1.25

WordPad window minimized to taskbar

Calculator window minimized to taskbar

5 In the taskbar, click the **Calculator** button to restore the Calculator window. Then, click the **WordPad** button to restore the WordPad window.

More Knowledge | Keeping More Than One Program Window Open at a Time

The ability to keep more than one window open at a time will become more useful as you become more familiar with Microsoft Office. For example, if you want to take information from two word processing documents to create a third document, you can open all three documents and use the taskbar to move among them, copying and pasting text from one document to another. Or, you could copy a chart from Excel and paste it into Word or take a table of data and paste it into PowerPoint. You can even have the same document open in two windows.

Activity 1.07 | Hiding and Displaying Windows

There is a shortcut that enables you to temporarily hide all open windows and view the desktop, and also a way to display just one window and hide the rest.

1 Move the pointer to the lower-right corner of the desktop to point to the **Show desktop** button. Notice that all open windows become transparent to give you a *peek* at the desktop—all desktop items display, as shown in Figure 1.26.

This only works if the Aero interface is turned on.

Figure 1.26

Outlines of transparent windows

Show desktop button

2 Move the pointer away from the **Show desktop** button and notice that the windows display again.

3 Point to the **Show desktop** button, but this time click the button. Notice that all open windows are hidden, and no outlines display.

4 Click the **Show desktop** button again to display all open windows.

5 In the taskbar, locate and click the **Calculator** button to make the Calculator the active window. Notice that the background of the Calculator icon on the taskbar is brighter than the icons for the other open windows.

6 Point to the **Calculator** title bar, hold down the left mouse button, and then *shake*—move the window back and forth quickly—the window.

All windows except the shaken window are hidden.

7 Shake the **Calculator** window again to display all of the open windows.

Objective 3 | Resize, Move, and Scroll Windows

When a window opens on your screen, it generally opens in the same size and shape as it was when last used. If you are using more than one window at a time, you can increase or decrease the size of a window, or move a window so that you can see the information you need.

As you work within a program, the information you create will likely grow larger than the screen can display. When the information in a window extends beyond the right or lower edges of the window, scroll bars display at the bottom and right. Using the *horizontal scroll bar*, you can move left and right to view information that extends beyond the left or right edge of the screen. Using the *vertical scroll bar*, you can move up and down to view information that extends beyond the top or bottom of the screen.

Activity 1.08 | Customizing and Using the Taskbar

When you have a number of windows open, you can use the taskbar to quickly review the contents of each document to determine which one to use. You can also move the taskbar to the top, left, or right edges of the desktop.

1 On the taskbar, point to—but do not click—the **Windows Explorer** button 🖿, and then compare your screen with Figure 1.27.

A thumbnail of the window displays. A *thumbnail* is a miniature representation of a window or a file. If two documents are open in the same program, two thumbnails will display. The Aero interface must be turned on for this feature to work.

Figure 1.27

Thumbnail of the
Computer window

2 On the taskbar, point to—but do not click—the **Calculator** button. Move the pointer and point to the **WordPad** button.

3 Click the **Start** button 🌐, point to **All Programs**, click **Accessories**, and then click **Paint**.

If the Paint window is maximized, click the Restore Down button 🗗.

Paint is a simple drawing program that comes with Windows 7. Four programs are now open, and there are icons on the taskbar for other unopened programs, such as Snipping Tool.

4 Hold down the [Alt] key, and then press the [Tab] key. Compare your screen with Figure 1.28.

The screen displays thumbnails of the windows that are open, including the desktop; if the Aero interface is not turned on, only the program icons display.

Figure 1.28

[Alt] + [Tab] enables you to move between open windows

Calculator window

Paint window

WordPad window

Computer window

Desktop

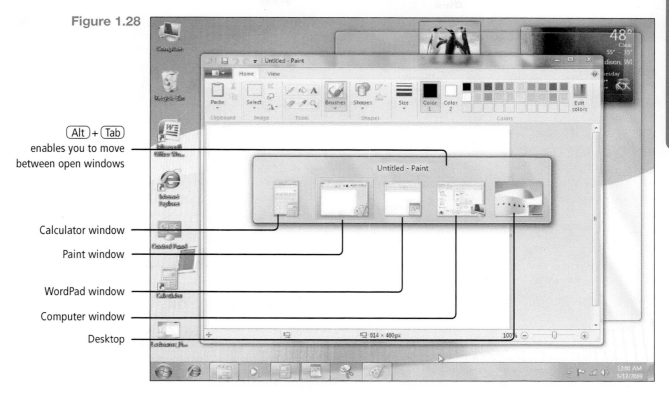

5 Continue to hold down [Alt], but press [Tab] several times. Notice that the selected window moves from left to right in the list of thumbnails.

When you release the [Alt] key, the window in the active thumbnail becomes the active window on the desktop.

6 Move to the **Calculator** window, and then release the [Alt] button.

7 On the taskbar, point to the **Windows Explorer** window, and then right-click.

A *jump list* displays frequent destinations you might want to jump to from the Windows Explorer window. If you display a jump list for a program such as a word processor or a spreadsheet, a list of recently edited files also displays, enabling you to quickly open any desired files.

8 Right-click an open area of the taskbar, and then from the shortcut menu, click **Properties**.

9 In the **Properties** dialog box, be sure the Taskbar tab is selected. Under **Taskbar appearance**, click the **Taskbar location on screen arrow**, and then click **Right**. Compare your screen with Figure 1.29.

Figure 1.29

Taskbar tab ——

Screen location of the taskbar ——

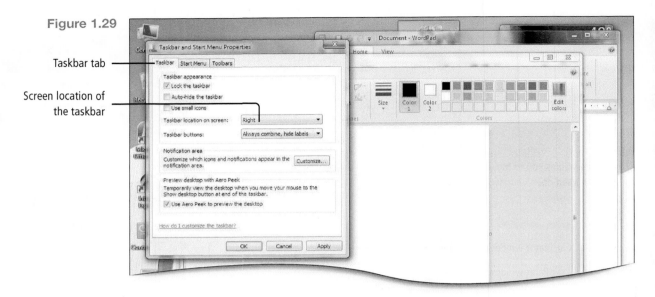

10 At the bottom of the **Properties** dialog box, click **OK**.

> The taskbar displays on the right side of the desktop. This is an ideal location if you are using a widescreen monitor or a portable computer with a wide monitor because it gives you more vertical space on the screen for your documents.

11 In the taskbar, click the **Snipping Tool** button ✂. In the **Snipping Tool** window, click the arrow to the right of the **New** button to display a list of potential snips. From the list, click **Full-screen Snip**.

12 Near the top of the **Snipping Tool** window, click the **Save Snip** button 🖫. In the **Save As** dialog box, in the left column, click **Desktop**. In the **File name** box, using your own last and first names, type **Lastname_Firstname_1A_Windows** Click in the **Save as type** box and be sure **JPEG file** is selected.

13 At the bottom of the **Save As** dialog box, click **Save** to save the snip on the desktop.

14 In the upper right corner of the **Snipping Tool** window, click the **Close** button ✖. Notice that your file displays as an icon on the desktop.

15 Use the procedure you practiced in Steps 8 through 10 to return the taskbar to the bottom of the desktop.

Activity 1.09 | Resizing, Moving, Scrolling, and Closing Windows

In the following activity, you will resize and move the Windows Explorer window. You will also use the vertical scroll bar in the window to view information that does not fit in the window.

1 On the right end of the taskbar, click the **Show desktop** button to hide all of the windows.

2 On the taskbar, click the **Windows Explorer** button 📁 to display the Windows Explorer window.

3 Move the pointer to the lower right corner of the window to display the diagonal resize pointer,  and then compare your screen with Figure 1.30.

> When the mouse pointer is in this shape, you can use it to change the size and shape of a window.

Figure 1.30

Diagonal resize pointer

Show desktop button

4 Hold down the left mouse button, *drag*—move the mouse while holding down the left mouse button and then release at the appropriate time—diagonally up and to the left until you see a scroll bar at the right side of the window, and then release the mouse button. Adjust as necessary so that the Windows Explorer window is the approximate size of the one shown in Figure 1.31.

> Notice that a vertical scroll bar displays on the right side of the window, and another one displays on the right side of the Navigation pane. A scroll bar is added to the window whenever the window contains more than it can display.

Figure 1.31

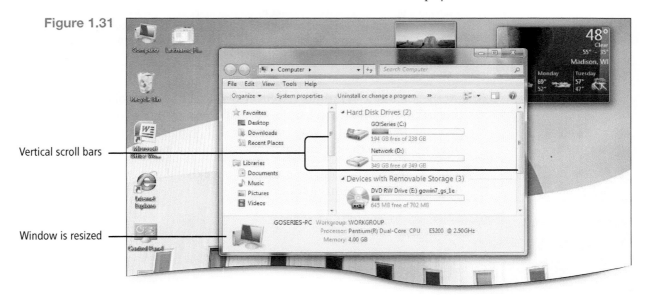

Vertical scroll bars

Window is resized

5 In the **Windows Explorer** window **file list**, at the bottom of the vertical scroll bar, point to the **down arrow** ▼ and click two times. Notice that information at the bottom of the window scrolls up so that you can see the information that was not visible before, as shown in Figure 1.32.

Figure 1.32

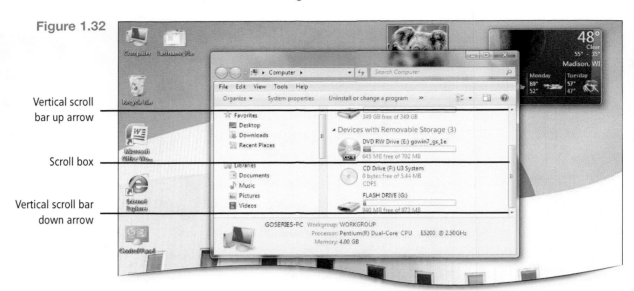

Vertical scroll bar up arrow

Scroll box

Vertical scroll bar down arrow

6 On the same scroll bar, point to the **up arrow** ▲, and then click and hold down the left mouse button.

> The window scrolls to the top of the file list. You can click and hold down the left mouse button on the up or down scroll arrows to scroll rapidly through a long list of information.

7 Point to the scroll box, and then drag it downward.

> The *scroll box* displays within the vertical and horizontal scroll bars and provides a visual indication of your location within the information displayed. It can also be used with the mouse to reposition the information on the screen. Moving the scroll box gives you more control as you scroll because you can see the information as it moves up or down in the window.

Note | Moving a Screen at a Time

You can move up or down a screen at a time by clicking in the gray area above or below the vertical scroll box. You can also move left or right a screen at a time by clicking in the area to the left or right of a horizontal scroll box. The size of the scroll box indicates the relative size of the display to the whole document. If the scroll box is small, it means that the display is a small portion of the entire document.

---

8 At the top of the **Windows Explorer** window, point to a blank area in the title bar to the left of the Minimize, Maximize, and Close buttons. Hold down the left mouse button, drag the window up as far as it will go past the top edge of the window, and then release the mouse button. Notice that the window is maximized.

9 Click in the title bar and drag down. Notice that the window is restored to its original size, but not its original location.

 In the **Windows Explorer** window title bar, click the **Close** button ![close]. In the taskbar, right-click the **Paint** button ![paint], and then click **Close window**. Use the same technique to close the **Calculator** window ![calc].

11 In the taskbar, click the **WordPad** button to display the WordPad window. Using the title bar, drag the WordPad window to the right edge of the desktop until it changes shape to occupy the right half of the desktop, and then release the mouse button.

> You can use this method to open two windows side by side if you drag a second window to the left border.

12 Click in the WordPad window, type your first and last names, and then press [Enter]. Locate the **Lastname_Firstname_1A_Taskbar** icon on the desktop—you may have to click the two snip files to find the correct file.

13 Drag the **Lastname_Firstname_1A_Taskbar** file to the line below your name in the WordPad document, and then release the mouse button. Compare your screen with Figure 1.33.

> The contents of the file you dragged are pasted into the WordPad document.

Figure 1.33

Your name ——

File dragged into WordPad document ——

File icon ——

14 Drag the **Lastname_Firstname_1A_Windows** file to the line below the figure you just inserted into the WordPad document. In the WordPad title bar, click the **Save** button ![save].

15 In the **Save As** dialog box, in the **Navigation** pane, click **Desktop**. In the **File name** box, type **Lastname_Firstname_1A_WordPad** and then click **Save**.

16 If you are to print your document, hold down [Ctrl] and then press [P] to display the Print dialog box. Be sure the correct printer is selected, and then click **Print**. If you are to submit this document electronically, follow your instructor's directions.

17 **Close** ![close] the WordPad window.

End You have completed Project 1A ——————————————

Project 1B Manage Files and Folders

Project Activities

In Activities 1.10 through 1.18 you will create folders, and then copy, move, rename, and delete files and folders. You will add tags to files and use the Windows 7 search features to search for files. Your screens will look similar to those in Figure 1.34.

Project Files

For Project 1B, you will need the following files:

36 sample files, and two folders containing 14 additional files

You will save your documents as:

Lastname_Firstname_1B_Renamed_Folder

Lastname_Firstname_1B_Compressed_Folder

Lastname_Firstname_1B_Search_Folder

Project Results

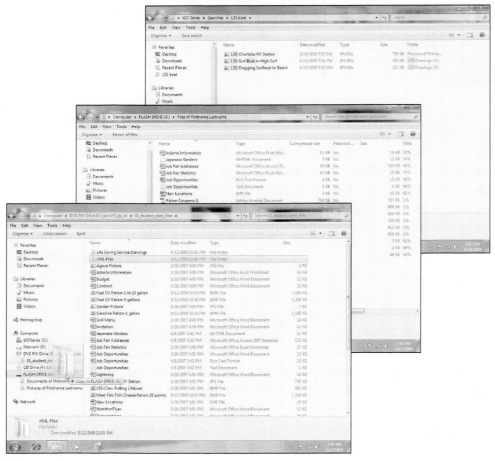

Figure 1.34

Objective 4 | Create, Move, and Rename Folders

Information that you create in a computer program is stored in the computer's memory, which is a temporary storage location. This data will be lost if the computer is turned off. To keep the information you create, you must save it as a file on one of the drives available to you. For example, a five-page term paper that you create in a word processing program such as Microsoft Word, when saved, is a *file*. Files can be stored directly on a drive, but more commonly are stored in a folder on the drive. A *folder* is a container for programs and files, represented on the screen by a picture of a common paper file folder.

Use folders to organize your files so that you can easily locate them for later use. Folders and files must be created and stored on one of the drives attached to your computer. Your available drives fall into three categories: 1) the nonremovable hard drive, also called the *local disk*, inside the computer; 2) removable drives that you insert into the computer, such as a flash drive, an external hard drive, or a writable CD or DVD; or 3) a shared network drive connected to your computer through a computer network, such as the network at your college.

Activity 1.10 | Opening and Navigating Windows Explorer

Windows Explorer is a program that enables you to create and manage folders, and copy, move, sort, and delete files. In the following activity, you will create a folder on one of the three types of drives available to you—the local disk (hard drive), a removable drive (USB flash drive, an external hard drive, or some other type of removable drive), or a network drive. If you are using a computer in a college lab, you may have space assigned to you on a shared network drive. You can create these folders on any drive that is available to you. For the rest of this chapter, a flash drive will be used.

1 On the taskbar, click the **Windows Explorer** button ⊞. If this button is not available, click the **Start** button ⊕, point to All Programs, click Accessories, and then click Windows Explorer.

> The Windows Explorer window opens, with the Navigation pane displayed on the left, and the Libraries pane displayed on the right. You may also see a Details pane just above the taskbar and a Preview pane on the right side of the window.

More Knowledge | **Using Libraries**

Libraries are folders used to sort files with similar content. By default, Windows 7 sets up four libraries: Documents, Music, Pictures, and Videos. Each of these libraries is assigned two folders—a user folder and a public folder. For example, the Documents library contains the My Documents subfolder for the current user, along with the Public Documents subfolder on the hard disk, which contains files that can be shared with all users. If you have other fixed drives on your computer, or permanent network drives, you can add other folders to a library so that all files of a similar type can be accessed quickly using the library.

Another Way

On the right side of the title bar, click the Maximize button ⬜.

2 If the window is not maximized, drag the title bar to the top of the screen.

3 On the Command bar, click the **Organize** button, and then point to **Layout**. If the Details pane does not display at the bottom of your window, click Details Pane. If the Navigation pane does not display on the left side of your window, repeat the procedure and click Navigation Pane. Compare your screen with Figure 1.35.

Figure 1.35

Organize button

Libraries pane

Navigation pane

Details pane

4 In the **Navigation** pane, if necessary scroll down, and then click **Computer**.

The file list displays a list of hard drives, removable storage devices, network drives, and other devices connected to the computer.

5 In the **Navigation** pane, if necessary, to the left of **Computer**, click the open arrow ▷. Notice that the arrow changes to a filled arrow pointing downward at an angle ◢.

The open arrow indicates that there are other folders and drives to be displayed. When you click the open arrow, the next level of folders and drives displays. The list of drives in the Navigation pane matches the list of drives in the file list.

6 Insert your USB flash drive or other removable drive. If an AutoPlay dialog box displays asking what you want Windows to do, click the Close button. In the **Navigation** pane, under **Computer**, click your removable drive—for this chapter, the removable drive name will be FLASH DRIVE (G:); yours will be different.

7 Compare your screen with Figure 1.36. Notice that the file list in the figure is empty; your storage device or drive may already contain files and folders.

Figure 1.36

File list is empty; yours may have files and folders

Flash drive (your drive name and letter will vary)

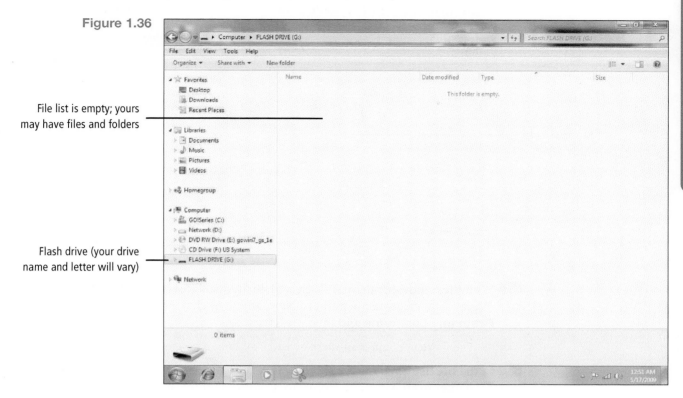

More Knowledge | **Computer Storage Devices**

The hard drive (local disk) is usually identified on your computer by the notation C: (and sometimes D:, E:, and so on for additional drives). ***Flash drives***—also known as ***USB drives*** or ***thumb drives***—are small storage devices that plug into a computer's Universal Serial Bus (USB) port, which provides a connection between a computer and a peripheral device such as a printer, a mouse, a keyboard, or a USB drive.

You may also have access to files on another type of storage device, a ***CD***—Compact Disc, or a ***DVD***—Digital Video (or Versatile) Disc. CD and DVD drives are optical storage devices that come in two formats—read-only and read-write. If you are using files stored on a read-only CD or a DVD disc, you will need to open a file from the disc, and then save it to a writable drive, or copy a file to another disk and then open it.

Activity 1.11 | Creating a New Folder

It is always a good idea to create a new folder when you have a new category of files to store. You do not need to create a new folder for each type of file, however. You can store many different kinds of files in the same folder.

> **Another Way**
>
> If you accidentally press Enter before you have a chance to name the folder, you can still rename it. Right-click the folder, click Rename from the shortcut menu, type a new name, and then press Enter.

1 With the flash drive selected, in the Command bar, click the **New folder** button.

A new folder—named *New folder*—is created with the name of the folder displayed in the ***edit mode***. Edit mode enables you to change the name of a file or folder, and works the same in all Windows programs.

2 With *New Folder* selected, substitute your name where indicated, and type **Pictures of Firstname Lastname** and then press Enter. Click anywhere in the blank area of the file list to deselect the new folder and compare your screen with Figure 1.37.

Figure 1.37

New folder button

Renamed folder

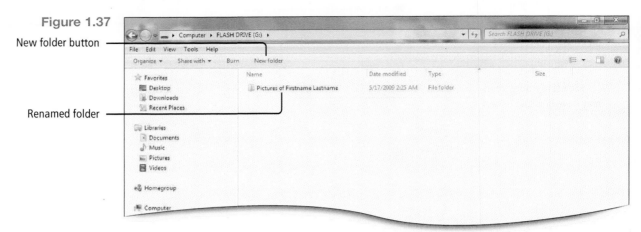

3 With the removable drive still selected, in an open area of the **file list**, right-click to display a shortcut menu, point to **New**, and then click **Folder**. Type **Documents of Firstname Lastname** and then press Enter.

The shortcut menu is an alternative way to create a new folder.

4 In the **file list**, click the **Name** column heading several times to sort the folders and file names from *a* to *z* and from *z* to *a*. Notice that the arrow in the Name column heading points up when the folders are displayed in *ascending order* (*a* to *z*), and points down when the folders are displayed in *descending order* (*z* to *a*). Stop when the folders are sorted in descending alphabetical order—from *z* to *a*.

5 In the **file list**, move the pointer to the line at the right of the **Name** column heading to display the resize pointer ⊹, as shown in Figure 1.38. Drag the resize pointer ⊹ to the right or left to make the column slightly wider than the longest folder name.

Figure 1.38

Name column heading with arrow indicating sort order

Folders in descending alphabetical order

Resize pointer

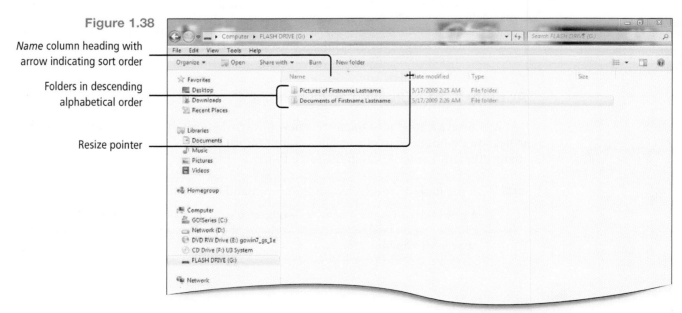

Activity 1.12 | Moving and Renaming Folders

Your student files and folders for this chapter are stored on a CD* or another location chosen by your instructor. You can move the folders, including the files in the folders, from another location to your flash drive or other storage device.

1 Navigate to the location where your student files for this chapter are stored. They may be stored on a CD, in a course management system, on a hard drive, or on a shared network drive. In this chapter, the data CD is used.

2 In the **Navigation** pane, on the data CD, click the open arrow ▷ to display the folder on the disc. Click the **01_student_data_files** folder, and then compare your screen with Figure 1.39. If your files and folders do not display the way they display in the figure, on the Command bar, to the right of the *Change your view* button, click the *More options* arrow, and then click Details.

There are two folders and a number of files in this folder. The total number of files and folders is displayed in the Details pane at the bottom of the screen. There are more files in the two folders, but they are not included in the totals in the Details pane—only the files and the folders currently displayed in the file list are counted.

Figure 1.39

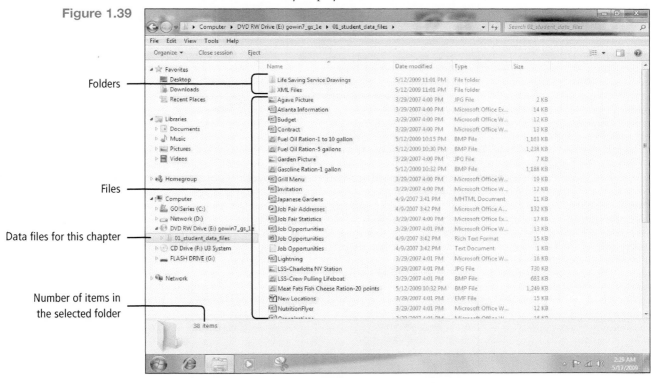

3 In the **file list**, move the pointer to the right border of the **Name** column heading to display the ↔ pointer. Double-click to resize the border to the widest folder or file name. Repeat this procedure to display the full **Date modified** and **Type** column contents.

> **Note** | Changing the Columns that Display in the File List
>
> If one or more of the columns displayed in Figure 1.39 do not display, right-click anywhere in the file list column titles, and then click the desired column.

4 In the **Navigation** pane, if necessary, click the open arrow ▷ to the left of your flash drive. Be sure your student files and folders from the data CD still display in the file list.

*Please note: Your custom textbook may not be accompanied by a CD. If this is the case, student files can be found at www.pearsoncustom.com/customphit/datafiles.

5 Near the top of the **file list**, locate the **XML Files** folder. Click on the folder, hold the mouse button down, and drag the folder to the **Navigation** pane directly on top of your storage drive, as shown in Figure 1.40. Notice that a folder displays attached to the pointer, and a ScreenTip says *Copy to FLASH DRIVE (G:)*—your folder or drive name will vary.

Figure 1.40

ScreenTip indicates copy location

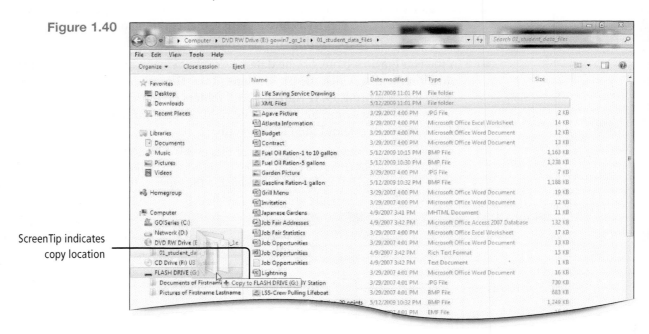

6 Release the mouse button.

7 Repeat the procedure you just practiced to copy the **Life Saving Service Drawings** folder to your flash drive, and notice that a message box indicates the progress of the copy, as shown in Figure 1.41.

The message box displays because the size of the *Life Saving Service Drawings* folder is much larger than the size of the *XML Files* folder and takes a few seconds to copy. The original files remain on the CD.

Figure 1.41

Message box indicates progress of the copy

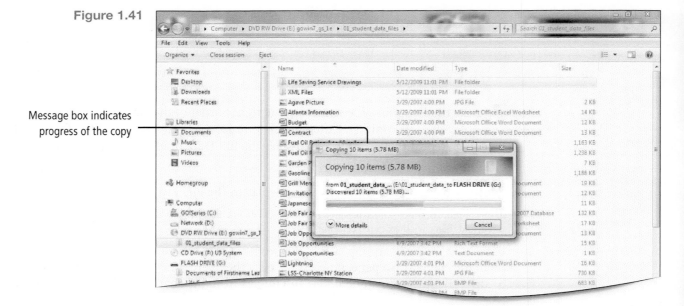

8 In the **Navigation** pane, click the flash drive or other device where you are storing your files and folders. In the **file list**, right-click the **Life Saving Service Drawings** folder, and then from the displayed shortcut menu, click **Rename**.

9 With the folder name in edit mode, type **LSS Drawings** and then press Enter.

> The folder name is changed. When text is selected, typing replaces all of the selected text.

10 Use the skills you practiced earlier to create a **Full-screen Snip**. Click the **Save Snip** 🔲 button. In the **Save As** dialog box, in the left pane, scroll down to display the **Computer** drives. Click your flash drive, and then in the Command bar, click the **New folder** button. Name the new folder **Windows Chapter 1** Press Enter, and then press Enter again to open the new folder. In the **File name** box, type **Lastname_Firstname_1B_Renamed_Folder** Click **Save**, and then **Close** 🔲 the Snipping Tool window.

Objective 5 | Copy, Move, Rename, and Delete Files

Copying files from one folder to another is a frequent data management task. For example, you might want to make a backup copy of important information, copy a file from a CD to a local disk, or copy information from your local disk drive to a removable drive. Copying files works the same regardless of the type of drive.

Performing other operations on files, such as deleting them or moving them, also works the same regardless of the type of drive. As you accumulate files, you will likely need to delete some to reduce clutter on your hard drive. You might also want to move documents into other folders on another drive to *archive* them—place them somewhere for long-term storage. Finally, you may want to change the names of file to make the names more descriptive. All of these tasks are functions of your Windows 7 operating system.

Activity 1.13 | Copying Files

1 In the **Navigation** pane, under **Computer**, scroll to the location where your student data files for this chapter are stored. Locate and click the folder named **01_student_data_files** to display the files and folders in the folder.

2 In the **Navigation** pane, scroll as necessary to display your flash drive or other storage device. Be sure your student data files and folders still display in the file list.

3 Near the middle of the **file list**, locate the **Garden Picture** file, and then drag it to your storage device. Recall that dragging also includes releasing the mouse button at the destination location.

> When you drag a file or folder from one device to another, it is copied, which means that the original file remains on the original drive and a copy of the file is placed on the new drive. If you drag a file or folder to another place (such as a folder) on the same drive—for example, from one folder to another—the file or folder is moved and no longer resides in the original location.

4 Locate the **Grill Menu** file, right-click the file, and then click **Copy**.

> This creates a copy of the Grill Menu file and places it in a temporary storage area called the *Clipboard*. Files in the Clipboard can be placed in other folders using the Paste command.

5 In the **Navigation** pane, click your storage device. In the **file list**, right-click in an open area, and then from the shortcut menu, click **Paste**. Notice that the file is copied to the open folder.

6 Click the **Name** column heading as necessary to sort the folders in ascending order—the arrow in the column heading should be pointing up. Compare your screen with Figure 1.42.

> The file list should display five folders—the three that you created and the two that you copied. In addition, the two files that you copied should display below the folders. When you sort a folder in ascending order, the folders always display first.

Figure 1.42

Folders display first

Folders and files sorted in alphabetical order by Name

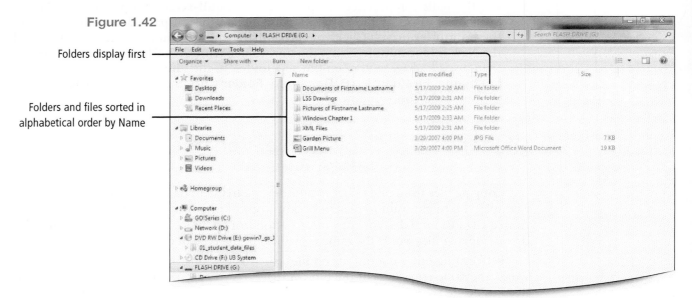

7 Display the files and folders in the **01_student_data_files** folder again. Click the **Atlanta Information** file, hold down Shift, and then click the **Fuel Oil Ration-1 to 10 gallon** file.

> By holding down the Shift key, you select the two files you click and all of the files in between.

8 In the **Navigation** pane, scroll as necessary to display your storage area. Drag the selected files to your storage area.

9 Click the **Agave Picture** file, hold down Ctrl, and then click the **Fuel Oil Ration-5 gallons** file, and then the **Gasoline Ration-1 gallon** file. Notice that by using the Control key, you can select several files that are not next to each other, as shown in Figure 1.43.

Figure 1.43

Selected files

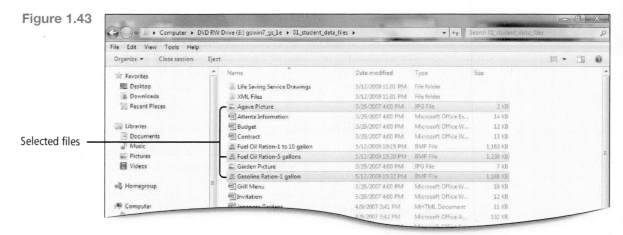

10 Drag the selected files to your storage area.

11 In the **file list**, click the **Invitation** file, and then use the vertical scroll bar to scroll to the bottom of the file list. Hold down Shift, and then click the **Volunteers** file. In the Detail area, notice that the number of files displays, as shown in Figure 1.44. If the total size of the files does not display, in the Details pane, click Show more details.

Figure 1.44

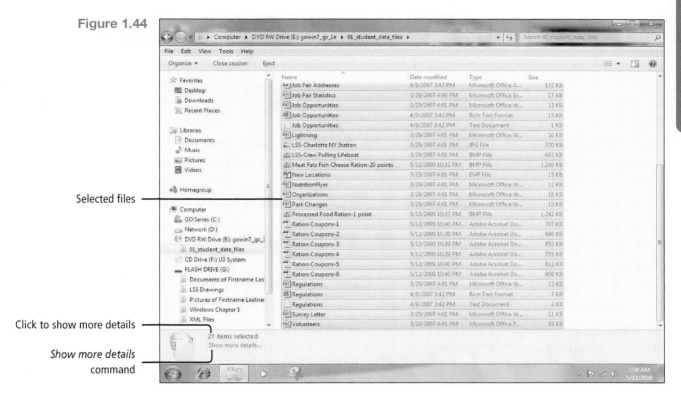

12 Drag the selected files to your storage area.

More Knowledge | File Extensions

The files you see may display three or four letters following the file name, such as *.docx*. These are *file extensions*, and most files have these extensions—although they may or may not display on your system. Files created by Microsoft Office programs have a standard set of extensions that identify the type of program used to create the file. For example, Microsoft Word documents end in *.doc* or *.docx*, Excel worksheets end in *.xls* or *.xlsx*, PowerPoint presentations end with *.ppt* or *pptx*, and so on. The default setting in Windows 7 is to hide the file extensions.

Activity 1.14 | Moving, Renaming, and Deleting Files

In the following activity, you will move files from one location on your removable drive to another location on the same drive. You will also rename and delete files.

1 In the **Navigation** pane, scroll as necessary and then click on your flash drive or other storage device.

> Your storage device should display five folders at the top, and a total of 36 files in the drive—41 objects, as displayed in the Details pane.

2 In the **file list**, click the **Type** column header to sort the files by file type. Move the pointer to the right border of the **Type** column heading to display the ⊕ pointer. Double-click to resize the border to the widest file type.

3 In the **file list**, use the wheel in the middle of your mouse, or the vertical scroll bar, to scroll down until you can see all of the **Microsoft Office Word Document** files.

4 Click the **Budget** file, hold down Shift, and then click the **Survey Letter** file to select all of the Word documents. Drag the selected files to the **Documents of Firstname Lastname** folder.

> The files are moved to the new folder, and no longer display in their original location.

5 In the **Navigation** pane, click the **Documents of Firstname Lastname** folder, and then compare your screen with Figure 1.45.

Figure 1.45

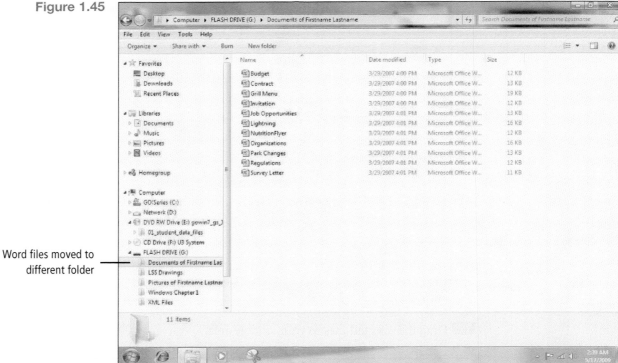

Word files moved to different folder

6 In the **Navigation** pane, click on your flash drive or other storage device. Using the technique you just practiced, select the three **JPG Images**, and then drag them to the **Pictures of Firstname Lastname** folder.

Alert! | What if your file types differ?

Files can be associated with several different programs, and will display a different file type in the Type column. For example, the three files labeled JPG in Figure 1.46 could be called JPEG files on your computer.

---

7 Select the six **BMP Files** and drag them to the **Pictures of Firstname Lastname** folder. If you do not see files labeled *BMP File*, select the six files beginning with *Fuel Oil Ration-1 to 10 gallon* and ending with *Processed Food Ration-1 point*.

8 In the **Navigation** pane, click the **Pictures of Firstname Lastname** folder, and then compare your screen with Figure 1.46.

Figure 1.46

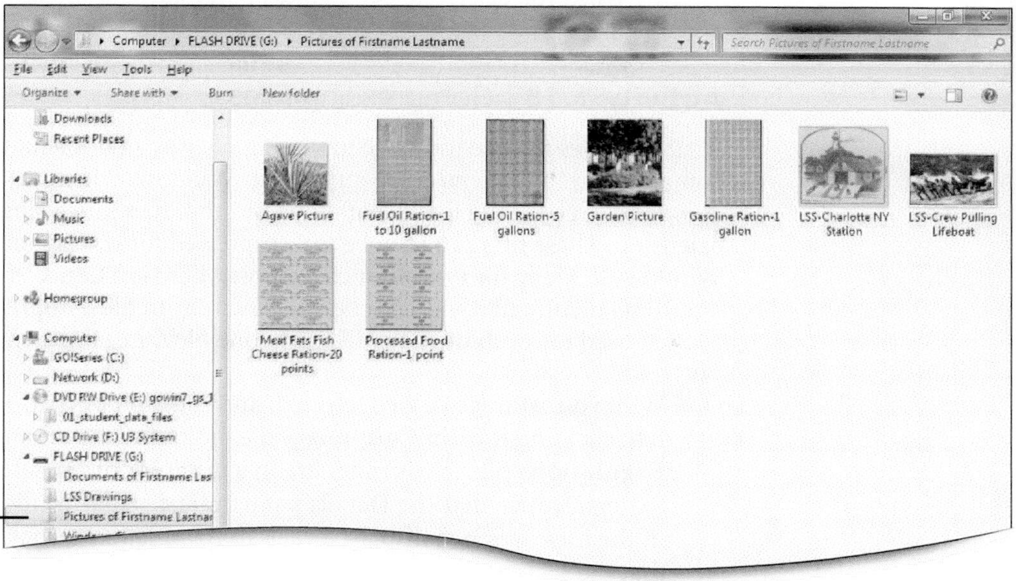

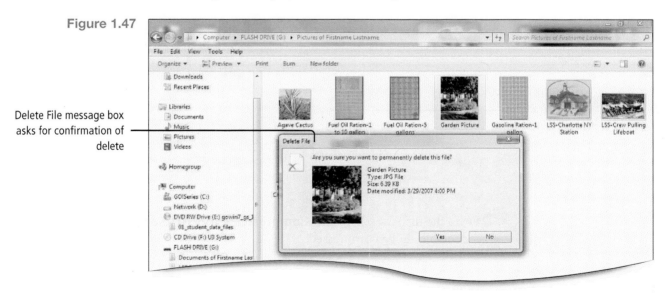

Picture files moved to new folder

9 If thumbnails do not display for the files, on the Command bar, to the right of the **Change your view** button, click the **More options arrow**, and then click **Large Icons**.

10 In the **file list**, right-click the **Agave Picture** file, and then click **Rename**. Type **Agave Cactus** and then press Enter.

11 In the **file list**, right-click the **Garden Picture** file, and then click **Delete**. The **Delete File** message box displays, as shown in Figure 1.47.

Figure 1.47

Delete File message box asks for confirmation of delete

Another Way

In the Navigation pane, click your flash drive or other storage location name.

12 In the **Delete File** message box, click **Yes** to send the file to the Recycle Bin.

13 In the upper left corner of the window, click the **Back** button to move back to your main storage area.

14 In the **file list**, right-click the **XML Files** folder, and then click **Delete**. In the displayed **Delete Folder** message box, click **Yes**.

> When you delete a folder, all files in the folder are also deleted.

Activity 1.15 | Compressing Files

Some files may be too large to send quickly as an e-mail attachment. For example, files containing graphics tend to be quite large. Windows 7 includes a feature with which you can *compress*—reduce the file size of—one or more files into a single file that uses a *.zip* file extension. These files can then be uncompressed for editing on any other computer running Windows 7. Many file types—such as most Microsoft Office 2007 files, Adobe Acrobat files, and JPEG picture files—do not benefit much from file compression. However, compression is often used to combine many files into one file for easy distribution.

1 With your storage device selected, and four folders and 16 files displayed in the **file list**, click the **Ration Coupons-1** file, hold down ⇧Shift, and then click the second **Regulations** file. If your files are in a different order, select all 16 files, but not the folders. Notice that the Details pane indicates that 16 files are selected. If the total size of the files does not display, under *16 items selected*, click *Show more details*. Notice that the 16 files have a total size of 5.00 MB.

2 In the **file list**, right-click any of the selected files, and then from the displayed shortcut menu, point to **Send to**. Compare your screen with Figure 1.48.

Figure 1.48

Compressed (zipped) folder command

Selected files

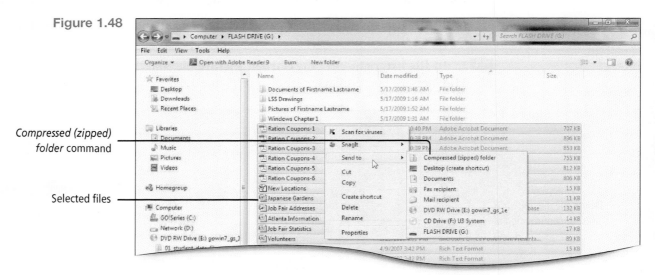

3 From the displayed list, click **Compressed (zipped)** folder, and then wait a moment for the files to be compressed.

> The compressed folder displays the name of the file you right-clicked, but displays in edit mode so you can change the file name.

Note | To Work with Third-Party Zip Programs

If you are using a third-party zip program, such as WinZip™ or PKZIP™, you will need to use that program to complete this task—the procedure listed below will not work.

---

4 With the compressed folder name still in edit mode, type **Files of Firstname Lastname** and then press Enter. Notice that the compressed folder size is approximately 4.9 MB, which is not a great space savings. Compare your screen with Figure 1.49.

Figure 1.49

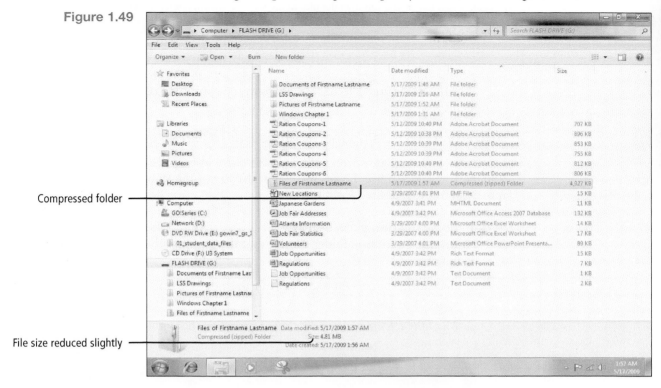

Compressed folder

File size reduced slightly

5 In the **file list**, double-click the **Files of Firstname Lastname** compressed folder. Compare your screen with Figure 1.50.

The files in the compressed folder are listed, along with their original sizes and their compressed sizes. The percent of space saved is indicated for each file. Some of the files show very little space savings, while in others the space saved is considerable. To extract the files from the compressed folder, you would click the *Extract all files* button on the Command bar. You can also open the files directly from the compressed folder.

Figure 1.50

Original file size
Extract all files button
Compressed file size

Files in compressed folder

Percent of space saved
Compressed folder

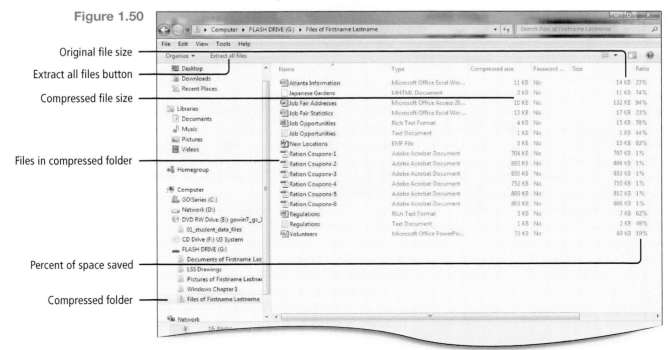

> **More Knowledge** | Adding More Items to a Compressed Folder
>
> You can add more files to an existing compressed folder by dragging files and dropping them on the compressed folder. You can drag the files to the folder from anywhere, and you can also drag folders into a compressed folder.

6 Use the skills you practiced earlier to create a **Full-screen Snip**. **Save Snip** 🖫 to your **Windows Chapter 1** folder as **Lastname_Firstname_1B_Compressed_Folder** and then **Close** 🗙 the Snipping Tool window.

Activity 1.16 | Using the Address Bar to Navigate Drives and Folders

In previous activities, you have used the Navigation pane to move between drives and folders. You can also use the address bar at the top of the Windows Explorer window to move quickly to a desired location.

1 In the **Navigation** pane, display your flash drive, and then click the **Pictures of Firstname Lastname** folder. Notice that the path to the current folder displays in the address bar.

2 In the Address bar, to the right of your flash drive name, click the **arrow**, and then compare your screen with Figure 1.51.

All of the folders on the flash drive—including the compressed folder—display in a menu.

Figure 1.51

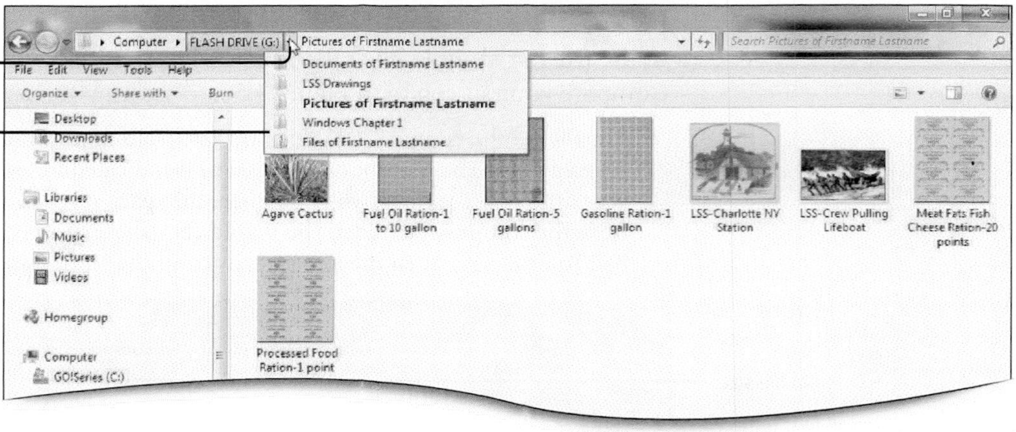

Flash drive arrow

Folders in flash drive, including compressed folder

3 From the menu, click the **LSS Drawings** folder. Notice that the contents of the *LSS Drawings* folder display in the file list.

4 In the address bar, click the **arrow** to the right of **Computer**. Notice that all of the available drives display.

5 To the left of **Computer**, click the **arrow**, and then compare your screen with Figure 1.52.

The top-level items in the Navigation pane display in a menu, along with commands for the Control Panel and the Recycle Bin.

Figure 1.52

Top-level items in Navigation pane

Opens the Control Panel

Opens the Recycle Bin

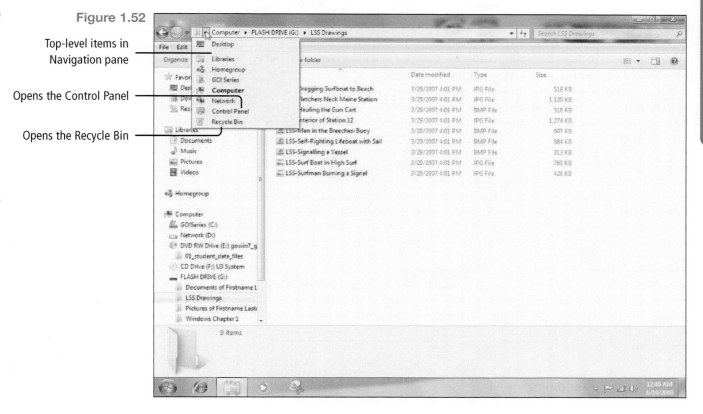

6 Click anywhere in the **file list** to close the menu.

Objective 6 | Find Files and Folders

As you use a computer, you will likely accumulate a large number of files and folders. It's easy to forget where you stored a file, or what you named it. Windows 7 provides several search functions with which you can find files and folders. You can also add tags to files. *Tags* are custom file properties that help you find and organize your files. Tags are part of a file's *metadata*—items that record and display information about a file, such as a title, a rating, the file name, and the file size.

Activity 1.17 | Adding Descriptions and Tags to Files

1 Be sure your storage device is selected, with the contents of the **LSS Drawings** folder displayed in the file list. Also be sure the **Details** pane is open at the bottom of the window.

2 Click the first file in the **file list**—**LSS-Dragging Surfboat to Beach**. Move the pointer to the line at the top of the **Details** pane to display the ⬍ pointer, and then drag the top of the Details pane to display three lines of details.

3 In the **Details** pane, click in the **Tags** box—to the right of the word *Tags.* Type **LSS** and then press →. Type **LSS Boat** and then press →. Type **Surfboat** and then compare your screen with Figure 1.53. Notice on the left side of the Details pane that the file type for this file is JPG—one of a number of image file types.

> When you add a tag, a semicolon immediately displays to the right of the insertion point. Semicolons separate multiple tags.

Figure 1.53

Selected file —

New tags added —

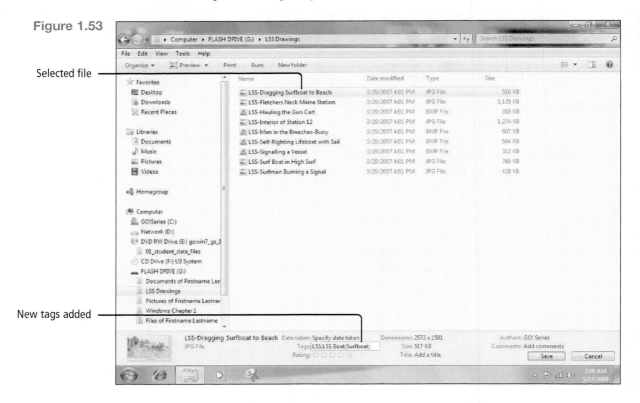

4 Press Enter to confirm the tags. Using the procedure you just practiced, add the same three tags to the **LSS-Surf Boat in High Surf** file. Notice on the left side of the Details pane that the file type for this file is JPG or JPEG.

5 Click the **LSS-Self-Righting Lifeboat with Sail** file. Notice that there is no place to add a tag.

> This image is a bitmap image, which does not support tags. Most Microsoft Office 2007 and 2010 default file formats support tags, as do many other file formats.

6 In the **Navigation** pane, click the **Pictures of Firstname Lastname** folder, and then click the file **LSS-Charlotte NY Station**. Add the following tags: **LSS** and **LSS Boat** and **LSS Boat Ramp** and then press Enter.

7 In the **Details** pane, click the **Title** box, type **Life Saving Station at Charlotte, NY** and then press Enter.

8 In the **file list**, right-click the **LSS-Charlotte NY Station** file, and then from the shortcut menu, click **Properties**. In the **Properties** dialog box, click the **Details tab**.

> The items you entered in the Details pane display, and there are several other categories of tags that you can add, including a rating of the picture or document.

9 In the **Properties** dialog box, under **Description**, click the fourth **Rating** star from the left. Under **Origin**, click the **Copyright** box, type **Public Domain** and then compare your screen with Figure 1.54.

Figure 1.54

Selected file

Rating tag

Copyright box

Title added

New tags added

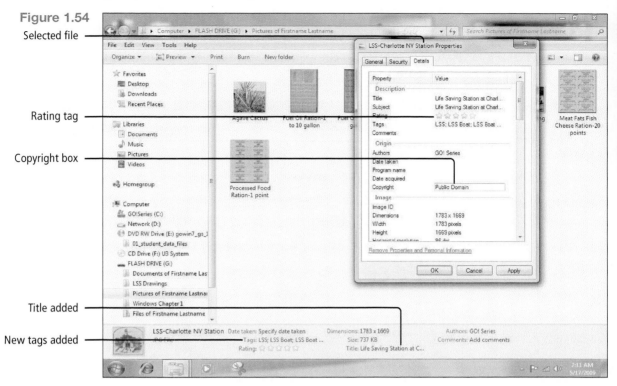

10 At the bottom of the **Properties** dialog box, click **OK**.

Activity 1.18 | Finding Files and Folders and Creating a Search Folder

1 In the **Navigation** pane, click your storage location name. Be sure your storage device is selected, and four folders, one compressed folder, and 16 files display in the file list.

2 Near the upper right corner of the window, click in the **Search** box, type **J** and then in the **file list**, examine the results of your search, as shown in Figure 1.55. If your search results do not display in the list format, to the right of the *Change your view* button [icon], click the *More options* arrow, and then click Details.

The program found all files and folders with words that begin with the letter *J*, along with all file types (file extensions) with words that begin with the letter *J*—in this case, all JPEG image files. Your files may display in a different order.

Figure 1.55

Letter to search for

File types beginning with the letter *J*

Files beginning with the letter *J*

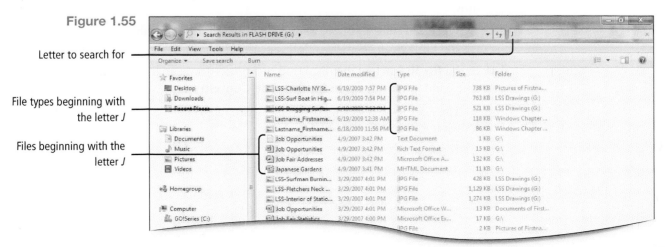

3 With the letter *J* already in the **Search** box, type the letter **P** and examine the search results. Notice that the only files, folders, or file types in your storage device that begin with the letters *JP* are the JPEG image files.

4 Press Bksp, and notice that the search results again display all files, folders, and file types that contain the letter *J*.

5 Now type **ob** to complete the word *Job*. Notice that five files display, as shown in Figure 1.56.

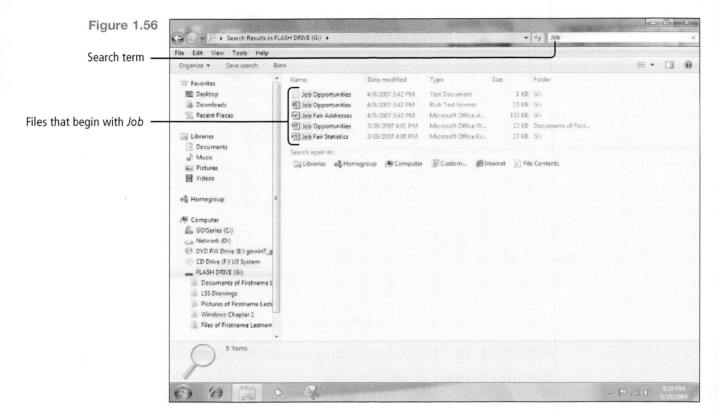

Figure 1.56

Search term

Files that begin with *Job*

6 Press Bksp three times, type **LSS** and then notice that files and folders from various locations display in the file list.

7 Press Spacebar, type **boat** and then notice that only one file or folder meets this search condition, even though you added *LSS Boat* as a tag to several files. Also notice that the file that was found had both search words, but they do not have to be next to each other.

> When you enter a word or phrase in the Search pane, only the file names, folder names, and file types are searched.

8 In the **file list**, below the displayed file, notice the search alternatives that are available. Under **Search again in**, click **File Contents**. Notice that three files display.

> The *File Contents* search extends the search to include tags, text that is a portion of a file name, or text inside the file.

9 On the Command bar, click the **Save search** button. In the displayed **Save As** dialog box, click **Save**. Compare your screen with Figure 1.57.

> A *search folder* is saved on your computer under **Favorites**—not on your removable storage device. A search folder retains all of the search conditions you specified during your search, and recreates the search every time you click the search folder. As you add more pictures with the *LSS Boat* tag to your removable storage device, the search folder will find them. It is important to remember that the search folder will only search the location you specified—it will not search the rest of the computer.

Figure 1.57

New search folder ———

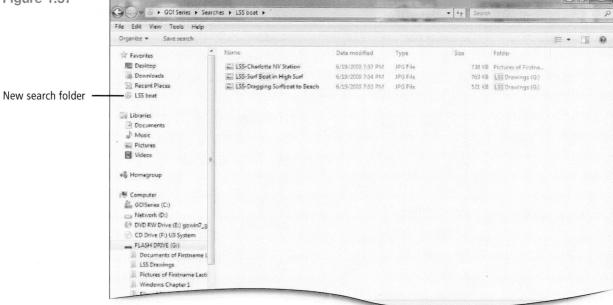

10 Use the skills you practiced earlier to create a **Full-screen Snip**. Save the snip to your **Windows Chapter 1** folder as **Lastname_Firstname_1B_Search_Folder** and submit all three file snips from Project 1B as directed. If you are directed to print the files, use the skills practiced in Activity 1.9 to create a WordPad document, add your name, drag the three snip files from this project, and then print the document. It is not necessary to save the WordPad file once you have printed it.

11 In the title bar, click the **Close** button to close the Windows Explorer window. Select and **Delete** the files and shortcuts you saved on the desktop, and then **Close** the gadgets that you added to the desktop.

More Knowledge | Using Wildcards in Searches

When you are searching for a particular type of file, you can specify the extension by using a wildcard, followed by the extension. A *wildcard* takes the place of one or more characters in a search. For example, if you wanted to search for all of your Excel 2007 files in the My Documents folder, select the folder, and then type *.xlsx* in the Search box. All files with the .xlsx extension will display. If you want to display all of your Excel files, including older versions (with the .xls extension), type *.xls. This search will locate all .xls and .xlsx files. Similarly, you can search for all files beginning with *Fun* by typing *Fun**, which will return all files with those first three letters, including *Fundamentals of Business* and *Fun with Trombones*.

End **You have completed Project 1B** ———————————

Summary

Windows 7 is a robust operating system that enables you to easily locate information and programs. It enables you to create, rename, move, copy, and delete files and folders. You can add key words and other information to the files to make searching easier and more accurate.

Key Terms

Active window	Folder	ScreenTip
Address bar	Gadget	Scroll box
Aero	Gadget controls	Search box
All Programs	Graphical user interface (GUI)	Search folder
Archive		Shake
Ascending order	Hard drive	Shortcut menu
CD	Hardware	Snip
Click	Horizontal scroll bar	Snipping Tool
Clipboard	Icon	Start button
Close button	Jump list	Start menu
Command bar	Libraries	Status area
Compress	Library pane	Submenu
Computer icon	Local disk	System tray
Context-sensitive command	Maximize	Tags
	Menu	Taskbar
Descending order	Menu bar	Thumb drive
Desktop	Metadata	Thumbnail
Desktop background	Minimize	Title bar
Details pane	Mouse pointer	Toolbar
Dialog box	Navigation pane	USB drive
Double-click	Notification area	Vertical scroll bar
Drag	Operating system	Wildcard
Drive	Paint	Window
DVD	Peek	Window name
Edit mode	Pinned programs area	Windows
Favorites	Pointer	Windows Aero
File	Recycle Bin	Windows Explorer
File extension	Restore	WordPad
File list	Right-click	
Flash drive	Screen saver	

Screen ID

Identify each element of the screen by matching callout numbers shown in Figure 1.58 to a corresponding description.

Figure 1.58

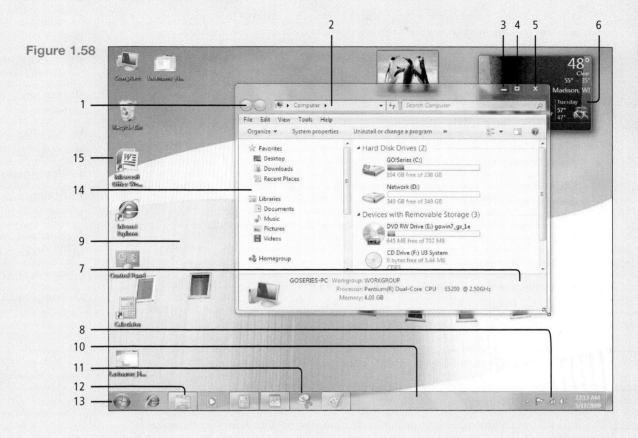

_____ A. Address bar

_____ B. Back button

_____ C. Close button

_____ D. Desktop

_____ E. Details pane

_____ F. Gadget

_____ G. Icon

_____ H. Maximize button

_____ I. Minimize button

_____ J. Navigation pane

_____ K. Notification area

_____ L. Snipping Tool button

_____ M. Start button

_____ N. Taskbar

_____ O. Windows Explorer button

Matching

Match each term in the second column with its correct definition in the first column. Write the letter of the term on the blank line in front of the correct definition.

_____ 1. The Windows 7 user interface that features a three-dimensional look, with transparent window frames, live previews of open windows, and multiple color schemes.

_____ 2. A program that captures a screen or part of a screen.

_____ 3. Displays information about the drive, folder, or file selected in the file list.

_____ 4. A set of instructions that coordinates the activities of your computer.

_____ 5. A computer interface that shows documents as they will look in their final form and uses icons to represent programs.

_____ 6. A simple drawing program included with Windows 7.

_____ 7. Displays the Start button and the name of any open documents; it may also display shortcut buttons for other programs.

_____ 8. Command at the bottom of the Start menu that takes you to all available programs on your computer.

_____ 9. To remove the window from the screen without closing it.

_____ 10. To increase the size of a window to fill the screen.

_____ 11. The bar at the right side of a window that enables you to move up and down to view information that extends beyond the top and bottom of the screen.

_____ 12. The bar at the bottom of a window that enables you to move left and right to view information that extends beyond the left and right edges of the screen.

_____ 13. Move the mouse pointer while holding down the left mouse button, and then release at the appropriate time.

_____ 14. Work that you save and store on a drive, such as a Word document or a PowerPoint presentation.

_____ 15. A program that enables you to create and manage folders, and copy, move, sort, and delete files.

A All Programs

B Details pane

C Drag

D File

E Graphical user interface

F Horizontal scroll bar

G Maximize

H Minimize

I Operating system

J Paint

K Snipping Tool

L Taskbar

M Vertical scroll bar

N Windows Aero

O Windows Explorer

Multiple Choice

Circle the correct answer.

1. In the Windows Explorer window, this pane displays Favorites, Libraries, Computer, and Network information.
   - **a.** Preview
   - **b.** Navigation
   - **c.** Details

2. The working area of the Windows 7 screen—consisting of program icons, a taskbar, a Start button, and gadgets—is the:
   - **a.** desktop
   - **b.** window
   - **c.** Notification area

3. The arrow, I-beam, or other symbol that shows the location or position of the mouse on your screen is the mouse:
   - **a.** button
   - **b.** cursor
   - **c.** pointer

4. The area on the right side of the taskbar that keeps you informed about processes that are occurring in the background, such as antivirus software, network connections, and other utility programs, is the:
   - **a.** Quick Launch toolbar
   - **b.** Notification area
   - **c.** program icon

5. Custom file properties such as names, places, and descriptions that are added to files are called:
   - **a.** jump lists
   - **b.** details
   - **c.** metadata

6. You can activate this by pointing to an object and clicking the right mouse button.
   - **a.** active window
   - **b.** shortcut menu
   - **c.** gadget

7. When you create a new folder, the folder name displays:
   - **a.** in edit mode
   - **b.** in the Details pane
   - **c.** on the desktop

8. When you create a search folder, it displays in the Navigation pane under this category:
   - **a.** Favorites
   - **b.** Computer
   - **c.** Libraries

9. A dynamic program—such as a clock, a stock market ticker, or a weather window—that displays on the desktop is a:
   - **a.** gadget
   - **b.** tag
   - **c.** snip

10. The three or four characters to the right of the period in a file name is called:
    - **a.** metadata
    - **b.** a wildcard
    - **c.** a file extension

Skills Review | Project **1C** Using Windows 7

Apply a combination of the 1A and 1B skills.

In the following Skills Review, you will copy files from your student data disk to a flash drive, create and rename folders, and move files. You will also add tags to files and search for files using the Search box. Your completed documents will look similar to the ones shown in Figure 1.59.

Project Files

For Project 1C, you will need the following files:

36 sample files, and two folders containing 14 additional files

You will save your documents as:

Lastname_Firstname_1C_Screen_Saver
Lastname_Firstname_1C_Desktop
Lastname_Firstname_1C_Folders
Lastname_Firstname_1C_Tags

Project Results

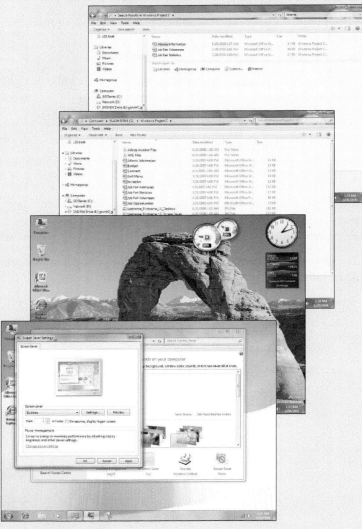

Figure 1.59

(Project 1C Using Windows 7 continues on the next page)

Content-Based Assessments

1 Turn on your computer and if necessary follow the log-on instructions required for the computer you are using.

2 Move the pointer to an open area of the desktop, and then right-click. From the shortcut menu, move the pointer to the bottom of the list, and then click **Personalize**. At the bottom of the **Personalization** window, click the **Screen Saver** button. Click the **Screen saver box arrow**, and then from the displayed list, click **Bubbles**.

3 If the **Snipping Tool** does not display on your taskbar, click the **Start** button, point to **All Programs**, click **Accessories**, right-click **Snipping Tool**, and then click **Pin to Taskbar**. On the taskbar, click the **Snipping Tool** button. In the **Snipping Tool** window, click the arrow to the right of the **New** button, and then click **Full-screen Snip**.

4 In the **Snipping Tool** window, click the **Save Snip** button. In the **Save As** dialog box, in the left pane, scroll down to display the **Computer** drives. Click your flash drive, and then in the Command bar, click the **New folder** button. Name the new folder **Windows Project C** Press Enter, and then press Enter again to open the new folder. In the **File name** box, type **Lastname_Firstname_1C_Screen_Saver** Be sure the **Save as type** box displays *JPEG file*. Click **Save**, and then **Close** the Snipping Tool window.

5 If you want to use the Bubbles screen saver, at the bottom of the Screen Saver Settings dialog box, click OK; otherwise, click Cancel.

6 At the bottom of the **Personalization** window, click **Desktop Background**. Use the vertical scroll bar to display the **United States** desktop backgrounds, and then click the picture of the **stone arch**. Click **Save changes** to apply the new background, and then **Close** the Personalization window.

7 Click the **Start** button, point to **All Programs**, and then click **Accessories**. Right-click **WordPad**, point to **Send to**, click **Desktop (create shortcut)**, and then click in any open area of the desktop.

8 In an open area of the desktop, right-click to display a shortcut menu, and then click **Gadgets**. Double-click the **Clock** gadget, double-click the **Stocks** gadget, and then double-click the **CPU Meter** gadget. **Close** the Gadgets window. Point to the **CPU Usage** gadget, and then click the **Larger size** button. Drag the **CPU Usage** gadget to the top of the desktop.

9 Use the skills you practiced to create a **Full-screen Snip** of the desktop, **Save** it in the **Windows Project C** folder as **Lastname_Firstname_1C_Desktop** and then **Close** the Snipping Tool window.

10 On the taskbar, click the **Windows Explorer** button. If this button is not available, click the Start button, point to All Programs, click Accessories, and then click Windows Explorer. Insert your student data CD*. In the **Windows Explorer** window, in the **Navigation** pane, click the drive that contains your student data files. To the left of the drive name, click the open arrow to display the **01_student_data_files** folder, and then click that folder to display the folders and files in the file list.

11 In the **Navigation** pane, in the drive that contains your student files, be sure the folders display. In the **file list**, drag the **XML Files** folder to the **Windows Project C** folder on your flash drive.

12 At the top of the **file list**, click the **Type** column heading. Widen the **Type** column so you can see all of the file types. Click the first **Adobe Acrobat** document—*Ration Coupons-1*—, hold down Shift, and then click the last **Adobe Acrobat** document—*Ration Coupons-6*. Drag the selected files to the **Windows Project C** folder on your flash drive. Then, select all of the files with a **Type** that begins *Microsoft Office*. Drag these 15 files to the **Windows Project C** folder on your flash drive.

13 In the **Navigation** pane, locate your flash drive, and then click the **Windows Project C** folder. On the Command bar click the **New Folder** button, and then name the folder **Adobe Acrobat Files** Select the six **Adobe Acrobat Files** and drag them to the folder you just created. In the **Navigation** pane, expand the **Windows Project C** folder, and then click the **Windows Project C** folder to display the folder contents.

14 In the **file list**, right-click the file **Volunteers**, and then click **Rename**. Rename the file **Job Fair Volunteers** In the same list of files, right-click the **Lightning** file, and then from the shortcut menu, click **Delete**. In the message box, click **Yes**.

15 At the top of the **file list**, click the **Name** column heading as necessary to display the folders and files in ascending (*a* to *z*) order. Use the skills you practiced to create a **Full-screen Snip** of the Windows Explorer window, **Save** it in the **Windows Project C** folder as

(Project 1C Using Windows 7 continues on the next page)

*Please note: Your custom textbook may not be accompanied by a CD. If this is the case, student files can be found at www.pearsoncustom.com/customphit/datafiles.

Skills Review | Project **1C** Using Windows 7 (continued)

Lastname_Firstname_1C_Folders and then **Close** the Snipping Tool window.

16 In the **file list**, click the **Job Fair Statistics** file. In the **Details** pane, click to the right of **Tags**. In the **Tags** box, type **Atlanta** press →, and then type **Job Fair** Add the same tags to the **Atlanta Information** file.

17 In the **Search** box, type **Atlanta** and then press Enter. In the **file list**, click **File Contents** to include files with the word *Atlanta* in the files or in the file tags. If necessary, change the display to Details. Use the skills you practiced to create a **Full-screen Snip** of the Windows Explorer window, **Save** it in the **Windows Project C**

folder as **Lastname_Firstname_1C_Tags** and then **Close** the Snipping Tool window.

18 Submit all four snips as directed. If you are directed to print the files, use the skills practiced in Activity 1.9 to create a WordPad document, add your name, drag the four snip files from this project, and then print the document. It is not necessary to save the WordPad file once you have printed it.

19 Remove all desktop and taskbar shortcuts that you created in this project, and then **Close** all three gadgets that you added.

 You have completed Project 1C _____

Getting Started with Internet Explorer 8

OBJECTIVES

At the end of this chapter you will be able to:

PROJECT 1A

Use Internet Explorer 8 to Navigate and Search the Internet, Create and Manage Favorite Internet Sites, and Save and Print Web Pages.

OUTCOMES

Mastering these objectives will enable you to:

1. Start Internet Explorer 8 and Identify Screen Elements
2. Navigate the Internet
3. Create and Manage Favorites
4. Search the Internet
5. Save and Print Web Pages

Monkey Business Images/Shutterstock

In This Chapter

Lake Michigan City College is located along the lakefront of Chicago—one of the nation's most exciting cities. The college serves its large and diverse student body and makes positive contributions to the community through relevant curricula, partnerships with businesses and nonprofit organizations, and learning experiences that enable students to be full participants in the global community. The college offers three associate degrees in 20 academic areas, adult education programs, and continuing education classes on campus, at satellite locations, and online.

The Internet got its start in the 1960s as an experiment by the Department of Defense as a way for large computers to communicate with other large computers. The Internet has evolved into the largest online computer network in the world—one accessed by hundreds of millions of people every day.

Today, using the Internet, you are able to locate old classmates, communicate with friends by using email or chat, or find phone numbers, directions, and maps so you can arrange visits. The Internet enables you to explore the museums of the world or shop for items that are unavailable at your local mall, all with the click of a button. You can control your finances or improve your mind with educational opportunities any time of day and from any location. The Internet gives you a greater connection to the world.

This introduction to Internet Explorer 8 provides a basic overview of Internet Explorer 8 features and how to use them to explore the Internet. You will practice accessing Web sites, navigating the Internet, saving your favorite Web sites, searching for information, and saving and printing Web pages.

Project 1A College and Career Information

In Activities 1.1 through 1.15, you and the students in Mr. Tony Adair's CIS 101 course will use Internet Explorer 8 to find information about opportunities after graduating from Lake Michigan City College. Some students are interested in transferring to a four-year college and others want to begin a job and work before thinking about more college. Your completed projects will look similar to those shown in Figure 1.1.

Project Files

For Project 1A, you will need the following file:

New blank Word document

You will save your documents as

Lastname_Firstname_1A_College_Money
Lastname_Firstname_1A_Career_Info

Project Results

Figure 1.1

Project 1A College and Career Information

Objective 1 | Start Internet Explorer 8 and Identify Screen Elements

Internet Explorer 8 is a software program that enables you to view the contents of the World Wide Web. Software of this type is called a *Web browser.* By using Internet Explorer as your Web browser, you can connect to the Internet to search for information, display Web pages, and receive email. Internet Explorer also assists with downloading and transferring files from the Internet, displaying the graphics on a Web site, playing audio and video files associated with a Web site, and executing small programs found in Web sites.

Activity 1.1 | Starting Internet Explorer 8

In the following activity, you will start Internet Explorer 8 and identify features of the Internet Explorer program window. The way you start Internet Explorer 8 will vary depending on the version of Windows you are using and the way your system has been set up by you, your college, or your organization. The standard installation of Windows places Internet Explorer at the top of the Start menu.

1 On the Windows taskbar, click the **Start** button ⬤, and then using Figure 1.2 as a guide, locate Internet Explorer on your system.

> Organizations can customize the arrangement of programs on the Start menu. If Internet Explorer is used as the standard browser program on your computer, it displays at the top of the Start menu. In other cases, Internet Explorer will display in the All Programs list. If the Internet Explorer logo displays as an icon on your desktop, you can double-click the desktop icon to start the program. The Internet Explorer logo might also display on the Quick Launch toolbar.

Figure 1.2

Internet Explorer icon on the desktop

Internet Explorer on the Start menu

Internet Explorer on the Quick Launch toolbar

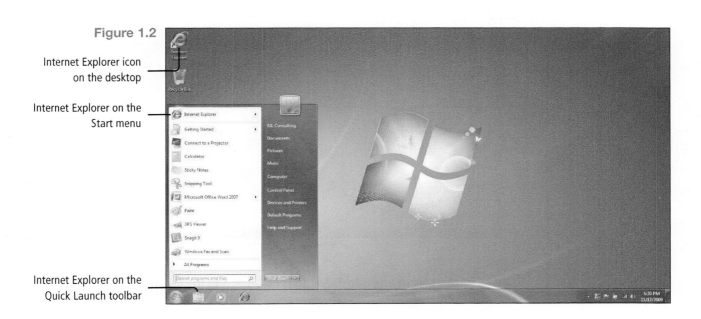

Alert! | Are you sure that you have an Internet connection?

To complete the activities in this chapter, your system must be connected to the Internet. This connection might be through your college or organization's network or your personal *Internet Service Provider (ISP).* An Internet Service Provider is a company that provides an Internet connection through a regular telephone line, a special high-speed telephone line, or a cable. These services are provided by companies such as AT&T, Yahoo!, Verizon, or Comcast, or by local cable and telephone companies.

---

2 On your system, click **Internet Explorer**. In the upper right corner, **Maximize** ▫ the window if it is not already maximized.

> Each time you start Internet Explorer 8 when your system is connected to the Internet, the home page that has been set on your system displays. Your *home page* is the Web page that displays every time you start Internet Explorer 8 and can be any Web page. In a college environment, the home page is usually set to the college's Web page. On your own system, you can choose any Web page.
>
> A *Web page* is a document on the World Wide Web that displays as a screen with associated links, frames, pictures, and other features of interest. A *Web site* is a group of related Web pages published to a specific location on the World Wide Web; for example, all the various screens—pages—that comprise your college's Web site. Each Web site has its own unique address, called a *Uniform Resource Locator* or *URL*.

3 In the **Address bar**, type **microsoft.com**, and then press Enter. As you type the first few characters in the Address bar, Internet Explorer 8 recalls sites that you have visited in past browsing sessions. These sites are displayed as a drop-down list directly beneath the Address bar. Matching characters are highlighted in blue. Compare your screen with Figure 1.3.

> Because Web sites are regularly updated, your screen might look slightly different than Figure 1.3. The Windows Live toolbar is an optional toolbar to make searching easier. It is not a default feature of Internet Explorer 8.

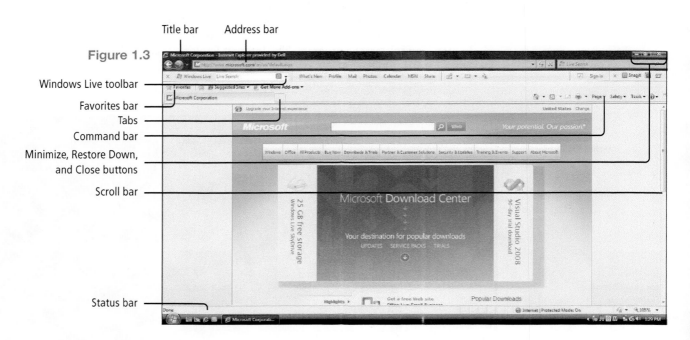

Figure 1.3

Title bar   Address bar

Windows Live toolbar

Favorites bar

Tabs

Command bar

Minimize, Restore Down, and Close buttons

Scroll bar

Status bar

4 Click the **Favorites** button 🌟, and then click **Add to Favorites** 🌟 to display the **Add a Favorite** dialog box. Compare your screen with Figure 1.4.

Figure 1.4

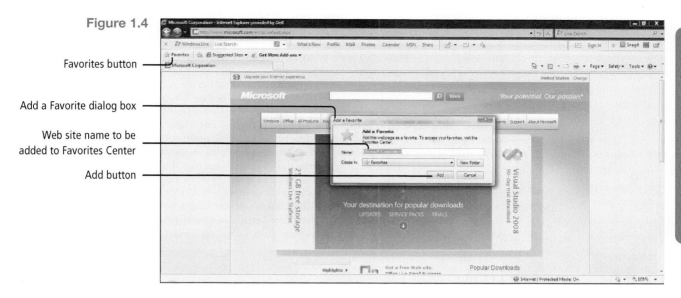

Favorites button

Add a Favorite dialog box

Web site name to be added to Favorites Center

Add button

5 In the **Add a Favorite** dialog box, click the **Add** button. Take a moment to review the Microsoft Internet Explorer 8 screen elements shown in the table in Figure 1.5.

The Web page has been added to your Favorites Center.

Internet Explorer 8 Screen Elements	
Screen Element	**Description**
Title bar	Identifies the program as Windows Internet Explorer and also displays the name of the active Web page.
Minimize, Restore Down, and Close buttons	Provide a way to vary the size of the window you are viewing.
Command bar	The toolbar located immediately above the right side of the browser window that can provide quick access to commands such as Home, Page, Safety, and Tools.
Address bar	Displays the address of the active Web page.
Favorites bar	The toolbar located immediately above the left side of the browser window that can provide quick access to a favorite Web site.
Mouse pointer	Displays as a pointing hand when you point to a link (Link Select pointer).
Hyperlinks	When clicked, display other Web pages in this site, or other Web sites. Links can also take you to a document, email address, picture, or sound clip.
Scroll bar	Allows vertical or horizontal navigation of a Web page.
Status bar	Provides information about the security of a site and information about a link's destination as you point to a link.
Tabs	Allow multiple Web sites to be open at the same time.

Figure 1.5

The default home page installed when Windows is set up on your computer is a Microsoft site because Internet Explorer 8 is a Microsoft program. Schools, organizations, and individuals that have Web sites often change the default settings to display their own site as the home page. As part of the installation process, ISPs such as AT&T, Yahoo!, or Comcast might set their Web site as the default home page. Many people want their home page set to sites such as MSN and Yahoo! to make accessing email and other frequently used features easier. These home pages, including MSN, act as *portals* or launching sites to other Web pages. They contain links to frequently visited sites, up-to-the-minute news, weather reports, maps, and directories. The portal pages are customizable so that you can replace the standard links and information presented on the page with features you use.

On school, lab, and business computers, changing the home page is usually not recommended. However, on your personal computer, you can change the home page. To do so, display the page you want to set as the home page. Then, on the Command bar, click the Home down arrow and then click Add or Change Home Page. In the Add or Change Home Page dialog box, review the choices, click one of the option buttons, and then click Yes. The *Command bar* is the toolbar located immediately above the right side of the browser window that can provide quick access to commands such as Home, Page, Safety, and Tools.

Objective 2 | Navigate the Internet

Most Web pages contain links that you can use to navigate to other sites on the Internet. Internet Explorer 8 also provides commands that are accessible on the toolbars, a History list, and the Address bar, all of which you can use to navigate the Web. Internet Explorer 8 has tabs that enable you to have multiple Web sites open at the same time. In Activities 1.2 through 1.6, you will use each of these tools to access different Web sites.

Activity 1.2 | Navigating the Internet

1 Click the **Back** button to return to your home page, and then notice that the **Forward** button becomes available.

2 On the **Address bar**, point to, but do not click, the **Forward** button, and then compare your screen with Figure 1.6.

A ScreenTip identifies the Web page that will display when you click the button. A *ScreenTip* is a small note that displays information about a screen element and is activated by pointing to a button or other screen object.

Figure 1.6

Back button
Forward button
ScreenTip
Home button
Refresh button
Stop button

3 On the **Address bar**, click the **Forward** button 🔵 to redisplay the **Microsoft.com** home page.

4 On the Command bar, click the **Home** button 🏠.

Regardless of how many Web pages you view or Web sites you visit, clicking the Home button returns you to the site that is set as the home page on the system at which you are working.

Activity 1.3 | Accessing Web Sites from the Address Bar

1 Near the top of the **Internet Explorer** window, click anywhere in the **Address bar**.

The existing Web address is highlighted indicating that it is selected.

2 With the current Web address selected, type **www.usa.gov** Press [Enter], and then compare your screen with Figure 1.7.

The USA.gov site's home page displays. When an existing Web address is selected, typing a new address replaces the selected text. As you type, a history list might display. Internet Explorer displays a list of all the sites you have accessed recently that begin with the characters you type. If you see the site you are typing in the history list, you can click the site name in the list rather than type the complete address.

Figure 1.7

Web site address in
Address bar

Home page of USA.gov
Web site (your screen will
likely differ)

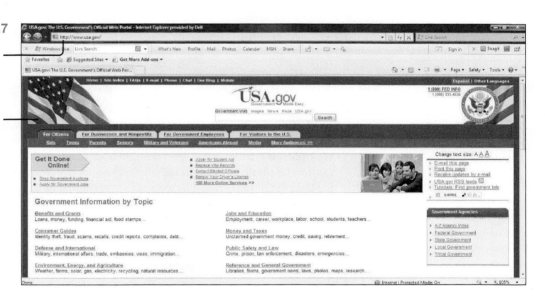

3 Take a moment to study the table in Figure 1.8 that describes how Web addresses are formed.

Parts of the Web Address

Parts of the Web Address	Description
http	The abbreviation of Hypertext Transfer Protocol—the standard *protocol* for retrieving Web sites. A protocol is a set of rules for transferring data over the Internet. Another protocol is *ftp*, or *File Transfer Protocol*. FTP is a protocol that enables individuals to copy files from one computer to another on a network.
://	Three characters identified by Internet creators for separating the protocol from the rest of the Web address. These three characters were identified because they had never appeared together in computer programs and other computer-related contexts.
www.USA.gov	The domain name. In this case, the domain name includes the abbreviation for World Wide Web *(www)*, the name of the organization, and top-level domain—*.gov* stands for government. Not all domain names start with www, but many do. Other domain types include *.com* (commercial), *.edu* (education), *.org* (organization), *.net* (network), and *.mil* (military). Most countries have their own domain types such as *.ca* for Canada and *.fr* for France.

Figure 1.8

4 Click the **Address bar** again, type **www.bls.gov** and press Enter. Compare your screen with Figure 1.9.

> The U.S. Department of Labor, Bureau of Labor Statistics Web site displays. Because sites are regularly updated, your screen will likely not match Figure 1.9 exactly. The *.gov* in the Web address is called a top-level domain and identifies the site as a government site. A *top-level domain*, or *TLD*, is the highest level of the Domain Name System expressed as the last part of the domain name and is represented by a period followed by three or four letters. The *domain name* is the part of a text-based URL that identifies the company or organization that owns the Web site.

Figure 1.9

Web address

U.S. Department of Labor, Bureau of Labor Statistics Web site

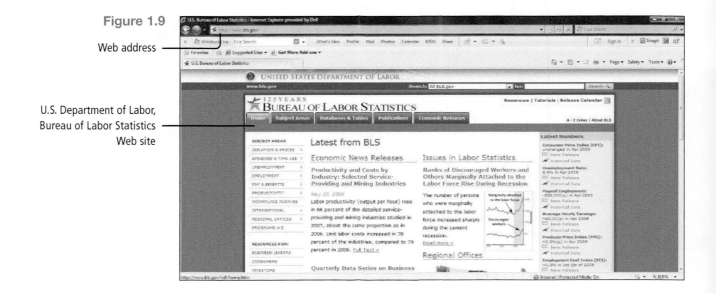

5 At the right end of the **Address bar**, click the **Address bar down arrow** ⏷ and point to but do not click the **http://www.usa.gov** Web address. Compare your screen with Figure 1.10.

The list of recently accessed Web sites on your computer will differ from those shown in Figure 1.10. The sites listed represent those most frequently visited on your system.

Figure 1.10

Site to select

Address Bar down arrow

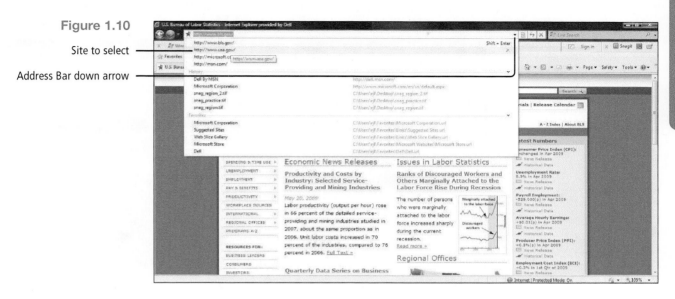

6 In the displayed list, click the **http://www.usa.gov** Web address to display that Web site. Then, in the **Address bar**, type **www.ed.gov** and press Enter.

The U.S. Department of Education Web site displays.

7 On the **Address bar**, locate the **Recent Pages button down arrow** ⏷ to the right of the Forward button, and then click the arrow to display the most recently visited Web sites. Click the listing for the **USA.gov** Web site. Then, click the **Forward** button ◉ to return to the **U.S. Department of Education** Web site. Compare your screen with Figure 1.11.

The U.S. Department of Education Web site displays, and the Forward button is unavailable because you have used it to return to this Web site.

Figure 1.11

Forward button (which is unavailable because you used it to get to this site)

Recent Pages button down arrow

8 On the Favorites bar, if necessary, click the **Favorites Center** button to display the task pane. Click **Microsoft Corporation**. Compare your screen with Figure 1.12.

The *Favorites Center* enables you to view the Favorites, Feeds, and History lists. With Internet Explorer 8, you can add Web pages directly to the Favorites bar for easy access. The *Favorites bar* is the toolbar located immediately above the left side of the browser window that can provide quick access to a favorite Web site.

Figure 1.12

Web address

Favorites bar

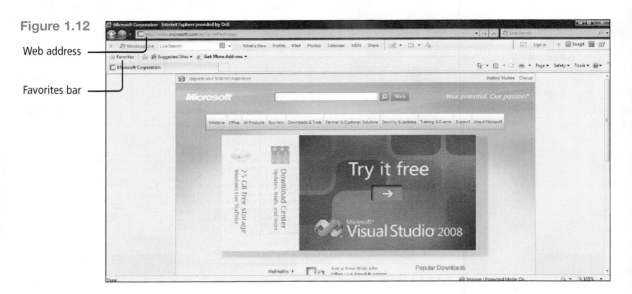

9 In the **Address bar**, click and type **www.psu.edu** and press Enter. Compare your screen with Figure 1.13.

Internet Explorer displays the Penn State Web site. The top-level domain *.edu,* is the domain type reserved for colleges and universities.

Figure 1.13

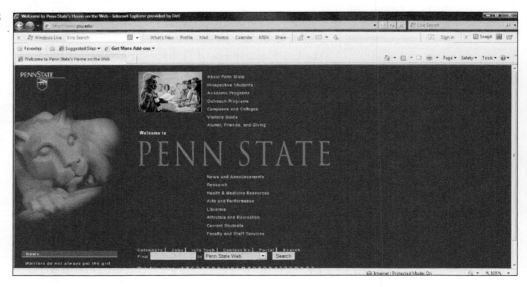

Activity 1.4 | Opening a Second Web Site

1 Near the right of the **Welcome to Penn State's Home on the Web tab**, position your mouse pointer over the **New Tab** button ▢ , but do not click. Compare your screen with Figure 1.14.

> A ScreenTip displays, indicating a new tab will be opened.
>
> *Tabs* in Internet Explorer 8 enable you to have multiple Web pages open at the same time without having to open multiple instances of the browser.

Figure 1.14

New Tab

ScreenTip

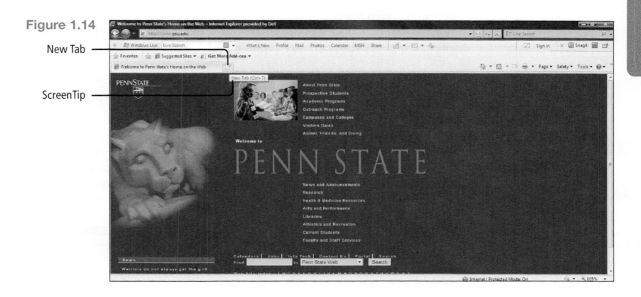

2 Click **New Tab** ▢ .

> A new tab displays that enables you to view another Web site while keeping the Penn State Web site open.

3 In the **Address bar**, type the URL for the Web site of your school, and then press Enter. Compare your screen with Figure 1.15.

> Your school's Web site displays and the name of the Web page displays on the New Tab along with a Close Tab button.

Figure 1.15

Your school's Web site in a new tab

Close Tab button

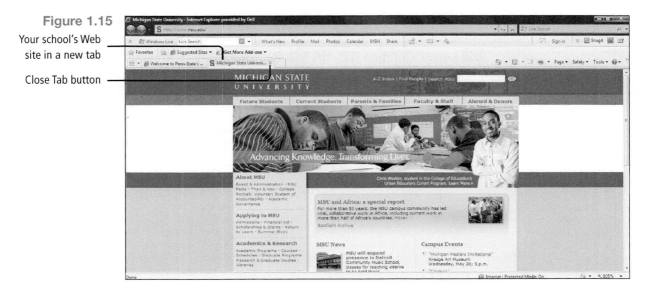

4 Use the **Close Tab** button ⊠ to close the tab displaying your school's Web page.

5 On the Command bar, click the **Home** button 🏠 to return to the home page that is set on your computer.

Activity 1.5 | Displaying Web Pages with Hyperlinks

Most Web sites contain *hyperlinks,* which provide another navigation tool for browsing Web pages. Hyperlinks are text, buttons, pictures, or other objects displayed on Web pages that, when clicked, access other Web pages or display other sections of the active page. Linked Web pages can be pages within the same Web site or Web pages on sites of other companies, schools, or organizations. In this activity, you will use hyperlinks to display Web pages about college financial aid.

1 In the **Address bar**, type **www.students.gov** and then press Enter. Move the mouse pointer to various parts of the screen to locate areas where the **Link Select pointer** 🖑 displays, as shown in Figure 1.16.

> Internet Explorer displays the students.gov home page. As you review Figure 1.16, notice that the mouse pointer displays as a pointing hand—the *Link Select pointer*—when you point to an item that links to another Web page. Web sites contain Web pages with links that connect to other pages on the site. These other pages contain links that lead to still other pages and also link back to the home page of the Web site.

Figure 1.16

Scholarships & grants link

Link Select pointer

2 Locate and then click the link for **Scholarships & grants**. Compare your screen with Figure 1.17.

> The Scholarships & grants page displays. The address in the Address bar still shows the *students.gov* Web site, but the URL has expanded to identify the *path* for this page. A path is the sequential description of the storage location of the HTML documents and files making up the Web page and stored in the hierarchy of directories and folders on the Web server.

Figure 1.17

Expanded URL path

students.gov Home link

Scholarships & grants
page title

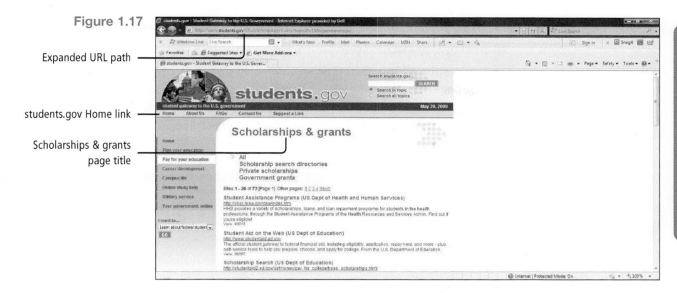

Alert! | Is the Web page available?

Because Web sites are updated frequently, the links on the Web sites also change. If the Scholarships & grants link on the *students.gov* Web site does not display, choose another link to follow.

---

3 On the **Address bar**, click the **Back** button .

The *students.gov* home page displays.

4 Scroll down as necessary to locate the link for **State financial aid** and click it. Compare your screen with Figure 1.18. Click on your state to try to find information about your state's financial aid. One or more links to information about financial aid in your state will display below the list of states. Click any one of these links.

Internet Explorer opens the individual state's financial aid links in a new window. Each Web page contains settings that control whether linked pages open in a separate window or in the same window. In addition, settings that are active on your computer control the linked page's display.

The new Web page opens in a separate window on top of the State financial aid window.

Figure 1.18

5 When you are finished viewing the information, return to the State financial aid Web page by clicking the **Close** button ⊠ in the upper right corner of the new window.

6 Click in the **Address bar**, type **www.fafsa.ed.gov** and press Enter. Compare your screen with Figure 1.19.

Before you can apply for financial aid such as scholarships, grants, or loans, you will need to fill out a FAFSA or Free Application for Federal Student Aid. The TLD, *.gov*, shows that the application is completed at a government Web site.

Figure 1.19

Web address showing *.gov* as the TLD

FAFSA Web site

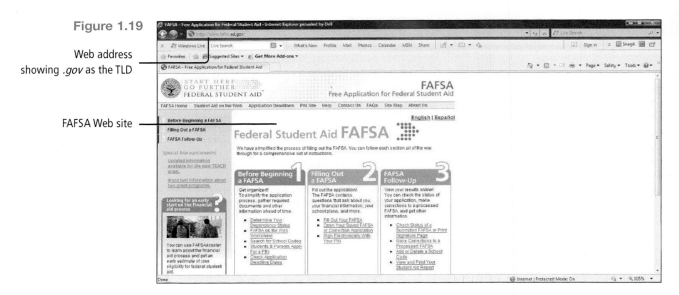

7 At the top of the FAFSA Web page, locate and then click the link for **PIN Site**. Compare your screen with Figure 1.20. The PIN Federal Student Aid Web site displays in a new window. You can see that the new Web page opens in a separate window on top of the FAFSA window.

Notice that the top-level domain name (*.gov*) in the Address bar shows that this is a government Web site. Both you and your parents can apply for a Federal Student Aid PIN at this site. Your PIN, or Personal Identification Number, serves as an electronic signature for your FAFSA.

Figure 1.20

PIN Web site

PIN Site link

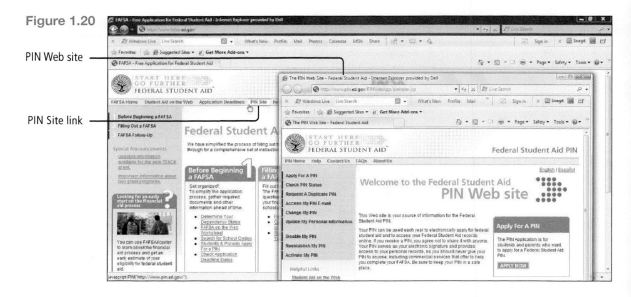

8 On the displayed Web site's title bar, click the **Close** button ⊠ to close the new window. Then click the **Home** button 🏠 to return to your home page.

Activity 1.6 | Using Internet Explorer 8 History

The Internet Explorer 8 *History* feature tracks recently visited Web sites. You can display the History list by using the Favorites Center button, and then clicking the History tab to view a site that you recently visited. You can view the History list by Date, Site, Most Visited, and by Order Visited Today. You can also use the Search History option to locate sites. In this activity, you will use the History list to display recently visited sites.

1 On the Favorites bar, click the **Favorites** button ⭐, and then if necessary, click the **History** tab. The History list displays on the left side of the Internet Explorer window. If necessary, click the down arrow to locate and click **View By Date**, and then click **Today**. Compare your screen with Figure 1.21.

The listings of items on your computer may differ from those shown in the figure. However, many of the listings shown for Today should be the same. Notice that the sites accessed today display in alphabetical order.

Figure 1.21

Favorites button —

Pages visited Today —

2 In the **History** list, click **bls** (**www.bls.gov**), and then compare your screen with Figure 1.22.

The Web site name associated with the URL displays as a link below the URL. If you click the link, the Web site will open. This is another way to open a Web site. You can also locate and open a Web site by clicking the **View By Date down arrow** and choosing the Search History option. Then type keywords into the Search for box.

Figure 1.22

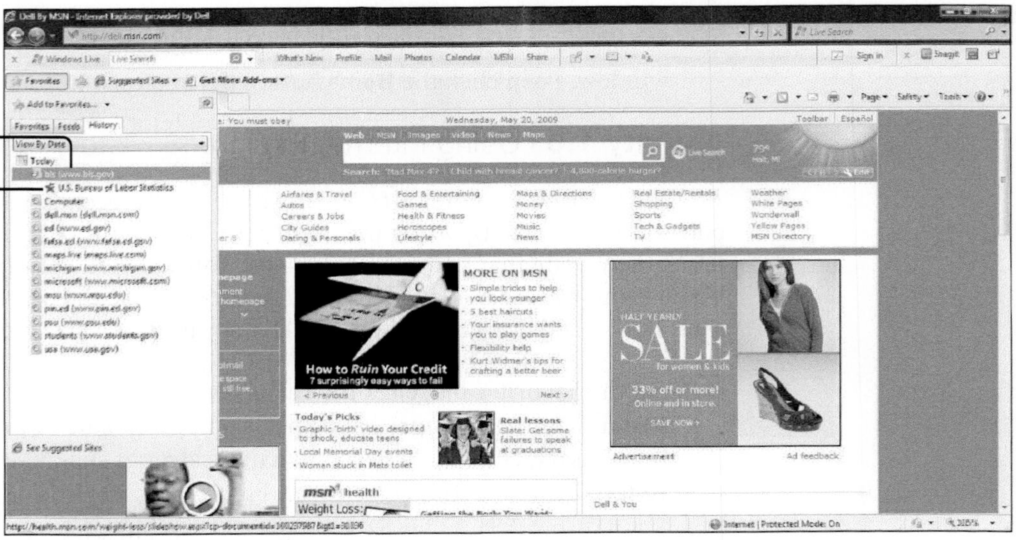

URL of a recently visited site

Associated Web site name

3 Scroll down the **History** list as necessary, and then click **usa (www.usa.gov)** to display the associated Web site name for the USA.gov Web site. Click on the Web site name link to open the **USA.gov** Web site.

More Knowledge | Setting History Options

By default, Internet Explorer 8 tracks sites visited in the last 20 days. To reduce the amount of disk storage space required to maintain the History list, you can customize the settings to change the number of days tracked and to clear the list. You can change the options that control and clear the History list by setting Internet Options under the Tools command. You can choose to delete temporary files, history, cookies, saved passwords, and Web form information. You can also choose to set the amount of disk space to use.

Objective 3 | Create and Manage Favorites

The History list automatically tracks sites that you visit each time you start Internet Explorer 8—many of which you may never visit again. The Favorites list works differently. The Favorites list contains Web addresses for sites you plan to visit frequently. You intentionally add addresses to the Favorites list and Internet Explorer 8 keeps the list for you. When you install Internet Explorer 8, a short list of Microsoft sites is added to the Favorites list. You can delete these addresses, add new addresses, and organize favorite site addresses into folders. For example, you may have a folder for Travel Sites, for College Sites, and so on. In Activities 1.7 through 1.9, you will add a new favorite, create a new folder, navigate to a site listed in the favorites, and delete a favorite.

Activity 1.7 | Adding an Address to the Favorites List

In this activity, you will display a Web page and add it to the Favorites list, using the Add to Favorites button.

1 In the **Address bar**, type **www.prenhall.com/go** and then press (Enter).

2 On the Favorites bar, click the **Favorites** button [icon], and the Favorites tab, if necessary. Then click **Add to Favorites** to display the **Add a Favorite** dialog box. Compare your screen with Figure 1.23.

The Add a Favorite dialog box displays with the title of the Web site indicated in the Name box.

Figure 1.23

Favorites button

Name of Web page

Add button

3 In the **Add a Favorite** dialog box, click **Add.**

You can also add a shortcut to a favorite directly to the Favorites bar by clicking the Add to Favorites Bar button.

4 On the Favorites bar, click the **Favorites** button ☆. Click the **Favorites** tab, if necessary, to display the Favorites. Click the **Add to Favorites down arrow**, and then click **Organize Favorites**. Near the bottom of the **Organize Favorites** dialog box, click the **New Folder** button. In the new folder that was added to the list, type **Textbook Sites** and then press [Enter].

The folder is created and displays in the listing of all folders and Web site favorites that is already established. When you have a number of sites that are related to a specific topic, you can create a new folder and use it to store related site addresses. The Organize Favorites dialog box displays a list of folders and links contained in the Favorites list and command buttons for creating folders, renaming folders and links, moving links to folders, and deleting folders and links from Favorites.

5 In the **Organize Favorites** dialog box, click the **GO! Web page**, and then click the **Move** button. In the **Browse For Folder** dialog box, click the **Textbook Sites** folder, and then click **OK**. In the **Organize Favorites** dialog box, click the **Close** button ☒.

Another Way

To move a Web site after the folder is created, in the Organize Favorites dialog box, drag the Web site to the desired folder.

Internet Explorer 8 adds the GO! Web page address to the Textbook Sites folder in the Favorites list.

6 Click the **Home** button 🏠 to display your home page.

Activity 1.8 | Displaying a Favorite Web Site

In this activity, you will use the Favorites list to display a Web site.

1 If necessary, on the Favorites bar, click the **Favorites** button ☆. Click the **Favorites tab**, click the **Textbook Sites** folder, and then notice that the link to the GO! Web site displays, as shown in Figure 1.24.

Figure 1.24

Favorites list

Textbook Sites folder

New item in the list (GO! site)

2 Click the link to the **GO! Web site.**

The GO! Web site displays.

Activity 1.9 | Deleting a Web Address from Favorites

In this activity, you will remove an address from the Favorites list.

1 On the Favorites bar, click the **Favorites** button ⭐, click the **Add to Favorites down arrow**, and then click **Organize Favorites**. Compare your screen with Figure 1.25.

Figure 1.25

List of folders and links in the Favorites list

Command buttons

2 In the **Organize Favorites** dialog box, scroll down if necessary and click the **Textbook Sites** folder to list its contents. Click the **GO! Web page** link one time to select it.

3 In the **Organize Favorites** dialog box, click the **Delete** button, and then compare your screen with Figure 1.26.

Figure 1.26

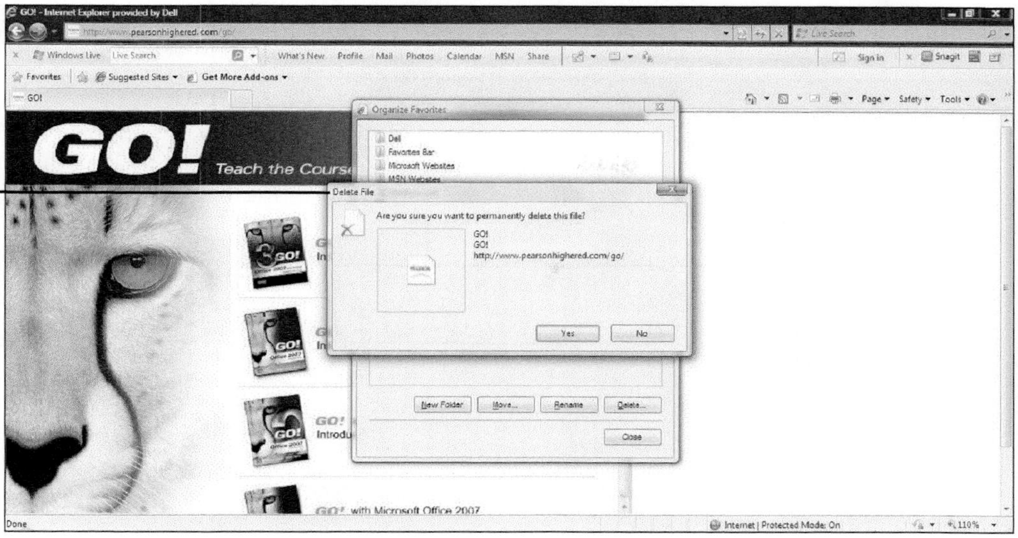

Delete File dialog box

4 In the **Delete File** dialog box, click **Yes**, and then in the **Organize Favorites** dialog box, click the **Close** button ⊠ .

> Internet Explorer 8 removes the GO! Web site from the Favorites list and closes the Organize Favorites dialog box.

5 On the Command bar, click the **Home** button 🏠 to display your home page.

Objective 4 | Search the Internet

When you know the name of an organization or the Web address you want to locate, accessing the site is easy and straightforward. When you want to locate information about topics from a variety of sources or find sites for businesses, journals, and other sources, it presents a greater challenge because of the large number of sites available on the Internet. There are several Web sites with search capabilities called *search engines*, programs that search for keywords in files and documents or other Web sites found on the Internet.

Internet Explorer 8 includes an Instant Search box that connects to a default search engine (such as Live Search or Bing) and easily allows you to add additional search engines. With Internet Explorer 8, Instant Search makes it easier to search for keywords within the text of the current Web page. In this activity, you will search the Internet for topics related to student financial aid.

Activity 1.10 | Adding a Search Engine and Searching the Internet

1 On right side of the **Address bar**, click the **Search down arrow**, and then click **Find More Providers**.

> The Add-ons Gallery: Search Providers Web page opens. It enables you to add additional search providers to Internet Explorer.

2 In the **Add-ons Gallery: Search Providers** list, scroll down or go to page 2 to locate **Google Search Suggestions**. Then click the **Add to Internet Explorer button**. In the **Add Search Provider** dialog box, click the **Make this my default search provider** check box. Compare your screen with Figure 1.27.

Figure 1.27

Google added as a
search provider

Make Google the
default search provider

3 Click the **Add** button.

Google now displays as the default search provider in the Instant Search box.

4 On the **Address bar** in the **Instant Search** box, type **"student financial aid"** including the quotation marks, and then press Enter. Compare your screen with Figure 1.28.

You can begin a search by typing a single word, a phrase, a question, or a statement. You can easily change the size of the Instant Search textbox by dragging the edge. This makes it easier to see all of the characters in a long search string. Typing *student financial aid* without the quotation marks directs the search engine to look for three different terms. Placing the text in quotation marks ensures that the search engine looks for sites that contain the entire phrase. You can see that the number of sites found during this particular search that contain the phrase *"student financial aid"* is quite large. Internet Explorer 8 displays links to the Web sites in a ranked order based on the quality and quantity of the content at the Web sites it returns. Several factors are considered, such as how closely the site matches the search phrase, the number of references to the search text contained in the site, the number of other links to that site, and how recently the site has been updated.

Figure 1.28

Instant Search box

Sites containing specific
search phrase

5 On the right side of the screen, under **Sponsored Links**, click the first link. Compare your screen with Figure 1.29.

> *Sponsored links* are sites that pay to be displayed with results on a search engine site. Sponsored links are frequently placed near the top or on the right side of the search engine results page so they are easily seen and clicked. Sponsored links generally are commercial sites, so they stand to gain from increasing traffic to their Web site. The top-level domain is *.com* for commercial sites.

Figure 1.29

Web address of first sponsored site (yours will vary)

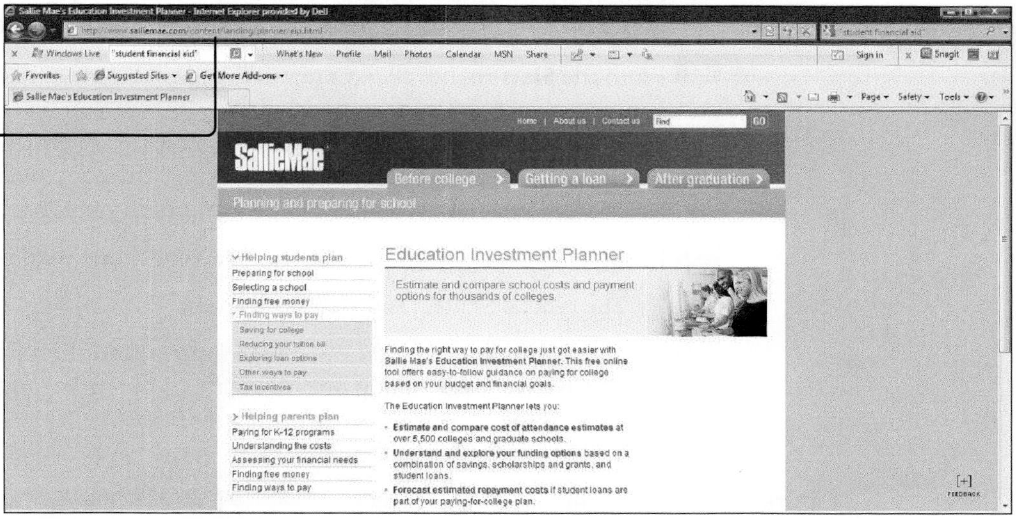

6 Click the **Back** button to return to your search results. Scroll as necessary, and then locate and click the link for **Federal Student Financial Aid**.

> The home page for student aid programs administered by the U.S. Department of Education displays. If you are interested in this information, you can print it or put it on your Favorites list to examine at a later time. Financial aid information found at a sponsored Web site (*.com*) is likely to be a loan opportunity, whereas a government financial aid Web site (*.gov*) is more likely to offer information on grant and scholarship opportunities.

7 On the Command bar, click the **Home** button to display your home page.

Objective 5 | Save and Print Web Pages

Saving a copy of a Web page on your system or storage device is referred to as *downloading*. Downloading means that you request a copy of a file or program from a remote server, such as a Web server, and save it on your local system or storage device. You can also download other types of Web files, such as graphics, and save them on your computer or disk so that you can review them later. When you download a Web page displayed in Internet Explorer 8, Internet Explorer 8 creates a new folder at the location you indicate to save all associated graphics, pictures, and other features of the Web page so that when you view the file offline, it resembles the entire page as it was displayed on the Web. Other techniques for accessing Web pages include setting a desktop shortcut to the Web page and sending a link to a Web page to someone through email. Setting a desktop shortcut creates an icon on your desktop for the Web page so that it opens very quickly. Both techniques are accomplished from the Page button on the Command bar.

Because of the widespread threat of system viruses, as a general precaution, avoid downloading or saving files from unknown Web sites, and be sure your virus protection program is up-to-date before downloading Web files on your system. You must also be careful not to violate copyright-protected Web materials.

Activity 1.11 | Downloading and Saving a Web Page

In this activity, you will download and save a Web page.

1 Determine where you will be storing your files for this chapter, for example, on your own disk or USB flash drive or on a network drive, and be sure that storage location is available. If necessary, check with your instructor or lab coordinator.

2 From the **Start** menu, click **Computer**, and then navigate to the drive—USB flash drive, computer hard drive, or network drive—where you will be storing your files. In the right pane of the **Computer** window, right-click an empty space. In the context-sensitive menu that displays, click **New**, and then roll over and click **Folder.** With **New Folder** selected, type **IE8 Chapter** and then press Enter. **Close** ☒ the window.

3 In **Internet Explorer**, in the **Address bar**, type **studentaid.ed.gov** and then press Enter.

The Federal Student Aid Web site displays.

4 On the Command bar, click the **Page** button, and then click **Save As**. In the left pane of the **Save Webpage** dialog box, navigate to the drive, and then to your **IE8 Chapter** folder. Compare your screen with Figure 1.30.

Figure 1.30

Selected storage location (yours may vary)

Default file name

Default file type

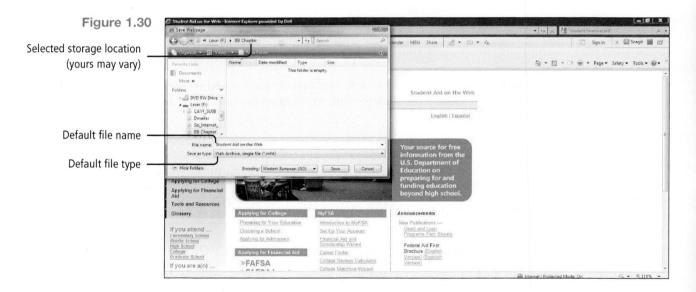

5 At the bottom of the **Save Webpage** dialog box, click the **Save as type arrow** and if necessary, click **Web Archive, single file (*.mht)**. Click in the **File name** box to select the existing text, and then replace the selected text by typing **Lastname_Firstname_1A_ College_Money** substituting your own names for Lastname and Firstname, and instead of spaces between words, use the underscore key, which is Shift + ⌐ . Then, in the lower right corner, click the **Save** button.

An *MHTML* file— which has a file extension of *.mht*—is a format used to save Web pages into a single archive, including all the page elements such as text and graphics.

6 Click the **Home** button ⌂. In the **Address bar**, type the drive, such as **f:** or the location where you saved the file, and the most recent files in that location will display. Compare your screen with Figure 1.31.

Figure 1.31

Location in Address bar

Files recently saved to the
drive and directory

7 Scroll down as necessary, and click the **IE8 Chapter folder**. In the **Computer** window, if necessary, double-click the IE8 Chapter folder. Then double-click the **Lastname_Firstname_1A_College_Money** MHTML document.

The Web page opens in a new tab. Notice the Address bar shows the Web page address as the location where you saved the Web page as a MHTML file. If you were looking at the actual Web page, the Address bar would display the URL as *http://studentaid.ed.gov/ PORTALSWebApp/students/english/index.jsp*.

Even though a Web page may look as if it is one single file, it is actually made up of several objects and files. Each graphic is its own file and the text content is another file. In addition, the Web page may be divided into *frames*. Frames are used to divide a Web page into separate panes that still display as one complete Web page. Navigation is controlled by one of the panes while viewing several different pages of content displayed within a single browser window. The MHTML format saves all of the objects, files, and frames together as one Web archive for viewing offline.

8 **Close** the new tab displaying the Federal Student Aid MHTML file.

9 If necessary, on the Command bar, click the **Home** button to display your home page.

More Knowledge | Downloading New Programs

Downloading, as you used it in Activity 1.11, saves a Web page and associated files in the folder you specify. You can also download entire software programs and other items from the Internet. For example, if you display the Microsoft.com Web site, you can download free trial programs, install them on your system, and try them before you purchase them. When sites offer free downloads, a **Download** link usually displays on the page. When you click the link, Internet Explorer 8 prompts you to save the file on your system. The prompt message also provides an option to open or run the program from the server.

It is generally recommended that you download and save the file on your system before trying to install it. After it is saved to your system, run the program file through your virus protection software before installing the new program. A good rule to follow is to be careful what you download, and download only from well-known and trusted sites.

Activity 1.12 | Downloading and Saving Graphics from a Web Page

1 In the **Address bar**, type **www.bls.gov** and then press Enter. On the **Bureau of Labor Statistics Web site home page**, scroll toward the bottom of the page, and then locate and click the **Career Information for Kids** link. Point anywhere in the displayed picture, right-click the mouse button to display a context-sensitive shortcut menu, and then click **Save Picture As**.

2 In the left pane of the displayed **Save Picture** dialog box, to the left of **Computer**, locate and click the small arrow. Navigate to your **IE8 Chapter** folder and double-click it so that its name displays in the **Save in** box. At the bottom of the dialog box, click in the **File name** box to select the existing text, and then replace it by typing **Lastname_Firstname_1A_Career_Info** Compare your screen with Figure 1.32. Leave the **Save as type** box as the default type—JPEG (*.jpg)—and then in the lower right corner, click the **Save** button.

> The file is saved as a JPEG file. The Save Picture dialog box closes and you are returned to the browser window.

Figure 1.32

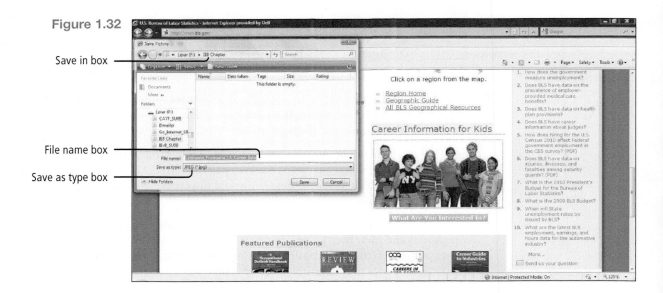

Save in box

File name box

Save as type box

3 On the Command bar, click the **Home** button 🏠 to display your home page.

Activity 1.13 | Printing Web Pages

Web pages are constructed to contain a variety of different elements—pictures, navigation panes, links, text, and so on. When you print Web pages, all the elements displayed on the Web page print unless you select the specific text, picture, or frame you want to print. Most of the options contained in the Print dialog box in Internet Explorer 8 are the same as those seen in the Print dialog box for other programs. However, the Print dialog box in Internet Explorer 8 contains options that enable you to print pages, frames within a Web page, or a table of pages that are linked to the active Web page.

Because frames and objects are placed so closely together on the Web page, selecting just the information you want to print can be a challenge without activating a hyperlink or selecting additional information as well. In this activity, you will review options in the Print dialog box and print a Web page.

1 From the **Start** menu, click **Computer**, and then navigate to the drive—USB flash drive, computer hard drive, or network drive—where you stored your files for this chapter. Locate and then double-click your MHTML file **Lastname_Firstname_1A_College_Money**. Compare your screen with Figure 1.33.

Figure 1.33

The Web site has been opened from a storage location

2 On the Command bar, click the **Print button down arrow** [icon], and then click **Page Setup** to display the Page Setup dialog box. Locate the three **Header: down arrows** and click **Empty** for each. Locate the section labeled **Footer:** Using the first down arrow, click **URL.** Using the second down arrow, click **Title.** In the third down arrow, click **Date in Short Format.** Compare your screen with Figure 1.34.

Figure 1.34

Page Setup dialog box

Footer section
Header section

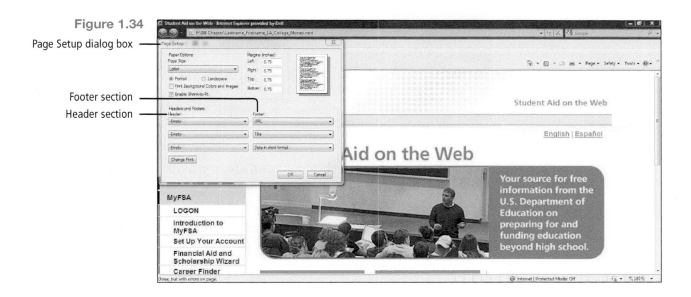

3 In the **Page Setup** dialog box, click **OK.** On the Command bar, click the **Print button down arrow** [icon], click **Print,** and then at the bottom of the displayed **Print** dialog box, click the **Print** button.

The saved Web page print. It is likely that two or more pages will print. At the bottom of each page, the footer you created displays.

4 On the Command bar, click the **Home** button [icon] to display your home page. Submit it as directed by your instructor.

Activity 1.14 | Printing Web Graphics

When you print a Web page, you print all of the elements that make up that Web page, both the graphics and text. It is possible to print only the graphics that are part of the Web page. In this activity you will create a document with a graphic that you have saved from a Web page and print the document.

1 From the **Start** menu, point to **All Programs**, click **Microsoft Office**, and then click **Microsoft Office Word 2007**.

> Microsoft Office Word, a word processing program, will open a new document. You will add text and graphics to this new document.

2 In the new **Word** document, type **Lastname_Firstname_1A_Career_Info** and then press Enter. On the **Insert tab**, in the **Illustrations group**, point to **Picture** (but do not click). Compare your screen with Figure 1.35.

Figure 1.35

Insert tab

Picture button

Text that has been added

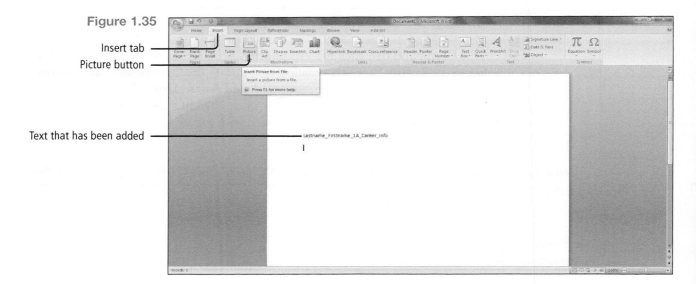

3 In the **Illustrations group**, click the **Picture** button to display the **Insert Picture** dialog box. Navigate to the file **Lastname_Firstname_1A_Career_Info** in your **IE8 Chapter** folder. This graphic was downloaded in Activity 1.12.

4 In the **Insert Picture** dialog box, click the file name, and then click **Insert**.

5 The Web graphic displays underneath your text in the new document. Compare your screen with Figure 1.36.

Figure 1.36

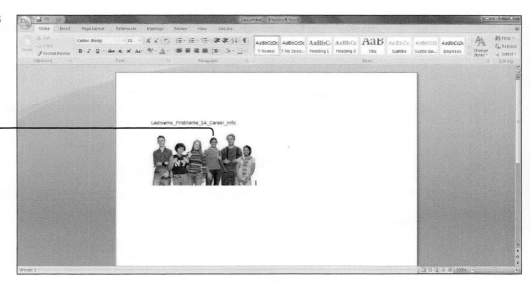

Web graphic that has
been inserted

6 From the **Office** button , click **Save As** and then navigate to your **IE8 Chapter** folder so that its name displays in the **Save in** box. At the bottom of the dialog box, click in the **File name** box to select the existing text, and then replace it by typing **Lastname_Firstname_1A_Career_Info** Leave the **Save as type** box as the default type, and then in the lower right corner, click the **Save** button.

> **More Knowledge** | Be Aware of Copyright Issues
>
> Almost everything you find on the Web is protected by copyright law, which protects authors of original works, including text, art, photographs, and music. If you want to use text or graphics that you find online, you will need to get permission. One of the exceptions to this law is the use of small amounts of information for educational purposes, which falls under Fair Use Guidelines. Another exception is to use work that is considered in the **public domain**. These works are created with the intention of letting anyone use them for any reason; also a work becomes public domain when the copyright has expired.
>
> Copyright laws in the United States are open to different interpretations, and copyright laws can be very different in other countries. As a general rule, if you want to use someone else's material, get permission first.

7 From the **Office** button , click **Print**, and then at the bottom of the displayed **Print** dialog box, click the **OK** button. Submit as directed by your instructor.

The document containing the saved Web graphic prints.

8 **Close** Word to return to the **Internet Explorer** window.

Activity 1.15 | Printing Selected Text from Web Pages

1 In the **Address bar**, type **www.denverpost.com** and press Enter.

The Denver Post Web site displays current information and news items.

2 On the Web page, drag your mouse over the first paragraph under the article heading in the left column to select it.

The paragraph will display as light text on a dark background.

3 On the Command bar, click the **Print button down arrow** , and then click **Print** to display the **Print** dialog box.

4 On the **General tab** of the **Print** dialog box, under **Page Range,** click the **Selection** option. Compare your screen with Figure 1.37. After comparing your screen, click **Print**.

Internet Explorer 8 prints only the selected text and not the entire Web page.

Figure 1.37

Print dialog box ——

General tab ——

Page Range area ——

Selection option ——

5 On the Internet Explorer title bar, click the program's **Close** button ☒ .

End **You have completed Project 1A** ——————————————

Summary

In this project, you explored basic Internet Explorer 8 features such as starting the browser, navigating among Web pages, and working with Favorites. You learned how to search for Web sites containing information about topics you specify and how to download and save Web pages and graphics. You learned how to print a Web page, a graphic saved from a Web page, and selected text on a Web page.

Key Terms

Command bar

Domain name

Downloading

Favorites bar

Favorites Center

File Transfer
    Protocol (FTP)

Frames

History

Home page

Hyperlinks

Internet Explorer 8

Internet Service
    Provider (ISP)

Link Select pointer

MHTML

Path

Portal

Protocol

Public domain

ScreenTip

Search engine

Sponsored link

Tabs

Top-level domain
    (TLD)

Uniform Resource
    Locator (URL)

Web browser

Web page

Web site

Matching

Match each term in the second column with its correct definition in the first column. Write the letter of the term on the blank line in front of the correct definition.

_____ 1. A protocol that enables individuals to copy files from one computer to another on a network.

_____ 2. A Microsoft software program that enables you to view the contents of the World Wide Web.

_____ 3. A company that provides an Internet connection through a regular telephone line, a special high-speed telephone line, or a cable.

_____ 4. Software that enables you to use the World Wide Web and navigate from page to page and site to site.

_____ 5. The unique address used to locate a Web page or Web site.

_____ 6. A small note that displays information about a screen element and is activated by pointing to a button or other screen object.

_____ 7. An Internet Explorer 8 feature that enables you to view the Favorites, Feeds, and History lists.

_____ 8. The toolbar located immediately above the right side of the browser window that can provide quick access to commands such as Home, Page, Safety, and Tools.

_____ 9. A browser feature that enables you to have multiple Web pages open at the same time without having to open multiple browsers.

_____ 10. The sequential description of the storage location of the HTML documents and files making up the Web page and stored in the hierarchy of directories and folders on the Web server.

A Command bar

B Downloading

C Favorites Center

D File Transfer
    Protocol (FTP)

E History

F Internet Explorer 8

G Internet Service
    Provider (ISP)

H MHTML

I Path

J ScreenTip

K Sponsored link

L Tabs

M Uniform Resource
    Locator (URL)

N Web browser

O Web page

_____ 11. An Internet Explorer 8 feature that tracks recently visited Web pages and sites.

_____ 12. A site that pays to be displayed with results at a search engine site.

_____ 13. To request a copy of a file or program from a remote server, such as a Web server, and then to save it on your local system or storage device.

_____ 14. A format used to save Web pages into a single archive, including all the page elements such as text and graphics.

_____ 15. A document on the World Wide Web that displays as a screen with associated links, frames, pictures, and other features of interest.

Multiple Choice

Circle the correct response.

1. The part of a text-based URL that identifies the company or organization that owns the Web site is called a:
   a. Top-level domain   b. Public domain   c. Domain name

2. The Web page that displays when you start Internet Explorer 8 is called a:
   a. Portal   b. Home page   c. Sponsored link

3. A group of related Web pages published to a specific location on the World Wide Web is called a:
   a. Favorites bar   b. Home page   c. Web site

4. A home page that contain links to frequently visited sites, up-to-the-minute news, weather reports, maps, and directories is called a:
   a. Portal   b. Favorites Center   c. Public domain

5. The highest level of the Domain Name System expressed as the last part of the domain name and represented by a period followed by three or four letters is called the:
   a. FTP   b. TLD   c. ISP

6. The toolbar located above the left side of the browser window that provides immediate access to a favorite Web site is called the:
   a. History   b. Command bar   c. Favorites bar

7. Text, buttons, pictures, or other objects displayed on Web pages that, when clicked, access other Web pages or display other sections of the active page are called:
   a. Hyperlinks   b. Link Select pointers   c. ScreenTips

8. The method used to divide a Web page into separate panes that appear to be one complete Web page is called:
   a. Tabs   b. Portals   c. Frames

9. A program that searches for keywords in files and documents or other Web sites found on the Internet is called a:
   a. Search engine   b. Portal   c. File Transfer Protocol

10. The set of rules for transferring data over the Internet is called a:
    a. Path   b. Protocol   c. Public domain

Apply **1A** skills from these Objectives:

1. Start Internet Explorer 8 and Identify Screen Elements
2. Navigate the Internet
3. Create and Manage Favorites
4. Search the Internet
5. Save and Print Web Pages

Skills Review | Project **1B** Playing Music from a Favorite Link

In the following Skills Review project, you will open a Web site, save it in Favorites, and locate and listen to a radio station that is near Lake Michigan City College. You can use the radio tuner to locate radio stations in your area and, if you have a sound card, you can listen to the radio as you work. Your screen will look similar to Figure 1.38.

Project Files

For Project 1B, you will save your file as:

Lastname_Firstname_1B_Radio

Project Results

Figure 1.38

(Project 1B Playing Music from a Favorite Link continues on the next page)

Content-Based Assessments

Skills Review | Project **1B** Playing Music from a Favorite Link (continued)

1 On the Windows taskbar, click the **Start** button, and then locate **Internet Explorer 8** on your system. On your system, click **Internet Explorer**. In the **Address bar**, type **http://windowsmedia.com/radiotuner** Press ⏎.

2 On the Favorites bar, click the **Favorites** button, and if necessary, click the Favorites tab. Then click **Add to Favorites** to display the **Add a Favorite** dialog box.

3 In the **Add a Favorite** dialog box, change the name to **Radio Station Guide** and then click the **Add** button.

Each category under Genres can be clicked to display additional stations. You can use links to visit a radio station or listen to the station. You can locate more stations by looking in the More Stations section or by using the Search box.

4 In the **Top Stations** list, click the first station to open the Windows Media Player.

5 In the Windows Media Player that displays, notice the buttons to pause the music and to close the Windows Media Player when you are finished listening.

The Windows Media Player opens and the station plays. This may take a few seconds as the streaming process occurs. Depending on the active settings on your system, Internet Explorer 8 may present a message box asking if you want to play the station in Internet Explorer. If you are prompted, click Yes to play the station.

6 On the Command bar, click **Page** and then click **Save As** to display the **Save Webpage** dialog box. In the **File name** box, type **Lastname_Firstname_1B_Radio** Change the **Save as type** to **Web Archive, single file (*.mht)**. In the **Save in** box, navigate to the **IE8 Chapter** folder that you created earlier in this chapter.

7 In the **Save Webpage** dialog box, click **Save**.

8 In the **Address bar**, type the drive—for example **f:**—and the location where you saved the file, and the most recent files in that location will display. Scroll down as necessary, and click the file name that you saved in Step 6.

9 On the Command bar, click the **Print down arrow** to open the **Print** dialog box. Click the **Print** button to print the saved Web page. Submit it as directed by your instructor.

10 In the **Windows Media Player** window, click the **Stop** button to stop the live broadcast, and then click the Media Player's **Close** button to close the pane.

11 Click the **Close** button to close Internet Explorer.

End **You have completed Project 1B**

Content-Based Assessments

Skills Review | Project **1C** Searching for Multimedia

In the following Skills Review, you will search for free downloads of multimedia for your music appreciation class at Lake Michigan City College.

   The Internet provides opportunities to locate and download several types of multimedia, such as animated graphics and sound or video files. However, the ease with which it is possible to copy these files does not always make it legally acceptable. The Fair Use Guidelines for Educational Multimedia allow for the use of copyrighted materials for educational purposes under certain circumstances. These circumstances address the purpose of use and the quantity of materials to be used. In addition, consideration must be given to whether the work has been put into the public domain, and there must be no effect on any potential market. Follow these instructions to perform a search for copyright-free sound files. Your screen will look similar to Figure 1.39.

Project Files

For Project 1C, you will save your file as:

Lastname_Firstname_1C_Multimedia

Project Results

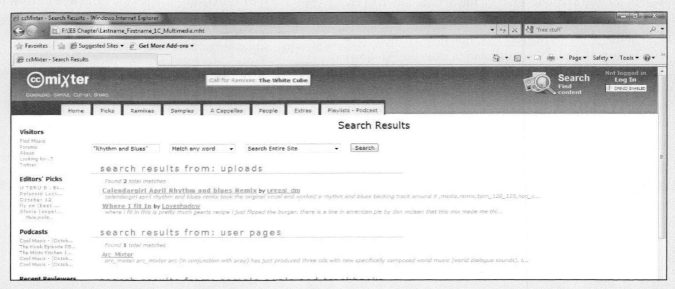

Figure 1.39

(Project 1C Searching for Multimedia continues on the next page)

Content-Based Assessments

Skills Review | Project **1C** Searching for Multimedia (continued)

1 On the Windows taskbar, click the **Start** button, and then locate **Internet Explorer 8** on your Start menu. On your system, click **Internet Explorer**.

2 In the **Address bar**, type **ccmixter.org** and then press Enter.

The ccMixter Web site displays. This site offers copyright-free and royalty-free sound files that are available for listening, downloading, remixing, and sharing through a Creative Commons license.

3 In the upper right corner, click the **Search Find Content** link.

4 In the **SearchFind content** pop-up that displays, in the **Search Text** box, type **"Rhythm and Blues"** including the quotation marks. Leave the default Match and What choices selected. Click the **Search** button.

5 On the Command bar, click **Page** and then click **Save As** to display the **Save Webpage** dialog box. In the

File name box, type **Lastname_Firstname_1C_ Multimedia** Change the **Save as type** to **Web Archive, single file (*.mht)**. In the **Save in** box, navigate to the **IE8 Chapter** folder that you created earlier in this chapter.

6 In the **Save Webpage** dialog box, click **Save**.

7 In the **Address bar**, type the drive—for example **f:**— and the location where you saved the file, and the most recent files in that location will display. Scroll down as necessary, and click the file name that you saved in Step 5.

8 On the Command bar, click **Print down arrow** to open the **Print** dialog box. Click the **Print** button to print the saved Web page. Submit it as directed by your instructor. **Close** Internet Explorer.

End **You have completed Project 1C** ———————————————

Content-Based Assessments

Apply **1A** skills from these Objectives:

- **1** Start Internet Explorer 8 and Identify Screen Elements
- **4** Search the Internet
- **5** Save and Print Web Pages

Mastering | Project **1D** Searching for Picture Space

In this project, you will search for free photographic services for the Alumni Club at Lake Michigan City College. The festivities on Homecoming Weekend were a great success and brought in alumni from around the state. Many sites on the Internet offer free space for storing and sharing pictures. From these sites, friends and family can view pictures and order copies of those pictures they want to keep. You can locate these services by searching the Internet. Follow these steps to locate and explore sites to determine which one best meets your needs. Your screens will look similar to Figure 1.40.

Project Files

For Project 1D, you will save your files as:

Lastname_Firstname_1D_Photo_1
Lastname_Firstname_1D_Photo_2

Project Results

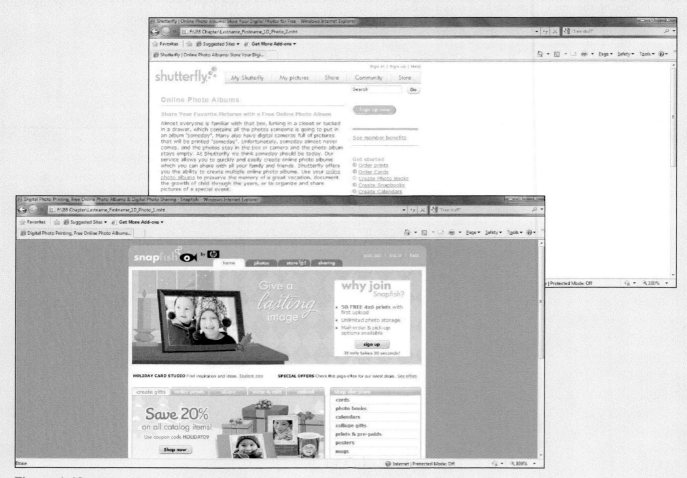

Figure 1.40

(Project 1D Searching for Picture Space continues on the next page)

Content-Based Assessments

Mastering | Project **1D** Searching for Picture Space (continued)

1 Open **Internet Explorer 8**.

2 On the **Address bar**, in the **Search** box, type **"free online photo albums"** and then press Enter. Several Web sites that offer free photographic services, such as storage and online photo albums, display.

3 In the list of **Web Results**, click the first link to display a Web site providing a free online photo album that is not a sponsored site. Scroll down the Web page until you locate information about how that online photo album works.

4 On the Command bar, click the **Page** button, and then click **Save As** to display the **Save Webpage** dialog box. In the **File name** box, type **Lastname_Firstname_1D_Photo_1** Change the **Save as type** to **Web Archive, single file (*.mht)**, and then in the **Save in** box, navigate to the **IE8 Chapter** folder that you created earlier in the chapter.

5 In the **Save Webpage** dialog box, click **Save**. Click the **Back** button to return to the search results.

6 Click another link in the list of Web Results to display another Web site providing a free online photo album. Scroll down that Web page until you locate information about how that online photo album works.

7 On the Command bar, click the **Page** button, and then click **Save As** to display the **Save Webpage** dialog box. In the **File name** box, type **Lastname_Firstname_1D_Photo_2** Change the **Save as type** to **Web Archive, single file (*.mht)**, and then in the **Save in** box, navigate to the **IE8 Chapter** folder that you created earlier in the chapter.

8 In the **Save Webpage** dialog box, click **Save**.

9 Use the **Address bar** to open each of the two saved files and then on the Command bar, click the **Print** button to print each of the saved files. Submit them as directed by your instructor.

10 **Close** Internet Explorer.

 You have completed Project 1D —————————————————

Apply **1A** skills from these Objectives:

1. Start Internet Explorer 8 and Identify Screen Elements
3. Create and Manage Favorites
4. Search the Internet
5. Save and Print Web Pages

Mastering | Project **1E** Locating Free Items

In the following project, you will search for free coupons, offers, and programs available on the Internet as marketing giveaway items for a club at Lake Michigan City College. As you become more familiar with the Internet, you will find free items such as software programs, computer equipment, computer services, and so on—available from Web sites. Not all of these offers are legitimate. Search the Internet for free items and review some of the offers. As you explore and evaluate the sites, remember that you should download programs and information only from sites you know and trust. Determine which sites make legitimate offers and which do not. Several criteria will help you with this determination. The following set of questions will be helpful as you perform an evaluation of a Web site:

- Is the site attractive and professional looking?
- When was the last time that the Web site was updated? Are there broken links or misspelled words?
- Who owns or sponsors the site? Do they seem qualified to make this type of offer?
- Are you required to provide personal data such as name, location, age, or credit or financial information in order to receive "free" items?

Your screens will look similar to Figure 1.41.

Project Files

For Project 1E, you will save your files as:

    Lastname_Firstname_1E_Free_1
    Lastname_Firstname_1E_Free_2

Project Results

Figure 1.41

(Project 1E Locating Free Items continues on the next page)

Content-Based Assessments

Mastering | Project **1E** Locating Free Items (continued)

1 Open **Internet Explorer 8**.

2 On the Address bar, in the **Search** box, type **"free stuff"** and then press Enter.

3 In the list of **Web Results**, click on the first link to display a Web site providing free stuff that is not a sponsored site. Scroll down the Web page until you locate the answers to the set of questions in the previous list to help you determine the legitimacy of the free offers.

4 On the Favorites bar, click the **Favorites** button, and then click **Add to Favorites** to open the **Add a Favorite** dialog box.

5 In the **Add a Favorite** dialog box, click the **New Folder** button. In the **Folder Name** box, type **Free Stuff** Click **Create**, and then click **Add** to add the Web site to the folder. A new folder named Free Stuff displays in the list of Favorites and the current Web site has been added to it.

6 On the Command bar, click the **Page** button, and then click **Save As** to display the **Save Webpage** dialog box. In the **File name** box, type **Lastname_Firstname_1E_Free_1** If necessary, change the Save as type to Web Archive, single file (*.mht), and then navigate to the **IE8 Chapter** folder that you created earlier in the chapter. Click **Save**.

7 Use the **Address bar** to open the saved file and then on the Command bar, use the **Print** button to print the saved file. Submit it as directed by your instructor.

8 On the **Address bar**, click **Back** to return to the Web Results. Scroll down the list to choose another Web site offering free stuff. Click the link to that Web site and answer the same set of questions to determine the legitimacy of the free offers.

9 On the Favorites bar, click the **Favorites** button, and then if necessary, click Add to Favorites to display the Add a Favorite dialog box. Be sure the **Free Stuff** folder is displayed in the **Create in** box, and then click the **Add** button.

10 On the Command bar, click the **Page** button, and then click **Save As** to display the **Save Webpage** dialog box. In the **File name** box, type **Lastname_Firstname_1E_Free_2** If necessary, change the Save as type to Web Archive, single file (*.mht), and then navigate to the **IE8 Chapter** folder that you created earlier in the chapter. Click **Save**.

11 Use the **Address bar** to open the saved file and then on the Command bar, use the **Print** button to print the saved file. Submit it as directed by your instructor.

12 On the Favorites bar, click the **Favorites** button if necessary, scroll down, and then click on the **Free Stuff** folder to display the two Web sites that you added to the folder.

13 Click anywhere outside the **Favorites** list to close it. **Close** Internet Explorer.

End You have completed Project 1E

Content-Based Assessments

Apply 1A skills from these Objectives:

- Start Internet Explorer 8 and Identify Screen Elements
- Search the Internet
- Save and Print Web Pages

Mastering | Project **1F** Protecting Your Privacy

In this project, you will search the Internet for information about yourself or other members of your family as part of your sociology project at Lake Michigan City College. The World Wide Web stores information about individuals in addition to companies. Many businesses store data about their clients and customers in databases on the Web so that they can place orders online. Families often store family trees on Web sites so that others can track their family history. Search the Internet for information about yourself to see what information is stored about you and others with your name. You might prefer to search for information about your family name to see if family tree data is available. The World Wide Web provides a means to easily gather personal information about you and your family. One of the best ways to learn about protecting your family and yourself is to look at the privacy policies of Web sites that you visit. Locate and review the privacy policy at any Web site you find that contains information about you or your family. Answer these questions:

- How does the Web site collect information about you?
- How is the information used?
- Are there options for you to prevent the collection and sharing of your personal data?

Your screen will look similar to Figure 1.42.

Project Files

For Project 1F, you will save your file as:

    Lastname_Firstname_1F_Privacy

Project Results

Figure 1.42

(Project 1F Protecting Your Privacy continues on the next page)

Content-Based Assessments

Mastering | Project **1F** Protecting Your Privacy (continued)

1 Open **Internet Explorer 8**.

2 In the **Address bar**, type **www.whitepages.com** and then press Enter to display the **WhitePages** home page.

3 Under **Find People**, type your first name, last name, your city, and your state in the appropriate boxes. Click the **Find** button. A number of results are displayed. Take a moment to review them.

4 Scroll down to the bottom of the results page. Click the **Privacy** link. Read the privacy policy to determine the answers to the questions listed at the beginning of this project.

5 On the Command bar, click the **Page** button, and then click **Save As** to display the **Save Webpage** dialog box. In the **File name** box, type **Lastname_Firstname_1F_Privacy** If necessary, change the Save as type to Web Archive, single file (*.mht), and then navigate to the **IE8 Chapter** folder that you created earlier in the chapter. Click **Save**.

6 Use the **Address bar** to open the saved file and then on the Command bar, use the **Print** button to print the saved file. Submit it as directed by your instructor.

7 **Close** Internet Explorer.

End **You have completed Project 1F** ─────────────────────

Outcomes-Based Assessments

Rubric

The following Outcomes-Based Assessment is an open-ended assessment. That is, there is no specific correct result; your result will depend on your approach to the information provided. Make Professional Quality your goal. Use the following scoring rubric to guide you in how to approach the problem and then to evaluate how well your approach solves the problem.

The *criteria*—Software Mastery, Content, Format and Layout, and Process—represent the knowledge and skills you have gained that you can apply to solving the problem. The *levels of performance*—Professional Quality, Approaching Professional Quality, or Needs Quality Improvements—help you and your instructor evaluate your result.

	Your completed project is of Professional Quality if you:	Your completed project is Approaching Professional Quality if you:	Your completed project Needs Quality Improvements if you:
1-Software Mastery	Choose and apply the most appropriate skills, tools, and features and identify efficient methods to solve the problem.	Choose and apply some appropriate skills, tools, and features, but not in the most efficient manner.	Choose inappropriate skills, tools, or features, or are inefficient in solving the problem.
2-Content	Construct a solution that is clear and well organized, contains content that is accurate, appropriate to the audience and purpose, and is complete. Provide a solution that contains no errors of spelling, grammar, or style.	Construct a solution in which some components are unclear, poorly organized, inconsistent, or incomplete. Misjudge the needs of the audience. Have some errors in spelling, grammar, or style, but the errors do not detract from comprehension.	Construct a solution that is unclear, incomplete, or poorly organized, contains some inaccurate or inappropriate content; and contains many errors of spelling, grammar, or style. Do not solve the problem.
3-Format and Layout	Format and arrange all elements to communicate information and ideas, clarify function, illustrate relationships, and indicate relative importance.	Apply appropriate format and layout features to some elements, but not others. Overuse features, causing minor distraction.	Apply format and layout that does not communicate information or ideas clearly. Do not use format and layout features to clarify function, illustrate relationships, or indicate relative importance. Use available features excessively, causing distraction.
4-Process	Use an organized approach that integrates planning, development, self-assessment, revision, and reflection.	Demonstrate an organized approach in some areas, but not others; or, use an insufficient process of organization throughout.	Do not use an organized approach to solve the problem.

Outcomes-Based Assessments

Apply a combination of the 1A skills.

GO! Think | Project **1G** Exploring Copyright Laws

Use the skills you practiced in this chapter to locate information on copyright laws and the appropriate use of copyrighted information for educational purposes. The major focus of legislation in this area includes findings on Fair Use.

Project Files

For Project 1G, you will save your files as:

Lastname_Firstname_1G_Copyright
Lastname_Firstname_1G_Fair_Use

Conduct a search to locate the Web site of the government organization that oversees copyright law and a Web site of an educational institution that pertains to Fair Use. Explore these Web sites to locate information on copyright and Fair Use. Save the government Web page as **Lastname_Firstname_1G_Copyright** Save the educational institution Web page as **Lastname_Firstname_1G_Fair_Use** Print each Web page and submit the documents as directed.

 You have completed Project 1G ————————————————

Computer Ethics, Copyright, and Plagiarism

OBJECTIVES

At the end of this chapter you will be able to:

1. Define Ethics, Systems of Personal Ethics, and Personal Ethics
2. Determine How to Make Ethical Choices
3. Decide Which Ethical Guidelines to Follow
4. Define Intellectual Property and Copyright
5. Understand Permissible Use of Copyrighted Material
6. Describe Copyright Infringement
7. Explain the Consequences of Copyright Infringement and How to Avoid Infringement
8. Define Fair Use
9. Explain How to Protect Your Work Against Infringement
10. Define Plagiarism

From Chapter 1 of *Go! with Ethics in Cyberspace Getting Started*, First Edition, Alan Evans. Copyright © 2010 by Pearson Education, Inc. Published by Pearson Prentice Hall. All rights reserved.

Introduction

The Internet has changed the way the world works. Now you can easily order merchandise from online merchants or auction sites with a few clicks of the mouse. Information is readily available on almost any imaginable topic, and most of the time, the information is accessible free of charge. In addition, with social networking tools like MySpace and Facebook, you can easily set up a profile of yourself and your interests and you can connect with your friends across cyberspace. Life is more convenient with the Internet!

However, what happens when you buy a product on the Internet, such as on eBay, and it doesn't arrive? What if the seller disappears with your money? Or, what if you receive a failing grade on your latest research paper for your history class because the Web sites you used for source material were inaccurate? Finally, what if you read rumors on MySpace about getting fired from your last job for shoplifting, and the rumor is completely untrue? Unfortunately, not everyone on the Internet is your friend, and many people behave unethically.

In this chapter, you will explore some of the ethical issues that you will encounter online, and you will learn strategies for detecting unethical behavior and protecting yourself from less scrupulous individuals. First, you will explore what ethics are and where they come from.

Objective 1
Define Ethics, Systems of Ethical Conduct, and Personal Ethics

What are ethics? *Ethics* is the study of the general nature of morals and of the specific moral choices made by individuals. Ethics are the guidelines you use to make decisions each day. For example, if you are standing in line at a convenience store and you see someone drop a dollar, the decision that you make about whether you tap the person on the shoulder and tell him about it or pick up and keep the dollar is an ethical choice you must make.

Does everyone have the same ethical values? Ethics vary widely from country to country and person to person. For example, in Western cultures (especially in America), privacy or secrecy is viewed as an inalienable right. However, in many Eastern cultures, people are perceived as having something to hide if they behave in a secretive manner. Every culture has its own unique system of ethical conduct. In this chapter, you will explore a few of the more common ethical systems.

In what types of ethical systems do individuals make their own decisions? *Relativism* is a theory in which there are no universal definitions of right and wrong; it is the individual's decision about how to act. With this system, individuals or groups of people can have completely opposing opinions about an ethical issue, and neither side is wrong. There are two relativism philosophies—subjective relativism and cultural relativism.

What is subjective relativism? With *subjective relativism*, each individual decides for himself what is right and wrong, and therefore, no one's views are more valid than anyone else's. This may seem like an ideal theory, but it doesn't work well in the real world. If everyone can just make their own decisions about right and wrong, then we would have a rather chaotic world. Consider if everyone could choose whether stealing from others is acceptable. You may feel that stealing is unethical, whereas the person next to you feels there is no problem with relieving a weaker individual of his property. You would never know when you could feel safe with your possessions and would constantly be worrying about some less ethical person stealing the lunch you just purchased.

What is cultural relativism? *Cultural relativism* means that right and wrong are defined by the accepted moral code of a society at a given place and in a given point in time (attitudes can change). For instance, in the United States, it is normally accepted that you will wear clothing (or at least cover certain strategic areas) when going out in public. Cultural relativism usually works better in practice if the alternative is leaving moral decisions up to individuals with no guidelines (as subjective relativists would).

Do some ethical values vary depending on the situation? Another ethical philosophy is *situational ethics*. The situational ethics theory, developed by American professor Joseph Fletcher, says that decision making should be based on the circumstances of a particular situation and not on fixed laws. Fletcher believed that other moral principles can be ignored to follow the overriding principle of love (meaning unconditional love for all people). This type of ethical system, because it depends solely on an individual's interpretation of what will increase love, is probably not ideal in a real-world setting either. Some people do change their values based on the situation, often for convenience. For example, a person might feel that stealing is wrong, but when he needs a ream of paper for his home laser printer, he may take it out of the supply closet at work because he doesn't have time to go to the office supply store. This is not an example of situational ethics as defined by Fletcher, but rather a case of a person with "flexible" ethics.

Are laws passed to guide people's ethical actions? *Rule utilitarianism* is an ethical theory that espouses establishing moral guidelines through specific rules (or laws). The idea behind this system is that if everyone adheres to the same moral code, society as a whole will improve and people will be happier. Many societies follow this system in general terms, including the United States.

Do religions influence ethics? Some ethical systems are based on religious traditions. For example, the expression **Judeo-Christian ethics** refers to the common set of basic values shared between Jewish and Christian religious traditions. These include behaviors like respecting property rights, treating others with kindness, respecting elders, and not interfering with other people's personal relationships.

Are there people who have no ethics? Everyone has a system of ethics to which they adhere. You may not agree with someone's ethical choices, but that doesn't mean they don't possess ethics. However, sometimes people act in a manner that violates the beliefs of the group or the geographical area in which they live. **Unethical behavior** means not conforming to a set of approved standards of social or professional behavior. This is different than **amoral behavior**, which is when a person does not know what is right or wrong and has no interest in the moral consequences of his actions.

Is unethical behavior a euphemism for illegal activity? Unethical behavior does not have to be illegal. **Laws** are groups of rules and principles that direct actions within a community. Laws are enforced by government agencies (such as the police, the Federal Bureau of Investigation, the Food and Drug Administration, and so on) and interpreted by the courts. It is not possible to pass laws that cover every potential behavior that human beings can engage in. Therefore, **societal ethics** provide a general set of unwritten guidelines for people to live by. However, as the interpretation of ethics varies from person to person, ethics are difficult and even impossible to enforce, and just because an action isn't illegal doesn't mean that it isn't unethical.

An example of an unethical but not illegal practice is supermarket slotting fees. These are fees that some supermarkets charge to produce companies and product manufacturers for the privilege of having their products placed on their store shelves. This is considered unethical by many people because it puts smaller companies at a disadvantage. Most smaller companies cannot afford to pay the fees. It is difficult to prove your product will sell to consumers if you cannot get it on to store shelves. Ice cream company owners Ben and Jerry faced this daunting problem when they first tried to get chain grocery stores to carry their fledgling products.

Which system of ethics works best? There is no clear superior choice among ethics systems. Most societies use a blend of the different systems. Regardless of the ethical system of the society in which you live, all ethical decisions are greatly influenced by personal ethics.

What are personal ethics? Every day you undertake specific actions and make statements to others. You make decisions about how to behave based on a set of criteria. Maybe you strive to be as happy as you possibly can be or maybe you try to ensure that others around you are safe and secure. Perhaps you are seeking to eliminate a source of discomfort or conflict in your life. Most likely, your words and actions are predicated on a combination of various goals. To select these words and actions, you follow a set of *personal ethics*, which is a set of criteria by which you make decisions that affect your personal life. Many people have well-defined principles they follow on a consistent basis. Other people behave less consistently and may not choose the same actions for a similar situation. Each person's personal ethics are unique to himself.

Your personal ethics may dictate that lying is inappropriate. But sometimes pressure to avoid unpleasant consequences may cause you to adjust this principle, and you may lie as a result. For instance, if you are applying for a job with an employer that you know has a high pay scale, you might consider exaggerating how much you are making at your current job in an attempt to gain a higher starting salary. Is an exaggeration a lie? Is it justified behavior to avoid being underpaid? You know you are worth a higher salary and will work hard for the company if it gives you the job. On the other hand, if you tell the truth, you may start at a lower salary making it tougher in the short term to maintain your lifestyle. The consequences of lying on most job applications can result in termination if you are caught. Weighing all these complex factors and deciding on a course of action is an ethical decision.

How do a person's ethics develop? There are many contributors to our ethical development, as Figure 1.1 illustrates. You may have thought about some of these factors, but others may have influenced you without your conscious knowledge. Surely, your family has a major impact on establishing the values you cherish in your life. You may also have a cultural bias toward certain moral positions.

Your religious affiliation is another major factor in the development of your ethical life. Most religions have established specific codes of ethical conduct. How these sets of ethics interact with the values of the larger culture is often challenging. Issues such as abortion, the use of the death penalty, and a country's involvement in war all can cause conflict between people's personal ethical systems and the established legal and societal ethics systems.

Define Ethics, Systems of Ethical Conduct, and Personal Ethics | **Ethics in Cyberspace**

As you mature, your life experiences will offer you opportunity to develop your personal ethics. Does the behavior you see around you make sense within the ethical systems of your family, your church, or your educational institution? Has your experience led you to abandon some ethical rules and adopt others? Have you modified how and when you apply these laws of conduct depending on what is at stake?

Finally, your daily life experiences influence your personal ethics. How well did things work out with the last ethical decision you made? If your decision was accepted by your family, peers, and society at large, you will likely make the same decision again under similar circumstances. Conversely, if you received criticism or a penalty for your actions, this might cause you to alter your ethical code in the future. Also, as you face decisions with higher stakes (changing jobs, getting married, and buying a home), the ethical framework you make decisions in may tend to shift.

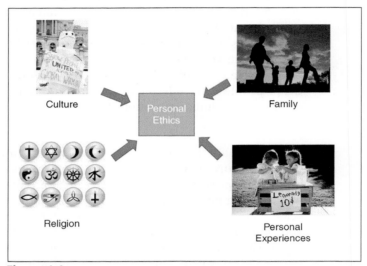

Figure 1.1
Many influences affect the development of your personal ethics. 1-1a: Courtesy of © Kirsten Hammelbo/Courtesy of www.istockphoto.com. 1-1b: Losevsky Pavel/Shutterstock. 1-1c: Emir Simsek/Shutterstock. 1-1d: www.indexopen.com.

Objective 2
Determine How to Make Ethical Choices

Do all decisions involve an ethical component? Not all choices require an ethical evaluation. For instance, if you buy a new iPod, you might choose green from the available color choices. The decision to choose green is a personal preference and doesn't involve an ethical decision.

Ethical choices involve *voluntary actions*—not situations where you react instinctively or are coerced. Suppose you see a toddler crossing the street and you notice a speeding car careening toward the child. You leap into the street and knock the toddler out of the path of the car, but you land on the child and break his leg. Yes, you harmed another human being—which is usually considered unethical—but you reacted by reflex in a scary situation. Therefore, you did not make an unethical decision even if your actions lead to harming a child.

What important points do you need to consider when making ethical choices? Each person has his or her own system of analyzing a situation and then applying personal ethics to that situation. However, asking three questions before taking action can be useful in helping you determine whether you are behaving in an ethical manner. These questions are:

- **If everyone took the same action, would society as a whole benefit?** You finish your bottle of energy drink and have to decide whether to toss the bottle out your car window or look for a trash receptacle. If everyone threw their trash wherever they felt like it, the world would soon look like a garbage dump. This would not benefit society.

- **Will your actions respect individuals or are you treating them as an ends to a means?** A casual acquaintance of yours (we'll call him Tom) works at the local arena in the ticket office. Your favorite band is coming to the arena, and tickets are already sold out. You don't really like Tom all that much, but you invite him over to your house for a barbeque and pretend to be his friend because you know he can get tickets that were held in reserve by management. Your treatment of the acquaintance is unethical because you are using him to satisfy your desire to see the concert.

- **Would an impartial observer consider your action fair to all parties involved in the decision?** Consider a scenario in which you go to a yard sale and find a rare t-shirt from an old rock concert that you know will sell for $4,000 on eBay. The person selling the shirt obviously is unaware of its value because it is priced at $4 and judging by the looks of his property, this person could use the money. You buy the shirt for $4 and leave. A neutral party analyzing this situation would probably not consider your actions ethical because the transaction was not fair to the person selling the t-shirt—you could have informed him of its value or offered him a more reasonable amount of money.

How does making ethical choices in a business setting differ from making personal ethical choices? Most personal ethical decisions involve few people, unless there is a great impact on society. When making ethical choices in the business world, careful consideration needs to be given to the stakeholders of the business. **Stakeholders** are those people or entities who are affected by the operations of a business. Before making an ethical choice for a business, you need to consider the effect it will have on all the stakeholders.

Imagine you are the plant manager of a small manufacturing company. The company has lost some key customers lately due to lower-priced competition from another company. You are under pressure to keep costs under control so that the company can compete effectively on price. You are concerned about the well-being of your employees if the plant has to make cutbacks due to lost sales. Your operation generates a small amount of liquid toxic waste, which costs $1,500 per month to have taken away. There is a storm drain out behind the plant into which you could empty the waste. Because it is summertime, there are thunderstorms almost every day. You think that if you dump the waste down

Determine How to Make Ethical Choices | **Ethics in Cyberspace** the drain just before a thunderstorm, the water will flow through the storm drain and sufficiently dilute the waste, minimizing any hazard. It is illegal to dump this waste in your state, but you rate the likelihood of getting caught as extremely low. Eliminating the disposal costs would help you keep the price of your product competitive and potentially save jobs at your company. If your company is caught dumping wastes, the fines and the negative publicity may cause you to suspend business temporarily, make cutbacks in your production, or go out of business altogether. Although it is laudable to try and protect your friends' jobs, consider the potential effect on these stakeholders:

- **Customers**—Customers who depend on your product to run their businesses may have increased costs from seeking other suppliers or may not be able to operate at all if your company closes.

- **Suppliers**—Other companies who sell you raw materials are dependent upon your business. If your business were forced to close or cut back, their sales would be impacted and they might be forced to terminate employees or even cease operations.

- **Employees**—Getting caught might mean temporary or permanent lay-offs for your employees, and the negative publicity may keep your employees from getting other jobs if prospective employers think they were involved in the illegal activities.

- **Shareholders (investors)**—If the company loses money because of your actions, shareholders will not receive a fair return on their investments.

- **Financial lenders**—If the company suffers financial setbacks because of your actions, banks who have loaned your company money may not be repaid. This, in turn, can potentially affect the bank's stakeholders in a negative way.

- **Society**—Perhaps there is a leak in the storm drainage system and the toxic waste seeps into local wells used for drinking water before the runoff from the thunderstorms can dilute it. Or, the waste was not sufficiently diluted by the thunderstorms and ends up in local creeks killing off fish and wildlife.

Obviously, there are many factors to consider in a business ethics decision that might not immediately occur to you. No matter what ethical choices you make, some people are not going to agree with them. That doesn't necessarily mean you are right and they are wrong (and vice versa) because many ethical choices (unless prohibited by law) are a matter of personal interpretation. However, common sense dictates that you should always strive to obey the law (unless you look particularly fetching in an orange jumpsuit).

Objective 3
Decide Which Ethical Guidelines to Follow

With computers and the Internet becoming ubiquitous tools in our personal and work lives, more and more ethical decisions revolve around or involve technology. *Cyberethics* refers to an ethical code that is followed when using computers and the Internet. Just as with other ethical

Ethics in Cyberspace | Computer Ethics, Copyright, and Plagiarism

codes, cyberethics are subject to the influences and interpretations of personal ethics.

Why should I be concerned about cyberethics? Aside from being an "ethical" individual, you need to be aware of the ways that unethical people may try to take advantage of you in cyberspace. Unfortunately, the convenience and global communication provided by the Internet comes with a price—it is often easier for unethical people to operate using the Internet. Among the main reasons are:

- **Anonymity**—Communications and transactions on the Internet are often conducted without knowing who the parties are or who is involved—at least without certainty (see Figure 1.2). If you inquire about the status of an order at Amazon.com, you can feel somewhat secure that you are dealing with an official representative of Amazon.com. But what about someone you met in a chat room? All you might know about that person for certain is his screen name. So when he tells you that you can get a better deal at XYZBookDealers.com than on Amazon.com, how do you know you can trust that person?

- **Quick, convenient exchange of information**—When information is in digital form (such as music or a video), it is easy to reproduce it or transfer it from one person to another. This makes violating owner-ship rights much easier (and harder to detect because of the anonymity factor mentioned previously).

- **Impersonal nature of computer communications**—People often say things in an e-mail or on a blog that they wouldn't say to someone in person. For some individuals, impersonal communications are an excuse to communicate in an unprofessional or even hostile manner. This can lead to people making claims about others that are inaccu-rate or just blatantly untrue, which potentially increases the likeli-hood of legal action.

"On the Internet, nobody knows you're a dog."

Figure 1.2
Anonymity, while sometimes a good thing, can facilitate unethical behavior. Courtesy of © The New Yorker Collection, 1993, Peter Steiner from cartoonbank.com. All Rights Reserved.

Decide Which Ethical Guidelines to Follow | **Ethics in Cyberspace**

What cyberethics guidelines should I follow? Because of the potential for problems, most schools and businesses have adopted **_acceptable use policies_**—which are guidelines regarding usage of computer systems—relating to the use of their computing resources. Your school most likely has a policy similar to Figure 1.3 that you should be familiar with. You can usually find it on your school's Web site, either under the Information Technology department section or the Student Policies section. If you can't locate it, check with the help desk personnel at your school; they can likely direct you to the appropriate Web page.

In making acceptable use of resources you are expected to:

- use resources only for authorized purposes;
- protect your user ID, password, and system from unauthorized use;
- access only information that is your own, that is publicly available, or to which you have been given authorized access;
- be considerate in your use of shared resources;
- demonstrate respect for principles of open expression;
- be aware of copyright laws as they apply to computer software and other materials that you may access with College computing resources.

Unacceptable use of resources may include but is not limited to:

- use of another person's system access, user ID, password, files, or data, or giving the use of one's system, user ID, password, files, or data;
- use of computer programs to decode passwords or access control information;
- attempt to disguise the identity of the account or computer you are using;
- attempt to gain unauthorized access to resources and data, including other's passwords;
- attempt to circumvent, subvert, or disable system or network security measures;
- engage in any activity that might be purposefully harmful to systems or to any information stored thereon, such as creating or propagating viruses, disrupting services;
- image files or make unauthorized modifications to College data;
- make or use illegal copies of copyrighted materials, software, or music, store such copies on College systems, or transmit them over College networks;
- creation or display of threatening, obscene, racist, sexist, or harassing material which is in violation of existing law or College policy;
- use of College system for any other illegal activity;
- monopolizing systems, overloading networks with excessive data, degrading services, or wasting computer time, disk space, printer paper, printer toner, manuals or other resources;
- use the College's system or networks for personal profit;
- installation of unauthorized hardware or software onto any College owned computer/network (the Information Technology Department is responsible for all installations, requests for exceptions

Figure 1.3
An excerpt of the Acceptable Use of Technology Policy from Montgomery County Community College, Blue Bell, PA.

Among other things, these policies usually cover the following:

- Keeping your account access (logon ID and password) secure from others

- Not running a business with college assets

- Prohibition of attempts to gain access to portions of the computer systems you are not authorized to use

- Illegally copying legally protected materials, such as CDs and DVDs

- Creation, distribution, or display of threatening, obscene, racist, sexist, or harassing material

- Prohibiting the installation of unauthorized software on the college's computers

- Conducting any illegal activities with college computing systems

If you have a job, you should also familiarize yourself with your employer's policy because it may differ substantially from your school's policy. For instance, most schools consider any work products—such as research papers, poems, musical compositions, and so forth—generated with school computing resources to be the property of the students who created them, unless the students were paid to create the works. With many employers, any work products created using company-provided computing resources are deemed to be the property of the company, not the employees who created them. Certain colleges and universities consider faculty-generated work products to be the property of the institution.

What guidelines should I follow if my school or employer doesn't have an acceptable use policy? The Computer Ethics Institute—*www.computerethicsinstitute.org/*—which was founded by the Brookings Institute, developed a well-known set of guidelines you can follow. They are known as the Ten Commandments of Computer Ethics and they are listed in the table in Figure 1.4.

Thou shalt not use a computer to harm other people.
Thou shalt not interfere with other people's computer work.
Thou shalt not snoop around in other people's computer files.
Thou shalt not use a computer to steal.
Thou shalt not use a computer to bear false witness.
Thou shalt not copy or use proprietary software for which you have not paid.
Thou shalt not use other people's computer resources without authorization or proper compensation.
Thou shalt not appropriate other people's intellectual output.
Thou shalt think about the social consequences of the program you are writing or the system you are designing.
Thou shalt always use a computer in ways that ensure consideration and respect for your fellow humans.

Figure 1.4
The Ten Commandments of Computer Ethics.

In the absence of clear policies, following the Ten Commandments of Computer Ethics should help you steer clear of most unethical behavior. But the Ten Commandments won't necessarily cover every area of cyberethics, nor do they provide specific guidelines. For additional guidance, you should investigate the behavior guidelines known collectively as netiquette.

What is Netiquette? As usage of the Internet grew, users developed certain conventions for communicating and exchanging information over various Internet services, such as e-mail, online chats, online role-playing games, and so on. This collection of guidelines is known as **netiquette**. The core rules of netiquette are outlined at *www.albion.com/netiquette/* and like the Ten Commandments of Computer Ethics, are designed to show respect for other computer users and to avoid annoying or harassing other people in cyberspace. You should explore these rules on your own. A summary of the core rules are:

- **Remember the human**—It is easy to forget when you are staring at a computer screen that you are communicating with other human beings. Therefore, you should remember to treat others with respect;

when communicating, act as if the person on the other end is standing in front of you.

- **Adhere to the same standards of behavior online that you follow in real life**—Most people are law-abiding in real life. Emulate real life with your online actions.

- **Know where you are in cyberspace**—Rules vary according to what part of cyberspace you inhabit. Passing on unsubstantiated rumors about an upcoming Indiana Jones film is acceptable in a movie fan blog. Posting these rumors in a response to a journalist blog entry on the *New York Times* Web site is not. Be sure to learn the acceptable behaviors for the part of the Internet you are surfing.

- **Respect other people's time and bandwidth**—Forwarding piles of useless e-mail to friends and family wastes their time. Consider if something is important before you pass it on.

- **Make yourself look good online**—For a job interview, a first impression is important. That is why you always show up on time in appropriate attire and well groomed. On the Internet, often the only impression you make is through your writing. Be clear, concise, and on topic, and people will be more likely to respect you.

- **Share expert knowledge**—The Internet is mostly about sharing information. If you are an expert in an area, share your knowledge to help others. A great place to do this is Yahoo! Answers. In Figure 1.5, you can view an example of a question on Yahoo! Answers. Everyone is an expert at something!

Figure 1.5
Yahoo! Answers is a free service that allows people to post questions that other "experts" can answer. It is an excellent place to share your knowledge.

- **Help keep flame wars under control**—*Flaming* is when people express an opinion with strong emotion, usually when they disagree with someone else's opinion. **Flame wars** occur when two or more people keep escalating an argument by exchanging messages. It is best not to perpetuate arguments by keeping the communication going with escalating anger.

- **Respect other people's privacy**—Don't go snooping around other people's computer files without their permission.

- **Don't abuse your power**—If you have an advantage over others, such as access to all company e-mail, don't abuse the privilege by reading private e-mails.

- **Be forgiving of other people's mistakes**—If someone makes an error, point it out politely and constructively.

Being familiar with the proper rules of netiquette should ensure that you don't inadvertently disrupt the Internet experience of other people and should assist you in behaving in an ethical manner.

You will explore some of the biggest ethical challenges facing users of cyberspace, and you alone will decide how to behave in ethical situations. Neither anyone nor anything, including the content in this text, can tell you how to behave. However, if you are aware of the unethical behavior that can take place in cyberspace, you can protect yourself from unethical practices and be better able to make informed, personal ethical choices. Next, we explore one of the biggest areas of ethical concern in cyberspace—the misuse and theft of intellectual property.

Objective 4
Define Intellectual Property and Copyright

The Internet has a wealth of information. With a few clicks of the mouse, you can locate a picture of almost anything by using Google image search or by searching on photo sites such as Flickr. If you have to prepare a research paper on global warming, you can easily find millions of sources on the subject, including professionally written articles. Does that mean you can freely use all these wonderful resources you locate on the Internet? No, you can't, because they are most likely someone else's property. Just as you wouldn't walk over to your neighbor's house and steal his garden hose, you can't just take property you find on the Internet.

What is property? Property comes in two general types: real and personal. **Real property** is considered immovable, such as land or a home, and it is often called real estate. **Personal property** comes in two types: tangible and intangible. We are all familiar with **tangible personal property**, which is something that has substance—you can touch it—and can usually be moved from place to place. Examples of tangible personal property are this textbook, an iPod, or a car. If someone walks past your desk while you are in the bathroom at school and steals your iPod from your book bag, the action is easily recognizable as theft. However, what if someone tries to steal your ideas? This action moves into the realm of one of the biggest problems in cyberspace—the theft of intangible personal property or intellectual property.

What is intellectual property? *Intangible personal property* cannot be touched—or potentially even seen—yet, it still has value. Most intangible property is classified as intellectual property. *Intellectual property* is property that is a product of a person's mind and is usually considered an expression of human creativity. Examples of intellectual property are art, music, songs, movies (or any type of video), designs, logos, patents for inventions, formulas (or methods of production), and computer software. It is important to distinguish the intellectual property from the physical medium that carries it. A music CD is not intellectual property. The music that is contained on a CD is the intellectual property, whereas the CD itself is merely a transport or delivery device. Likewise, a poem is intellectual property, but the piece of paper on which it is written is not. Just as tangible personal property is protected by law from theft, intellectual property is also protected.

Who came up with the idea of protecting intellectual property? John Locke was an English philosopher who developed many prominent theories about property rights, so perhaps he is considered the "father" of intellectual property rights. However, in the United States, the authors of the Constitution of the United States recognized that encouraging creativity was ultimately beneficial to society. As written in Article 1, Section 8 of the U.S. Constitution, Congress has the power to "promote the Progress of Science and useful Arts by securing for limited Times to Authors and Inventors the exclusive Right to their respective Writings and Discoveries." Giving a person exclusive control of the disposition of his intellectual property gives him a significant opportunity to make money from it. People might not be as motivated to generate creative ideas if they are unable to profit from them.

How is intellectual property categorized? Intellectual property is divided into broad categories: copyright, patents, trademarks and service marks, and trade dress. Each category has its own laws of protection.

According to Title 17 of the United States Code (17 USC 102), *copyright* protection can be granted to authors of "original works of authorship." In the United States and the European Union, copyrightable works include:

- Literary works, including computer software
- Musical works, including any accompanying words
- Dramatic works, including any accompanying music
- Pantomimes and choreographic works
- Pictorial, graphic, and sculptural works
- Motion pictures and other audiovisual works
- Sound recordings
- Architectural works

U.S. copyright law does not protect ideas, but rather the unique expression of an idea. You can't copyright common phrases, such as "bad boy" or "good girl," discoverable facts, such as water freezes at 32 degrees Fahrenheit, or old proverbs, such as, "To err is human, to forgive divine." However, you can copyright a creative twist on an old phrase, such as the one in Figure 1.6.

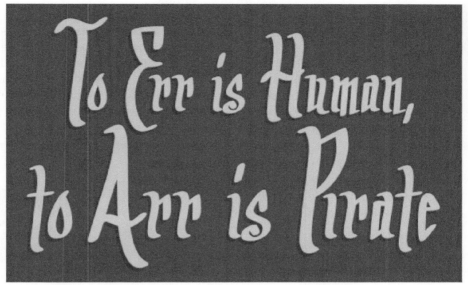

Figure 1.6
Although a parody of an old proverb, this phrase (offered on a t-shirt from Threadless.com) is sufficiently creative to allow it to be copyrighted.

Generic settings and themes of a story also can't be copyrighted. J.R.R. Tolkien wrote the *Lord of the Rings Trilogy*, which is about all types of monsters, wizards (Gandalf), and a young lad (Frodo) who overcomes great personal hardships and peril to save a land from the control of an evil being—Sauron. This didn't preclude writers, such as Terry Brooks, from creating stories like the *Sword of Shannara* in which a lad—Shea Ohmsford—overcomes personal peril and hardships to defeat an evil being—the Warlock Lord—who is bent on taking over the world. Mr. Brooks was merely precluded from using the same characters and plot lines as J.R.R. Tolkien but not the basic idea of a lone person overcoming odds against the forces of evil.

Patents are used to grant inventors the right to stop others from manufacturing, using, or selling (including importing) their inventions for a period of 20 years from the date the patent is filed. Generally, patents are not renewable but may be extended under certain circumstances. There are three basic types of patents:

- **Utility patents** are granted for inventing or discovering a novel and useful process, machine, product, or composition of matter (chemical entities and so on), which would include new improvements to existing products or methods.

- **Design patents** cover a new ornamental design for a product.

- **Plant patents** are granted for discovering or inventing a new type of plant.

A *trademark* is a word, phrase, symbol, or design—or a combination of all of these—that uniquely identifies and differentiates the goods of one party from those of another. A *service mark* is essentially the same as a trademark, but it applies to a service as opposed to a product. The Nike swoosh and McDonald's Golden Arches, shown in Figure 1.7, are both trademarks, whereas the FedEx logo is a service mark.

Similar to a trademark, a *trade dress* applies to the visual appearance of a product or its packaging. This would include interior decorations or the external design and ornamentation of a building, such as restaurants. The signature look of a TGI Fridays restaurant—red and white striped table cloths and the eclectic décor—or the unique shape of the Coca Cola glass bottle, shown in Figure 1.7, are examples of trade dress.

Figure 1.7
Instantly recognizable images such as the Nike swoosh, McDonald's Golden Arches, the Federal Express logo, and the Coca Cola glass bottle, all need protection from other companies that may try to produce look-alikes. 1-7a: Courtesy of McDonald's Corporation. 1-7b: Courtesy of PRNewsFoto/NIKE, Inc./AP Wide World Photos. 1-7c: Courtesy of © Dorling Kindersley/The Coca-Cola Company. 1-7d: Courtesy of FEDEX Corporation.

If I work for a company and develop intellectual property, do I own it? The answer to this question depends on the terms of your employment contract with your employer. Most companies—pharmaceutical companies, advertising agencies, movie production companies, and so on—in which intellectual property that has potential develops during employment, require their employees to sign agreements that any intellectual property developed while working for the company becomes the company's property. Mattel, the makers of Barbie dolls, filed a lawsuit against MGA Entertainment, which makes the successful line of Bratz dolls shown in Figure 1.8. Mattel alleged that Carter Bryant, the designer of the Bratz dolls, came up with the design for them while working at Mattel. Mr. Bryant's employment agreement with Mattel stipulated that Mattel was the owner of anything he designed while employed by Mattel. The court found for Mattel in this action and granted them damages of $90 million related to the violation of the employment agreement that Mr. Bryant had with Mattel. The court also awarded Mattel $10 million for copyright infringement. Mattel will now probably seek an injunction to stop MGA from making the Bratz dolls. Before you invent a new gasoline additive to solve the energy crisis, make sure you don't have an agreement in place with your employer that means it owns it instead of you!

Figure 1.8
Who actually owns the designs to the Bratz line of dolls depended on whether the creator designed them while he was working at Mattel. Coutesy of John Sleezer/Kansas City Star/Newscom.

How long does copyright last? Current copyright law in the United States grants copyright for the life of the author (creator) plus 70 years for original works. ***Works made for hire*** or ***works of corporate authorship***, which is when a company or person pays you to create a work and then that person or company owns the copyright to the work when it is completed, have copyright terms of 120 years after creation or 95 years after publication, whichever is shorter. After you die, the copyrights you own are transferred to your heirs. Therefore, if you write a best-selling novel in 2015 and die in 2082, your heirs can continue to earn money from the copyrighted novel until the year 2152. Copyright laws and terms of copyright are modified from time to time. The table in Figure 1.9 summarizes significant U.S. legislation on copyright.

Name of Law (Act)	Significant Points
Copyright Act of 1790	First U.S. copyright law—Copyright term of 14 years with 14-year renewal established.
Copyright Act of 1909	Extended copyright term to 28 years with a 28-year available renewal.
Copyright Act of 1976	Term extended to either 75 years or life of author plus 50 years. Renewal option eliminated. Registration no longer required.
Copyright Term Extension Act (CTEA) of 1998	Term now life of author plus 70 years. Works of corporate authorship now 120 years after creation or 95 years after publication, whichever endpoint is earlier. Extended term to 95 years from publication for works published prior to January 1, 1978.
Digital Millennium Copyright Act (DMCA) of 1998	Increased penalties for copyright violation on the Internet. Criminalized the production and dissemination of technology, devices, or services that could be used to circumvent measures that protect access or duplication of copyrighted works.
Artist's Rights and Theft Prevention Act of 2005	Designed to prohibit the piracy of movies by filming them in a theater. Made it illegal to distribute unreleased software—including beta software—which will later be sold for profit.

Figure 1.9
Major U.S. legislation affecting copyright.

If someone owns copyright to work, what exactly do they own?
Copyright holders own a bundle of rights that grant them the ability to exclusively do things with the copyrighted work. Section 106 of the U.S. 1976 Copyright Act grants these specific rights to a copyright holder:

- **Reproducing the work**—This means copying the entire work or just part of the work. Violations of this right may involve burning a copy of a music CD, photocopying a magazine article, copying software DVDs, or printing a cartoon character, such as Calvin from the *Calvin and Hobbes* cartoon strip, on a messenger bag using a Web site such as *www.cafepress.com.*

- **Preparing derivative works based upon the original work**—This means developing any media based on the original work regardless of what form the original is in. The X-Men were originally characters in a comic book, but they now appear in movies and video games. Andrew Lloyd Webber's *Phantom of the Opera* was developed into a movie script from the original play. You can't develop a derivative work without the copyright holder's permission, so you cannot just develop and sell your own movie script based on the X-Men or *Phantom of the Opera.*

- **Distributing the work to the public**—This means any method of distribution but usually involves selling the work. However, the copyright holder could also loan, rent, or give away the work. Copying a music CD and selling it (or even giving it) to your friend would be a violation of this right.

- **Public performance of the work**—Obviously, this applies to any audiovisual work such as plays, movies, songs, choreographic works, and literary readings. In the case of audio recordings, this also means digital audio transmission. You can't put a copy of the latest Batman movie up on YouTube or show the movie at your annual company meeting without permission of the copyright holder because that would constitute a public performance.

- **Public display of the work**—This usually applies to works of art such as paintings, photographs, and sculpture. Putting copies of photographs that someone else holds copyright to on your blog is a violation of this right.

When does copyright protection begin? Copyright begins when a work is created and fixed into a tangible, physical form, as illustrated in Figure 1.10. For example, if you make a video of your cat, as soon as you save the video to tape, your hard drive, or a DVD, the video is subject to copyright protection. There is no need for the video to be registered or even published for it to be protected.

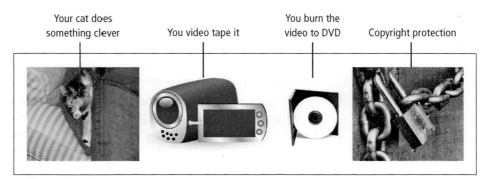

Your cat does something clever   You video tape it   You burn the video to DVD   Copyright protection

Figure 1.10
The copyright formula in action. 1-10b: Courtesy of Shutterstock. 1-10c: Courtesy of Aliciahh/Shutterstock.1-10d: Courtesy of Steven Paul Pepper/Shutterstock.

Can rights to a copyrighted work be sold? Rights to copyrighted work obviously have value if there is a demand for the work. Rights can be sold or granted for free to various individuals or entities in perpetuity or for a limited period of time. For instance, if you make a video of your band and your band is going to appear at a local bar, you might grant the bar owner the right to play your video in his bar for a specific period of time leading up to your performance. Or, you might grant the right to produce and sell DVDs of your performance to a distributor such as CD Baby—*www.cdbaby.com*—so you can earn some money from your fans. When your band appears at a local Battle of the Bands competition, you might grant the promoter the right to sell your CDs to fans at the concert and provide you with a percentage of the profits. Figure 1.11 shows many of the ways you can sell or grant rights to your copyrighted work.

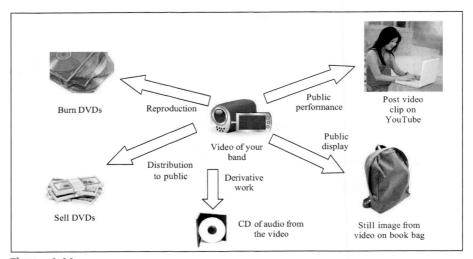

Figure 1.11

Exercising some of your rights from your copyrighted video. 1-11a: Courtesy of mashe/Shutterstock.1-11b: Courtesy of MalibuBooks/Shutterstock. 1-11c: Courtesy of Elnur/Shutterstock. 1-11d: Courtesy of Johanna Goodyear/Shutterstock.

Is buying a copyrighted work, such as a music CD or a book, the same as buying the copyright? In most cases you will encounter, buying a copyrighted work does not mean you are buying the copyright. When you buy a copyrighted item, such as a book, you own only the physical item. The copyright is unaffected and still resides with the copyright holder. Pearson Education, Inc. owns the copyright to this book. However, buying copyrighted works is covered by a rule of law known as the ***first sale doctrine***. You have the right to sell, lend, give away, or otherwise dispose of the item you purchase. This is the legal principle that allows public libraries to operate by lending out copyrighted material.

When you buy software, all you have usually bought is a license to install the software and use it on a specific number of computers. There may be other restrictions such as prohibition against using the software for profit. Check your license. For music CDs, all you have bought is the right to listen to the music in a private setting—your home, car, and so on. You cannot broadcast the music publicly, such as on the Internet. When you buy a DVD of a movie, again you have just bought the right to view the movie privately. You don't have the right to set up a screening for 50 of your closest friends in a local bar.

Are all works, such as music, books, movies, and so on, protected by copyright? Some works that were created never had a copyright holder. Examples are old traditional folk songs, the origin of which is unknown. For copyrighted works, they can lose their copyright protection. The term of protection can expire, the owner might not renew the copyright to extend the term—if renewal was available—or the owner may have intentionally relinquished the rights. Works without copyright protection are considered in the ***public domain***. Works in the public domain are considered public property and therefore, anyone can modify, distribute, copy them, and even sell them for profit.

When is a work considered in the public domain? It is difficult sometimes to determine when works enter the public domain. Factors that can influence the determination are the date of publication, whether the work was published, if copyright was applied for, if a notice is published, and many other factors. Copyright terms vary between countries, but many countries have similar laws. Under U.S. and European Union laws, a work is probably in the public domain if the following is true:

- The work was created or published before January 1, 1923 or at least 95 years before January 1 of the current year, whichever is later.

- The last surviving author died at least 70 years before January 1 of the current year.

However, there are exceptions to these rules. Therefore, you should probably only consider a work in the public domain that has provable, objective evidence that it is in the public domain or is clearly stated as being in the public domain.

The basic assumption you need to make is that all intellectual property you find on the Internet is protected by copyright (unless otherwise stated).

Objective 5
Understand Permissible Use of Copyrighted Material

Under what circumstances can copyrighted material be used? Many Web sites that contain copyrighted material also contain lengthy legal documents that delineate the *terms of use*—the terms governing your use of material—for the material that you download from the site. It is important for you to find and read the terms of use *before* using any copyrighted material on the site. Failure to read the terms of use does not absolve you from liability for using copyrighted material without permission. The terms of use Web page from Photos.com, as shown in Figure 1.12, clearly spells out your rights regarding photos downloaded from its Web site.

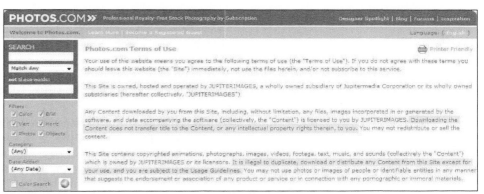

Figure 1.12
Excerpt of the Terms of Use from Photos.com. Notice how the highlighted portions severely limit your actions.

What if a Web site does not have terms of use? Ferreting out the terms of use on a particular site can sometimes be tricky. Look for links that say, Terms of Use, Restrictions, Copyright, Rules, FAQ, or even Contact Us. Sometimes, the usage terms are not displayed until you attempt to download copyrighted material. If you have done a thorough search and can't find them, then follow the instructions for contacting the organization that maintains the Web site and ask about the terms of use.

Can you use copyrighted material if it isn't permitted in the terms of use or there are no terms of use? Copyright holders can always grant permission to use copyrighted material to an individual or organization. Depending upon the material used and the specific nature of the usage, there may be a payment necessary to secure the rights to the copyrighted work. Sometimes though, simply asking permission is enough to get you the rights to use the work for a specific purpose free of charge.

Whom do you contact for permission? Whom to contact to obtain permission depends on the nature of the intellectual property. Sometimes it can be difficult to tell who actually owns the copyright, or the particular rights you need, to a piece of media. The creator may not be the copyright holder any longer. They may have sold their rights to another party.

The table in Figure 1.13 provides some suggestions about possible contacts for permission.

	Type of Media	Who to Contact
	Books or periodicals	Publisher or author
	Web site text	Webmaster, Web site owner, or author
	Photos, sculpture, paintings, or other art	Artist or photographer, publisher if it's print media, museum or gallery management if it's on display, or Web site owner
	Movies or video	Uploader if it's original video on a Web site, the production company (may not own the rights, but should know who does), film distributor, or screenwriter

Figure 1.13
Contacts for various types of media. 1-13c: Courtesy of Regien Paassen/Shutterstock. 1-13d: Courtesy of Ben Jeayes/Shutterstock.

What information is provided in a permission request? The most important items to include are a description of the work you are requesting permission to use—the exact parts if the entire work is not being requested—and the scope of your use. Be sure to include all of these key points:

- **Who you are**—Are you an individual or requesting permission on behalf of an organization or business? Be sure to include complete contact information (name, address, phone number, and e-mail address).

- **Which work you are requesting permission to use**—Make sure to describe the work completely and accurately. "That cool picture you posted on Flickr" isn't going to be sufficient because the photographer might have hundreds of pictures posted online!

- **Complete details of your usage of the work**—The copyright holder will be interested in why you are using the work, the context in which the work will be used, if the work is being used as part of a money-making project, where the work will be used (Web site, book, magazine, and so on), how frequently the work will be used, and if you are making any modifications to the work. You may be required to illustrate exactly how the work will be used, such as showing a mock-up of a Web page or the layout of a page in a book.

- **The timing of the request**—Be sure to indicate the date you intend to begin using the work and suggest a deadline for responding to the request. This might help speed up a response to your request for permission.

Be sure you receive a written response to your request authorizing the usage you requested. You should never assume that no response is an indication of a tacit approval on the part of the copyright holder. Remember, copyright holders are under no obligation to grant your request or even to respond to it. As the owner of the work, they alone decide if and when it can be used by someone else. Therefore, you should always have a back-up plan in case your request for permission is denied or ignored.

Objective 6
Describe Copyright Infringement

What happens if you use copyrighted material without permission of the copyright holder? A violation of the holder's rights is known as *copyright infringement*. According to section 501 of Title 17 of the United States Code (17 USC 501), "Anyone who violates any of the exclusive rights of the copyright owner . . . is an infringer of the copyright or right of the author." Examples of copyright infringement are:

- Right-clicking on a photo you find on a Web site and saving it to your hard drive,

- Copying a music CD and giving it to a friend,

- Using a peer-to-peer file sharing service, such as BitTorrent, to download a new action movie—in other words, you did not buy the movie from an authorized agent of the copyright holder.

- Taking a photograph of a work displayed in a museum and using it in a work you are publishing.

- Setting up a fan Web site dedicated to your favorite TV show that features clips from the TV show and the theme music from the show.

- Copying a copyrighted software program and giving it to your friend.

- Singing a copyrighted song in a video with your friends and then posting it on YouTube.

When judges consider cases of infringement, they generally examine the extent to which there is a substantial similarity between the copyrighted work and the infringing work. Obviously, if you copy an image from the Internet or burn a copy of a CD, that would be an exact copy and clearly is infringement. What if you wrote a play based on characters from *Star Wars*? Or, what if you wrote a story with a similar plot to an episode of your favorite TV show? The courts will have to determine how similar the characters and plot are to the copyrighted works and if infringement exists. This is a subjective process, and infringement cases are usually decided on the merits of each case.

Is putting a URL that points to a copyrighted Web site on a site (such as a MySpace page) considered copyright infringement? A URL is a specific direction for finding a specific Web page on the Internet. It is not debatable or open to interpretation, and therefore, it is considered a fact. Because facts cannot be copyrighted, you can list all the textual URLs you want on your Web site without committing copyright infringement. However, be sure you do not take copyrighted material, such as a logo or character, to use as a picture link to a Web site, such as using a picture of Mickey Mouse to link to the Disney Web site, as this may constitute infringement.

What are the most common types of copyright infringement in cyberspace? Illegally copying or using software, music, video, and photographs top the list of digital rights violations on the Internet. Aside from the copyright laws mentioned earlier, many court cases have helped frame the context of digital copyright infringement in the United States. The table in Figure 1.14 lists some of these cases.

Year	Case Name	Major Issue(s)	Significant Outcomes
1976	*Sony v. Universal Studios*	Universal alleged that manufacturing and marketing of VCRs allowed people to violate their copyrights on television shows and movies.	Time shifting (watching a show at a different time than when it was broadcast) did not have a significant effect on the market for the copyrighted work. Time shifting for personal use is permissible.
1999	*RIAA v. Diamond Multimedia Systems Inc.*	Recording Industry Association of America (RIAA) alleged that the Rio portable music player (MP3 player) allowed users to violate music copyright.	Copying a recording to make it portable is deemed "space shifting" and permissible under U.S. copyright law.
2001	*RIAA v. Napster*	RIAA sued Napster for allowing users to violate copyright by downloading copyrighted songs.	Napster was forced to shut down because they were unable to block 100% of illegal downloads of copyrighted material. Napster later reopened as a site that sells legally licensed music.
2005	*MGM Studios, Inc. v. Grokster, Ltd.*	MGM and a group of other movie studios, songwriters, recording companies, and music publishers sued Grokster and Streamcast for allowing members to download copyrighted music and videos.	The U.S. Supreme court decided that peer-to-peer file sharing companies Grokster and Streamcast can be sued for copyright infringement when their users illegally exchange copyrighted files.

Figure 1.14
Major court cases involving digital rights violations.

Ethics in Cyberspace | Computer Ethics, Copyright, and Plagiarism

How are music and video copyrights usually infringed? The major sources of infringement for music and video are:

- **Peer-to-peer file sharing**—Peer-to-peer (P2P) networks, such as Limewire, BitTorrent, and Morpheus, are virtual networks deployed across the Internet that enable two computers running common P2P software to connect directly with each other and access files stored on the other computer's hard drive. These networks provide users with access to files on millions of other computers and have the ability to upload and download files from multiple computers simultaneously. Although peer-to-peer networks can be used to exchange files legally, they are often used to exchange copyrighted materials such as music and movies.

- **Direct exchange or copying**—Many people freely burn copies of CDs and DVDs for their friends or allow their friends to copy the entire contents of their portable media player (iPod).

- **Uploading to file-sharing sites**—Many of the files on sharing sites such as YouTube are from copyrighted material. Just because you can record a television show for personal use because of the *Sony v. Universal Studios* decision, it doesn't mean you can upload it on YouTube for everyone to watch.

Are people who upload music videos or clips from TV shows to YouTube liable for copyright infringement? Although many people think that YouTube would be responsible for any infringement, anyone who uploads copyrighted material could be held responsible. Currently, Viacom has lodged a $1 billion damage suit against YouTube and its parent company Google for copyright infringement related to the many television shows and movies to which it holds copyright. The suit alleges that YouTube has permitted 160,000 clips of unauthorized Viacom-owned content to be viewed billions of times. Google is defending itself by pointing to the 1998 Digital Millennium Copyright Act, which is designed to protect Internet companies from copyrighted content uploaded by their users. If YouTube wins the suit, Viacom could still go after individual uploaders or even viewers of the material for compensation. And if YouTube loses the suit, it may have to come to the uploaders for compensation.

Why would YouTube be able to collect damages from users for uploading protected content? Although users might not have paid attention when uploading videos, they did agree not to infringe copyright when uploading the files, as shown in see Figure 1.15. Therefore, YouTube has potential legal recourse to recover damages from users who ignore the terms of use on their Web site. If you have uploaded copyrighted material to YouTube or any other file sharing site, you should remove it immediately.

Describe Copyright Infringement | **Ethics in Cyberspace**

You said you have copyright to the video or permission to upload it. Do you?

Figure 1.15
Those who upload videos to YouTube agree not to infringe copyright.

Why would a band object to uploading a music video to YouTube or a Web site? Wouldn't it be free publicity for them? Each time someone plays a video that is uploaded to a Web site, the performer (singer or band), the songwriter, and the music publisher lose money. If the person listening to the song forgoes buying the music, the performer and his record company lose money. However, a song played on a Web site is considered a live performance. Songwriters and music publishers (organizations that promote songwriters' compositions to record companies and take a cut of royalty payments) are entitled to a royalty every time a song is played live, on the radio (or other broadcast medium), or on the Internet. Normally, royalty fees are paid by radio stations and other entities performing music to Performing Rights Organizations (PROs) such as The American Society of Composers, Authors and Publishers (ASCAP), Broadcast Music, Inc. (BMI), and SoundExchange. The PROs then forward the royalties to the songwriters and music publishers. Because you are not paying royalties to a PRO when the video is viewed on YouTube, someone is losing revenue.

How significant is the loss of revenue from music and video infringement? It is difficult to quantify the impact on revenue. A recent June, 2008 study by the University of Hertfordshire revealed that on average there are 842 illegally copied songs on the average 14-to-24-year-olds' digital music players. This accounts for 48 percent of the average collection of music. So potentially, music revenue might be cut in *half* by illegal file swapping. If you copy 40 songs from a friend's iPod instead of buying them on iTunes for $.99 each, you've potentially deprived numerous entities (record companies, performers, and songwriters) of $39.60 of revenue.

Ethics in Cyberspace | Computer Ethics, Copyright, and Plagiarism

How are the rights of software copyright holders usually violated?
Illegally using copyrighted software is often referred to as *software piracy*.
If you have ever given a friend a copy of a copyrighted software program
to install on his computer, then you are intimately familiar with a common
method of infringement. The Business Software Alliance (*www.bsa.org*),
an organization that has among its goals the prevention of software
piracy, provides a few other examples of software piracy that you may
not have thought about:

- Taking advantage of upgrade offers without possessing a required
  older version of the software

- Using software designed specifically for academic or non-commercial
  use for commercial purposes

- Installing a licensed copy of software on more computers than the
  license permits

- Downloading copyrighted software from peer-to-peer networks

- Buying pirated copies of software on Internet auction sites

- Counterfeiting software (copying it for the express purpose of selling it
  as if it were the real, licensed product)

- Selling computers preloaded with illegal copies of software already
  installed

You need to exercise caution when buying software online to ensure that
it is a real, fully licensed copy. Otherwise you might not even be able to
use the software that you bought. Most modern software requires a serial number for installation. And usually, the first time you launch the
software after installation, this serial number is checked against a database to ensure the software has not been installed on more computers
than the license allows. This is a form of *digital rights management*.
If you are buying illegally copied software on the Internet, you might not
be able to activate it because too many other people have already
installed it with the serial number you have.

How widespread is software piracy? In some countries, such as China,
it can be described as rampant. As the table in Figure 1.16 shows, piracy rates can exceed 90 percent in some areas of the world. Although less
of a problem in the United States on a percentage basis, the U.S. still
leads the world in lost revenue from software piracy.

Describe Copyright Infringement | **Ethics in Cyberspace**

Country	Percentage of Installed Software that Is Pirated	Estimated Economic Loss (U.S. $ in Millions)
Bangladesh	92	$92
Brazil	59	$1,617
China	82	$6,664
France	42	$2,601
Kenya	81	$28
India	69	$2,025
Russia	73	$4,123
United Kingdom	26	$1,837
United States	20	$8,040

Figure 1.16
2007 software piracy statistics for selected countries per the Business Software Alliance.

Why is photographic infringement widespread on the Internet? The Web is a visual medium. Therefore, many pictures are displayed on Web sites. With the proliferation of camera phones and according to IDC, a marketing intelligence firm, forecasted sales of 8.5 million digital cameras per year by 2011, it is not surprising that millions of photos are uploaded to the Internet every day. Photo-sharing sites like Flickr, Picasa, and Photobucket give anyone the ability to post and share photos online. Of course the widespread availability of images also gives rise to people appropriating them for their own use. Need a picture of the Grand Canyon for your PowerPoint presentation? Using Google image search or Flickr's search feature will probably enable you to find an appropriate image. And right-clicking and saving it to your hard drive is simple, which is a major reason why infringement of photo copyright is so widespread on the Internet.

Who owns the copyright to a photo? When the photo is taken, the photographer owns the copyright, assuming the photographer was taking photographs in a public place or had permission from the property owner to take photos. In the U.S., you are free to take photos in public places such as streets, public parks, or sidewalks. Property owners can prohibit photography on their premises, so be sure to enquire about the right to take photographs in privately owned space. But if the photographer was working on a "work for hire" basis (his employer was paying him to take the photos), usually the copyright will belong to the employer.

Do people in the photograph have any rights to the photograph? The Fourth Amendment to the U.S. Constitution and various other laws and court cases have recognized Americans' rights to certain amounts of privacy. Being photographed without your consent generally falls under the realm of privacy. Usually, if a photographer takes a picture with you in it that he knows he wants to sell for publication, he will ask you to sign a *model release*. A model release usually grants the photographer the right to use an image of the model (or subject of the photo) commercially. If a picture of you is published without your consent, you might have the basis for a lawsuit. However, be aware that there are many times when you agree to allow your photograph to be taken and used commercially (usually for publicity). You may agree to these conditions when you enter a contest, buy a ticket for a museum, or enter an event such as a marathon or a concert. So make sure you read the conditions of sign-up forms and the back of tickets to ensure you understand any rights you are surrendering.

What happens when a photographer sells or transfers rights to a photograph? Often the photographer will sell the rights to the image for publication on a Web site, in a magazine, and so on. Selling the rights might not transfer copyright depending upon the type of rights sold. The most common rights are:

- **Exclusive photo rights**—The purchaser of these rights is the only one who may use the photo. These rights can be limited to a specific industry or might specify no publication in vehicles of competing organizations. For instance, you may take a photo of Old Faithful that a travel magazine wishes to use on their cover. The rights may preclude you from selling exclusive rights to other travel periodicals but not from selling the rights to a souvenir company.

- **One time or lease rights**—Rights to photos can be sold for a certain number of instances (someone can publish the photo three times in their magazine) or for a specific duration (display the photo for a year on their Web site).

- **All rights**—This transfers all rights to the photo to the buyer.

How do you know if a photo on the Web is copyrighted? Usually information is attached to a photo to indicate it is copyrighted or that all rights are reserved. If there is not information attached, the safest course of action is to assume that the photo is protected by copyright. Figure 1.17 shows an example of information attached to a photo that is copyright protected. Or, there may be information that says the photo is in the public domain or free for anyone to use. If there is no information on copyright, your safest assumption is that you can't use it without permission of the copyright holder.

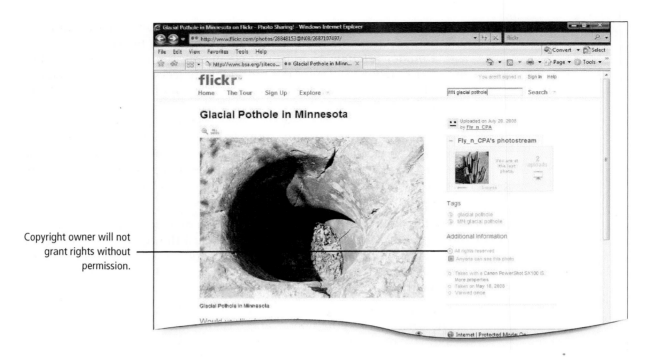

Copyright owner will not grant rights without permission.

Figure 1.17
Although this photographer's work is available to anyone searching Flickr, he has reserved all rights so you cannot use his photo without permission.

Objective 7
Explain the Consequences of Copyright Infringement and How to Avoid Infringement

What happens to people who infringe on someone's copyright?
Infringing copyright risks a potentially long and costly legal battle. At best, you might receive a slap on the wrist, but the worst-case scenarios can involve large fines and jail time. The penalties vary depending upon the laws relating to the type of property being infringed and the country whose laws are in effect. In the United States (17 USC 504), statutory civil penalties for software infringement can be up to $150,000 per software program copied. And this is in addition to the $250,000 fine and 5-year jail sentence for the criminal charges that can be levied against you by the United States government.

How will you know if someone thinks you have infringed on their copyright? If you used a picture of Mickey Mouse on your Web site without permission, you might receive a *cease and desist letter* from the Walt Disney Corporation. This letter is a request to immediately stop the alleged infringement. The letter should describe the alleged infringement and require you to reply by a certain date to indicate that the infringement has ceased. If you receive such a letter, you should take it seriously. In our example, be sure you remove the picture of Mickey from your Web site and respond by the due date in a letter indicating what you have done to stop the infringement.

Ethics in Cyberspace | Computer Ethics, Copyright, and Plagiarism

What if you don't believe you committed copyright infringement?
Seek competent legal advice from an attorney specializing in intellectual property law and have the attorney assist you in crafting a reply to the cease and desist letter explaining your side of the story. You may be able to prove you did not infringe if you have proof you received permission to use the material or if you can make a successful argument for a fair use exception (we discuss fair use later in this chapter). Because the next step taken against you might be a formal legal action, the help of an attorney is critical at this stage. If the issuer of the cease and desist letter is not satisfied with your response or your actions, the next step is most likely a lawsuit against you.

What happens if a person loses a court case and is found guilty of infringement? If someone is found guilty of infringement, the court might provide for the following types of relief for the copyright holder:

- Issue an *injunction*—a court order prohibiting a certain action—that forces you to stop the infringement. This can include recalling or destroying all copies of printed matter containing the infringing material, stopping the performance or display of the infringing work (in the case of music, a play, art, or a video), removing the material from your Web site, and so on.

- Confiscation and destruction of the infringing items, such as an entire piece of artwork, t-shirts you were selling with infringing images, and so on.

- Make the violator pay actual damages or statutory damages per the copyright statues. *Actual damages* are provable losses sustained by the company such as lost revenue. *Statutory damages* are prescribed by law and in the U.S. currently range from $750 to $30,000. However, if the court finds there was *willful infringement* (such as intentionally ignoring a copyright notice that was clearly evident), under U.S. law, the penalties can be increased up to $150,000.

Why would anyone risk copyright infringement? With such serious penalties, you would think everyone would respect copyright. Why run the risk of a large fine just to enhance a MySpace page with a cool image? Here are a few reasons why students have indicated that they risk copyright infringement:

- **Low likelihood of getting caught**—People often base their actions on their chances of being discovered. If you download three songs from a P2P Web site or copy a CD from a friend, are you likely to get caught? Probably not, but that still doesn't make it an ethical action. You are still depriving an artist of his livelihood. However, some people will always commit acts that are illegal (or generally accepted as unethical) if they think they can escape notice.

- **Everyone is doing it (the tax cheat defense)**—Many U.S. citizens who cheat on their taxes state the reason for doing so as "Everyone else does it so why should I miss out?" However, numerous surveys have been done that prove that the vast majority of Americans do not cheat on their taxes. But, this herd mentality tends to affect some people's actions, especially if the likelihood of getting caught is low.

Explain the Consequences of Copyright Infringement and How to Avoid Infringement | **Ethics in Cyberspace**

- **No one would come after an individual**—Many students are under the impression that only large corporations with a lot of money are being sued for copyright infringement. But if you ask the over 20,000 individuals who have been sued for illegal file sharing by the RIAA since 2003, you might have a different opinion. Most of these cases were settled out of court for amounts ranging from $3,000 to $4,000, but court awards have gone higher. The RIAA is tending to target *supernodes* (people who offer thousands of music files on P2P networks for sharing) for their legal action, but they can just as easily target you for downloading a couple of CDs of songs.

- **I'm only downloading one song . . . it isn't worth that much**—Whether you are stealing one candy bar from a convenience store or a Corvette from the mall is irrelevant. They are both still crimes. Because copyright infringement is also prohibited by law, copying one song is still stealing.

Now let's explore the concept of fair use, which is one way (besides obtaining permission to use copyrighted material) that you can steer clear of copyright infringement and keep yourself from being tied up in unnecessary legal entanglements.

Objective 8
Define Fair Use

Are there any instances in which you can use copyrighted work without permission of the copyright holder? In original copyright law, there were no exceptions to obtaining the copyright holder's permission to use the work. However, a number of court cases over the years served to develop the doctrine of fair use. In 1976, the concept of fair use was added to the copyright laws and is now codified in section 107 of the Copyright Act (17 USC 107). *Fair use* provides for people to use portions of a copyrighted work for specific purposes without receiving prior permission from the copyright holder. However, there are no specific rules on exactly what amount of use constitutes fair use, which means each case has to be decided on its own merits.

What types of activities constitute fair use? A list of examples of approved fair use activities from U.S. court cases is provided in the 1961 Report of the Register of Copyrights on the General Revision of the U.S. Copyright Law. Although this list is not all-encompassing, it provides a good start for evaluating fair use activities. Following are some examples:

- Quotation of excerpts in a review or criticism for purposes of illustration or comment.

- Quotation of short passages in a scholarly or technical work, for illustration or clarification of the author's observations.

- Use in a parody of some of the content of the work parodied.

- Summary of an address or article, with brief quotations, in a news report.

Ethics in Cyberspace | Computer Ethics, Copyright, and Plagiarism

- Reproduction by a library of a portion of a work to replace part of a damaged copy.

- Reproduction by a teacher or student of a small part of a work to illustrate a lesson; this is commonly known as educational fair use.

- Reproduction of a work in legislative or judicial proceedings or reports.

- Incidental and fortuitous reproduction in a newsreel or broadcast, of a work located in the scene of an event being reported.

Copying a CD or DVD that you own to serve only as a backup copy in case yours is damaged is also usually—but not definitively—considered fair use, as established by certain court cases. However, under the Digital Millennium Copyright Act, it is illegal to circumvent any technology that is employed to prevent media from being copied. Therefore, if you have a CD, DVD, or MP3 file that has copy protection technology—also known as digital rights management—in place, you are not legally entitled to copy it even though there are probably software programs available on the Web that could allow you to do so. This represents a conflict between the body of case law and a legal statute and remains a source of confusion and frustration for consumers.

What factors do the courts consider when determining fair use?
There are four factors used to consider whether usage of copyrighted material is considered fair use:

- **The purpose and character of the use**—A major factor here is whether the user will profit from the work. Profiting from the work usually precludes a fair use exemption except in the case of transformative works (like parody). For use to be **transformative**, the work must be altered in some manner that causes the user or viewer of the work to derive another meaning from the work. Satire is a technique that is used to poke fun at political views, moral principles, or social mores usually in an attempt to provoke change or draw attention to a particular issue. Parody is considered transformative and therefore is usually viewed as fair use.

- **The nature of the copyrighted work**—Factual works have less copyright protection under the fair use doctrine than creative or fictional works. Commonly known or discoverable facts cannot be copyrighted although a unique expression of facts can be copyrighted. "The sky is blue" or "The diameter of the moon is 2,160 miles" can't be copyrighted. Therefore, excerpts from factual works are much more likely to be considered fair use.

- **The amount and substantiality of the portion used in relation to the copyrighted work as a whole**—The courts look primarily at whether you used only as little of the work as possible to accomplish your goal. You should also stay away from using parts of a work that are key to making it special or creative. For instance, using a small passage from *Gone with the Wind* that is incidental to the main plot would most likely be considered fair use. Using key lines from the last scene where Rhett leaves Scarlett would be viewed much less favorably.

Define Fair Use | **Ethics in Cyberspace**

- **The effect of the use upon the potential market for or value of the copyrighted work**—If your use would affect the ability of the copyright holder to sell or otherwise profit from his protected work, this tends to argue against fair use because there is little that is "fair" about affecting someone's ability to earn money. Copying a song from a band's CD and posting it on YouTube as a video (with still pictures of the band) would not be considered fair use. Although you could argue that using a different medium for the work (video) is transformative because people can listen to the song for free on YouTube, you damage the market value of the song.

Does being a student who uses educational (academic) fair use give me a defense for using any copyrighted material I want? Unfortunately, this is what many students and some instructors think. However, even educational fair use has to be reasonable and meet the four tests cited previously to be deemed a defense against copyright infringement.

Educational fair use greatly facilitates teaching and learning, which tends to be a fluid process. As lesson plans change frequently based on current events, teachers and students might find it difficult to obtain the permissions they need in a timely fashion to ensure content in classroom discussions, multimedia, and research papers are current. Because there are no fixed guidelines on the quantity of material that can be used and still be considered fair use, various groups of educators have met to develop guidelines to assist teachers and students. The Consortium of College and University Media Centers developed suggested guidelines for various types of media, excerpts of which are summarized in the table in Figure 1.18. The full text of the guidelines can be found on the American Distance Education Consortium Web site at *www.adec.edu*.

Media	Quantity
Motion media	Up to 10% or 3 minutes, whichever is less
Text material	Up to 10% or 1,000 words, whichever is less
Music, lyrics, and music videos	Up to 10%, but in no event more than 30 seconds, of the music and lyrics from an individual musical work (or in the aggregate of extracts from an individual work)
Illustrations and photographs	a) One artist: No more than 5 images b) Collections of works: No more than 10% or 15 images, whichever is less
Numerical data sets (databases and spreadsheets)	Up to 10% or 2,500 fields or cell entries, whichever is less

Figure 1.18
Suggested fair use guidelines.

Again, these are only suggested guidelines and depending upon the individual case, you may be able to make a successful argument under the fair use doctrine to use a greater percentage of a given work. Many educational institutions publish their own guidelines, so be sure to inquire about your school's guidelines.

Objective 9
Explain How to Protect Your Work Against Infringement

What work do I have that could be infringed upon? The answer to this question depends on whether or not you are creating valuable intellectual property. Are you a prolific, capable photographer who uploads thousands of images to Flickr? Are you writing a blog that is read by a lot of people every day? Are you posting original research that you have done to Web pages on the Internet? Do you have a band and have you posted videos of original performances on YouTube? If so, you might just have intellectual property worth protecting.

Is copyright protection automatic? Registering copyright for works you think will be valuable is always a good idea. Although you do have copyright without registration, registering your copyright provides certain advantages, as shown in the table in Figure 1.19.

Advantages (Per the U.S. Copyright Office)	Explanation
Registration establishes a public record of the copyright claim.	Much harder for someone to argue they were unaware your material was copyrighted. Can make it easier for a person or entity to locate you and request permission to use your work.
Before an infringement suit may be filed in court, registration is necessary for works of U.S. origin.	You can sue someone for infringement and recover damages.
If registration is made within three months after publication of the work or prior to an infringement of the work, statutory damages and attorney's fees will be available to the copyright owner in court actions.	Without timely registration, only actual damages can be recovered.
Registration allows the owner of the copyright to record the registration with the U.S. Customs Service for protection against the importation of infringing copies.	Important for protecting your work—especially CDs and DVDs—from being infringed upon by people pirating copies from overseas.

Figure 1.19
Advantages of registering copyright.

How do you register work for copyright protection? Instructions and forms for registering work for copyright protection can be found on the U.S. Copyright Office Web site at *www.copyright.gov*. Registration can be done online and requires the payment of a small fee ($35 at time of publication). Although you can file online, the Library of Congress might still require you to submit a hard copy of your work. It can take quite a while to receive your notice of registration (up to eight months), but your registration is effective when the Copyright Office receives your registration form.

Posting a copyright notice with your work is also a great deterrent to copyright infringement as it clearly establishes the work is copyrighted. A simple format is to use the word copyright (or the copyright symbol—©), the year the work was first published, the copyright holder's name, and optionally, the location of the copyright holder. For example, either of these notifications for this book would be appropriate:

Copyright 2010 Pearson Education, Inc., Upper Saddle River, NJ

or

© 2010 Pearson Education, Inc.

Will it cost $35 to register each picture if there are 400 pictures? A copyright registration form can be filed for a collection of works. The stipulation is that the works must be published as a collection. A group of images or a collection of blog postings published online prior to registration should meet this criterion.

Can government copyright records be searched to determine if a work is copyrighted? The records are open to the public, and records from 1978 forward are searchable in an online database, as shown in Figure 1.20. For a search of records prior to January 1, 1978, you need to take a trip to Washington, DC, and do the search yourself in the paper records or pay the Copyright Office $150 per hour to conduct a search for you. Because the personnel at the copyright office are probably more proficient at searching than you are, a paid search is often the best option.

Online searching is available for works published after 1977.

Instructions for paper file searches are detailed by following this link.

Figure 1.20
Begin your copyright search online or find out how to search offline at *www.copyright.gov/records*.

What if the creator of the work doesn't mind people using it but doesn't want to be hassled constantly by permission requests? *Copyleft*—a play on the word copyright—is designed for this situation. Copyright laws are designed to allow copyright holders to prevent other people from copying, modifying, or distributing the creator's work. Copyleft is a term for various licensing plans that enable copyright holders to grant certain rights to the work while retaining other rights. Usually, the rights (such as modifying or copying a work) are granted with the stipulation that when users redistribute their work (based upon the original work) they agree to be bound by the same terms of the copyleft plan used by the original copyright holder. The General Public License (GNU) is a popular copyleft license that is used for software. For other works, the Creative Commons, a non-profit organization, has developed a range of licenses that can be used to control rights to works.

Creative Commons (see Figure 1.21) has various types of licenses available based on the rights you want to grant. The company—located on the Web at *www.creativecommons.org/about/licenses*—provides a simple form to assist you with selecting the proper license for your work and the following licenses you can choose from:

- **Attribution**—This condition lets others "copy, distribute, display, and perform your copyrighted work—and derivative works based upon it—but only if they give credit the way you request."

- **Noncommercial**—This condition lets others "copy, distribute, display, and perform your work—and derivative works based upon it—but for noncommercial purposes only."

- **No Derivative Works**—This condition lets others "copy, distribute, display, and perform only verbatim copies of your work, not derivative works based upon it."

- **Share Alike**—This condition lets others "distribute derivative works only under a license identical to the license that governs your work."

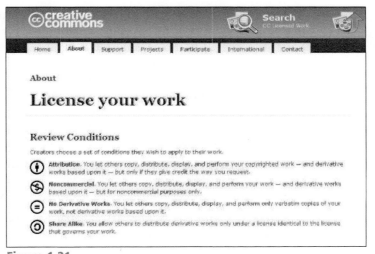

Figure 1.21
The Creative Commons Web site.

What are the advantages and drawbacks of licenses designed by Creative Commons? The obvious advantage is that people won't hassle you with endless permission requests. They should know exactly how you are willing to have your work be used. Also, many advocates of copyleft schemes feel that creativity is encouraged when people are free to modify others' work instead of worrying about infringing on copyright.

Opponents of Creative Common's licenses often complain that these licenses have affected their livelihoods. With millions of images out on Flickr with Creative Common's licenses that permit free commercial use, professional photographers might have a tougher time selling their work. Also Creative Common's licenses are irrevocable. If you made a mistake and selected the wrong license for your work or you later find out a work is valuable and you've already selected a license that allows commercial use, you're out of luck. Also, many people find Creative Common's licenses confusing. If there is a Creative Commons disclaimer at the bottom of a blog, does that mean all the blog entries apply to that license or just some of them? What actually constitutes commercial use? Is displaying Google Adsense ads on your blog commercial use?

You need to carefully consider the value of your intellectual property and decide how best to protect your rights. You should proceed carefully before giving up some of your rights with any copyleft license, especially if it is irrevocable.

Objective 10
Define Plagiarism

Is plagiarism a form of copyright infringement? *Plagiarism* is the act of copying text or ideas from someone else and claiming them as your own work product. Using ideas from other sources and integrating them into your work is acceptable only if you disclose your source and identify the content you use with quotation marks. Changing a few words, but keeping the essence of someone else's idea is still plagiarism even if you don't copy the text exactly. Although the following examples don't involve copying words or ideas without attribution, they are still examples of plagiarism under the academic definition:

- **Turning in work that someone else did for you**—Copying the Excel file that was due for homework in your computer literacy class from a classmate is still plagiarism, even though the file is not a text file.

- **Failing to identify a quotation with quotation marks**—"Whoops, I forgot" is not a suitable defense!

- **Falsifying quotations or sources**—Sometimes, students feel that attributing an idea of their own to a highly regarded source makes their idea sound more credible. Students have been known to enhance a paper that is thin on research sources by adding a list of sources and attributing them to various parts of the document.

- **Copying too much material from other sources**—If a work consists mostly of quotes and ideas from other sources, even though the source has been identified, it is difficult to justify this as original, creative work.

Plagiarism is usually considered an academic offense of dishonesty and is not punishable under U.S. civil law. However, it certainly is prohibited by almost all academic institutions, and the penalties usually are severe, such as a failing grade on the assignment, a failing grade for the course, or being dismissed from the institution. Although plagiarism is not technically copyright infringement, it can easily turn into copyright infringement if too much material is stolen from other sources, such as an entire chapter of a book or an entire research paper.

Why does plagiarism get so much press today when it has been a problem for centuries? Unfortunately, quick access to volumes of information on the Internet has made it easier than ever to commit plagiarism. Just a few clicks of the mouse can copy large quantities of information. Essay paper mills are Web sites that sell prewritten or custom written research papers to students. The essays are often written by graduate students or professional ghostwriters. For custom work, you can even specify what type of grade you would like to get. Some students choose to buy papers to earn them a grade of "C" if they think that it is less likely to arouse suspicion from the professor. Although it is illegal in most states to sell essays that will be turned in by students as their own work, the mills get around this by putting disclaimers on their Web sites that the papers should be used only for research purposes and not as the student's own work. Fortunately, there are good tools available to professors for detecting this type of plagiarism.

What can professors do to detect plagiarism? Sometimes, just reading a student's work product is a dead giveaway. If the level of writing suddenly improves dramatically from earlier assignments, most professors immediately become suspicious. Most colleges allow professors to test students orally on the content of papers that they suspect are not the student's own work product. If a student is unfamiliar with the content of the paper and the sources used, charges of academic dishonesty are usually brought against the student.

Typing suspicious phrases from a paper into Google and searching for hits is also an effective way to find unaccredited sources. Often, the plagiarized material turns up in the first page of Google results so professors don't even have to search hard to discover it. Also, most school libraries subscribe to online, searchable databases of periodicals that contain the full text of published articles. This aids professors in ferreting out plagiarism from printed sources.

Because of rampant plagiarism in recent decades, specialized electronic tools such as turnitin.com have been developed. Turnitin.com is a Web site to which educational institutions subscribe. The subscription enables professors to upload student papers, which are then checked against Web pages from the Internet—both current pages and archived pages that are no longer live—student papers previously submitted to Turnitin, and databases of published journals and periodicals. Customized reports, such as the one shown in Figure 1.22, are generated to determine the amount of suspected plagiarism in the paper. Professors also have the option of letting students upload their papers and check them for inadvertent plagiarism to give them a chance to cite unaccredited sources before turning in their final product.

Define Plagiarism | **Ethics in Cyberspace**

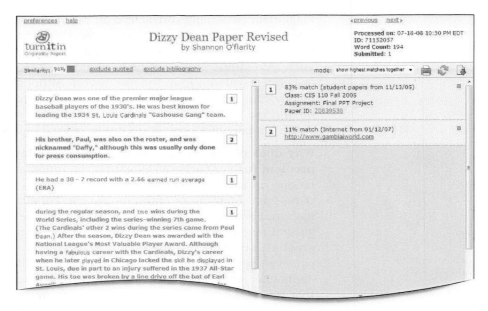

Figure 1.22
The turnitin.com originality report for this paper clearly shows that most of the paper was plagiarized from one turned in previously by another student with some small additions that were directly lifted from the Internet.

Why do students plagiarize? There are many reasons that students commit plagiarism. These include:

- **Pressure and deadlines outside of school**—Students, especially community college students, have a lot going on in their lives besides schoolwork. Often students are juggling jobs, family responsibilities, and relationships with their friends. Sometimes, they run out of time to get everything accomplished. This pressure to meet a deadline often results in a student taking the easy way out—plagiarism.

- **Poor time management and lack of advanced planning**—Many students have trouble assessing the amount of work that is necessary to complete an assignment. Coupled with poor management of time and responsibilities, this can lead some students to seek shortcuts to completing an assignment.

- **The feeling that everyone does it**—Certain students are under the impression that plagiarism is rampant and because "everyone else is cheating," they must also cheat to remain competitive. Why spend 15 hours on an assignment and risk an average grade when your friend is copying his work and getting As?

- **Perception of poor writing skills**—Many students feel that the sources they are consulting for research express thoughts and ideas much more eloquently than they are able to do. However, the only way to improve your writing skills is to write! Most instructors would rather see a paper that expresses a student's ideas passionately with a few grammar mistakes rather than see work that is stolen from others.

How can I avoid committing plagiarism? Learn to follow this simple maxim: *When in doubt, cite your source.* If you are taking an exact quote from a work, cite the source. If you are paraphrasing someone else's idea but still maintaining the essence of their original, creative idea, cite the source.

How do I cite a printed source properly? There are many different styles of citations you can use that have been developed by organizations such as the American Psychological Association (APA) and the Modern Language Association (MLA). Be sure to ask your professor which style is preferred and ask for relevant examples. Regardless of the style, your objective is to make sure that readers of your work have enough information to find the sources that you cite in your work. In Figure 1.23, you can see the important information to be included in your citation.

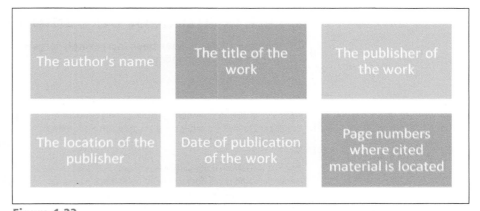

Figure 1.23
Information to include in a citation from a printed work.

How does citing a source from the Internet differ from citing a printed source? Depending on the citation style you are using, there are specific formats to follow that delineate what information to include and exactly how to present it. Regardless of the style being used, you usually need to obtain at least the following information for your citation:

- Author's name.

- Title of the Web page or the title of the Web site if you are citing the entire site.

- Date of creation or revision of the Web site. Note that the dates are usually shown directly under the title, at the top or bottom of the page. If the date is not provided, you can leave this information out of your citation.

- The full **uniform resource locator (URL)**—the Web address—of the Web page.

- The date the Web page or site was accessed. This is the date on which you viewed the Web page. Be sure to keep a record of this as you do research because Web pages can change frequently.

Define Plagiarism | **Ethics in Cyberspace**

Figure 1.24 provides an example of the pertinent information to gather from an article on a Web site. Keep in mind that this information does not necessarily appear in the same place on every Web page so you may have to look around to find it.

Figure 1.24
Relevant information used in Web page citations should be easy to locate. Don't forget to note the date you accessed the Web page.

Remember to properly cite your sources and don't use too much material from published sources. Being proud of your own work and respecting the work of others should keep everyone happy—especially when it comes to the grade you will receive on your work!

Ethics

Summary

In this chapter, you learned what ethics are and how your personal ethics develop. You explored various methods for making ethical choices. You learned how to determine which ethical guidelines to follow in a given situation and how to research the guidelines that various institutions (such as your school or your employer) have established. The concepts of intellectual property and copyright protection were explained. You examined the various permissible uses of copyrighted material and learned how to properly request permission to use copyrighted material. The consequences of copyright infringement were evaluated. The concept of fair use was defined and the extent to which it protects students and educators was explored. The various methods available to protect your copyrighted work were explained. Finally, you learned what plagiarism is and how to avoid committing it by citing your sources.

Key Terms

Acceptable use policies

Actual damages

Amoral behavior

Cease and desist letter

Copyleft

Copyright

Copyright infringement

Cultural relativism

Cyberethics

Digital rights management

Ethics

Fair use

First sale doctrine

Flame wars

Flaming

Injunction

Intangible personal property

Intellectual property

Judeo-Christian ethics

Laws

Model release

Netiquette

Patents

Personal ethics

Personal property

Plagiarism

Public domain

Real property

Relativism

Rule utilitarianism

Service mark

Situational ethics

Societal ethics

Software piracy

Stakeholders

Statutory damages

Subjective relativism

Supernodes

Tangible personal property

Terms of use

Trade dress

Trademark

Transformative use

Unethical behavior

Uniform resource locator (URL)

Voluntary actions

Willful infringement

Works made for hire

Works of corporate authorship

Key Terms | **Ethics in Cyberspace**

End-of-Chapter Assessments

Matching

Match each term in the second column with its correct definition in the first column by writing the letter of the term on the blank line in front of the correct definition.

_____ **1.** Criteria by which you make ethical decisions.

_____ **2.** General unwritten rules that guide people's behavior.

_____ **3.** People or entities affected by business decisions.

_____ **4.** Ethical guidelines that involve the use of computer systems and the Internet.

_____ **5.** Expressing an opinion in an online forum with strong emotions.

_____ **6.** Property that is an expression of human creativity.

_____ **7.** Legal protection for works of original authorship.

_____ **8.** Defines how you may use copyrighted material.

_____ **9.** Ability to use a portion of a work without obtaining permission.

_____ **10.** Passing off another's ideas as your own.

A Copyright

B Cyberethics

C Fair use

D Flaming

E Intellectual property

F Personal ethics

G Plagiarism

H Societal ethics

I Stakeholders

J Terms of use

Ethics

Fill in the Blank

Write the correct answer in the space provided.

1. The _____ gives you the right to resell your text book or loan it to a friend even though you don't own the copyright.

2. Works that lack copyright protection are said to be in the _____.

3. Many Web sites list _____, which delineate the rights you have to use copyrighted work you download from the site.

4. For permission to use a quote from a book, you should contact the _____ or the _____.

5. _____ occurs when you use copyrighted material without first obtaining the copyright holder's permission.

6. Textual URLs pointing to a Web site do not constitute copyright infringement because the URL is deemed to be a _____, which cannot be copyrighted.

7. _____ is a common method of infringement for music and video and involves two computers running common software to swap files.

8. Uploading a video of a band performing a song to YouTube without their permission is a violation of their right to control _____.

9. _____ occurs when someone copies a copyrighted software program and gives it to another person to install on another computer.

10. Usually, the _____ owns the copyright to a photo.

11. A _____ constitutes a request to immediately stop an alleged incidence of infringement.

12. You may be able to use a portion of a copyrighted work without receiving permission from the copyright holder under the _____ doctrine.

13. _____ refers to technology in place on CDs, DVDs, or MP3 files that prevents the media from being copied.

14. The granting of certain rights to a work by a copyright holder while retaining other rights is known as _____.

15. Appropriately _____ your source is the best way to protect yourself from plagiarism.

Fill in the Blank | **Ethics in Cyberspace**

End-of-Chapter Assessments

Multiple Choice

Circle the letter of the item that correctly answers the question.

1. Under current Unites States law, the term of copyright for a work created today lasts:
   a. Forever
   b. Until the author's death
   c. For 75 years from date of creation
   d. For the life of the author plus 70 years

2. Which of the following has an effect on the development of a person's personal ethics?
   a. Religious affiliation
   b. Influences of family members
   c. Daily life experiences
   d. All of the above

3. Which of the following are not business stakeholders?
   a. Employees
   b. Competitors
   c. Society
   d. Financial lenders

4. Unethical people sometimes find it easier to get away with their behavior on the Internet because of:
   a. The anonymity of online identities
   b. Ease of information exchange
   c. Impersonal nature of electronic communication
   d. All of the above
   e. None of the above

5. The collection of conventions for communicating and exchanging information over the various Internet services is known as:
   a. Cyberethics
   b. Cyber-road rules
   c. Netiquette
   d. Surfing etiquette

6. Which of the following is not an example of intellectual property?
   a. The design for the fastest motorboat in the world
   b. The latest iPod
   c. The theme song NBC played during the Olympics
   d. A poem about trees

(Multiple Choice—continues on the next page)

Ethics in Cyberspace | Computer Ethics, Copyright, and Plagiarism

End-of-Chapter Assessments

Multiple Choice

(Multiple Choice—continued)

7. Which of the following does not constitute intellectual property?

   a. The music contained on a CD

   b. The art on the box containing a DVD of *Spiderman 4*

   c. A DVD of *Spiderman 4*

   d. A poem published in a local newspaper

8. Which of the following cannot be granted copyright protection?

   a. The architectural plans for the new sports stadium to be built in your town

   b. The invention of a new interface for the Apple iPod

   c. A play written by your drama professor

   d. The picture you took last week of your cat

9. The Nike swoosh is an example of a:

   a. Service mark

   b. Trademark

   c. Copyright

   d. Patent

10. When does copyright protection begin?

   a. When a work is published

   b. When a work is registered

   c. When a work is created and fixed in a physical form

   d. When a work is first thought of in someone's mind

End-of-Chapter Exercises

Apply the objectives in this chapter by answering the following questions:

1. What (or who) had the biggest influence on your personal ethics? Are there circumstances that you think you would face during the course of your life that would compel you to make choices that went against your core ethical beliefs?

2. Describe something that one of your friends or coworkers did (no names please!) that was not illegal but that you consider to be unethical. Did this person's actions become public knowledge and did they suffer any negative consequence from the action? Could you ever envision any circumstances in which you would do the same thing they did even though you believe it is fundamentally unethical?

3. You catch the company cleaning staff dumping your employer's garbage into another company's trash dumpster. Your boss asks you to "look the other way" because he told the cleaning staff to take this action in order to cut down on your company's trash hauling expenses. Since there is no legal ordinance in your township prohibiting this action, your boss tells you that "no one is at risk of getting hurt." Explain how you feel about your boss's actions. What would you do in this situation? What possible risks does your company and its employees face even though the action is not illegal?

4. You (lead singer), your roommate (lead guitar), and two of his friends (bass player and drummer) form a band. You and your roommate co-write a song called *College Rocks* for the band. The entire band records the song.
   - Who owns copyright to *College Rocks*?
   - What rights do the copyright holder(s) have to *College Rocks*?
   - The bass player leaves the band and joins another band. Does he have a right to perform *College Rocks* with his new band? Can the new band sell t-shirts with the lyrics to *College Rocks* on it?

5. You find a really cool photo of a woman riding an ostrich on Flickr and download it to your computer. There was no copyright information attached to the photo or displayed on the page of Flickr where you obtained the photo. You are planning on modifying it by using Photoshop to combine it with a photo you have of yourself on a bicycle so it looks like you are chasing the woman. Then you plan to print the modified photo on baseball caps that will be sold at a local rodeo. Consider the following and fully explain your answers:
   - Who do you think owns the copyright to the unmodified photo? How would you find out?
   - Do you own the copyright to the modified photo?

(End-of-Chapter Exercises–continues on the next page)

Ethics in Cyberspace | Computer Ethics, Copyright, and Plagiarism

End-of-Chapter Exercises

(End-of-Chapter Exercises–continued)

- Could you be sued for copyright infringement by the copyright holder of the picture of the woman? If not, explain why. If you could be sued, what types of damages could the copyright holder potentially get from you?
- What if you donated the proceeds of the sales from the hats to charity? Would that change your answer to the previous question?

6. How would you find out if the book *Watership Down* written by British author Richard Adams is in the public domain? If you have an idea for a sequel to *Watership Down* featuring some of the same characters as the original, explain how you could write and publish it without committing copyright infringement.

7. Lucinda works for the Fun Stuff Advertising Agency as an ad copywriter. In her spare time, she is an avid artist. One day her boss tells her the art department has a backlog of work and asks her to design a logo for the Fizzy Cola ad campaign she is currently working on. Lucinda creates the logo on her company owned computer and it is a big hit with the client. The logo is featured in a nationwide television and print advertising campaign for Fizzy Cola. Describe the pertinent facts that must be considered to determine who owns the copyright to the logo: Fun Stuff, Fizzy Cola, or Lucinda.

8. You take a photograph of several students playing with a Frisbee on the quad at Humongous State University (HSU). A classmate of yours is a summer intern at an ad agency who is working on a new ad campaign for Mattel Toys, who markets Frisbees. Your classmate shows the picture around the office and decides it would be good to use in the ad campaign. The representative from Mattel loves it, and it is used in print ads across the United States including a billboard down the street from the college. The week after the billboard appears the following happens:

- You receive a cease and desist letter from HSU indicating that you did not have permission to photograph the college library which appears in the background of the picture.
- You receive a letter from the attorney of one of the students in the picture indicating you are being sued for violating the privacy rights of the student.

Based on what you have read in this book and by doing a little extra research on the Internet (if necessary), explain the legal principles governing each of these situations, what you should have done to avoid being involved in the situations, and whether these complaints have any legal merit.

Privacy and Other Ethics Issues

OBJECTIVES

At the end of this chapter you will be able to:

1. Define Privacy and the Associated Risks in Cyberspace

2. Describe the Ethical and Legal Issues of Employee Monitoring

3. Define Cyberbullying and Describe Methods for Mitigation

4. Describe Major Threats to Online Privacy and Methods to Combat the Threats

5. Define E-waste and Describe Methods for Disposing of E-waste

6. Describe Web Content Filtering and Its Effect on Free Speech

7. Define the Digital Divide and Describe Methods for Bridging It

8. Describe Methods to Evaluate the Accuracy of Digital Information

9. Define Online Reputation and Describe Methods for Protecting Your Online Reputation

From Chapter 2 of *Go! with Ethics in Cyberspace Getting Started*, First Edition, Alan Evans. Copyright © 2010 by Pearson Education, Inc. Published by Pearson Prentice Hall. All rights reserved.

Introduction

Two of the major ethical issues in cyberspace are violation of digital assets copyright, such as software and movies, and plagiarism. However, there are many more ethical choices that users of the Internet are faced with every day.

In this chapter, you will explore the ethical ramifications of violating privacy rights, such as employers monitoring the behavior of employees, and methods you can take to protect your privacy rights from being violated by unethical individuals. In addition, we explore other important ethical issues such as the generation and disposal of e-waste, assurance of equal access to cyberspace resources for everyone—bridging the digital divide—and Web content filtering that restricts access to information.

Objective 1
Define Privacy and the Associated Risks in Cyberspace

Every day it seems like we encounter another issue regarding the disposition of private information in some sector of cyberspace. Perhaps it is a news item about people in your community suffering financial losses from having their identities stolen. Maybe you have heard about the latest data breach from a government agency that allowed supposedly secure data to be accessed by a hacker. Or, maybe you were surprised when the grocery clerk at the supermarket called you by name even though you had never seen him before.

Consider the effect cyberspace has on your day-to-day life. Back in the 1980s, most people paid for purchases with cash. Today, debit and credit cards have largely replaced cash. But whereas cash leaves virtually no trail, a record of your debit and credit card transactions can exist in multiple companies' records. E-mail, text messaging, social networking, and other forms of electronic communication are now the norm. Because of the persistence of digital information, your correspondence may be stored somewhere on the Internet, such as in multiple computers, for years to come. The last time you visited your favorite Web site, the owner of that site probably kept track of what you looked at while you were visiting. Events constantly transpire to make you wonder if privacy is a casualty of the information age.

What is privacy? Simply stated, **privacy** is the right to be left alone to do as one pleases as long as there is not a violation of laws or harming of others. Information privacy means that information is controlled in terms of the manner and time frame in which it is disclosed to others. If you worship owls in your living room, perhaps you don't want your neighbors to know this because they might think you strange. However, you may choose to share your views with other owl worshipers because you know they would understand your interest in owls. As long as you aren't hurting the owls—there are laws against cruelty to animals, keeping endangered species, and so on—you should have the right to keep your personal preferences confidential. Someone who obtains or reveals personal information without your consent is said to have committed an **invasion of privacy**.

Isn't privacy a basic right guaranteed to all Americans? Many Americans think that individual privacy is protected by the Constitution or the Bill of Rights. Our forefathers didn't specifically address the right to individual privacy; however, the Fourth Amendment to the Constitution does reference the right of people to be "secure." The Fourth Amendment states:

"The right of the people to be secure in their persons, houses, papers, and effects, against unreasonable searches and seizures, shall not be violated and no Warrants shall issue, but upon probable cause, supported by Oath or affirmation, and particularly describing the place to be searched, and the persons or things to be seized."

This provision against "unreasonable search and seizure" by government entities as interpreted by the courts, has been interpreted by U.S. society to a reasonable expectation of privacy in any place that is not public or subject to public view. This would include your home and places designed to ensure privacy, such as a public bathroom stall or a phone booth. The right to privacy is a societal norm in the United States. Therefore, it is unethical to violate someone's privacy without his consent.

Can you modify your behavior to protect your privacy? You can modify your behavior to protect your privacy, but would you want to? Would you rather carry cash that can be stolen instead of a debit card that needs a password to be used? For example, do you want to stop purchasing items on the Internet? The electronic exchange and tracking of information makes our lives easier in that it enables us to purchase items without having to leave the comfort of our homes. Tracking activities at a Web site enables the Web site owner to customize the user experience each time the user visits the site. For example, the Amazon Web site makes recommendations to users visiting the site based on the users' previous visits to the site and previous purchases. Only 7 percent of Americans, in a recent poll by the Ponemon Institute (*www.ponemon .org*), said they would be willing to change their behavior to protect their privacy. Although Americans are often vocal about their concerns over loss of privacy, most do not exert pressure on their legislators to enact laws to preserve privacy rights.

Which privacy areas are of concern to most people? Privacy concerns vary widely among individuals. You might not care if your supermarket knows what brand of cereal you buy every week, but your neighbor might consider that a breach of her privacy. The following general types of information are usually of concern to most people:

- **Confidentiality of personal information**—Data such as gender, race, religion, sexual orientation, political affiliation, reading preferences, daily activities, and group memberships are often a source of concern because people want to prevent discrimination, ostracizing, and general embarrassment.

- **Protection of financial information**—Financial information is an area of concern because people want to guard themselves against fraud or identity theft. However, financial transactions can also reveal information about a person's personal life. For example, a company can analyze your purchases through financial transactions.

- **Non-disclosure of medical information**—Most concerns about medical information are related to the ability to obtain insurance or employment. People are also concerned about embarrassment regarding the treatments of certain illnesses. Also, some illnesses might be used correctly or incorrectly to interpret someone's activities or sexual preferences.

In addition to individuals, organizations have valid reasons for maintaining privacy. For example, companies like Coca Cola and other manufacturers often have trade secrets or formulas that they want to protect from falling into the hands of competitors. Some companies might want to keep secret the fact that they participate in an activity that is potentially objectionable to large segments of society. For example, some companies use animal testing for cosmetic products. In these cases, maintaining privacy is a way to avoid adverse or negative publicity.

What ethical responsibilities do you have with regard to privacy? If you are in possession of information about another individual and you do not know whether or not the person would want that information disclosed, you should keep that information confidential. By respecting an individual's right to privacy, you are behaving in an ethical manner.

For example, in the course of employment in a retail clothing store, employees are continually exposed to sensitive information, such as the customers' payment information (credit card numbers), contact information (home or work address and phone numbers), clothing sizes, and even social security numbers. A customer has a reasonable expectation that her credit card numbers will be kept private. You have an "ethical contract" with your customers to protect the information they wish to keep private.

This ethical contract doesn't apply only to employment situations. If your friend John was drunk and made a fool of himself at a small dinner party at your home, you need to respect John's privacy and not describe his antics on your MySpace page. Ethical responsibility regarding privacy is mostly a matter of thinking before acting. Consider if it was you who acted silly. Would you want someone describing you dancing on the top of a table with a t-shirt tied around your head as a bandana after your hometown baseball team just won the World Series? Although your friends might think it was amusing and you might get over your embarrassment relatively quickly, how would a prospective employer feel about your antics? How about your parents? Don't you have a right to privacy when attending a private party in the confines of a friend's home? Put yourself in the other individual's position before you disclose personal or embarrassing information.

Objective 2
Describe the Ethical and Legal Issues of Employee Monitoring

What do employers monitor? Think you aren't being closely watched by your employer? Think again! There are few privacy laws related to the workplace, and most recent court cases tend to support the employer's capability to monitor their employees. A 2005 survey by the American Management Association and the ePolicy Institute (*www.epolicyinstitute .com*) showed that of the employers surveyed, they monitored the following:

- 73% monitored e-mail messages
- 66% monitored Web surfing
- 48% monitored with video surveillance
- 45% monitored keystrokes and keyboard time
- 43% monitored computer files in some other fashion

You need to think carefully about what you are doing at work and what you want your employer to know about because there is a high probability that your employer watches your activities.

Why do employers monitor employees? The two main reasons are to prevent theft—including *industrial espionage*, which is spying by competitors to gain access to sensitive information, and other forms of *white collar crime*, which are non-violent crimes committed by office workers such as fraud, bribery, and stock manipulation—and to measure productivity. Monitoring for theft isn't new because television cameras have been around for years, and productivity monitoring has been a consistent process for assembly line workers for decades. The rise of the Internet has enabled a new type of productivity drain.

Cyberloafing, or cyberslacking, is doing anything with a computer—usually involving the Internet—on company time that is not related to your job while you are being paid to do your job. Examples of cyberloafing activities are surfing the Web, playing games, reading personal e-mail, running another business, such as an eBay business, and watching videos. Estimates of business productivity losses due to cyberloafing top $50 billion annually. Although many employers don't mind the occasional personal e-mail answered at work, they would probably not appreciate it if you spent four hours of your day playing *World of Warcraft* online (see Figure 2.1)!

Figure 2.1
Your boss may be watching to ensure your honesty and productivity.
Courtesy of © Neal Aspinall/Images.com.

Do I have a legal right (in the United States) to a reasonable expectation of privacy in the workplace? The 1986 Electronic Communications Privacy Act (ECPA) is the federal law that most closely applies to privacy in the workplace. Among the provisions of the act are prohibitions

Ethics in Cyberspace | Privacy and Other Ethics Issues

against the unauthorized monitoring of electronic communications, which includes e-mail. The law specifically exempts *service providers* from its provisions, and the courts have interpreted this to mean employers who routinely provide electronic communication services such as Internet access, e-mail, and cellular phone texting service. When cases have come to court, the court's view is usually that because the employer is paying for the equipment and software, the employees don't have an expectation of privacy that they could easily enjoy by communicating on their own time with their own electronic devices.

Shouldn't people be allowed some privacy at work? Many employees feel that an employer should allow some leeway during the day to take care of personal business that can be conducted only during normal work hours. With the lengthening of the U.S. work week over the past several decades, this is not an unreasonable expectation. But the allowances an employer will make vary widely from employer to employer. You need to understand the difference between acceptable and unacceptable conduct at your place of business. And even though your employer might allow you to do some personal tasks during the day, it doesn't mean those tasks won't be monitored.

Is it ethical for employers to monitor employees? Just because an action is legal doesn't mean it is ethical. It is difficult to argue that an employer doesn't have the right to take measures to prevent theft and detect low productivity. The ethical issue here is whether or not the employees are made aware they are being monitored. An ethical employer should treat employees with respect and dignity and inform the employees that they are being monitored. Also, employers have an ethical responsibility—a legal one, too, depending on the jurisdiction—to not place monitoring devices in sensitive locations such as bathrooms and dressing areas.

Do employers have a legal obligation to notify employees they are being monitored? In most cases—although it can vary from state to state—the employer does not need to inform the employees in advance that they are being monitored. However, most employers include this in published employee policies to avoid confusion and conflict. If you aren't sure if your employer monitors employees, check with the human resources department at your employer.

Can an employer monitor employee phone calls? Yes, an employer can monitor phone calls as long as they are business-related. The ECPA specifically exempts personal calls from monitoring so if your employer monitors your calls, they are supposed to stop when they realize you are making a personal call. Your employer may specifically state that no personal calls are to be made from certain business phones, in which case, you can assume that all calls from those phones are monitored. The number of phone calls, the duration of the calls, and the specific numbers dialed are often reviewed by employers for judging worker productivity. Ten calls per day to a spouse may be noted in a performance review. With the rise of cellular phones, it is easy to maintain your privacy on phone calls at work. Simply make all personal calls on your cell phone.

Describe the Ethical and Legal Issues of Employee Monitoring | **Ethics in Cyberspace**

However, to be fair to your employer, you should keep personal calls at work to a minimum because you are supposed to be working. Spending three hours a day on personal calls does not constitute turning in an honest day's effort!

How are computers monitored? Employers use a variety of software programs to monitor employee computer usage. Certain software packages keep track of every Web site you visit and the duration of your stay. Checking the baseball scores might take only three seconds and go unnoticed, but spending two hours updating your fantasy football team might get flagged. *Keystroke loggers* are software packages that record every key stroke you make on your computer. Originally they were used to monitor performance for people with input-intensive jobs like clerks and secretaries. Now these programs can be used to invade your privacy because they record everything you type, even that nasty e-mail about the boss that you thought better of sending and deleted!

In addition to monitoring keystrokes, computer software can also be used to monitor the contents of your hard drive, so you don't want to collect 4,823 illegal MP3 files on your work computer. Some programs even keep track of how long your computer is idle, which can give your manager a good idea of whether you were working or away for a three-hour lunch.

Your employer might not tell you that your computer use is being monitored, so you should assume that anything you do on your company-provided computer is subject to scrutiny. If you need to do personal work on your lunch hour or other breaks, bring in your personal laptop to avoid the monitoring.

Are all my e-mail communications subject to monitoring? E-mail sent from employer-owned systems can be monitored. Also, the courts have indicated that e-mail sent from third-party systems, such as Yahoo and Gmail, are subject to monitoring if they are sent on employer-provided computer systems. Instant messaging is also subject to monitoring. About the only exception to communications monitoring are phone text messages.

In the case of *Quon v. Arch Wireless, et al.* Ninth Circuit, June 18, 2008, No. 07-55282, the 9th U.S. Circuit Court of Appeals ruled in June 2008 that employers can view phone text messages only if they have the employee's permission or a valid legal warrant. The distinction between text messages and e-mail are that the text messages are stored by a third party and that the employer does not directly pay for storage of those messages. E-mail is usually stored on a company-owned server or on a third-party server for which the third party is paid specifically to store the messages.

Again, the best defense against monitoring of personal instant messaging, text messaging or e-mail is to use your own computing device to send the communications.

Ethics in Cyberspace | Privacy and Other Ethics Issues

Figure 2.2
You can save yourself a lot of angst about your communications being monitored in the workplace by using your own cell phone or computer for personal communication. Courtesy of Photos.com.

What protects employees from those who monitor and then misuse personal information? People who monitor employees have a duty to protect your right to privacy and not to disclose any information that they may inadvertently see during the course of monitoring. The acceptable computer use policies at most companies include guidelines for network administrators and other people who have higher levels of access to sensitive information.

In addition to the procedures for preventing abuse of data that is monitored, companies need strong policies to safeguard customer and employee data. Companies need to prevent data theft and loss from happening because these crimes can lead to identity theft. Consider the 2007 theft of the data backup device stolen from a college intern's car. The intern was working for the state of Ohio at the time and the stolen device contained data on 1.3 million taxpayers and employees. Procedures for investigating employee misuse of computers and data and the sanctions that will be imposed for violations must be detailed.

Whether monitoring employees' work habits or safeguarding data, management must ensure that compliance with the policies is tested periodically. Periodic reviews of procedures and compliance helps ensure that established company policies are working as designed. An ethical company strives to prevent misuse of personal data and accidental data loss. This helps the company maintain the trust of its employees, customers, and the public.

Describe the Ethical and Legal Issues of Employee Monitoring | **Ethics in Cyberspace**

Objective 3
Define Cyberbullying and Describe Methods for Mitigation

What is cyberbullying? *Cyberbullying* is just like normal bullying, but it involves the use of digital technologies such as the Internet, cell phones, or video. Instead of a bully chasing you at recess on the playground, cyberbullying involves minors (children) harassing, threatening, humiliating, embarrassing, or tormenting other minors by means of technology. Cyberbullying is not an adult behavior. *Cyber-harassment*—threatening or annoying others in cyberspace—or *cyberstalking*—threatening an individual via electronic communications—are incidents that involve adults. Cyberbullying is a child-on-child process that might result in criminal charges depending upon the type of incident.

How does cyberbullying take place? There are many direct and indirect methods of cyberbullying. The main ones are:

- **Instant messaging or text messaging**—Often groups of children will bombard a victim with thousands of text messages. Sometimes a bully will create an IM account and pretend to be the intended victim and act in such a way as to embarrass or anger the victim's friends.

- **Password theft**—If students discover someone's password, they may log onto their accounts and send harassing, threatening, or lewd messages while pretending to be the victim.

- **Blog and Social Networking sites**—Children often post nasty rumors about other kids on these sites. This exposes the victim to widespread humiliation and embarrassment, especially as other people add comments to postings and start their own rumors. Often these sites feature cruel polls, such as a vote about who is the "fattest" kid in the class.

- **Embarrassing photos or videos**—Usually candid photos or videos—often nude or semi-nude photos that have been taken discretely with cell phone cameras—are sent through cell phones or e-mails. These can circulate widely and end up on Web sites all over the world.

- **Malware**—Computer-savvy cyberbullies often send viruses or Trojan horse programs to their victims in attempts to disable their computers or spy on them.

- **Junk e-mail or text messaging**—Bullies often sign their victims up with hundreds of marketing or porn sites in an attempt to flood their accounts with annoying messages.

Why is cyberbullying unethical? Most bullying involves harassment, spreading of false rumors or revealing embarrassing, personal details about an individual. The individual's right to privacy (just to be left alone and do his own thing) is violated by these actions, which are considered unethical in our society. Children have the same expectations of anonymity when they use Internet services as adults and should respect the privacy of others. Unfortunately, some children fail to treat their peers with respect and behave unethically.

Ethics in Cyberspace | Privacy and Other Ethics Issues

Why does cyberbullying take place? Children are often more trusting than adults and may be more willing to reveal personal information, such as passwords, to their friends. Because younger people are so comfortable using the Internet, they often forget to exercise the same precautions over sensitive information that they would exercise in the real world. And sometimes children just want to fit in with the "popular kids," so they reveal a lot of information about themselves in the hopes of being accepted. Unfortunately, these behaviors make it easier for cyberbullies to commit their unethical activities.

How do cyberbullies typically behave? Although every cyberbullying incident can be slightly different, there are common characteristics that cyberbullies share. According to *www.stopcyberbullying.org*, there are four main categories of cyberbullies:

- **The Vengeful Angel**—These people don't view themselves as bullies but think they are avenging some wrong, protecting a friend, or retaliating against another cyberbully. They often think they are teaching their victim a well-deserved lesson.

- **The Power Hungry (*Revenge of the Nerds*)**—Some bullies like to show off their power or intimidate others through fear. Many of these bullies just want to show how much smarter they are than the intended victim. They enjoy making people feel powerless.

- **Mean Girls**—These bullies, who do not have to be female, are either bored or searching for a cruel form of entertainment. They usually work in groups because they enjoy having an audience for their pranks. Fortunately, these bullies frequently lose interest if they don't get a sufficiently entertaining reaction from their victims.

- **Inadvertent Cyberbully**—These people are not intentionally being cyberbullies, but are usually just thoughtless. They dash off a mean e-mail, IM, or text message and hit send before thinking about the consequences. They frequently respond out of anger or frustration for something that happened to them.

Are the consequences of cyberbullying serious? For many adults, their job and their families define who they are and affect how happy and successful they feel. For children, their standing in peer groups is a critical component of their self worth. Adults have freedom in their lives to change bad situations, such as changing jobs, when they feel their esteem is under attack. Children often feel powerless because they have such limited options. You might have been mortified in sixth grade if someone had sent around a picture of you in your underwear when you were changing in the locker room. Children don't usually have the option of changing schools without uprooting the entire family. Aside from developing severe feelings of depression, rage, frustration, and powerlessness, children have committed suicide over cyberbullying incidents.

How do you overcome cyberbullying? There are no easy answers to overcoming cyberbullying, but educating and informing children about the consequences of cyberbullying are effective solutions. Often, when children are educated about the behaviors of cyberbullies, they recognize that some of the actions they take contain aspects of bullying.

Define Cyberbullying and Describe Methods for Mitigation | **Ethics in Cyberspace**

Children need to suffer consequences for their actions, such as having their cell phones taken away if they send thousands of text messages to a cyberbullying victim. Children also need to be educated about the possible effects on their intended victims, such as anger, depression, and even suicide. Programs that teach children to manage their anger—always useful in later life—by stepping back and taking a critical look at situations that enrage them before they act can be effective in preventing cyberbullying incidents. Finally, when someone understands that it is unethical to take a facilitator role in other cyberbullying schemes, they are less inclined to participate, such as not forwarding a hurtful e-mail or making a nasty post on someone's blog.

What can adults do to prevent cyberbullying? Parents need to be alert to changes in their children's behavior which may indicate they are victims of cyberbullying or becoming bullies themselves. If a child is suddenly spending a lot less time or more time online, what is the reason? Is your child suddenly depressed or getting sick frequently to avoid going to school? Maintaining open channels of communication with children is important because they need to be able to inform a trusted adult—parent, teacher, counselor, or religious leader—when they are being harassed or bullied.

Objective 4
Describe Major Threats to Online Privacy and Methods to Combat the Threats

There are many threats to personal privacy from individuals, such as hackers, behaving unethically online. Computer viruses and spyware can cause havoc by disrupting your computing experience or by collecting personal information, such as credit card numbers, to be used in the commission of *cybercrimes*—criminal activities conducted with the aid of a computer or the Internet. Most individuals are aware of these threats and can combat them by using software solutions such as anti-virus programs, anti-spyware programs, and firewalls. Obviously, hacking, creating viruses, and deploying spyware are unethical activities, and we don't expect you to engage in these activities. However, because there are unethical individuals who will attempt to take advantage of you with these methods, you need to know how to protect yourself. In this section, you explore threats to your privacy that require more diligence to defend yourself against. You will also look at suggestions for how to protect your privacy online.

How can I possibly be a threat to myself? People are often too eager to reveal information about themselves, especially when it appears that the request is coming from a legitimate source. Have you filled out a warranty form online for a product you bought lately? Have you obtained a customer loyalty card at a pharmacy or a supermarket? Have you filled out a survey to potentially win a prize? Think about how much information you voluntarily gave up performing these activities. In addition, if you have a MySpace, Facebook, Blogger, or Twitter account, you are probably constantly revealing information about your likes and dislikes—what movie you saw this weekend, which concert you attended last night, presents you received for your birthday, and so on. Con artists and scammers take advantage of this tendency to reveal one's self, and they collect information by using a technique called social engineering.

How does social engineering work? *Social engineering* uses social skills to generate human interaction that leads to individuals revealing sensitive information. Social engineering often doesn't involve the use of a computer or face-to-face interaction. Telephone scams are common because it is often easier to manipulate someone when you don't have to look at them. The two main types of social engineering are as follows:

- *Pretexting*—Pretexting involves creating a scenario that sounds legitimate enough that someone will trust you. For example, you might receive a phone call during which the caller says he is from the bank and that someone tried to use your account without authorization. The caller then tells you he needs to confirm a few personal details such as your birth date, social security number, bank account number, and whatever other information he can get out of you. The information he obtains can then be used to empty your bank account or commit some other form of fraud. Often pretexting is used to gain access to corporate computer networks. People will sometimes call random extensions in a large business claiming to be from technical support. Eventually, the caller will find someone who has a problem and is happy that someone is willing to help. The scam artist will then elicit information such as logons and passwords from the victim as part of the process for "solving the problem."

- *Phishing*—Phishing usually involves sending e-mails—although instant messaging, phone texting, and telephoning can also be used—that appear to come from an official source, such as your bank, eBay, Paypal, and so on. Phishing messages are used to gather sensitive information from unsuspecting individuals. The e-mail, as shown in Figure 2.3, usually gets your attention by mentioning something that might make you upset: unauthorized access to your account, large payments made from your account, and so on. The e-mail might then contain a link to a Web site where you are asked to enter sensitive information about your account, such passwords, social security number, birth date, and so on. The phishing Web site is made to look as close to the official Web site as possible and may even feature logos and text copied directly from the legitimate site. These e-mails are insidious because they often disguise the links to look like the official links of the real organization. In addition, the fake Web sites often use computer programming to alter the address bar in your browser so that it looks like you are on the official site instead of a phishing site.

Figure 2.3

Example of a phishing e-mail from Ginormous National Bank. Obviously, actual phishing attempts appear to be from real financial institutions.

How do you avoid falling for social engineering schemes? Be wary of all unsolicited phone calls when you are being asked for personal information. Hang up and call the appropriate institution (your bank, for example) using a phone number from a source you trust, such as your bank statement, credit card statement, and so on. You will quickly ascertain whether there is an actual problem. Also, never respond to e-mails or click on links they contain, especially in e-mails that are trying to "verify" sensitive information. Bank personnel never send e-mails asking for personal information such as your account number because they already know it! Instead, contact the appropriate institution directly and see if the e-mail is legitimate.

The latest version of the popular Web browsers, such as Internet Explorer and Firefox, contain anti-phishing measures that check Web sites against a database of known phishing sites and warn you if you browse to a suspect site. For additional protection, anti-phishing software comes with most Internet Security Suite software packages such as Norton Internet Security (see Figure 2.4). The Norton Internet Security toolbar will alert you if you browse to a known phishing site. It would be a good idea to purchase a security product that does help protect you against phishing scams.

Ethics in Cyberspace | Privacy and Other Ethics Issues

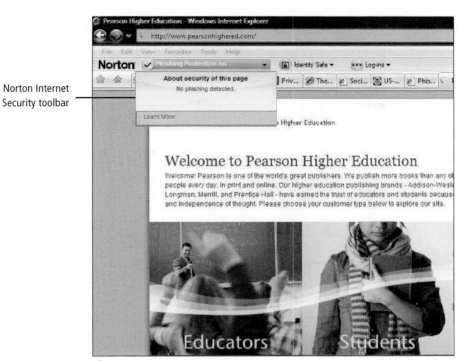

Norton Internet Security toolbar

Figure 2.4
Not sure if you are on the real Pearson Higher Education Web site? Norton Internet Security's tool bar gives you added assurance.

What do you do if you think you have fallen victim to a phishing or other social engineering scheme? If you have suspicions of being a victim of phishing or social engineering, immediately contact the appropriate institution—your bank, Paypal, Amazon.com, and so on. Ask for the fraud division and explain what happened. They should be able to freeze your account, assist you in changing passwords, or close your old account and open a new one for you. Don't be embarrassed to call for help; this type of scam fools even seasoned professionals sometimes.

What is identity theft? When someone steals your personal information such as your name, address, social security number, and birth date and then uses that information to impersonate you and run up debts in your name, the crime is known as *identity theft* (see Figure 2.5). The identity thief will usually open new charge accounts in your name or will obtain loans at financial institutions. The first indication that you've been a victim is often not until you receive a charge card bill for items you never bought. Victims of identity theft spend months (and even years) trying to repair their credit and eliminate fraudulent debts.

Describe Major Threats to Online Privacy and Methods to Combat the Threats | **Ethics in Cyberspace**

Figure 2.5
How many people are posing as you? Identity theft can strike at any time!
Courtesy of © Dave Pilbosian/Courtesy of www.istockphoto.com.

Some identity thieves use your information to obtain medical services from doctors and hospitals. Identity theft victims have found themselves denied coverage because the thief's treatment sent them over the limit of covered services on their policy. The "2008 Identity Fraud Survey Report" by Javelin Strategy & Research reported that approximately 8.1 million American adults were victims of identity theft in 2007. Clearly, this is widespread problem against which you need to protect yourself.

How do identities get stolen? Many people believe that identity theft happens only through computers, but this is untrue. The "2008 Identity Fraud Survey Report" indicates that identity theft fraud through telephone and conventional mail tactics accounts for approximately 40 percent of identity theft. The U.S. Federal Trade Commission (*www.ftc.gov*) lists the following sources of identity theft that have nothing to do with computers or electronic data:

- **Theft of purses and wallets**—Many people carry valuable personal information such as their ATM PIN codes or social security cards. You should memorize both these numbers; do not carry them in your wallet.

- **Dumpster diving**—Thieves dig through trash to find bank statements and credit card bills, which often provide valuable personal information.

- **Pretexting**—Posing as bank or credit card company representatives often enables thieves to fool people into revealing personal information by phone.

Of course you are at risk from online attacks also. For example, responding to phishing e-mails often results in you handing over your information voluntarily.

What else do identity thieves do with my information? Although creative identity thieves can do numerous nasty things, the most common are:

- Request a change of address with financial institutions—The thief cleans out your bank account or maxes out your credit limit before you realize you aren't receiving statements.

Ethics in Cyberspace | Privacy and Other Ethics Issues

- Open bank accounts in your name and write bad checks—This ruins your credit rating.

- Obtain a mortgage in your name to purchase real estate—not necessarily the home in which you live—and then disappear with the proceeds, leaving you with the debt. This can be the toughest problem to repair.

How do you protect yourself against identity theft? It is impossible to fully protect yourself against identity theft but taking the following steps can decrease your risk of being a victim:

- Never reveal passwords, logon IDs, and PIN codes to anyone. Don't write them down and leave them in an easily accessible place. If you need to write them down because you just can't remember them, put the list in your safe deposit box at the bank.

- Think carefully before giving out personal information, especially online. Only give information that a company needs (for example, retail stores don't need your social security number or your birth date to sell you a television or pair of jeans).

- Don't respond to requests for personal information when someone calls you. Hang up and call the company directly to verify that the call is legitimate.

- Create secure passwords for your accounts. Combinations of letters, numbers, and symbols work best. For example, IUX34#WS7 is a strong password. Thieves are adept at guessing obvious passwords such as names, and even your pets' names, birth dates, portions of social security numbers, your address, and so on.

- Shop only with well-known online merchants. Check with the Better Business Bureau before dealing with a merchant for the first time to see if they have complaints lodged against them. Businesses should have valid contact information on their Web site such as a mailing address and phone number.

- Most states now allow you to freeze your credit history. This prevents anyone from checking your credit, including you, through the three main credit bureaus, and legitimate merchants won't open a new charge account without a credit check. You can always unfreeze your credit later if you need to apply for a loan.

For additional tips on preventing identity theft or for procedures to follow if you are a victim, check out the U.S. federal government site on identity theft at *www.consumer.gov/idtheft*.

What other steps can you take to maintain your online anonymity and privacy? Aside from the obvious steps of not giving out personal information and not identifying yourself on social networking sites and other Web pages, you should take the following steps:

- **Restrict access to your online information**—You may have good reasons for creating an account under your real name at Facebook or LinkedIn, such as networking to find a better job. But that doesn't mean you have to let everyone see your information. Check the options and restrict all or part of your account to just your trusted friends.

- **Exercise caution when using public terminals or networks**—The computer at the student union or the wireless network at the local coffee shop are convenient. That doesn't necessarily mean they are secure. Information thieves often hang around in places that offer public computer access—such as libraries—because people often leave a trail of information behind when they surf the Internet. You never know what monitoring software hackers may have installed on a public computer. Likewise, open wireless networks in public places offer hackers a chance to intercept messages you send and to possibly steal sensitive information such as credit card numbers. Therefore, when using public computers and wireless networks, you should take the following steps:

  - When you use a public computer at school, the library, and so on, always make sure you log out of all the accounts you accessed and close your browser.

  - Do not make financial transactions on public computers or open wireless networks.

  - Consider using portable privacy devices like the IronKey (*www.ironkey.com*), shown in Figure 2.6. The device plugs into a USB port on the computer you use. Instead of being stored on the computer, all sensitive files, such as cookies, Internet history (list of Web sites you have visited), and browser caches (copies of Web pages you surfed), are stored on the privacy device. Therefore, you don't leave an electronic trail for hackers to follow on the public computer. Many of these privacy devices use software such as the Anonymizer Safe Surfing Suite (*www.anonymizer.com*), which shields your Internet address from prying eyes. This makes it difficult or impossible for hackers to tell where you are surfing on the Internet. Password management tools are included with these devices so you can store logon information easily. The data is encrypted so even if you lose the device, your information should remain safe.

Figure 2.6
Products such as the IronKey help to protect your privacy when working on computers away from your home or office. Courtesy of IronKey.

Ethics in Cyberspace | Privacy and Other Ethics Issues

- **Create Strong Passwords**—Well-constructed passwords are difficult to guess and contain a combination of upper and lowercase letters, numbers, and symbols (such as # or &). The ideal length for secure passwords is at least 12 characters. Strong passwords do not contain dictionary words, letter or number sequences, such as 1234 or ABCD, or personal information, such as birth dates, street addresses, names of your pets, and so on. You should avoid using the same password for all the Web sites that you access to make it more difficult for thieves if they obtain one of your passwords. Web sites such as *www.passwordmeter.com* (see Figure 2.7) can help you evaluate the strength of your passwords.

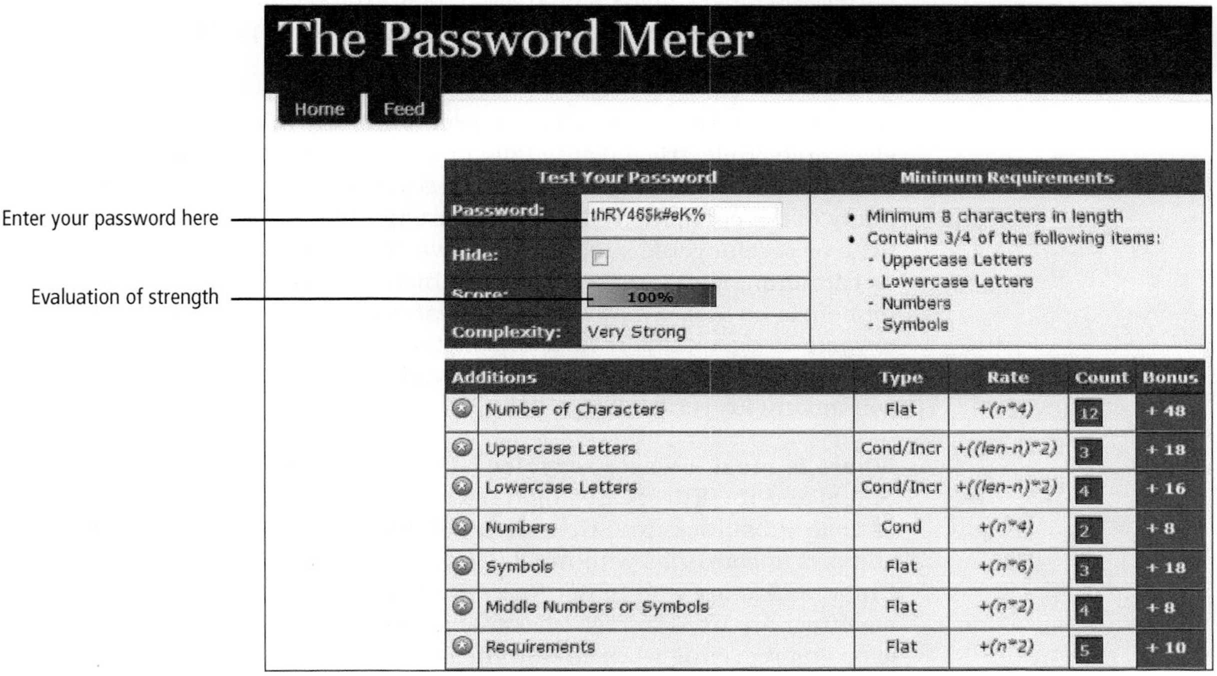

Figure 2.7
The Password Meter gives you a free evaluation of the strength of your password.

- **Change your passwords frequently**—You should change your passwords on a regular basis to improve your security. However, strong passwords that you constantly change can be challenging to remember. Therefore, you may want to use password management software to keep track of your passwords. Windows Vista, the Firefox browser, and security products (such as Norton 360) all have password management tools. The software stores all of your passwords for you to make logging onto your favorite Web sites a breeze. Even though you have different passwords for each site, you'll need to remember only one master password for the password management software to gain access to all your passwords.

Protecting your privacy requires the use of vigilance, common sense, and appropriate software programs. Enjoy the Internet, but practice caution to maintain your anonymity and privacy.

Objective 5
Define E-waste and Describe Methods for Disposing of E-waste

Did you ever throw away an old cell phone because it stopped working? Perhaps you bought a new computer and put your old one out on the sidewalk for trash collection. What will you do with your iPod when the battery no longer holds a charge? Replace the battery or get a newer iPod? All of these decisions impact a growing world problem of the disposal of electronic waste or e-waste.

What is e-waste and why is it a problem? Any broken or discarded electronic or electrical device falls in the category of *e-waste*. E-waste is much more difficult to dispose of or recycle than normal waste because many of the components of e-waste are not biodegradable or contain toxic or carcinogenic substances. E-waste can include substances such as cadmium, lead, and mercury—all highly toxic—and polychlorinated biphenyls (PCBs), which are known carcinogens. The problem is that e-waste also contains recoverable metals, such as gold, silver, and copper, whose prices are rising on the world market. This makes e-waste a valuable commodity for recycling.

Where is most e-waste recycled? Unfortunately, because the United States and the European Union have stringent laws about the handling of toxic substances and their disposal, much of the world's e-waste is shipped to countries with much less stringent pollution laws, such as China, Pakistan, and India. Risky methods, such as plastic and copper smelting, are used to recover valuable resources from the waste while exposing recycling workers and the surrounding environment to unsafe levels of toxic substances. The components that can't be recycled—mostly non-biodegradable—end up in landfills in developing countries. Although you could argue that the developing countries doing the recycling receive economic benefit, it can easily be argued that developed countries dumping their toxic wastes on less developed countries is unethical. Remember that analyzing the ethics of a situation involves considering whether a decision is fair to all involved. Is it fair for developed countries to use developing countries as their trash dump?

What can I do about the problem of e-waste? The main thing you can do is generate less e-waste, which sounds like an obvious solution. Use products for as long as possible by upgrading or refurbishing them. Do you need a brand new iPod when you can replace the battery pack in your old one? A 50-inch plasma TV sounds great until you consider discarding an old television that still works.

Donating products that you no longer need, but that still work, to someone who can use them is another great solution. Many manufacturers of electronic products provide resources on their Web sites for locating

Ethics in Cyberspace | Privacy and Other Ethics Issues

organizations to which you can donate your unwanted computers and electronic devices. Freecycle (*www.freecycle.org*) is a worldwide organization comprised of groups of people in local communities. Their objective is to reduce waste by encouraging people to give away for free their unwanted items to people in their local communities who can use them. You can probably find someone in a Freecycle group who can use that computer or cell phone you no longer need.

Buying products that are recycling friendly is another way to reduce e-waste. Green computing products use more renewable materials, such as bamboo, instead of non-biodegradable plastics. The [re]drive Turbo USB 2.0 External Hard Drive from Simple Tech (see Figure 2.8) uses bamboo, which is biodegradable and fast growing, and aluminum—easily recyclable—to create an environmentally friendly product. Web sites such as The Green Lounge (*www.thegreenlounge.org*) can keep you abreast of trends in green computing.

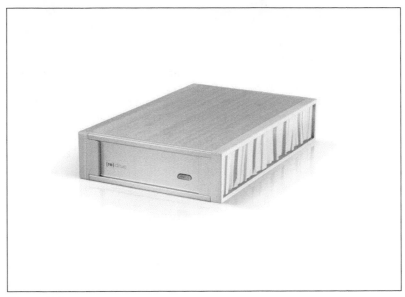

Figure 2.8
Bamboo and aluminum components help make this hard drive environmentally friendly. Courtesy of Erin Hartin/Fabrik, Inc./SimpleTech, Inc.

Recycling e-waste safely is the final step you can take. Many computer manufacturers sponsor their own computer recycling programs (see Figure 2.9). You can locate local recycling centers in your area by exploring sites such as Earth 911 (*http://earth911.org/*).

Figure 2.9
Many computer companies provide guidance on recycling and donation of unwanted computers in a number of different countries including the United States. If companies export wastes overseas for recycling or disposal, they have an ethical responsibility to train workers to recycle and reclaim materials in an environmentally friendly manner that minimizes worker exposure to toxic substances.

Keeping e-waste to a minimum and disposing of it safely is obviously good for the environment and society. By disposing of e-waste safely or recycling it in your own country, you are behaving ethically by treating residents of developing countries with respect instead of exploiting them.

Objective 6
Describe Web-Content Filtering and Its Effect on Free Speech

If you are an adult surfing the Web from home in the United States, you probably won't have trouble accessing sites on the Web and finding information on almost any topic you want. But what if you are restricted from seeing certain content on the Web "for your protection" or "for your own good"? Think this can't happen? It happens every day in the United States and many other countries and is a constant subject of ethical controversy. As usual, whether you find this practice to be ethical or unethical is a matter of personal opinion.

What is Web content filtering? *Web content filtering* means using software to restrict the availability of information that someone can find while surfing the Web. There are two main situations in which Web content filtering is used:

- **Politically**—Certain governments, such as China, want to restrict the availability of opposing political views and other sensitive information from their citizens.

- **Protectively**—The objective is to protect a certain group of people from objectionable, inappropriate, or offensive content, such as not allowing children access to pornography.

What type of political content filtering takes place? Many countries restrict access to information, but China is one of the most active. China has passed numerous laws regarding censorship, and state-owned ISPs block Web sites with content that violates these laws. The Golden Shield Project, often referred to as the Great Firewall of China, is a government network of firewalls and Internet servers that block specific URLs from being accessed. Web sites that are blocked include, but are not limited to, the following topics:

- Pornography or obscenity
- References to outlawed groups such as Falun Gong
- Commentaries on free speech, democracy, or Marxism
- Descriptions or photographs of Tiananmen Square protests of 1989 or other more recent protests
- Discussions of the Dalai Lama, his teachings, or the International Tibet Independence Movement

China employs an Internet police force to enforce their Internet laws. Comments on blogs or other discussion sites that are deemed to violate these laws are often rapidly deleted. In 2006, Google came under fire by many international civil rights groups when it agreed to deploy a version of their search engine for China that was self-censored by Google to meet the Chinese guidelines. The civil rights groups argued that Google was facilitating the suppression of free speech by the Chinese government. Google merely contended that it was complying with Chinese laws in an effort to provide search services to the Chinese people. The issue is still furiously debated today.

Why do people feel content needs to be filtered to protect individuals? Most people would agree that protecting children from pornography is an admirable objective. Controlling content placed on the Internet is difficult, especially in America and other countries where free speech is a right. Laws designed to restrict Internet content are often not passed due to concerns about the violation of the right to free speech. Therefore, since almost anything can be placed on the Internet, filtering content is one of the few options available. Schools and libraries in the United States are required to have filtering software on their computers to qualify for certain types of federal funding. Filtering software, like Net Nanny (see Figure 2.10) can be configured to block various categories of objectionable material.

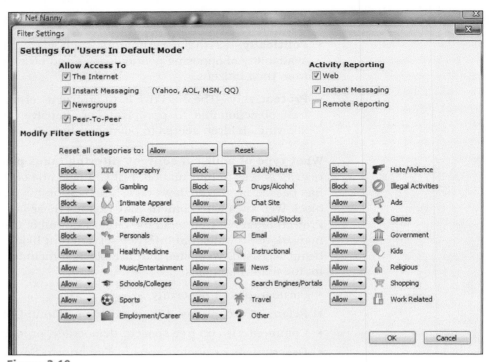

Figure 2.10
Net Nanny filtering software provides a wide range of content-blocking options.

Why is content filtering an ethical issue? Opponents of filtering software contend that when objectionable material—defined by arbitrary standards—is blocked, the infringement of free speech rights occurs. Actually, individuals are not prevented from exercising their right of free speech. But, infringing upon the rights of free access to information has generally been defined by the U.S. courts as a First Amendment (free speech) issue. Restricting free speech is not only illegal in the United States, but is also considered unethical. Supporters of content filtering contend that there are groups of people, like children, that need to be protected from objectionable material "for their own good" and that it would be unethical not to protect them.

But free speech is not necessarily a right of individuals in other countries. Although in the United States, we consider the restriction of free speech to be illegal, it is legal in many instances under Chinese law. So although you might consider the restriction of content to be unethical, the Chinese government has a different view. You need to consider ethical issues in the context of individual societies. In the case of free speech, for example, what is ethical in one country may be considered unethical in another.

Does content filtering actually protect people from objectionable content? In many instances, filtering software is effective. However, problems arise when the software is unable to discern between objectionable content and informational content. Content filtering software often

Ethics in Cyberspace | Privacy and Other Ethics Issues

looks for key words or phrases when determining whether or not to block a Web site. Sites that provide information on safe sex, support gay rights, or with information on breast cancer may be blocked because key-term filters might confuse them with pornographic sites. Sometimes the owners of pornography sites are adept at disguising the content of their sites in ways that fool the filtering software.

Because regulating the content of the Internet is not practical, content filtering remains one of the few options. Therefore, the debate over violating the rights of free speech—usually considered unethical—will rage on for the foreseeable future.

Objective 7
Define the Digital Divide and Describe Methods for Bridging It

Computers, the Internet, and other advanced technologies are becoming ubiquitous in the United States. Even the simple acts of ordering a sandwich at a local convenience store or running a gasoline pump often involve using touch screen computers. When you are doing research assignments for school—perhaps related to this book—the first resource you utilize is often the Internet. But what if you didn't have Internet access? What if you didn't even have access to a computer? What if you were unable to get clean drinking water because computer-controlled water purification systems were too expensive for your village to afford? Just like millions of other people around the world, in these instances you would find yourself on the wrong side of the digital divide.

What is the digital divide? The concept of a *digital divide* refers to the perceived gap between those people who have access to digital technology and those who do not. Although the term came into popular usage in 1996 after President Clinton and Vice President Gore began using the term in speeches, the concept of a division between haves and have-nots is hardly new. In the 1960s, Dr. Martin Luther King was one of the first social activists to recognize and articulate this problem in several speeches that he made. Dr. King said, "Modern man through scientific genius has been able to dwarf distance. Through our genius we have made this world a neighborhood. And yet we have not yet had the ethical commitment to make of it a brotherhood. But somehow, and in some way, we have got to do this." And these statements were made almost 20 years before the invention and popularization of the personal computer and 30 years before the widespread popularity of the Internet! Dr. King recognized that without equal access to technology, people might find themselves at a disadvantage.

Why is the digital divide an ethical issue? A key component of judging whether behavior is ethical is fairness. If certain groups are denied access to technology, they are put at an unfair disadvantage compared to those with access to the technology. And equal access to technology doesn't just mean computers. Many technologies contribute to improved quality of life such as new farming techniques, water purification equipment, transportation systems, and digital access to government services. Improving the quality of life of individuals tends to benefit society as a whole and therefore makes it a laudable ethical goal.

So we just need to give cheap computers to poor people to conquer the digital divide? If only it were that simple. The digital divide is not just about socioeconomic differences (poor versus rich). The divide also can be generational (youth versus senior citizens), geographic (urban versus rural . . . especially with Internet connectivity), or ethnic (racial). The gap in the digital divide is complex and is not as simple as throwing money at the problem to make it go away. First we need to consider the nuances that make up the gap.

What comprises the "gap" in the digital divide? There are two main components to the digital divide. The first is *physical access gap* which involves individuals who do not have ready access to technology (such as home PCs, the Internet, etc.) or when technology that is available elsewhere is not being used to effectively improve their lives. Do you have access to computer equipment? Is digital technology (such as kiosks to access government services) being used to improve the quality of your life? Do you posses a broadband Internet connection? Can you even get broadband access in the area where you live? Yes, having a dial-up connection to the Internet actually can put you on the wrong side of the digital divide because so much of the multimedia experience of the Internet today is dependent upon fast access speed. Many people only consider the physical access gap when considering the digital divide, but equally as important is the accessibility gap.

The *accessibility gap* refers mainly to the lack the knowledge (or varying degrees of knowledge) to use technology effectively (lack of computer literacy skills). Giving someone a computer without teaching them how to use it is of dubious value ... especially if they have never seen a computer before! Remember the first time you went on the Internet? Unless someone showed you what to do and where to start (such as how to use a Web browser), you probably struggled at first. But the accessibility gap also refers to physical limitations that prevent people from adequately accessing technology (such as the elderly and people with disabilities). To close the digital divide, physical access and accessibility issues must both be addressed.

Has the availability of inexpensive computers in the U.S. effectively eliminated the physical access gap? True, computers are relatively inexpensive in the U.S. But that still doesn't mean everyone can afford to own one. In many countries such as China and India, computers are still unaffordable to a large percentage of the population. Also, if you don't have a computer in your home, you are forced to rely on shared-access computers at your job, your school, the public library, or Internet cafes. And don't forget, the cost of accessing technology isn't limited to the cost of a computer and monitor.

If you actually want to do something with the computer, you are going to need software. Yes, there are free software programs available, but you may need to purchase a product like Microsoft Office to maintain compatibility with coworkers. And access to the Internet isn't free. While dial-up connections can still be relatively cheap, their slow speed will make your Internet experience rather inefficient or downright painful in many instances. Broadband connections cost $30 a month and up, which isn't necessarily in everyone's budget. And backup hardware and software and networking equipment is an additional expense if you are planning on establishing connectivity between multiple computers (or sharing Internet access). The cost of computing still presents a physical barrier for many individuals in the United States and other countries.

Won't the accessibility gap close on its own as computers become more user-friendly? This is a position that is popular in certain circles. Certainly, computers are becoming more user-friendly. That helps many people caught in the accessibility gap, but not all—don't forget about the physical gap! Children are exposed to technology at a much earlier age and use it on a regular basis. Many people equate the comfort level that today's generation has with technology with proficiency. Unfortunately, growing up with technology doesn't necessarily guarantee computer literacy. You still need to know how to use the technology effectively and efficiently. Being connected to the Internet or having an easy to use point-and-click interface doesn't help you if you don't know where to look for information or how to interpret what you find.

How do we close the digital divide? There are many organizations that are working on solutions, and you can start by getting involved or supporting them. Start by finding organizations in your community that provide computer access and training to underserved populations. Your local library, community college, community center, or social service organizations are great places to begin.

One of the most famous organizations working on closing the digital divide is The One Laptop Per Child Association, Inc. (*http://laptop.org*). OLPC is an organization funded by major corporations such as AMD, eBay, Google, and Red Hat with the goal of providing affordable laptops to children in developing countries. Individuals also provide support mostly by funding the purchase of individual computers for donation. The XO-1 laptop (see Figure 2.11) is a sturdy computer with flash memory instead of a hard drive that runs on a version of the Linux operating system. It features networking capabilities to foster working on shared projects by users and to enable many computers to access a single Internet connection. The specially designed graphical user interface called Sugar was designed to make collaboration easy for novice users. Millions of laptops have already been purchased by a number of developing countries.

Define the Digital Divide and Describe Methods for Bridging It | **Ethics in Cyberspace**

Figure 2.11
The XO laptop is designed to provide an inexpensive computing solution for the masses in developing countries. Courtesy of Fuse Project.

Other less well known organizations, such as EduVision, Inveneo, and Geekcorps (*www.geekcorps.org*), are working on various hardware, infrastructure, and training projects to shrink the digital divide. Geekcorps (see Figure 2.12) recruits technology professionals to work in various parts of the world with local partners to design and deploy communication infrastructure and to teach technology in small group settings. If you have the appropriate technology experience, you can volunteer to work for Geekcorps and possibly go overseas when participating in projects. But Geekcorps makes it easy for everyone to support them by doing something that many people already do on a regular basis—buy merchandise from Amazon.com. Following the link to Amazon on Geekcorps, Web site results in commissions to Geekcorps for all purchases you make in that visit to Amazon. So while the digital divide isn't going to be closed overnight, you can get involved and help shrink the divide in your part of the global community.

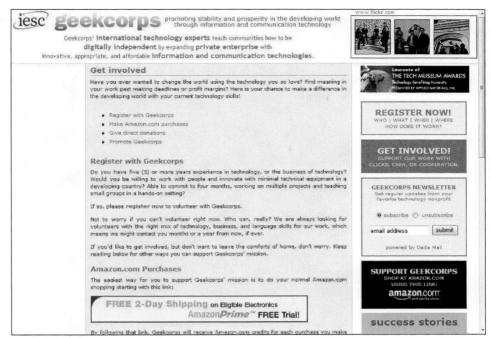

Figure 2.12
You can provide support to organizations such as Geekcorps and start bridging the digital divide.

Objective 8
Describe Methods to Evaluate the Accuracy of Digital Information

You can find almost anything on the Internet just by using a search engine such as Google or Yahoo. Everyone seems to receive helpful e-mails from friends and family warning you about a variety of issues, such as the police in your state giving out speeding tickets. Because any-one can put up a Web page on any subject imaginable or send off a quick e-mail, how can you distinguish fact from fiction? Determining the relia-bility of information you encounter in cyberspace can be a challenge. It is also critically important when you use the Web as a source of scholarly research. Your biology professor would probably give you a poor grade if you presented her with a research paper on the rare Pacific Northwest Tree Octopus (see Figure 2.13).

Figure 2.13
A joke Web site that looks real if you don't know that an octopus lives only in the ocean!

Is posting false information on the Internet unethical? Most people would agree that posting false information is unethical; however, that doesn't stop people from posting blatantly false or erroneous information on the Web because of the ease with which you can disseminate information on the Internet and often remain anonymous. In less than an hour, someone can create a credible looking Web site that presents "evidence" to support the premise that the 1906 San Francisco earthquake never took place. But given the overwhelming amount of historical evidence—including still photos and newspaper interviews with earthquake survivors—you know that a devastating earthquake did occur in California in 1906. Not only is trying to change history by lying unethical, but it is disrespectful to the memories of the people who suffered through a catastrophic event like an earthquake.

Why would someone disseminate false information? Certain Web sites portray facts in a distorted fashion to support an organization's point. The dissemination of false or distorted information is often used to further an agenda of hate speech, racism, or the perpetuation of stereotypes. Bogus or exaggerated claims are made to sell ineffective products, such as "miracle weight loss drugs." Organizations might distort facts, make sweeping generalizations, or state opinions as facts to support fund-raising campaigns, especially for causes that have an emotional component, such as cruelty to animals or impoverished people. Other individuals enjoy seeing how many people they can fool into believing information that is false.

Unfortunately, many inaccuracies on the Internet are unintentional. People writing content for Web pages may not check their facts to ensure they are accurate. Others perpetuate bad information by using an erroneous source of information and then using those facts to generate new Internet content for other Web sites. Obviously, if you are going to rely on information from a Web site—especially if you are doing scholarly research—you need to take steps to ensure that the information is accurate and the site is appropriate for your needs.

There are many instances of intentional misrepresentations on the Internet. Some Web sites, such as the Tree Octopus, or the last Web page (see Figure 2.14) are obvious attempts at humor or parodies of other legitimate Web sites. Because it sometimes can be difficult to tell fact from fiction on the Internet, you need a strategy for evaluating what you will encounter while surfing the Web.

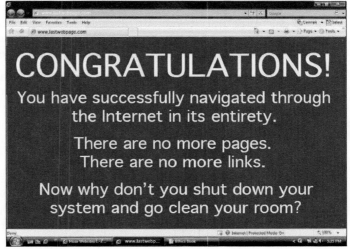

Figure 2.14
An obvious joke because there is no last page to the Internet.

What criteria should you use for evaluating the suitability of a Web site? Evaluation criteria are similar to those you use for printed resources that you would find in your school library. You need to consider the following:

- **Who is the author?**—Is information about the author —including contact information—readily available on the site? If you know the author's name, you can search the Internet or other resources to consider the expertise of the author. Is the author a noted leader in the field he is writing about and recognized as an authority by others you respect? Does the author have appropriate credentials such as college degrees or relevant work experience that gives you comfort to know he has expertise in the field? Although you might find what you consider to be good information on an anonymous blogger's Web site, you don't have any information about the blogger to consider him an authority on a subject.

- **Who is the publisher of the information or the owner of the Web site?** —Is the organization that owns or sponsors the Web site clearly identified? Is that entity an appropriate source of information for the topic you are researching? Is the publisher respected in the field and relied upon by others? Obviously, a respected journalistic body like the New York Times (*www.nytimes.com*) has more credibility than Billy Bob's Bodacious Blog!

  Carefully examine the URL for the Web site for clues. Domains—the portion of the web address after the dot—are often set up for specific purposes: *.gov* and *.mil* are for government and military entities, *.edu* is for educational institutions, and *.org* is mostly for non-profit organizations, although other entities can get *.org* addresses now. For instance, URLs for personal Web sites or less well known businesses need more scrutiny than a Web site like *www.irs.gov* when seeking tax advice. Educational entities (*.edu*) may have more scholarly credibility than Web sites in the *.com* domain, in which anyone can register a site.

- **What is the relationship of the author to the publisher?**—Is the author an employee of the publishing entity? Or, does the author have a more casual relationship with the publisher such as generating content for a fee? Employees *might* be held to a more stringent level of competence and be required to have more appropriate credentials than independent contractors.

- **The point of view or bias**—Writers tend to use information that helps them make their points to the reader. A good writer is objective and provides different points of view, even when they are detrimental to his argument. The writer should also acknowledge when he is presenting his opinion as opposed to facts, and controversial theories should be identified as such.

  Consider the organization and how it might be affected by the information. If you are reviewing information about products that the company publishing the Web site sells, be aware that the information presented may be intended to persuade people to buy the product. Corporate Web sites tend to paint the corporation in the most positive light, whereas a site not sponsored by the corporation might provide a more objective opinion about the company's operations and products. Also consider whether the publisher has a particular political, religious, or philosophical agenda that may encourage him to slant the information that is presented to support their causes.

- **Does the work cite sources?**—Just as your professors expect you to use footnotes and a bibliography in your research papers, scholarly publications on the Internet should also list their sources of information. When presented with a list of sources, check them. Are the sources respected publications or from authoritative and reliable authors on other Web sites?

- **Is the accuracy of the work verifiable?**—Can you find the sources listed in the bibliography? Do hyperlinks to other articles work so you can review the sources? For articles involving research, were the research methods, the data collected, and the interpretation of the results provided so that the research study could be reproduced if necessary?

- **Is the information presented current?**—Are dates of publication clearly indicated on the Web site? When the work is updated, are updates clearly identified and dated? Are the dates at which research information was gathered presented (for example, "based on a study conducted by XYZ Consultants in May, 2011")?

Finally, after following these steps, take a step back and consider what you have found. Decide why the page was placed on the Web. Was the main goal of the page to inform, persuade, or sell? Consider whether the page was intended to be a parody or a satire. The best indicator for this is the tone of the writing. Was the writer sarcastic? Did he tend to use a lot of humor or exaggerate to make points? Was the page supplemented with outlandish or humorous photographs? Decide if there are better places to find your needed research than on the Internet. Are the Web sites you are evaluating as credible as respected published periodicals or texts that you would consult in your college library? If after all of this analysis you feel comfortable, then you might have found a good source of reliable information on the Web.

Can I rely on the information I find in Wikipedia? Because anyone can add content to Wikipedia, the world's largest online encyclopedia, many people wonder if it is a reliable source of information. Wikipedia entries are reviewed by editors so there is some control over the accuracy of content. But just as any other source of information, articles in Wikipedia need to be evaluated based on the criteria described previously. Recent studies have shown that Wikipedia, for science and nature articles, contain about the same number of errors as the *Encyclopædia Britannica*. Many articles on Wikipedia have extensive footnotes and lists of sources so you can investigate the reliability of the source material. So treat Wikipedia as you would any other Web page upon which you might want to rely; evaluate it thoroughly before relying on it.

Is there a resource for finding quality sites for scholarly research? There are several resources on the Internet, most of which were created by librarians, that can be useful for quickly locating Web sites that are considered reliable, current, and suitable for academic research. Some of the more popular ones are the Librarian's Internet Index, The Internet Public Library, Infomine, and Academic Info. These are described in the table in Figure 2.15.

Web Site Name	Description	Web Site Address
Librarian's Internet Index	Publically funded Web site maintained by librarians that finds and evaluates high quality information sites. Currently has links to over 20,000 resources.	*www.lii.org*
INFOMINE	Built and maintained by librarians, INFOMINE focuses on resources relevant to university-level faculty, students, and research staff. Resources listed include databases, electronic journals, electronic books, articles, and directories of researchers.	*http://infomine.ucr.edu*
The Internet Public Library	Another librarian constructed information resource that strives to provide links to resources that have been evaluated by librarians and determined to contain high quality information. The IPL also serves as a research forum and an online test bed for new information technologies	*www.ipl.org*

Figure 2.15
Resources for finding quality Web sites.

The Librarian's Internet Index (see Figure 2.16) is easy to use as it closely resembles other search engines and subject directories. But, the pages indexed in LII have been carefully reviewed for accuracy and currency by librarians and other scholars who maintain the site. This doesn't mean you don't have to check facts, but it does provide you with an excellent starting point for your research.

Type in key terms to use the search engine feature.

Browse through evaluated Web pages by subject.

Figure 2.16
The Librarian's Internet Index can be used like a conventional search engine or you can browse through it by subject.

Following these guidelines should ensure that you are relying on accurate information for your research needs. There is one more category of false information that requires some additional measures to handle, and that is e-mail hoaxes.

What is a hoax? A *hoax* is anything that is designed to deceive another person either as a practical joke or for financial gain. It attempts to make someone believe something that is untrue. Hoaxes perpetrated in cyberspace that are designed to part suckers from their money are classified as cybercrimes. Cybercrime hoaxes generally target a single individual. In this section, you will explore hoaxes that target a large audience and are generally perpetrated as practical jokes, agents of social change (poking fun at the established norm in an effort to change it), or a waste people's valuable time. Although there are hoax Web sites, most cyberspace hoaxes are perpetrated by e-mail.

Why do people create e-mail hoaxes? As opposed to garnering financial rewards, the motives of e-mail hoax creators can be more complex. Many people start e-mail hoaxes just for the challenge of seeing if their "brain-child" can be spread globally. Other hoaxes start as innocent practical jokes between friends, but then take on a life of their own via the fast communication on the Internet. Many hoaxes become so well known that they are incorporated into society as true events even though they are false. Once this happens, they are known as **urban legends**. An example of an urban legend is the story about a man who wakes up in a bathtub full of ice water to discover he has had his kidney taken out. Hoaxes are similar

Describe Methods to Evaluate the Accuracy of Digital Information | **Ethics in Cyberspace** to acts of real world vandalism such as graffiti. Just as graffiti artists "make their mark on the world" hoaxers may consider they are making a similar mark when a bogus e-mail they created becomes widespread.

Sometimes hoaxes are based on misinformation or the venting of frustration. An e-mail hoax that reappears every time there is a spike in gasoline prices is the Gas Boycott, or Gas War hoax (see Figure 2.17). The e-mail touts the scheme as being invented by reputable businessmen to boost its credibility. The e-mail explains how boycotting certain gasoline companies will drive the price of gasoline down and urges recipients of the e-mail to join the fight. The originator of this hoax was probably frustrated by high gas prices and had a poor understanding of economics. Unfortunately, this tactic will have no effect on gasoline prices as it only shifts demand for gasoline from certain oil companies to other sources. Because it does not reduce the overall demand for gasoline, the price of gas will not decline. How many of you received this e-mail and thought it sounded like plausible idea?

Figure 2.17
The Gas War hoax is a typical e-mail hoax.

How can I tell if an e-mail is a hoax? Sometimes it is difficult to separate fact from fiction. Many hoax e-mails are well written and crafted in such a way that they sound real. Before hitting the Forward button and sending an e-mail to all your friends, first check it out at one of the many Web sites that keep track of e-mail hoaxes and expose them. Check sites such as *www.snopes.com, www.hoax-slayer.com* (see Figure 2.18), or *www.truthorfiction.com.* These sites are searchable, so you can enter a few key words from the e-mail you suspect may be a hoax and quickly find similar e-mails with an explanation of whether they are true or false.

Checking out e-mails before forwarding them on to friends, family, and coworkers will save other people's time and help end the spread of these time wasters.

Get alerts to new hoaxes by subscribing

Use keywords from a suspected e-mail to find similar hoaxes

Browse hoaxes by category

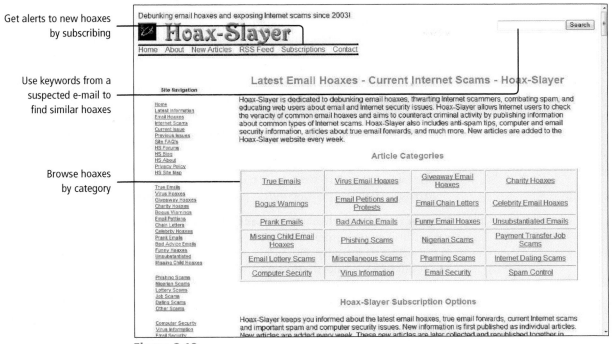

Figure 2.18
Hoax-Slayer.com is a useful resource for researching suspected hoaxes.

Not passing on information that is false is all part of being an ethical Internet user. It takes more effort on your part to check potential hoaxes, but think of all the time you'll save your friends and family by not sending out endless streams of hoax e-mails!

Objective 9
Define Online Reputation and Describe Methods for Protecting Your Online Reputation

There may already be quite a bit of information about you on the Internet. Chances are you've put quite a bit of it out there yourself possibly through social networking sites such as MySpace, Facebook, and LinkedIn. Most people strive to maintain a good reputation in the real world because this helps them get good jobs, make friends, develop business relationships, and generally makes life easier to conduct. But in the twenty-first century, your online, virtual reputation is just as important as your real-life one.

What exactly is my online reputation? Your *online reputation* is an extension of your real-life reputation. Your real-life reputation is the view held by the community, the general public, friends, family, and coworkers of your general character. Are you considered an honest person? Do you always speak your mind regardless of the consequences? Are you known for defending the rights of less fortunate individuals? These are examples of factors that contribute to society's view of the type of individual you are.

Your online reputation consists of the information that is available about you in cyberspace that can influence people in the real world regarding your character. Information is constantly added to the Internet about many of us, even by people we don't know. It can be challenging to control the information that contributes to your online reputation. If you go to a party this weekend and some of the guests take pictures of you or videos at the party, these people may post their media to Flickr or YouTube and identify—known as **tagging**—you in the pictures and video. Your friends might be writing about you on their MySpace pages as you read this. Perhaps someone you work with is talking about you on his or her blog. Even if what they are writing is true, false, misleading, embarrassing, or disturbing to you, it is becoming part of your online reputation.

Why is it so important to protect my online reputation? If you say something or do something you wish you hadn't in real life, people will forget about it eventually. However, given the **persistence of information**—the tendency for information on the Internet to remain on the Internet for long periods of time—pictures, videos, and narratives about you might never disappear. Even if you delete something, it probably still exists somewhere. Sites such as the Internet Archive—*www.archive.org*—feature utilities such as the Wayback Machine that can show you what a Web site looked like at a previous point in time. Ever wonder what Yahoo looked like way back in the dark ages, such as in 1996, of the Internet? A search

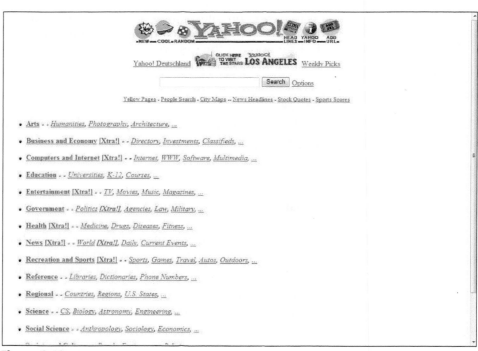

Figure 2.19
A much simpler Yahoo home page is preserved for posterity in the Internet Archive. Your Web pages might live on forever also.

Ethics in Cyberspace | Privacy and Other Ethics Issues

on the Wayback Machine shows you that it looked like Figure 2.19. Cyberspace has a much longer memory than humans. When reputation was spread only by word of mouth, it tended to encompass a small area. Now, you can move halfway around the world, and negative information about you is much more easily discovered.

Of course your reputation varies depending on who is interpreting the cyberspace information about you. You friends might be impressed by that picture on MySpace of you doing a headstand on your skateboard. Your mother is less likely to be impressed when she spots it and worries that you might get seriously injured by your tricks.

What are the ethical issues surrounding my online reputation? The main ethical issues are truthfulness and fairness. Does your online reputation portray accurately, or truthfully, the type of person you are? Would all third parties researching you on the Internet arrive at the correct conclusion about your nature and character based on the available information, or fairness related to that availability of information?

Obviously, you don't want your friends, family, or coworkers to post inaccurate or misleading information about you online that would portray your character in an inappropriate manner to others. Conversely, you shouldn't act unethically yourself by posting false information on the Internet in an attempt to artificially enhance your reputation.

Why should I care what others think of my online reputation?
According to the University of Massachusetts Center for Market research, 54 percent of college admissions officers research candidates on the Internet. Employers also routinely browse through social networking sites (such as MySpace and Facebook) and blogs to evaluate job applicants as part of making hiring decisions. And even after you are hired, if your employer finds things that it doesn't like on one of your sites you might be fired because of it. In early 2008, CNN producer Chez Pazienza alleged he was discharged by CNN because it felt he had violated CNN journalism standards on a personal blog that he writes called Deus Ex Malcontent. The most famous firing for blogging was also the first instance of this practice. Ellen Simonetti was a Delta Airlines flight attendant who was fired by Delta because the company objected to pictures that she posted on her blog.

How can an employer fire me for writing something on my own time?
Don't we have free speech in the United States? Yes, you do have a constitutional right to free speech. However, that doesn't mean your employer is going to agree with your opinions. In the majority of the states, the *employment at-will* principle governs the firing of employees. Employment at-will means that unless you are covered by an employment contract or a collective bargaining agreement, such as a union contract, employers can fire you at any time for any reason, unless the reason violates a legal statute such as race discrimination. You employer is not required to provide you with a reason for the firing, but can simply tell you not to report for work any longer. Therefore, it is a good idea to be aware of the attitudes and behaviors that your employer might find objectionable and steer clear of those issues on sites where you are easily identifiable (see Figure 2.20).

Besides losing my job, what other problems can a bad online reputation cause me? It could perhaps get you put in jail! Consider Joshua

Lipton who was arrested for a drunken driving accident in which another person was seriously injured. When the case came to trial, the prosecutor presented a picture of Lipton taken two weeks after the accident when he was attending a Halloween party. He was dressed as a prisoner in an orange jumpsuit labeled *Jail bird*. The prosecutor successfully argued that Lipton was not repentant over his actions, but was instead joking about them. Lipton was sentenced to two years in prison. The prosecutor had found the picture on a Facebook page from someone who attended the party.

Figure 2.20
Pictures posted on social networking sites can be used to defend or defame your character depending upon the context. Courtesy of www.istockphoto.com.

Can I take legal action against someone who damages my reputation? You can try. In this case, you would be filing a *defamation* suit—also called libel or slander suit. Defamation results when a false claim is made that portrays an individual, group, business, or product in a negative light, thereby damaging the reputation. *Libel* is defamation in written or visual depictions, and most cyberspace defamation suits revolve around libel. *Slander* usually relates to verbal statements and gestures; it is a more common source of legal action in the real world. Unfortunately, many defamation suits filed over statements made in cyberspace are dismissed by judges based on first amendment, free speech grounds. However, certain cases involving serious damage to reputations do make it all the way through to a trial.

What steps should I take to protect my online reputation? Exercise care in putting personal details about yourself on the Internet. Make sure there is a compelling reason to reveal information before doing so. Be vigilant about the access you grant to social networking sites. Make your profiles visible only to friends. Be selective about the friends you connect with on these sites. You need to be satisfied that they are people you can trust and not just casual acquaintances or friends of friends. If you are blogging, consider remaining anonymous.

You need to examine your own reputation periodically. Google yourself and see what information about you is available on the Web. If you see something that displeases you, ask the poster or the webmaster to remove the offending material. Don't have time to constantly monitor your reputation? Products such as MyReputation (see Figure 2.21) and Trackur provide automatic searches and updates regarding information posted about you online.

Figure 2.21
MyReputation from Reputation Defender provides comprehensive reports about the information about you that is on the Web and provides you with assistance in having the information removed.

Keeping your online reputation accurate and not unfairly damaging other people's cyberspace reputations is an integral part of being an ethical cyber-citizen.

End-of-Chapter Assessments

Summary

Engaging in ethical behavior on the Internet means you will exercise common sense and good judgment. Stop and think before you act to consider the ramifications of your actions and their effects on other individuals.

- Do you really want to pass on that unsubstantiated rumor about a classmate on your Facebook page?

- How would you feel if someone posted an embarrassing picture of you on the Internet?

- Is saving a little time on an English class assignment worth potentially failing the course and being kicked out of school because you copied the information for the paper directly from a Web site?

- Do you really want representatives from a federal law enforcement agency coming to your house, seizing your computer and leveling massive finds on you just because you wanted to save a few bucks and illegally download a copy of the movie *Spiderman 3*?

- If the band you were in recorded a cool new song would you want people swapping MP3 files of it on the Internet while you received no compensation for your hard work?

- Do you really need a new computer, or can you make your current one last another year and thereby avoid having it tossed into a landfill in India?

Being an ethical citizen in cyberspace takes extra time and effort. But the rewards of treating others fairly and with respect are worth it.

Key Terms

Accessibility gap	Hoax	Phishing
Cyberbullying	Identity theft	Physical access gap
Cybercrimes	Industrial espionage	Privacy
Cyber-harrassment	Invasion of Privacy	Slander
Cyberloafing	Keystroke loggers	Social engineering
Cyberstalking	Libel	Tagging
Defamation	Online reputation	Urban legends
Digital divide	Persistence of information	Web content filtering
Employment at-will		
E-waste	Pretexting	White collar crime

Ethics in Cyberspace | Privacy and Other Ethics Issues

360

Ethics

Matching

Match each term in the second column with its correct definition in the first column by writing the letter of the term on the blank line in front of the correct definition.

_____ **1.** The perceived gap between those with access to technology and those without access.

_____ **2.** Using a created scenario (usually over the phone) to trick an individual into revealing sensitive information.

_____ **3.** The tendency for information to endure.

_____ **4.** The right to be left alone to do as one pleases.

_____ **5.** Using the Internet to avoid working.

_____ **6.** Preventing access to objectionable material on the Web.

_____ **7.** An attempt to trick people into revealing sensitive information usually through the use of e-mail or another means.

_____ **8.** An attempt to trick someone into believing false information.

_____ **9.** Using the Internet to harass a classmate.

_____ **10.** Not having ready access to technology.

A Cyberbullying

B Cyberloafing

C Digital divide

D Hoax

E Persistence of information

F Phishing

G Physical access gap

H Pretexting

I Privacy

J Web content filtering

End-of-Chapter Assessments

Fill in the Blank

Write the correct answer in the space provided.

1. The _____ refers to people who lack the necessary skills to use a particular technology.

2. Software programs that keep track of all input via a computer keyboard are known as _____.

3. _____ is a false oral statement about an individual.

4. False information that becomes stories or facts that many people believe are known as _____.

5. _____ occurs when someone's personal privacy has been violated.

6. Playing an online game instead of working at your job is an example of _____.

7. The right of an employer to fire you at any time for any reason is known as the _____ doctrine.

8. Impersonating someone with the intent to defraud another institution, such as a credit card company, is called _____.

9. The tendency for information to remain somewhere in cyberspace for long periods of time—perhaps forever—is known as _____.

10. Personal information about you that is available in cyberspace and enables others to draw conclusions about the type of person you are is known as your _____.

11. False claims that are made about an individual that damages his reputation is collectively known as _____.

12. Written or visual depictions of defamation are known as _____.

13. A form of _____ is using a fake e-mail account to bombard a classmate with rude and insulting messages.

14. _____ software is often used to prevent children from accessing pornography sites.

15. Poor people in the United States who are unable to afford a computer or Internet access are said to be on the wrong side of the _____.

Multiple Choice

Circle the letter of the item that correctly answers the question.

1. The "digital divide":

   a. Is impossible to close

   b. Can be closed by providing individuals with inexpensive computers

   c. Requires ongoing community effort to bring technology resources to underserved populations

   d. Deals only with access to the Internet

2. Monitoring an employee's Internet use by an employer is:

   a. Illegal in the United States

   b. Legal in most areas of the United States

   c. Legal only if the employee is informed about the monitoring

   d. Legal only in Florida, California, Nevada, and New Jersey

3. Web content filtering is said to breach an individual's right to:

   a. Privacy

   b. Free information

   c. Self awareness

   d. Free speech

4. When many people believe a false story and the story becomes almost a universally accepted anecdote, the story is said to have become:

   a. An urban legend

   b. Folklore

   c. Wisdom

   d. An Internet reality tale

5. The right to privacy for Americans is:

   a. Specifically granted in the Fourth Amendment of the Constitution

   b. Granted by section 7 of the Bill of Rights

   c. Alluded to in the Fourth Amendment of the Constitution and interpreted by the courts as a right

   d. A key component of the Declaration of Independence

6. The two main reasons employers monitor employees are:

   a. Prevention of theft and measurement of productivity

   b. Prevention of theft and amusement

   c. Measurement of productivity and exercise of strict control of the workforce

   d. Provide laughs at the Christmas party and blackmail

(Multiple Choice—continues on the next page)

Multiple Choice | **Ethics in Cyberspace**

Multiple Choice

(Multiple Choice–continued)

7. All of the following are types of cyberbullies except:
   a. The Vengeful Angel
   b. The Power Hungry
   c. Mean Girls
   d. Sneaky Meany

8. Which of the following statements about identity theft is *not* true?
   a. A significant percentage of identity theft occurs through methods other than online information theft.
   b. Identity theft incidents occur online over 90 percent of the time.
   c. Identity thieves can take out mortgages in the victim's name and then disappear with the cash.
   d. Freezing your credit history is an effective method for preventing identity theft.

9. An effective way to mitigate the problems related to e-waste is to:
   a. Use electronic products for as long as possible
   b. Donate products that you no longer need to other individuals
   c. Buy electronic products that contain easily recyclable components
   d. All of the above

10. Which of the following is *least* important when evaluating the quality of a Web site for research purposes?
   a. The reputation of the author in the field being written about
   b. The relationship of the author to the Web site publisher
   c. The links on the Web site to other sites covering the same topic
   d. Sources cited in the work are from credible publications

Ethics in Cyberspace | Privacy and Other Ethics Issues

Outcome-Based Assessments

End-of-Chapter Exercises

Apply the objectives in this chapter by answering the following questions:

1. Does your school use filtering software in computer labs on campus? If so, what types of Web sites are filtered? Who should decide what sites should be blocked by filtering software? The government? Librarians? Educators? Would you install filtering software on your home computer to protect your children? What types of sites would you block, and why would you block those sites?

2. How do you normally dispose of your used electronic equipment? Use the Internet to find recycling programs in your area that are designed to handle e-waste. Is there a cost involved for dropping off materials to be recycled? What Internet sites can you use to locate organizations in your area that take donations of used electronic equipment?

3. Have you ever been the target of a phishing scam? What information was the scammer trying to obtain from you? Was the scammer successful in soliciting information from you? How can you protect yourself from phishing scams in the future?

4. Research identity theft on the Internet. What is the average amount of dollars lost per incident? How much time does the average victim spend clearing up an identity theft problem? Does your state allow you to freeze your credit report and if so, what is the procedure you must follow to do so? Prepare a checklist for victims of identity theft that provide them with the steps they need to follow if they have become a victim.

5. Does your employer or your school monitor your computer usage? If you aren't sure, find out. What types of activities are prohibited under the acceptable use policy at your employer or school? Have you ever violated the terms of the acceptable use policy? If yes, were you caught? How effective do you think monitoring is in preventing wrongdoing?

6. Google yourself. How many references did you find that you didn't know about? Are any of these damaging to your online reputation? Is there anything on any Web sites where you maintain pages— MySpace, Facebook, and so on—that might be damaging to your reputation? Is there anything on your friends' sites that might portray you in a bad light? If an employer searched for information about you online, what impression of your character would they form?

7. Have you or one of your friends ever been the victim of a cyberbully? If so, what exactly happened and how did you handle it? What procedures do you think should be put in place at an elementary school to decrease the chances of cyberbullying occurring?

8. Using the Internet, research organizations are taking steps to bridge the digital divide. What organizations are operating in your community to solve this problem? What are the underserved populations— that is, the people without appropriate access to technology—in the county where your college is located? What programs do you think should be developed in the county to help these underserved populations gain more access to technology?

Basic Computer Concepts

OBJECTIVES

Mastering these objectives will enable you to:

1. Define Computer and Identify the Four Basic Computing Functions
2. Identify the Different Types of Computers
3. Describe Hardware Devices and Their Uses
4. Identify Types of Software and Their Uses
5. Describe Networks and Define Network Terms
6. Identify Safe Computing Practices

In This Chapter

Computers are an integral part of our lives. They are found in homes, offices, stores, hospitals, libraries, and many other places. Computers are part of cars and phones, and they enable you to access bank accounts from home, shop online, and quickly communicate with people around the world by means of e-mail and the Internet. It is difficult to find a business or occupation that doesn't rely on computers. Whether it's a truck driver who keeps an electronic travel log or a high-powered stockbroker who needs up-to-the-second market information, computers can make these tasks faster, easier, more efficient, and more accurate.

Computers are all around us, which makes it important to learn basic computing skills and gain the knowledge to be a responsible computer user. Knowing how to use a computer makes you *computer fluent*.

This chapter looks at different types of computers and their functions. It discusses computer hardware and software and the benefits of networking. In addition, this chapter also discusses the importance of safe computing practices and the ways that you can protect your computer from various threats.

From Chapter 1 of *Go! with Basic Computer Concepts Getting Started,* First Edition, Shelley Gaskin, Victor Giol.

Objective 1 | Define Computer and Identify the Four Basic Computing Functions

What are the benefits of becoming computer fluent? Becoming computer fluent can benefit you in several ways. The advantage of being computer fluent is that it makes employees more attractive to potential employers. Many employers expect employees to have basic computer skills when they are hired. Computers have certainly changed the way we work. The traditional memo has given way to e-mail messages. Business reports can now be shared on a network, enabling a group of individuals to collaborate by adding their own notes and comments before the final report is finalized. Presentations are seldom delivered via overhead transparencies; presentation graphic software is widely used to share information with an audience in a conference room or via the company's intranet. Spreadsheet software is a key tool in presenting financial information and developing sound business plans.

On the other hand, if you are knowledgeable about computers and their uses, it also makes you a better consumer. You feel more comfortable when it comes to purchasing the right computer hardware and software for your needs, adding a peripheral for a specific use, or detecting basic problems when a system does not work properly. Also, if you have a basic understanding of today's technology, you can better understand and use *new* technologies.

What are the basic functions of a computer? A **computer** is a programmable electronic device that can input, process, output, and store data. The term **programmable** signifies that a device can be instructed to perform a task or a function when fed with a program or software. A computer takes data and converts it into information. **Data** represents text, numbers, graphics, sounds, and videos entered into the computer's memory during input operations.

Information is data that has been processed so that it can be presented in an organized and meaningful way. Think of data as the pieces of a jigsaw puzzle and information as the finished puzzle. Putting the pieces of the puzzle together gives you the overall picture. For example, CIS1100, the letter B, and the name Amy Stevens are pieces of data. Individually, these pieces of data seem meaningless. However, when processed, this data becomes the information on a grade report that indicates Amy Stevens received a grade of B in her CIS 1100 class.

These four basic computer functions work in a cycle known as the ***information processing cycle***. See Figure 1.1.

The functions of this cycle are:

- ***Input***—The computer gathers data or enables a user to enter data.
- ***Process***—Data is manipulated and converted into information.
- ***Output***—Information is displayed or shown to the user in a way that is understandable.
- ***Storage***—Data and/or information is stored for future use.

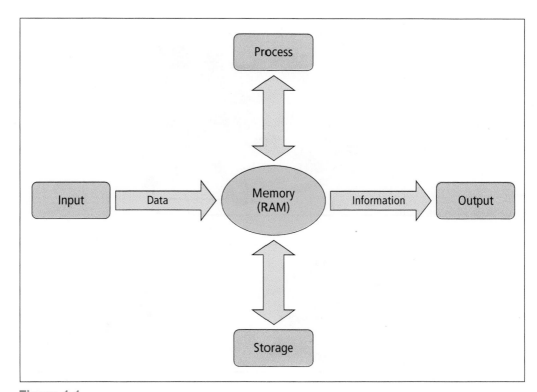

Figure 1.1

These are the four computer functions within the information processing cycle. Memory is not considered a function, but it is the center of flow of data and information within this cycle.

In the grade report, the instructor used a computer to enter, or input, the students' grades into the school's computerized grading system. A computer then processed this data along with data for other classes the students might have taken. In the example, the student Amy then received a written record of her grade or she accessed her grades online. The grade report was output by the computer. In addition, her grades remain stored in the system so they can be used to generate her transcript or to determine her future grade point average as she continues to take classes. See Figure 1.2.

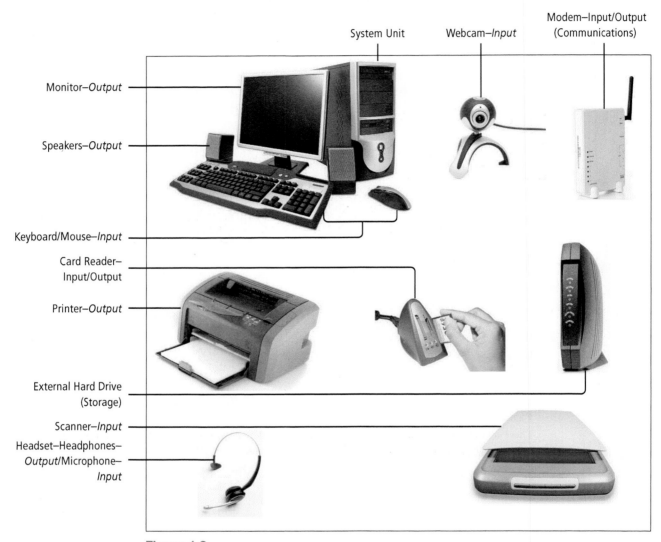

Figure 1.2
The components of a typical computer system and the appropriate step in the information processing cycle.

Objective 2 | Identify the Different Types of Computers

What are the different types of computers and what are their uses? Although computers come in a variety of sizes and shapes, the basic components required to complete the information processing cycle must be present in them. In addition to ***microcomputers***, the desktop and notebook computers and mobile devices that many of us are familiar with, there are also specialty computers, including servers, mainframes, supercomputers, and embedded computers. See Figure 1.3.

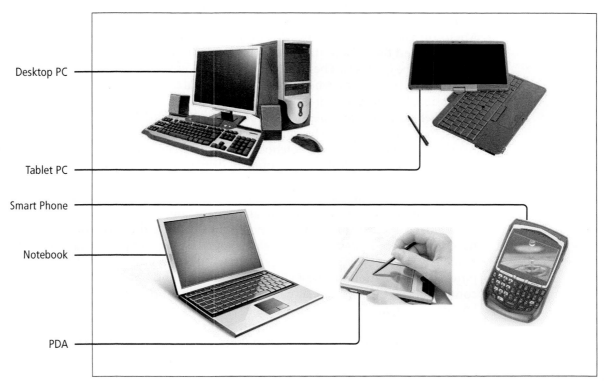

Desktop PC

Tablet PC

Smart Phone

Notebook

PDA

Figure 1.3
Types of microcomputers

Microcomputers

What are microcomputers? The term microcomputer means that the main component of a computer is a microprocessor, a tiny but powerful chip that is very small in size compared to a mainframe or a supercomputer. Microcomputers are classified as small, inexpensive, and designed for personal use or as part of a network of computers in a business environment. Computers in this category range in size from a desktop size system that is ideal when portability is not required to handheld devices that fit in your pocket. Some of the most common types of microcomputers include the following:

- ***Desktop computers*** are computers that sit on the desk, floor, or table, and typically have a detachable keyboard, mouse, monitor, and possibly other peripheral devices, such as digital cameras, scanners, and music players. Desktop computers are used in most homes and in business applications where portability is not needed. They can be configured in a multitude of arrangements depending on the specific needs and budget constraints. To ***configure*** means to put together by selecting a specific combination of components, features, and options.

- ***Gaming computers*** are mostly used by video game enthusiasts. They are usually configured with a fast CPU, large amount of memory, a special video card, joystick or game pad, and sound card with surround sound speaker system.

Desktop computers generally fall into two main categories: PCs or Macs. The PC, or personal computer, originally referred to as the IBM personal computer when it was released in the early 1980s, is now manufactured by a variety of companies including Hewlett-Packard, Dell, and Gateway. Today the term *PC* applies to any personal computer based on an Intel microprocessor, or on an Intel-compatible microprocessor. The Apple Macintosh computer, now known as Mac, is manufactured exclusively by Apple Inc. with an Intel microprocessor and can perform the same functions as the PC.

There are pros and cons to both types of computers, but in reality, both are good systems and the choice usually comes down to personal preference. The primary differences between the PC and the Mac relate to the different user interface, the application software, and the cost and availability of parts and accessories. The PC is typically used in a Microsoft Windows operating environment, and the Mac uses the Mac operating system. Although and the PC and the Mac each process information differently, both can perform the same types of tasks. The PC has a larger market share among general computer users and in business settings, whereas the Mac is popular with graphic design, advertising, and professional audio and film industries.

Notebook computers are ideal for people "on-the-go." Equipped with rechargeable batteries, they are designed to be portable, permitting them to be used in a variety of places. Averaging about 6 pounds, a notebook's size and weight can also limit its computing power. Notebooks typically have a built-in display screen, a keyboard, and a pointing device, although it is possible to connect them to detachable devices for more comfortable desktop use. A **docking station** enables the user to connect a notebook to a full-size keyboard, monitor, and other devices in an office setting.

Tablet computers are similar to notebooks because they are portable; however, they have some special features that set them apart. Tablet computers have a convertible **touch screen** that swivels, enabling the tablet to be used like a standard notebook computer in one position or like a clipboard in the second position. When used in the tablet configuration, the user can actually write directly on the screen using a special pen known as a **stylus**, which is a pointed device used to input information and access various features right on the device's screen. Tablets use advanced handwriting-recognition technology to convert handwriting to digital text. Many also use **speech-recognition** technology, which enables the user to record discussions or lectures, or to control the computer functions using voice commands.

Mobile devices include items such as **personal digital assistants (PDAs)**, **handheld computers** (Pocket PCs), and **smartphones**. These devices vary in size and purpose, but they are all ultra-lightweight and portable. PDAs were initially designed to provide a convenient resource for maintaining an organized calendar and list of business and personal associates. Handheld computers enable users to access personal productivity software and send e-mail over the Internet, while smartphones add Internet capability to the wireless communication aspects of cell phones.

The newest mobile devices are often referred to simply as "handhelds." Many handheld devices now include personal productivity software and enable the user to play music, take photos and video, make phone calls, and access the Internet. PDAs and Pocket PCs often use a stylus. It is not uncommon for these devices to use a small detachable keyboard for text and data entry. As the features of mobile devices continue to converge, permitting them to perform similar tasks, it becomes more difficult to differentiate between them. If you are in the process of buying one of these handhelds, you need to do some research and make sure that you get the features and functions you want.

Servers

What are servers? When computers are connected together in a ***network*** environment, ***servers*** are specialized computers that manage network resources through the use of administrative software (see Figure 1.4). They provide other computers with access to the network and can handle a variety of functions or may be assigned to just one particular type of task. Thus, within the same company, you might find a Web server that holds and delivers the organization's Web pages, a file server that handles the storage and retrieval tasks for all of the company's files, and a printer server that handles all print requests. Also, virtual servers (not real, but an abstraction) can manage other specialized servers without the added cost of additional hardware.

Figure 1.4
Network server

What are mainframe computers? **Mainframe computers** are large computers often found in large businesses, organizations, and government agencies where thousands of users need to simultaneously use the data and resources of their institution (see Figure 1.5). Mainframe computers **multitask**; that is, they can perform more than one task at a time. Mainframes can store vast amounts of data using a variety of storage. Mainframes are often used for high-security applications, bulk data processing such as data surveys and census, and statistics. Early mainframe computers were very large and required separate rooms to house them, while today's mainframes are significantly smaller, faster, and more powerful than their predecessors.

Figure 1.5
Mainframe computer

Supercomputers

What are supercomputers? **Supercomputers** are large, powerful, and ultrafast computers that perform specialized tasks. Some of these are used for research, processing intensive scientific calculations, and multi-scale simulations. Since June 2008, the IBM nicknamed "Roadrunner," at the Department of Energy's Los Alamos National Laboratory in New Mexico, holds top spot as the world's fastest supercomputer. (See http://www.top500.org/ for more information about Roadrunner.)

Supercomputers (see Figure 1.6) are the fastest and most expensive computers. Unlike a mainframe computer that can handle a number of programs simultaneously, the supercomputer is designed to run fewer programs at one time, but to do so as quickly as possible. They perform sophisticated mathematical calculations, track weather patterns, monitor satellites, and perform other complex, dedicated tasks.

Figure 1.6
Supercomputer

Embedded Computers

What are embedded computers? **Embedded computers** are small specialized computers built into larger components such as automobiles and appliances. Functions such as emission control systems, antilock braking systems (ABS), airbags, and stability control systems are common in today's vehicles. These computers use a specially programmed microprocessor to perform a set of predefined tasks, and may require little or no input from the user. Other examples include electronic appliances, microwave ovens, digital cameras, programmable thermostats, medical devices, and diagnostic equipment.

Objective 3 | Describe Hardware Devices and Their Uses

What is computer hardware? **Hardware** is the computer and any equipment connected to it. Hardware devices are the physical components of the computer. Items such as the monitor, keyboard, mouse, and printer are also known as **peripherals** because they attach to the computer. In Figure 1.3, the computer and different peripherals are matched with the individual steps of the information processing cycle.

The computer itself is known as the **system unit**, and it contains many of the critical hardware and electrical components. The system unit is sometimes referred to as the tower, box, or console. When the system unit is combined with the appropriate peripheral devices, the system can perform the four basic computer functions: input, process, output, and storage. Peripheral devices are used to input and output data and information, and the system unit processes and stores the data.

System Unit

What is inside the system unit? If you remove the cover from the system unit, you will find several key components inside. One of the most essential components is the **motherboard**, a large printed circuit board to which all the other components are connected (see Figure 1.7). The **microprocessor chip**, also known as the **central processing unit (CPU)** and RAM, the computer's main memory, are connected to the motherboard (see the table in Figure 1.8). The motherboard also provides some of the ports used to connect peripheral devices to the system. Ports are explained and illustrated later in this chapter.

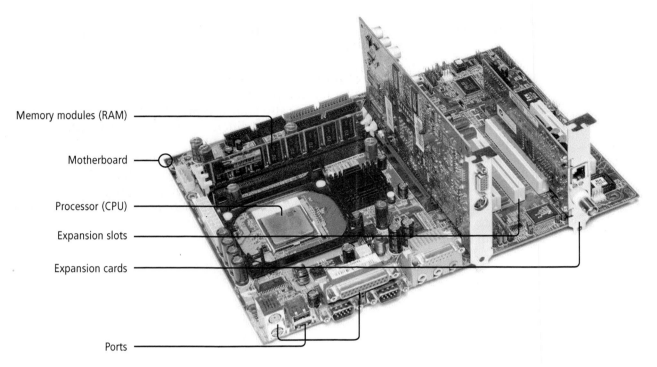

Figure 1.7
The motherboard and some of its components

Motherboard Features

Component	Description
Motherboard / System board	The main computer circuit board into which all components are plugged. It is installed safely inside the box or case called the system unit.
CPU	The central processing unit is responsible for getting data from memory, performing arithmetic and logical operations, and converting data to information.
Memory modules (RAM)	Temporary storage area where data is stored before processing, output, or storage. RAM is the center of flow of data and information within the information processing cycle.
Expansion slots	Slots or connectors on the motherboard that allow you to connect expansion cards.
Expansion cards	Removable circuit boards used to add new peripherals or increase the computer's capabilities. If the motherboard does not have a specific port to connect a peripheral device, the appropriate expansion card will allow you to do so.
Ports	Connecting points used as an interface between peripherals and the motherboard.

Figure 1.8
Motherboard features

Input Devices

Input devices are used to enter data into memory (RAM). The two most familiar input devices are the keyboard and the mouse, but they are not the only ones. See Figure 1.9.

Wireless Laser Mouse

Multimedia Keyboard

Underside of Wireless Laser Mouse

Microphone

Figure 1.9
Input devices

Keyboards

Are there different types of keyboards? The **keyboard** is the primary input device for computers. There are actually several different kinds of keyboards. The QWERTY keyboard is the one most common. It is based on the original typewriter keyboard and is named for the arrangement of the letters on the upper left alphabetic row of keys. Another style is the Dvorak keyboard, which arranges the letters and numbers in a different pattern for increased typing speed. Some ergonomic keyboards use a split keyboard arrangement, offsetting each half at an angle to reduce the incidence of repetitive stress injuries such as carpal tunnel syndrome.

Keyboard size and layout on notebook and tablet computers can differ slightly from a standard keyboard due to space constraints. Keyboards usually send information to the computer through a cable connected to a USB port; however, **wireless** or remote keyboards are gaining in popularity. A wireless keyboard communicates with the computer by infrared or radio frequency technology. These wireless devices require batteries.

What are all these other keys used for? In addition to the standard alphanumeric keys originally found on typewriters, computer keyboards have a variety of keys that provide additional functionality.

Control keys, such as the Ctrl, Alt, and Windows keys, often provide shortcuts or increased functionality to the keyboard when used in combination with another key. If you press the Shift key and a letter, the result is an uppercase, rather than a lowercase, letter. In the same way, using one of the control keys enables the standard keys to be used for additional purposes. For example, pressing Ctrl and the letter P opens the Print dialog box. Another example of a control key is the Esc key, which can often be used to stop, or *escape*, from a currently running task. A unique control key that is found only on Windows-based keyboards is the Windows key.

The **numeric keypad**, located at the right of the keyboard, provides an alternative method of quickly entering numbers. This is useful for individuals who are accustomed to using an adding machine or calculator.

Function keys are located above the standard row of number keys. Numbered F1 through F12, these keys are generally associated with certain software-specific commands. Pressing the F1 key will usually open the Help menu for a program; however, pressing one of the other function keys can produce different results, depending on the software program running.

Arrow keys are the keys located at the bottom of the keyboard between the standard keys and the numeric keypad. These keys enable the user to move the insertion point around the window one space at a time.

Toggle and other keys, which are located just above the arrow keys, are used for various purposes, including navigation and editing. The Insert, Num Lock, and Caps Lock keys are all examples of toggle keys. A **toggle key** works just like a light switch; press it once and the feature is turned on, press it again and it is turned off. If you've ever accidentally pressed the Caps Lock key and typed a long string of all capital letters, you've seen this feature in action. Pressing the Caps Lock key again allows you to return to normal keyboarding mode.

Multimedia and Internet control keys are typically found at the top edge of the keyboard. The precise placement and function of these keys usually depends on the keyboard manufacturer. However, most modern keyboards have at least a few keys or buttons that can be used for such tasks as muting or adjusting speaker volume, opening a **Web browser**, and sending an e-mail. Generally, each button has an icon that indicates its function.

The Mouse

Is there an easier way to control the action on the computer screen? Yes, the **mouse** is an input device (also called a pointing device) that, together with the keyboard, enables the user to control the operations of the computer. The mouse became popular with the introduction of graphical user interfaces, such as Microsoft Windows. This point-and-click device is useful for positioning the **insertion point** by translating hand movements into corresponding actions on the screen. The mouse is represented on the screen by a symbol called the **mouse pointer**. The user can move the mouse and position this pointer anywhere on the screen to move objects or make selections from available program icons or menus.

Some mice have a roller ball on the bottom that, as you move it, translates your movement into electrical impulses. Others use laser technology (optical) to control the pointer movement. Because the bottom of an optical mouse is sealed, dirt and debris are less likely to get inside and interfere with the mouse's internal mechanisms. This laser beam can be harmful if pointed to your eyes; do not look at it directly or point it at anybody else's eyes. See Figure 1.4. Just like a keyboard, the mouse can be wired or wireless. Notebook and tablet computers can use a mouse, but most of them have a built-in touchpad, a trackball, or track point to move the insertion point and mouse pointer. Most mice today are equipped with two buttons and a wheel button in the center that provides easy zoom and scroll functions.

How can the mouse be used more efficiently? Although there are different kinds of mice, the traditional mouse has two buttons and a scroll wheel. The palm of your hand should rest comfortably over the mouse in such a way that your index finger rests on the left mouse button and the middle finger on the right mouse button. The following provides a brief description of some of the ways the mouse can be used:

- **Click**—By default, the left mouse button is considered the primary button. When instructed to click, it is understood that the mouse pointer is moved to a certain location on the screen and the left mouse button is be pressed and released one time.

- **Double-click**—When instructed to double-click, it is understood that the mouse pointer is moved to a certain location on the screen and the left mouse button is pressed and released twice in rapid succession. It is important that the mouse does not move while double-clicking or the command will not produce the expected results.

- **Drag**—This means to press the left mouse button and continue to hold it while dragging, or moving, the mouse then releasing it. This action can be used to select large blocks of text, to move objects, or to resize other objects.

- **Right-click**—Pressing and releasing the right mouse button one time will open a **shortcut menu**. Shortcut menus are usually context-sensitive, which means they will vary depending on what or where you have clicked and what program you are using. The right mouse button is also known as the secondary button and is not typically pressed more than one time; no double-clicking for the right button. After the shortcut menu has been opened, you select the appropriate choice by clicking it with the left mouse button.

- **Right-drag**—This is done by pressing the right mouse button and continuing to hold it while dragging, or moving, the mouse. This action is used when copying or moving files or folders within different storage devices.

- **Scroll wheel**—If your mouse is equipped with a scroll wheel, it can be used to quickly move a page up or down in a window, thus the name of the action to **scroll**. It is an easy way to navigate through lengthy documents or websites.

    Are there other input devices? Although the keyboard and mouse are the two most common input devices, there are many other input devices. **Scanners** are similar to copy machines, but instead of producing a paper copy, they convert documents or photos to digital files that can then be saved on your computer. **Microphones** are used to digitally capture and record sounds. Game controls such as **joysticks** are used to control movement within video games. **Digital cameras** and **digital video recorders** enable you to capture digital images and movies and transfer them directly to your computer.

The Processor

What does the CPU do? The CPU (see Figure 1.10) is the brain of the computer and is responsible for executing program instructions and manipulating data to convert to information. It has two main parts—the ***control unit*** and the ***arithmetic logic unit (ALU)***. The control unit is responsible for obtaining and executing instructions from the computer's memory. Example: The user wants to print a document and selects the "Print" command from an icon on the screen. The CPU gets the command from memory (RAM), interprets the command, and sends the document as output to a selected printer. In other words, the CPU coordinates the internal activities and the activities of all the other computer components. The arithmetic logic unit (ALU) performs the arithmetic and logic functions for the computer. The ALU handles addition, subtraction, multiplication, and division, and also makes logical and comparison decisions. This enables the CPU to perform tasks such as sorting data alphabetically or numerically and filtering data to locate specific criteria.

Figure 1.10
Two sides of a CPU

Different CPUs

As important as the CPU is to your computer, you might expect it to take up a large amount of space in the console. However, the CPU is actually rather small, thus the term *microchip*. Over the years, manufacturers have successfully reduced the size of microprocessor chips while continuing to increase their computing power. In fact, Moore's law (formulated in 1965 by Gordon Moore, cofounder of Intel) addresses this increase in computing power, observing that current production methods enable CPU capacity to double about every 24 months or so!

Are there different brands of CPUs? Yes, the most well-known chip manufacturers include Intel and Advanced Micro Devices (AMD). Chip manufacturers often produce several different models of chips. Some of the chips that Intel makes include the *Intel® Core™ i7 processor Extreme Edition*, the *Intel® Core™2 Quad Processor* for desktops, and the *Intel® Centrino® 2 Processor Technology* for portable computers. AMD manufactures chips such as the *AMD Phenom™ II X4* for desktops, and the *AMD Turion™ X2 Ultra Dual-Core Mobile Processor* for portable computers. Intel and AMD chips are the mainstays for PCs. Using multiple processors (dual core or quad core) has several advantages over a single-processor CPU, including improved multitasking capabilities and system performance, lower power consumption, reduced usage of system resources, and lower heat emissions.

How is a CPU's processing power measured? One indicator of a CPU's processing power is its ***clock speed***. Clock speed measures the speed at which a CPU processes data (number of instructions per second) and is measured in ***megahertz (MHz)*** or ***gigahertz***

(GHz), depending on the age of the CPU. Early computers had CPUs that processed at speeds of less than 5 MHz, whereas modern processors can operate at over 3 GHz (the equivalent of 3,000 MHz) and newer processors continue to surpass these numbers.

What types of memory does a computer have? Memory is another critical computer component of a computer system. The term *memory* signifies storage. There are two basic types of memory: temporary or ***volatile*** and permanent or ***nonvolatile***.

Permanent memory includes ***Read-Only Memory (ROM),*** which is prerecorded on a chip. The information on a ROM chip cannot be changed, removed, or rewritten, and is generally inaccessible to the computer user. ROM is nonvolatile memory because it retains its contents even if the computer is turned off. ROM contains critical information, such as the program used to start up or boot—start— the computer.

Storage devices such as hard disks and flash drives and storage media such as CDs and DVDs are considered permanent or nonvolatile memory. These are presented later in this chapter.

Temporary memory, the computer's temporary or volatile memory, is ***Random Access Memory (RAM)***. RAM (see Figure 1.11) acts as the computer's short-term memory and stores data and program instructions waiting to be processed. RAM is considered volatile because its contents are erased when the computer is turned off.

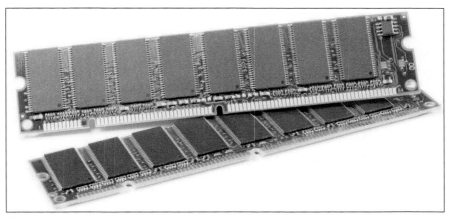

Figure 1.11
Random Access Memory (RAM) / RAM chips

Why is it important to have enough RAM? The more tasks your computer performs at the same time, or the more programs you have open, the more RAM it uses. We described RAM earlier as the center of the flow of data and information in the information processing cycle (see Figure 1.1). That flow slows down when there is not enough RAM. Your computer's RAM is like the top of your desk. The size of the desk that you need is determined by the work you do at a given moment. You may need to use a notebook computer, several books, a clipboard with notes, a holder for pens and pencils, and a telephone. If your desk is not big enough to fit these items, you cannot work with all of them at the same time. If you do not have a sufficient amount of RAM in your system, you might notice your computer slows down or even stops responding when you try to perform tasks.

Computer users often think this means they have too much information saved on their computers' hard drives. What it actually means is that they are running out of memory, not permanent storage space. To fix this problem, you can reduce the number of programs running at the same time, disable some features of the Operating System, or simply add more RAM to your system. Installing additional memory is one of the most inexpensive and easiest upgrades for your computer and often results in noticeable performance improvements.

Memory is measured in several units such as **megabytes (MB)**, which is approximately one million bytes, **gigabytes (GB)**, which is approximately one billion bytes, or **terabytes (TR)**, which is one trillion bytes. Study the table in Figure 1.12.

Units to Measure Memory

Name	Abbreviation	Number of Bytes	Relative Size
Byte	B	1 byte	Holds one character of data
Kilobyte	KB	1,024 bytes	Holds about a half page of double-spaced text
Megabyte	MB	1,048,576 bytes	Holds about 768 pages of typed text
Gigabyte	GB	1,073,741,824 bytes	Holds approximately 786,432 pages of text
Terabyte	TB	1,099,511,627,776 bytes	This represents a stack of typewritten pages almost 51 miles high
Petabyte	PB	1,125,899,906,842,624 bytes	This represents a stack of typewritten pages almost 52,000 miles high

Figure 1.12

Measuring memory—these units are used to measure the size and capacity of RAM and also of storage devices/media

RAM size requirements vary depending on the operating system in use. Older computers that run Windows XP should have between 512 MB to 1 GB of RAM. For newer computers, a minimum of 2GB possibly more is recommended.

Output Devices

Output devices display information after data has been processed in a useful format. This format can be text, graphics, audio, or video. Monitors and printers are the two most common output devices.

Monitors

What are monitors? Monitors are display devices that show images of text, graphics, and video once data has been processed. The image on a monitor is called **soft copy**; you can view it, but you cannot touch it. See Figure 1.13.

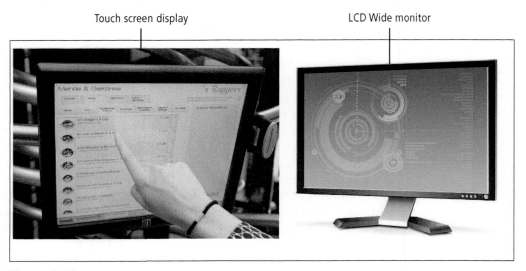

Touch screen display   LCD Wide monitor

Figure 1.13

Output devices—monitors

What is an LCD monitor? Monitors come in a variety of sizes and styles, but the standard today is the **LCD (liquid crystal display). Flat-panel** LCD monitors use a liquid crystal display and are thin and energy efficient.

What factors determine a monitor's display quality? The number of **pixels**, a monitor's display, is made up of millions of tiny dots known as pixels or picture element. Each pixel represents a single point on a display screen or in a graphic image. The number of pixels on the screen determines a monitor's sharpness and clarity, also known as its **resolution**. A higher number of pixels results in a clearer and sharper monitor resolution. A standard screen resolution might be expressed as 1024 x 768, which means there are 1,024 columns, each containing 768 pixels, for a total of more than 786,000 pixels on the screen. Monitor sizes are determined by measuring their screens diagonally.

Dot pitch is another display characteristic and refers to the diagonal distance between two pixels of the same color. Dot pitch is measured in millimeters with smaller measurements resulting in a crisper viewing image because there is less blank space between the pixels. For best viewing, monitors should have a dot pitch measurement of .28 mm or less. LCD monitors use an electric current to illuminate the pixels.

Refresh rate is the speed at which the pixels are reilluminated and it's measured in cycles per second, expressed as hertz (Hz). Refresh rates generally average between 75 and 85 Hz, which means the screen image is redrawn 75 to 85 times per second. Higher refresh rates result in less screen flicker and less eye strain.

What are touch screen monitors? Touch screen monitors are both input and output devices. They display images just like regular monitors but also enable users to touch their surfaces and make selections directly from the screen. These monitors are widely used in retail stores at checkout counters, in airports for passengers' fast check-ins, and HP has released a personal computer in which the monitor is also the system unit and uses touch screen technology.

Which monitor is best? Choosing the right monitor is always a combination of what you like, want, and can afford. A higher resolution, small dot pitch, fast refresh rate, and large monitor size are desirable, but all come with a higher price tag.

Printers

Using a monitor is a good way to view the information on your computer, but sometimes a soft copy isn't sufficient for your needs. **Printers** generate a **hard copies** or **printouts**, which are a permanent record of your work on paper. See Figure 1.14.

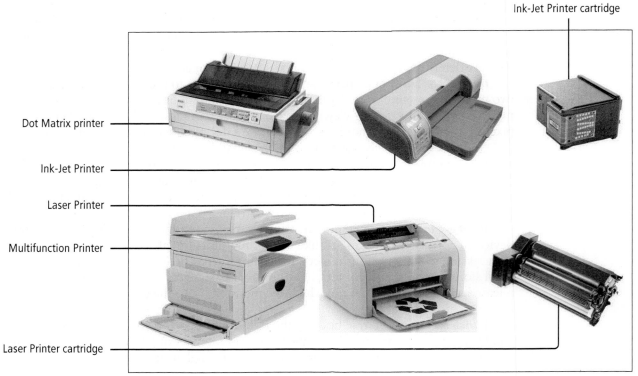

Figure 1.14
Output devices—printers

What types of printers are available? There are two categories of printers: impact and nonimpact. **Impact** printers have small hammers, similar to a typewriter's, that strike an ink ribbon against paper, leaving behind the image of the character or symbol. The **dot matrix** printer is an impact printer. Once very popular because of their low cost, dot matrix printers are still in use today, limited only to certain applications that require continuous forms or multipart forms (an original and several copies), such as invoices or purchase orders.

How does a nonimpact printer work? Nonimpact printers do not actually touch the paper when printing. There are a variety of nonimpact printers, but the two most commonly used with home computers are the ink-jet printer and the laser printer. The **ink-jet** printer uses a special nozzle and ink cartridges to spray ink in small droplets onto the surface of the paper. Ink-jet printers easily print in color, in black, and in grayscale to produce good quality printouts. They are relatively inexpensive to buy and maintain. **Laser printers** use the same process as photocopiers to produce their output. They use a special cylinder known as a drum, dry ink or toner, and a laser. Static electricity attracts toner to the surface of the drum, and the laser distributes the toner in the correct pattern. The drum transfers the toner to the paper and heat is used to permanently fuse the toner to the paper. Laser printers are generally more expensive to purchase than ink-jet printers, although they often print more quickly and are more cost effective. Lower-end laser printers print only in black and white; however, more expensive printers can produce color copies.

Computer Concepts | Basic Computer Concepts

How do you assess a printer's capabilities? When you select a printer, there are some key characteristics to consider.

Print speed is often expressed as **pages per minute (ppm)**. Print speed can vary depending on the manufacturer and model, and is also affected by whether the page is text-only, if it includes graphics, and if the printout is in color or in black and grayscale.

Just as with monitors, resolution is also important to print quality. For printing purposes, resolution is expressed as **dots per inch** or **dpi**. The higher the dpi, the better the print quality. Print qualities of 300 to 600 dpi are typical of most printers, although special photo printers can offer resolutions up to 1,200 dpi. Professional printers can reach even higher values.

Color output and its related cost is another important consideration. Ink-jet printers offer four- or six-color options. Many ink-jet printers use one cartridge for black ink and one or more cartridges for color. When available, printers that offer a separate cartridge for each color are a practical choice because you need to replace only one color at a time as the cartridges run out. Laser printers use separate toner cartridges for each color.

What are all-in-one printers? All-in-one printers bundle multiple capabilities in one device. All-in-one devices usually include:

- A printer, either ink-jet (color or black and grayscale) or laser (output)

- A scanner to convert text or images into files that can be stored and further manipulated by the computer (input)

- A facsimile (fax) function to send and receive documents via the telephone (communications)

- A copier function to duplicate documents (output)

- Network capabilities to enable this **multifunction device (MFD)** to work as part of a network environment both wired or wireless (communications)

Speakers and Multimedia Projectors

Are there other output devices? **Speakers** and **multimedia projectors** are also examples of output devices. Many computers include small speakers to enable the user to listen to CDs or DVDs and hear any auditory signals the computer sends. However, if you're serious about multimedia, you will probably want to invest in a better set of speakers for improved performance. Multimedia projectors are used to conduct presentations and training sessions. These projectors enable information to be displayed on a big screen so it can be easily viewed by a large group of attendees.

Under what category do digital cameras fall? A digital camera is a device that stores pictures digitally rather than using conventional film. After images are captured, they are stored in the camera's internal memory. Some cameras use removable flash memory cards as storage media. These cards can be read by a computer, which can then edit them and save them as files. So, the camera itself is a form of "hand-held" computer, which, if connected to a computer, serves as an input/output device. The same thing can be said to describe camcorders.

Storage Devices

What are storage devices? **Storage devices** are used to store the data, information, and programs for future use. This storage is often referred to as permanent memory because, unlike data that is in RAM, data saved to a storage device remains there until the user deletes or overwrites it. Data can be stored using internal hardware devices located in the system unit or in removable units that enable portability. See Figure 1.15.

Figure 1.15
Storage devices

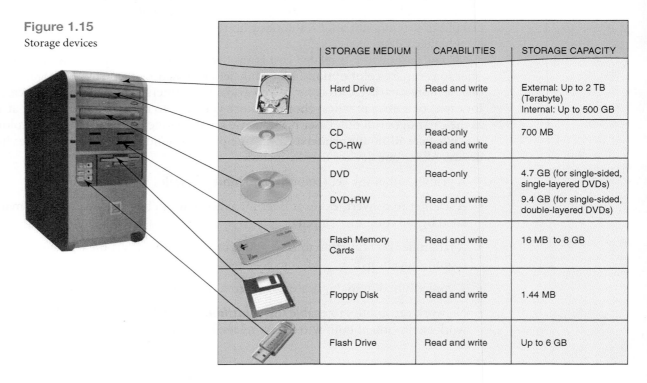

	STORAGE MEDIUM	CAPABILITIES	STORAGE CAPACITY
	Hard Drive	Read and write	External: Up to 2 TB (Terabyte) Internal: Up to 500 GB
	CD CD-RW	Read-only Read and write	700 MB
	DVD DVD+RW	Read-only Read and write	4.7 GB (for single-sided, single-layered DVDs) 9.4 GB (for single-sided, double-layered DVDs)
	Flash Memory Cards	Read and write	16 MB to 8 GB
	Floppy Disk	Read and write	1.44 MB
	Flash Drive	Read and write	Up to 6 GB

How is a storage device different than storage media? A **device** is a piece of hardware such as a hard drive or a DVD drive. Media is the removable part that actually contains the stored data. Media requires a device to **read** and **write** on it. Read is the action of retrieving or opening existing data and write is the action of saving or storing data. Following is a list of devices and their media:

• CD and DVD optical drives read and write on CDs and DVDs, which are the media.

• Card readers read and write on flash memory cards, which are the media.

• Flash drives or thumb drives are media that require a connection to a USB port for read/write operations.

• Tape backup drives read and write onto tape cartridges, which are the media.

• The exception to this is the hard drive, in which the hardware and the media are all contained in a sealed unit that cannot be taken apart.

How is data stored? Data is generally stored using one of three forms of storage: magnetic, optical, or flash memory:

• **Magnetic** storage uses tape or film covered in a thin, magnetic coating that enables data to be saved as magnetic impulses. It works in much the same fashion as an audiocassette or videotape works. Hard drives and backup tape drives are both forms of magnetic storage. Before magnetic storage can occur, media has to be formatted. This is the process in which media is divided into **tracks** and **sectors**. Tracks are magnetic concentric circles and sectors are segments within those circles Data is stored magnetically within the spaces created by these tracks sectors. Magnetic media has read/write capability, which means it is possible to use it over and over again, enabling you to delete or revise existing data and save new data.

- *Optical* storage uses flat plastic discs coated in a special reflective material. Data is saved by using a laser beam to burn tiny pits into the storage medium. A less intensive laser is used to read the saved data. The saved data is organized using tracks and sectors, similar to those used in magnetic media. *Compact discs (CDs)* and *digital video discs (DVDs)* are examples of optical media. Unlike magnetic media, not all optical storage is read/write capable. *CD-ROMs*—CD media that was burned once and from that moment on can only be read—and *DVD-ROMs*—DVD media that is burned once and from that moment on can only be read—are considered read-only media (ROM). The information contained on them can be read, but not changed or deleted, and it is not possible to save new data to them. If you purchase new software, music, or a movie, it is most likely on a CD-ROM or DVD-ROM. A record-only disc (CD-R) enables you to record, or *burn*, information to the disc one time only; information saved this way cannot be deleted or rewritten. A rewritable disc (CD-RW) enables information to be recorded, revised, or deleted, and new data can also be written to the disc, similar to magnetic media. The same possibilities are available in DVDs. However, there are currently two competing formats DVD-R/RW, known as "DVD dash," and DVD+R/RW, known as "DVD plus." The R/RW suffix indicates the DVD can be used to record and can also be rewritten. Although most DVD players can play either format, if you want to record to a DVD, you need to know which format the DVD recorder requires.

What is LightScribe? **LightScribe** is a disc-labeling technology that burns text and graphics onto the surface of a specially coated LightScribe CD or DVD. This is an alternative to printing a conventional sticker label and attaching it to a regular CD or DVD but it does require that you purchase LightScribe media. See Figure 1.16.

Figure 1.16
LightScribe direct disc labeling

- **Flash memory** uses solid-state technology. It is completely electronic and has no moving mechanical parts. Flash memory is a quick and easy form of rewritable storage and is often used in mobile devices such as PDAs, digital cameras, and MP3 players. Depending on the manufacturer, flash memory cards may be called Memory Stick, CompactFlash, Secure Digital, or MultiMediaCard. Typically, a device can use only one style of memory card; however, a computer equipped with the appropriate card reader can read any of them. Small, removable storage devices known as flash drives or thumb drives also use flash technology, require a USB port to connect to the system unit, and are very popular to transport data.

What are the main types of storage devices? Depending on the age and type of computer you have, you might find some or all of the following internal storage options:

- **Hard disk drive**—A hard disk drive is the computer's main internal storage device. Also referred to as a hard drive, its storage space is usually measured in gigabytes (GB), with newer computers ranging in size from 80 GB to 750 GB, although it is possible to find some specialized, high-end computers with storage space measuring up to 2 terabytes (TB). As with everything else in computing, these numbers tend to increase with each new model. Hard drives are traditionally permanent storage devices fixed inside the system unit.

- **Floppy disk drive**—This is a device that reads/writes floppy diskettes that have a maximum storage capacity of 1,450 MB. Because of this limited storage capacity compared to other media, you will seldom see floppy disks used by computer users today.

- **CD and/or DVD drives**—Your computer may have one or two of these optical drives in the system unit. It's important to know whether these drives are simple CD-ROM drives, which can only read CDs, or if it is a **CD-RW** drive, also known as a CD burner. A **CD burner** gives you the ability to save, or burn, files to a CD-R (compact disk recordable). You might also have a separate drive that can read and/or write DVDs.

Although CDs and DVDs look alike, DVDs are capable of holding much more information than CDs. A CD can hold up to 700 MB of data, but a DVD can store almost 10 GB! Because of their differences, a CD drive is unable to read DVDs, although a DVD drive can read CDs.

Is it possible to add a storage device to a system? If you are running out of hard disk space or your system doesn't have a particular storage device, it may be possible to add a storage device, provided your system has enough room for it. You would need an available drive bay, which is the physical location within the system unit, or you might consider removing an existing device and replacing it with another. For instance, if you only have a CD-ROM drive, you could remove that and replace it with a CD-RW/DVD drive, thereby giving you the ability to read and burn CDs and play DVDs too. It is also possible to purchase many of these units as external storage devices. An external storage device is a peripheral that attaches to the computer via a port and performs the same tasks as its corresponding internal device. One of the most popular of these today is the external hard drive, which can greatly increase a computer's storage capacity and make your data fully portable.

Are there other types of storage devices? Other storage devices you might be familiar with include flash drives, a currently popular form of data storage, and older but still reliable backup tape drives.

Flash drives are removable storage devices that use flash memory and connect to the computer by a USB port. Flash drives are also known as thumb drives, universal serial bus (USB) drives, and jump drives. The flash drive is typically a device small enough to fit on a keychain or in a pocket and, because of its solid-state circuitry and lack of moving parts, it is extremely durable. Available in several storage sizes ranging from 16 MB to 64 GB, a flash drive is a quick and easy way to save and transport files. As an example, a 64-MB flash drive, which is relatively small, holds the equivalent of almost 45 floppy disks! To use one of these devices, you simply plug it into a computer's USB port. The computer recognizes the new device and enables the user to save or retrieve files from the flash drive.

Backup tape drives are storage devices that resemble audiocassette tape recorders and save data to magnetic tape media. Although they are rarely used for home computers anymore, many businesses and organizations still rely on tape backup systems to safeguard their data on a daily basis. See Figure 1.17.

The capacity of the components found in your system unit is measured in terms of storage size or speed. Computer systems continue to increase in storage capacity and

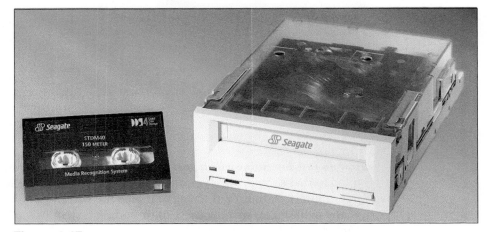

Figure 1.17
Tape backup drive and media

computing speed, while decreasing in size. Generally, higher measurements indicate a system that is quicker and more powerful than a system with lower measurements. However, it is important to balance size and speed with financial considerations too. Although it is tempting to consider buying a computer with the most power possible, a lesser computer may be more reasonably priced and still be sufficient for the typical user's needs. Recall that CPU speed is measured in megahertz (MHz) or gigahertz (GHz). The amount of RAM in a computer is generally measured in megabytes (MB), while storage space is usually measured in megabytes or gigabytes (GB), depending on the device.

Ports

What are ports? A **port** acts as an interface or connector between a system's peripheral devices and the computer, enabling data to be exchanged easily. Ports (see Figure 1.18) have different shapes and sizes. The same ports are typically found on a desktop too, although they might be arranged in a different order. Various input and output devices use different data exchange methods, requiring different types of ports and connectors (or plugs). If your computer does not have a particular port, you can buy an expansion card that connects to the motherboard and provides the needed connection.

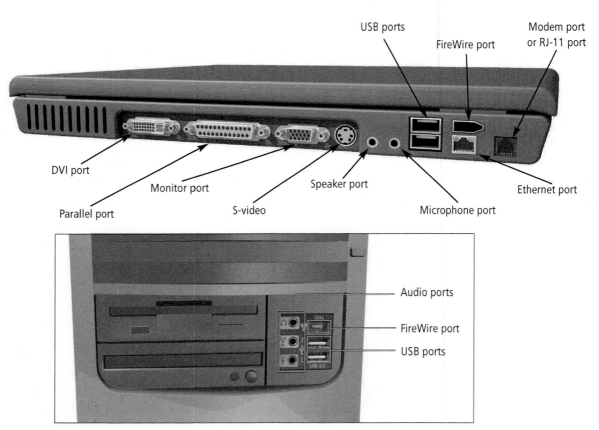

Figure 1.18
Ports

How do you determine which port a peripheral device needs? Manufacturers have attempted to make the process of connecting peripheral devices less complicated on newer computers. Rather than trying to match the size and shape of a connector to its port, many manufacturers now use a color-coding system that coordinates the colors of the connectors with their corresponding ports. Additionally, many newer desktop computers include ports, such as USB and audio ports, on the front panel of the system unit to provide easier access to them. Locating these ports on the front or back panels makes it a simple process to connect and disconnect devices that are used only occasionally, such as digital cameras, external hard drives, or MP3 players. Peripherals that are rarely disconnected, such as a keyboard or printer, are generally plugged into the ports on the back of the computer.

What are the different ports used for? Serial and parallel ports are two of the oldest types of ports found on a computer. **Serial ports** are ports that can send data only one bit at a time, so the data exchange rate is slow compared to newer technology. The maximum rate at which a standard serial port can transfer data is 115 **kilobits** or one thousand bits per second (Kbps). The mouse and modem are examples of devices that might use a serial port. A **parallel port** is a port that sends data in groups of bits, at transfer rates of up to 500 Kbps, so it is a considerably faster method of transferring data than the serial port. Older printers were often connected to a computer through a parallel port.

Are there faster ports? Over the years, newer ports have come into existence. One of these is the **universal serial bus (USB) port**. This type of port is able to interface with several different peripheral devices, which reduces the need for individual, dedicated ports. USB ports are also able to transfer data at extremely high rates of speed. Original USB ports, known as USB 1.1, are capable of speeds of 12 **megabits** or one million bits per second (Mbps). The newest version, USB 2.0, can attain a rate of 480 Mbps, 40 times faster than USB 1.1 technology and over 400 times faster than a serial port! USB 2.0 ports are backwards compatible, which means that older USB devices work with them; however, data will transfer only at the slower USB 1.1 speed. The higher data transfer capabilities of USB ports, coupled with their capability to work with multiple devices, have made the older serial and parallel ports obsolete. Because of the USB port's speedy data transfer rate and its capability to be used with numerous devices, new computers often include six or more USB ports. Devices using USB ports include keyboards, mice, printers, scanners, digital cameras, MP3 players, and PDAs. In general, it's a good idea to get a computer with as many USB ports as possible. See the table in Figure 1.19.

Ports and Their Uses

Port Name	Data Transfer Speed	Typical Use
Serial	115 Kbps	Mice / External modems
Parallel	500 Kbps	Printers / External Zip drives
USB 1.1	12 Mbps	Mice / Keyboards / Printers / Scanners / Game controllers
USB 2.0	400 Mbps	Same as USB 1.1 but at faster transfer rates. Also, camcorders, digital cameras, and MP3 players. It maintains compatibility with USB 1.1.
FireWire / FireWire 800	400 Mbps / 800 Mbps	Digital video camcorders / Digital cameras
Ethernet / Gigabit Ethernet	Up to 100 Mbps / Up to 1,000 Mbps	Network connections / Cable modems

Figure 1.19
Port speeds and uses

The **FireWire port**, developed by Apple and also known as IEEE 1394, is another means of transferring data quickly. The FireWire 400 has a data transfer rate of 400 Mbps, while the newer FireWire 800 transfers data at a blazing 800 Mbps! This port is typically used to connect devices that need to transfer huge amounts of data to a computer quickly, such as digital cameras or digital video recorders, or external hard drives. FireWire ports are standard on many Apple products, but are usually found only on higher-end Windows PCs and peripheral devices. Some peripheral devices offer users a choice of connecting using a USB port or a FireWire port.

What kind of port is used to connect to another computer? Connectivity ports, such as Ethernet and modem ports, are used to connect a computer to a local network or to the Internet. An ***Ethernet port***, also known as an RJ-45 jack, resembles a standard phone jack, but is slightly larger. The Ethernet port is used for network access and can also be used to connect a cable modem or router for Internet access. A ***modem port*** is the same size and shape as a phone jack and is used to connect the modem to a phone system, enabling ***digital subscriber line (DSL)*** or dial-up Internet access. DSL is a type of communications line in which signals travel through copper wires between a telephone switching station and a home or business. The maximum data transfer rate for a modem is 56 Kbps, whereas the most common Ethernet standard, Fast Ethernet, transfers data at the rate of 100 Mbps. However, Gigabit Ethernet, with a potential transfer rate of 1,000 Mbps, is becoming an option on higher-end systems and is standard on many Mac systems.

Even faster Ethernet technologies, such as 10 Gigabit Ethernet or 10 GbE exist, but they are currently used for network backbones and enterprise network infrastructures rather than home users.

Are there special purpose ports? Despite the prevalence of USB ports, which can be used for a variety of peripherals, there are still some devices that require special ports. These ports include Musical Instrument Digital Interface (MIDI), IrDA, Bluetooth, video, and audio ports.

MIDI ports are used to connect electronic musical devices, such as keyboards and synthesizers, to a computer, enabling musicians to create digital music files.

The ***IrDA port*** is used to enable devices such as PDAs, keyboards, mice, and printers to transmit data wirelessly to another device by using infrared light waves. In order to transmit information, each of the devices must have an IrDA port, and a clear line of sight, with no other objects blocking the transmission.

Bluetooth is another type of wireless technology that relies on radio wave transmission and doesn't require a clear line of sight. Bluetooth-enabled devices such as PDAs or other mobile devices can communicate only with each other over short distances, typically less than 30 feet.

Video ports include standard monitor ports, DVI ports, and S-video ports. A ***monitor port*** is used to connect the monitor to the graphics processing unit, which is usually located on the motherboard or on a video card. However, to get the best results from a flat-panel (LCD) monitor, the ***Digital Video Interface (DVI) port*** should be used instead. The DVI port transmits a pure digital signal, eliminating the need for digital-to-analog conversion and resulting in a higher quality transmission and a clearer picture on the monitor. The ***S-video port*** is typically used to connect other video sources, such as a television, projector, or digital recorder, to the computer.

Similar to video ports, ***audio ports*** connect audio devices, such as speakers, headphones, and microphones, to the computer's sound card. These jacks will be familiar to anyone who is used to using standard stereo components.

Evaluating Your System

Each computer might have a different configuration. The way a computer system is set up or the combination of components that make up the system is called its **configuration**. This is important when buying a computer, expanding an existing system, or when connecting computers together in a network environment.

Now that you have learned most of the hardware components of a typical personal computer, you are ready to explore the computer's configuration, specifications, and features. If you didn't buy your computer brand new, you might not know all the details about your computer. If you did buy a new computer, the easiest way is to check your paperwork; all the basic information should be there. However, if your computer isn't new or you didn't keep the paperwork, there are some ways to determine exactly what is in your system. Also if you start a new job or a new position and are given a computer system, you can do a number of things again to determine exactly what is in your system.

What kind of computer do you have? This is one of the easiest questions to answer. Like almost every other appliance you've used, you can probably find the manufacturer's name and a brand name or model number on the case of the computer. If not, check the back of the unit; there should be a metal tag that includes the manufacturer's name, model number, and serial number. This information might be necessary if you have to have service performed under warranty. Use the following steps to see your system properties, which will answer some questions.

If you are a Windows XP user and you have the My Computer icon on the desktop:

1 Right-click My Computer.

2 Select Properties and read the contents of the General tab.

If you do not have the My Computer icon on the desktop, follow these steps:

1 Click the **Start** menu, select **Settings**, and then click **Control Panel**.

2 From the next window, click **Performance** and **Maintenance**.

3 Then click **System** and read the contents of the **General** tab.

Windows Vista users can follow these steps:

1 Right-click the **My Computer** icon on the desktop and select **Properties**.

2 If the icon is not on the desktop, open the **Start** menu and then right-click the **Computer** button and select **Properties**. See Figure 1.20.

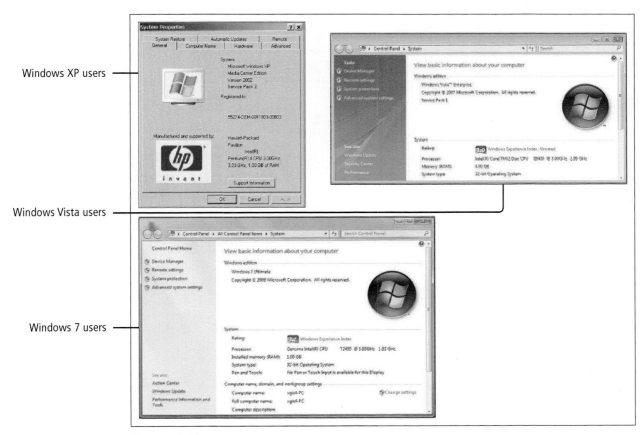

Windows XP users

Windows Vista users

Windows 7 users

Figure 1.20
Evaluating your system—General Properties

What operating system does the computer use? If you watch carefully as a computer boots up, you can often determine the operating system. You will usually see a ***splash screen*** showing the version of Windows that runs—for example, Windows ME, Windows XP, Windows Vista, or Windows 7, which is the working name for a new version of Windows to be released sometime in 2010.

How much memory is in the computer? What is the type and speed of the CPU? Figure 1.21 displays (for several versions of Windows) a window with information on the computer's operating system, the type and speed of the CPU, and the storage capacity of RAM.

How do you determine what drives are on the system and how much storage space is available? It's important to know how much information you can store on your computer, what disk drives are available, and how much room you have left on each drive. Is there enough storage space or are the storage devices getting full? Use My Computer (or Computer) to find the answers. If the desktop does not have a My Computer (or Computer) icon, you can access it through the Start menu.

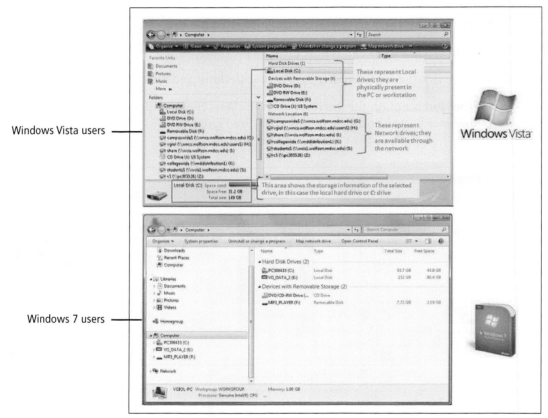

Figure 1.21
Using Windows Explorer to view the drives available to your computer

Figure 1.22 shows the Computer (or Windows Explorer) window in which the user can see all available local drives (devices within the system unit or peripherals to that unit) and network drives (devices available through a network). Also, right-click on any drive symbol, and select Properties from the shortcut menu. A new dialog box displays the drive's information similar to the one shown in Figure 1.22. The pie chart displayed on the General tab is a good visual tool that shows the size of your storage device and how much space is free.

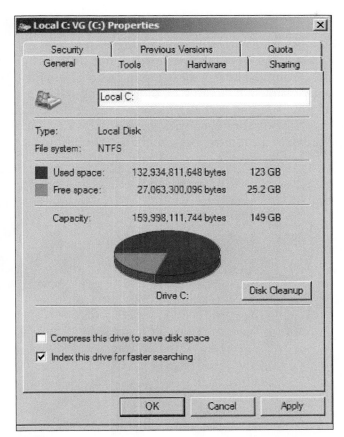

Figure 1.22

The properties of one of the storage drives (the hard drive)

Objective 4 | Identify Types of Software and Their Uses

So far we have described computer hardware, the physical components of the system. However, without software, the computer would just be a collection of useless electronic and mechanical parts. Software provides the instructions or commands that tell the computer what to do. To perform various tasks, the computer requires a set of instructions called **programs**. These programs enable individuals to use the computer without the need for special programming skills. There are two categories of computer software—**system software** and **application software**. Both types of software are required to work effectively with your computer.

System Software

System software provides the instructions that the computer needs to run. It contains the directions needed to start up the computer (known as the **boot process**), checks to ensure everything is in good working order, and enables you to interface or interact with the computer and its peripheral devices so that you can use them. System software consists of two main programs: the **operating system** and **utility programs**.

Operating Systems

What is the operating system? The **operating system (OS)** is a special computer program that is present on every desktop computer, notebook, PDAs, or mainframes. The operating system controls the way the computer works from the time it is turned on until it is shut down. As shown in Figure 1.23, the operating system manages the various hardware components, including the CPU, memory, storage devices, peripheral devices, and network devices. It also coordinates with the various software applications presently running and provides the interaction with the user (user interface).

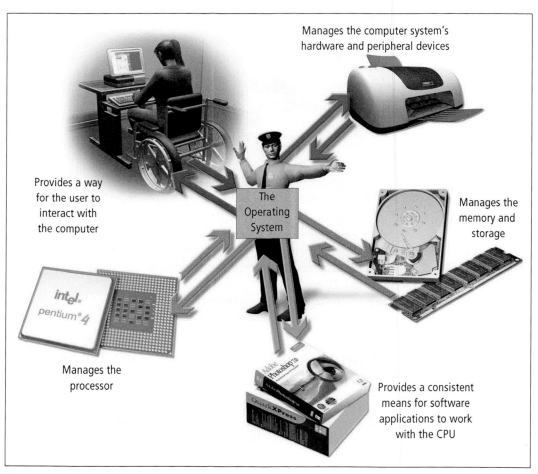

Figure 1.23
The operating system

Is it possible to communicate with the operating system? Although the operating system communicates with the computer and its peripherals, it also includes a **user interface** that you can use to interact and communicate with the computer. Early operating systems used a text-based or keyboard-driven interface. The early **Disk Operating System (DOS)** required knowledge of special commands that had to be typed accurately to achieve the desired results. This type of system was not very "**user friendly.**" Most current operating systems

Computer Concepts | Basic Computer Concepts

use a point-and-click format known as a **_graphical user interface (GUI)_**. GUIs are more user friendly and intuitive than DOS systems. Rather than typing specific commands, you can use a mouse to select from on screen objects such as **_icons_** (a graphical depiction of an object such as a file or program), **_menus_** (lists of available commands), or **_dialog boxes_** (windows used to make choices or give the system specific instructions as to the action you want to take or task to perform). GUI operating systems display information on the monitor in the form of rectangular boxes called **_windows_**. Although you interact with system software every time you use the computer, in some ways you don't notice it.

Do all computers need an operating system? Yes, the operating system is a critical part of a computer system. Without an OS to provide specific instructions, the computer would be unable to fulfill its four main functions. However, different computers require different types of operating systems. There are several popular operating systems available for home computers. They include Microsoft Windows, Mac OS, and Linux.

Microsoft Windows has the largest market share of the three main operating systems and is found on most of today's desktop and notebook computers. There have been many versions of Microsoft Windows, including Windows 3.0, Windows 95, Windows 98, Windows Me, Windows Vista, and Windows 7 to be released in 2010. Although a previous version of Windows might be found on an older computer, Windows Vista is the current version installed on most computers. A sample Windows Vista desktop is displayed in Figure 1.24.

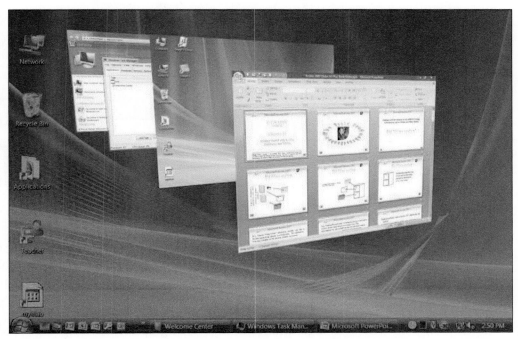

Figure 1.24
A sample of the Windows VISTA desktop

Why are there so many versions of Windows? Software developers are always updating and refining their software to adapt to new technology, respond to vulnerabilities, and improve their product. Because Microsoft also manufactures application software, some of its products have similar names and users can become confused. It's important to note that even though your computer might use Microsoft Windows for its operating system, it might not have Microsoft Office (an application software suite) installed.

Mac OS is an operating system designed specifically for Apple's Macintosh computers. Figure 1.25 shows the Mac OS desktop that is similar to Windows because it also uses a GUI. In fact, Apple was the first company to introduce a commercially successful GUI operating system for the consumer market. But, because of the popularity of the Windows-based PCs, Mac OS has a much smaller market share. If you are looking to purchase a PC or a peripheral for a PC, you have a variety of choices among different manufacturers. Only Apple manufactures Apple products and peripherals for its computers and they tend to be a bit pricier.

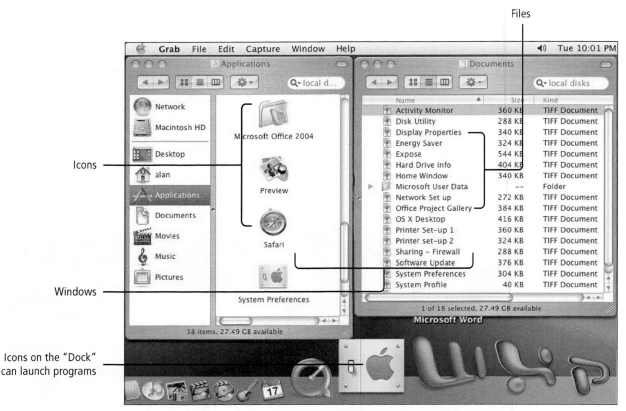

Figure 1.25
Mac OS desktop

Can Windows run on an Apple computer? Until recently, the Mac OS could not run on a PC, and the Windows OS could not run on a Mac. Software is available to start a Mac that will run Windows applications. Microsoft's Virtual PC for Mac features specifications such as:

• Access PC-only software, files, networks, and devices with your Mac

• Zero-configuration printing; better graphics handling; expanded preferences

• Cut and paste between platforms; share folders and other media between platforms

• Easily shut down virtual PC and relaunch right where it left off

• Use PC and Mac peripherals

Linux is an alternative operating system. Based on the UNIX operating system developed for mainframe computers, it also has a dedicated group of users. Linux is an **open-source** operating system, which means it is not owned by a single company and some versions are available at no cost.

How is open-source software different from other types of software? Open-source software makes its source code, essentially the program instructions, available to anyone who would like to see it. Programmers are encouraged to work with and change the code as they see fit, in the hope that having many "eyes" looking at the code will streamline and improve it. Proprietary software, such as Microsoft Windows, keeps this code secret and inaccessible to programmers who are not authorized by the software development company.

Why is Linux used? Linux is rarely used by novice computer users, although it is popular among developers and other technologically advanced individuals who prefer to use an alternative operating system. Some people appreciate the opportunity to work in this more "open" programming environment. However, one of the disadvantages of Linux is that, because no single company is responsible for it, technical support is not easily found. Users might find help from various resources such as user groups and Internet communities. Alternatively, some software companies have chosen to develop and sell a version of Linux that includes a warranty and technical support as a way of alleviating user concerns. Figure 1.26 shows an example of one version of the Linux operating system.

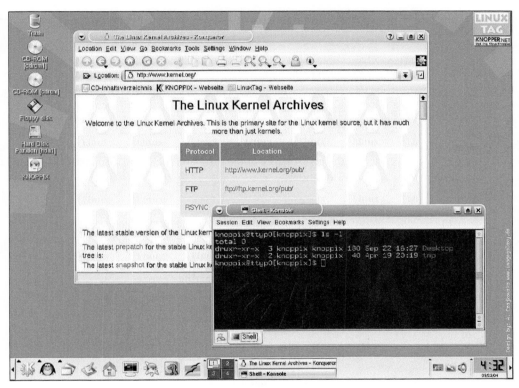

Figure 1.26

Example of one of the versions of the Linux operating system

Utility Programs

What are utility programs? Operating system software is the most critical software on the computer, because nothing can run without it. However, utility programs are another important component of system software. These small applications handle many important tasks involved with the management and maintenance of your system. Utility programs can be used to help back up important files, remove unwanted files or programs from your system, and schedule various tasks to keep your system running smoothly. Some of these utilities are included with the operating system, whereas others are stand-alone versions that you can purchase or download for free. The table in Figure 1.27 displays a variety of utility programs that ship with the Windows operating system and compares them with similar stand-alone products, describing the function of each utility.

Windows Utility Programs

Program	Function
Windows Explorer	Create folders, manage files, and compress/extract files. Read disk drive's properties including view storage capacity and free disk space, check drive for errors, defragment utility, and back up/restore utility
Windows Task Manager (Ctrl + Alt+ Delete)	Lets the user view the list of active applications, and switch or end any of them. Also, check the performance of the computer including CPU usage, RAM availability, and network utilization
Control Panel	
• System and Security	Review your computer's status Back up your computer Find and fix problems
• Network and Internet	View network status and tasks Choose home group and sharing options
• Hardware and sound	View devices and printers Add a device Connect to a projector Adjust commonly used mobility settings
• Programs	Install/uninstall programs Add desktop gadgets
• User Accounts and Family Safety	Add or remove user accounts Set up parental controls for any user
• Appearance and Personalization	Change the theme Change desktop background Adjust screen resolution
• Clock, Language, and Region	Change keyboards or other input methods Change display language Let Windows suggest settings
• Ease of Access	Optimize visual display
Administrative Tools	Schedule tasks
Security	
• Security Configuration Manager	Set account policies, local policies, network list manager policies, software restriction policies, and application control policies
• Firewall and Advanced Security	Set firewall and advanced security on local computer

Figure 1.27
Windows utility programs

Computer Concepts | Basic Computer Concepts

Application Software

Application software or applications are comprised of programs that enable you to accomplish tasks and use the computer in a productive manner. Applications are programs created to perform a specific task, solve a specific problem, or address a specific need.

How do system software and application software work together? System software is like the breathing you need to do to live; however, you don't usually think much about it unless something goes wrong. Application software might be compared to a musical instrument like a flute. When a musician combines each of these breaths and her flute, the result may be a beautiful melody (if she has practiced, of course!). Computer software works together similarly; the system software acts as the "breath," while the application software provides the "instrument," enabling you to create something.

There are many different kinds of application software, although they often fall into one of several general categories, each of which has a different purpose. These categories include financial and business-related software, graphics and multimedia software, educational and reference software, entertainment software, and communication software. You might be most familiar with productivity software, which includes the following applications.

- ***Word processing software*** is used to create, edit, format, print, and save documents and other text-based files. Word processing software enables you to create or edit letters, reports, memos, and many other types of written documents that you can print or attach to an e-mail message. Revisions to existing documents can be made quickly and easily, without having to re-create the entire document. Documents created with this type of software can also include pictures, charts, ***hyperlinks,*** and other graphic elements. A hyperlink is a connection to another area of a document or a connection to an Internet URL. Microsoft Word, Lotus Word Pro, and Corel WordPerfect are all examples of word processing programs. A document created using Microsoft Word 2007 is shown in Figure 1.28. Notice that the document

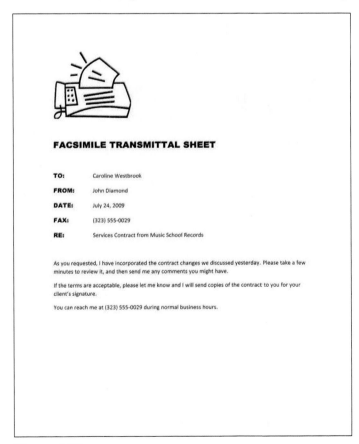

Figure 1.28

Sample document created with Microsoft Word 2007

contains a graphic element as well as text. Using word processing software replaces the use of conventional typewriters, on which editing was virtually impossible once the document was finished.

- **Spreadsheet software** enables the user to enter data in rows and columns format and:

    - Perform calculations on numeric data with user-defined formulas.

    - Convert part of the data into one or more charts, such as a column chart, a pie chart, or a line chart.

    - Work with lists to organize data and sort it in alphabetic or numeric order.

    - Create different scenarios and perform "what-if" analyses, the basis for sound decision making.

A key advantage of spreadsheet software is its capability to recalculate spreadsheets without user intervention. When data used in a calculation or a formula is changed, the spreadsheet software automatically updates the worksheet with the correct result. Microsoft Excel, Lotus 1-2-3, and Corel Quattro Pro are examples of spreadsheet programs. Figure 1.29 shows a worksheet and a chart created with Microsoft Excel 2007. The use of spreadsheet software replaces the old manual method of entering data in ledgers or journals and using a desktop calculator to do the math computations.

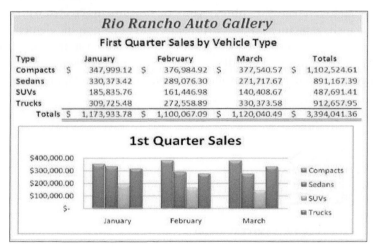

Figure 1.29

Example spreadsheet created with Microsoft Excel 2007

A database is a collection of data or unorganized facts. **Database software** is used to store, organize, update, and retrieve large amounts of data. **Relational database software (RDBMS)** stores information in tables, which enable users quick access to the data by connecting tables with common fields. **Data mining** is a function in some databases that looks for hidden patterns in the data to anticipate future patterns. This is commonly used in scientific applications and as a marketing tool to predict future consumer trends. Typically, database software can be used to manage various types of information, such as that found in large mailing lists, inventories, students' records, order histories, and invoicing. Databases help you to enter, store, sort, filter, retrieve, and summarize the information they contain and then generate meaningful reports. Common database programs include Microsoft Access, Lotus Approach, and Corel Paradox. Figure 1.30 shows a database object created in Microsoft Access 2007. Database software replaces an old manual filing system where information is stored in filing cabinets in a single location.

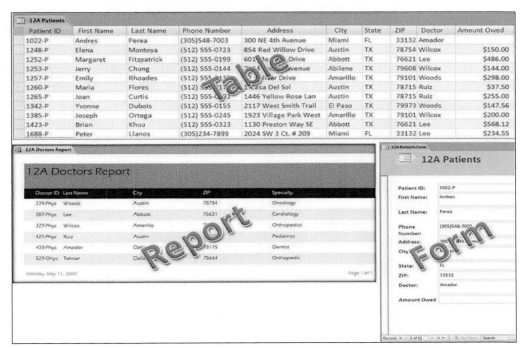

Figure 1.30

Examples of database software objects

Presentation software has become a standard in replacing flip charts, slide projectors, or overhead transparencies used by speakers and lecturers. This software is used to create electronic slides and project slide shows to visually present materials and ideas to large groups in a conference room or on the Web. Presentation software is also used to create audience handouts, speaker notes, and other materials that can be used during an oral presentation or for distribution to a group of participants. Microsoft PowerPoint, Lotus Freelance Graphics, and Corel Presentations are examples of presentation software programs. Figure 1.31 shows a presentation created with Microsoft PowerPoint 2007.

Figure 1.31

Example presentation created with Microsoft PowerPoint 2007

Communication and organizational software—Communication software can cover a broad range of tasks including videoconferencing and telephony. However, applications in the productivity category are most often used to send and receive e-mail. These applications typically include an address book (contacts list), a scheduler, a calendar, and task functions, which help users organize their personal and professional responsibilities. Microsoft Outlook, Lotus Notes, and Corel WordPerfect Mail are examples of communication and organizational software. Figure 1.32 shows an example of a calendar in Microsoft Outlook 2007.

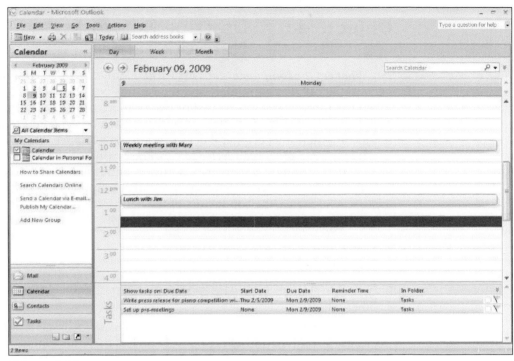

Figure 1.32

Example of a calendar in Microsoft Outlook 2007

What is a software suite? Although it is possible to buy any of the previous applications separately, most software manufacturers, including Microsoft, Corel, and Lotus, also group applications together into a package called a **suite**. There is an alternative suite called OpenOffice and it's free. It is designed as an open source software in such a way that users can report bugs, request new features, or change and improve the software.

Another advantage of using a suite is that because products from the same company have many common elements, such as basic window design and layout, toolbars containing similar tools, dictionaries, and media galleries, many users find this familiarity makes it easier to switch between the programs in a suite. Examples of suites include Microsoft Office, Corel WordPerfect Office, and Lotus SmartSuite.

What are some other common software applications? As mentioned earlier, there are many different types of application software besides productivity software, each one with a specific function. Some of these are the following:

- You might use Microsoft Publisher or QuarkXPress to create newsletters or brochures.

- Bookkeepers rely on special accounting packages such as Peachtree Accounting or QuickBooks to balance the books and handle other accounting functions.

- Graphic designers turn to packages such as Adobe Photoshop or Adobe Illustrator to develop creative artwork.

- You might use Microsoft Expression Web or Macromedia Dreamweaver to create your own Web site.

- **IM** (instant messaging) software enables users to communicate in real time like a phone conversation but using text only. The software can alert you if a member of your group is online at that moment.
- Web browsers are software used to locate and display Web pages and navigate through them. They also enable users to store their frequently used sites for quick access.

If you have a specific need, chances are there is software that will address those needs. Today the best way to find software is to do a Web search using a search engine.

Objective 5 | Describe Networks and Define Network Terms

What are the components of a network? Connecting one computer to another creates a network. Recall that computers and the various peripherals that are connected to them are called hardware. Networks consist of two or more connected computers plus the various peripheral devices that are attached to them. Each object connected to a network, whether it is a computer or a peripheral device, is known as a ***node***.

Why are computers connected to networks? Some of the benefits of computer networks include the capability to share data, software, and resources such as printers, scanners, Internet access, video conferencing, and VoIP. Computers can be connected to a network using several media, the conductors of the network signals:

- Existing telephone wires
- Power lines
- Coaxial cables
- Unshielded twisted pair (UTP) cables
- Fiber optic

Wireless networks use radio waves instead of wires or cables to connect. Most networks use a combination of media and wireless communications (see Figure 1.33).

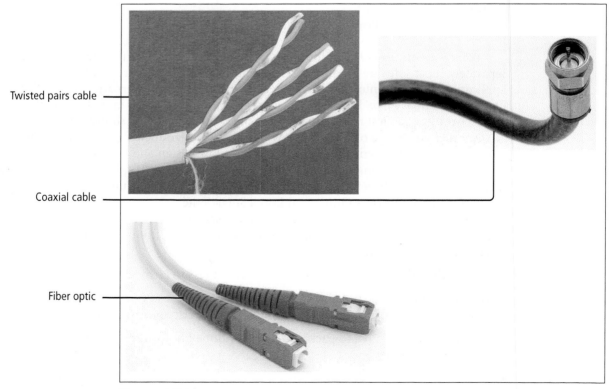

Twisted pairs cable

Coaxial cable

Fiber optic

Figure 1.33
Network media, the conductor of network signals

Today, using computer networks, institutions are able to **video conference**, that is, communicate audio and/or video between two or more individuals in different locations, optimizing communications, information sharing, and decision making.

Voice over Internet Protocol (**VoIP**) enables voice, facsimile, and voice-messaging communications over networks and the Internet.

Can networks be different sizes? A network that connects computers reasonably close together, say within a few city blocks in adjacent buildings, is called a **local area network (LAN).** See Figure 1.34.

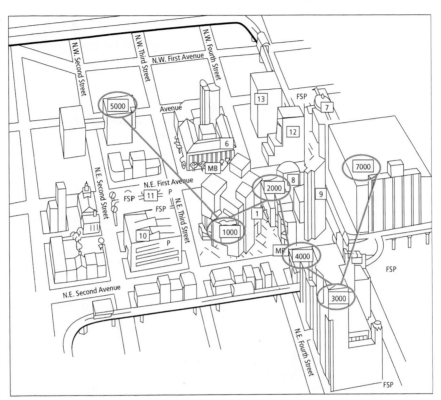

Figure 1.34

Example of a local area network, a college campus network that covers several buildings within a few city blocks

If the network grows to cover a larger geographic area or begins to include other networks, it becomes a **wide area network (WAN)**. An example is a state college campus that connects its computers with a LAN while all of its campuses connected together form a WAN. Because the different campuses are connected through WANs, students, faculty, staff, and administrators can easily and seamlessly use the resources of the entire network. Both LANs and WANs can be wired, wireless, or a combination of both. See Figure 1.35. The Internet is actually the largest WAN because it connects computer networks all around the world.

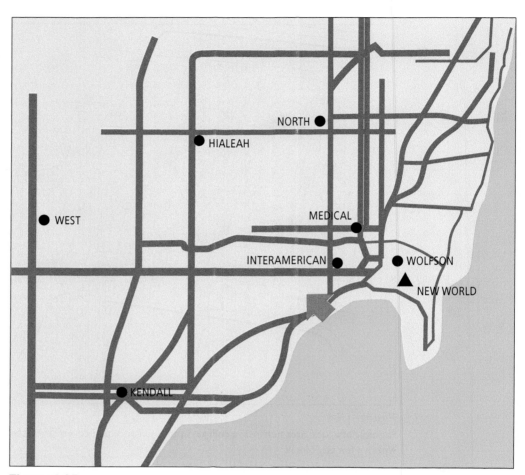

Figure 1.35

Example of a wide area network, which is a college network that links campus LANs in several cities within a county

Are networks public or private? They can be either. If you want to post information and make it available to any user, you post it on a website with no restrictions. If you want to protect certain information, you create an ***intranet*** in which access is restricted to authorized users only. Within an intranet, network administrators can limit the specific rights and privileges of different users.

How are networks configured? Networks can be configured in several ways. There are two main categories: peer-to-peer and client/server. ***Peer-to-peer*** or ***P2P networks*** are most commonly found in homes and small businesses. In a peer-to-peer network, each node can communicate with every other node without a dedicated server or hierarchy among computers. Peer-to-peer networks are relatively easy to set up, but tend to be rather small. This makes them ideal for home use, although not as desirable in the workplace. If a network grows to more than, say, ten to fifteen nodes, it is generally best to use the ***client/server network***. In a client/server network, the server manages and controls all network resources. A node can be a computer, printer, scanner, modem, an external hard disk, or any other peripheral device connected to a computer. Therefore, it isn't difficult to find more than ten nodes in an office or business setting.

How is a client/server network different from a P2P network? Client/server networks typically have two different types of computers. The **client** is the computer used at your desk or workstation to write letters, send e-mail, produce invoices, or perform any of the many tasks that can be accomplished with a computer. The client computer is the one most people directly interact with. In contrast, the server computer is typically kept in a secure location and is used by network technicians and administrators to manage network resources. If a server is assigned to handle only specific tasks, it is known as a **dedicated server.** For instance, a Web server is used to store and deliver Web pages, a file server is used to store and archive files, and a print server manages the printing resources for the network. Each of these is a dedicated server.

As a client/server network grows in number of nodes and geographical distance covered, servers are assisted by distance-spanning devices such as switches and routers to optimize data traffic.

Network topology describes the different types of network architecture used for client/server networks (see Figure 1.36). Just as there are different sizes and styles of buildings that are designed for different purposes, networks are designed to be physically configured and connected in different ways.

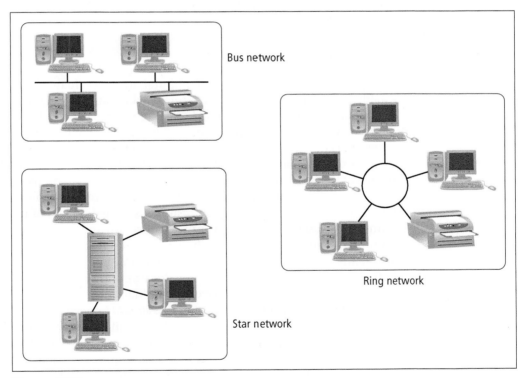

Figure 1.36
Common network topologies

Which topologies are used most often? The three most common layouts are explained in the following list:

- **Bus topology** connects each node to a single, central high-speed line known as a bus. No server is used, and although it is possible for each node to communicate with all the others, they can only do so one at a time. If one computer or device is sending over the network, all the others must wait until the transmission is complete before they can begin. Because this is an inexpensive and easy way to connect, this topology is often found in peer-to-peer networks.

- **Ring topology**, sometimes known as **token-ring topology**, connects each node to the next, forming a loop or a circle. The data that's sent is passed from node to node, traveling around the circle in only one direction. A token travels around the ring until one of the nodes is ready to send a transmission. The node then holds the token until the transmission is finished, preventing any of the other devices from sending until the token is released to make its way around the circle again. This type of topology gives each device an equal chance of being able to send data and prevents one node from doing all the communicating. This topology is being retired in favor of star topology.

- **Star topology** is the most frequent networking style used for businesses and homes. It offers a high degree of flexibility. Each node is connected to a special device known as a switch, which is centrally located. Each node must go through the switch to communicate with the others. If something happens to one node, the others are still able to communicate.

Objective 6 | Identify Safe Computing Practices

Being computer fluent implies you are a responsible computer user. This means more than just understanding the key components of a computer or the differences between hardware and software. Responsible computer users also know how to properly maintain their computers, back up necessary data, and protect themselves and others from security breaches and attacks.

Computer Maintenance

The first step to protect your computer and the valuable information it contains is to establish a regular maintenance routine. Backup utility programs, which may be part of your system software or purchased separately, enable you to back up your files. You can back up everything on your computer, just one or two important files, or anything in between. People often think that the computer is the most expensive item to replace if their hard drive fails. In reality, it is usually all the lost information that was contained on the hard drive that is the most costly to replace, if it is even possible to do so. Think about the types of files you might have on your own computer like financial records, your personal phone/address directory, resumes, scanned images of important documents, homework or school projects, your CD collection and purchased music files, and family photos and videos. Now imagine how you would re-create these files if they were irretrievably damaged. Would you be able to find them again? If you back up files on a regular basis and store the backups in a secure location, you lessen the impact that a mechanical failure or security breach will have on your data.

What other types of maintenance tasks should be performed? In addition to backing up files, regular file maintenance also helps to maintain order in your system. Several useful Windows utilities can be accessed from the System Tools folder. You can access the System Tools folder by clicking Start, clicking All Programs, and then clicking Accessories. Disk Cleanup scans the hard drive and removes unnecessary files such as those found in the Recycle Bin, in addition to temporary Internet files and other temporary files created by various programs. It is possible to adjust the settings and select which files to delete and which files to retain.

Similarly, the Disk Defragmenter scans the hard drive. However, rather than removing files, it attempts to reallocate files so they use the available hard drive space more efficiently. Recall that data is stored on hard drives in sectors and tracks. As file sizes change, they can outgrow their original location. When that happens, the remaining portion of the file may be stored elsewhere. If a file size decreases, or a file is deleted, this can create a blank area on the hard drive. Defragmenting a hard drive enables scattered portions of files to be regrouped and open spaces to be rearranged. This results in faster and more efficient file access, which improves the response time of the hard drive.

Is there a way to automate these maintenance tasks? Running these programs can be time-consuming, especially when you want to use your computer for other tasks. It is also easy to forget to do these things on a regular basis. That is why newer versions of Windows include a Task Scheduler. This utility enables you to create a task and select the best time for each task to run, in addition to how often, which makes the whole process automatic. Figures 1.37 and 1.38 show the steps to follow to reach the Task Scheduler dialog box for Windows Vista users and Windows 7 users, respectively.

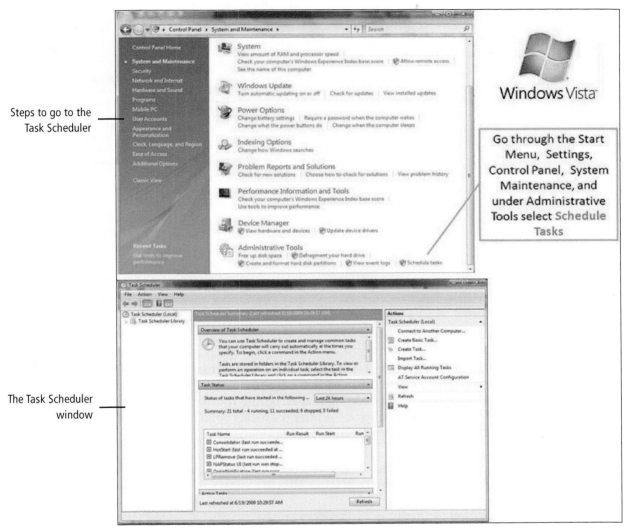

Steps to go to the Task Scheduler

The Task Scheduler window

Figure 1.37

Computer maintenance—Task Scheduler (Windows Vista users)

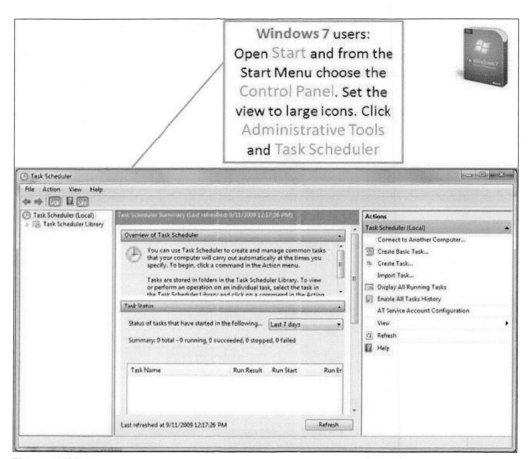

Figure 1.38

Computer maintenance—steps to set a task in the Task Scheduler (Windows 7 users)

Can changes to my system be undone? Sometimes when new software is installed on a computer, the results are not what you anticipated. Instead of playing a new game, you find your system stops responding each time you start it. Or, you might find the new driver you installed for your printer is causing conflicts. Even though you've tried to uninstall the software, the system is still not right.

Fortunately, if you are running a newer version of Windows, the System Restore utility come to the rescue. Periodically, Windows creates a ***restore point***, which records all the settings for your system. It's similar to taking a picture of how everything is currently set up. Figures 1.39 and 1.40 show steps to create a restore point for Windows Vista and Windows 7 users, respectively.

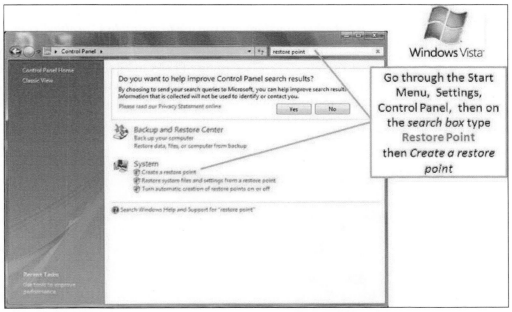

Figure 1.39
Computer maintenance—steps to create a Restore Point (Windows Vista users)

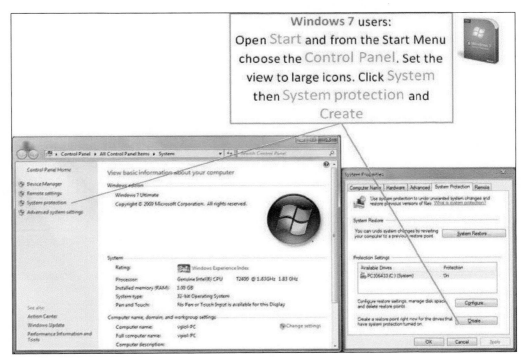

Figure 1.40
Computer maintenance—steps to create a Restore Point (Windows 7 users)

It is also possible to set manual restore points, and it is highly recommended that you set one before installing new software or hardware, or when making any major changes to your system. If you experience a problem with your system after the new software is installed, you can roll your system back to an earlier restore point when the system was working correctly. Think of it as an Undo button for your operating system. The good news is, returning to an earlier restore point affects only your system settings. It does not delete any of the data files you may have created during the interval.

What other functions can you use to maintain a "healthy" computer? Following are some of the other things that keep computers healthy:

- **Disk Cleanup**—This is a group of tasks intended to free disk space cause by Internet temporary files and hard drive unwanted files that accumulate from time to time. Part of this routine includes emptying the Recycle Bin. Figures 1.41 and 1.42 show the steps for accessing Disk Cleanup in Windows Vista and Windows 7.

Figure 1.41

Computer maintenance—steps to access Disk Cleanup (Windows Vista users)

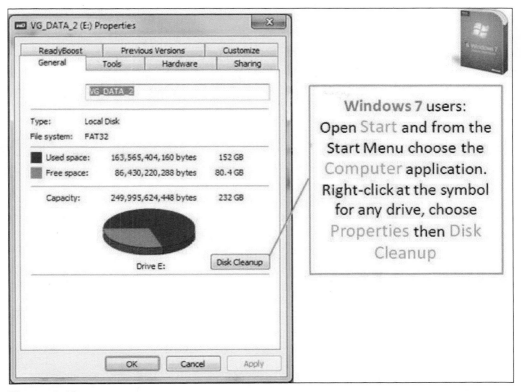

Figure 1.42
Computer maintenance—steps to access Disk Cleanup (Windows 7 users)

- **Activate and set up the Internet Pop-up Blocker**—This lets the user the select options to allow or to block advertising and other pop-up windows while surfing the Net. Figures 1.43 and 1.44 show the steps for accessing Pop-up Blocker in Windows Vista and Windows 7.

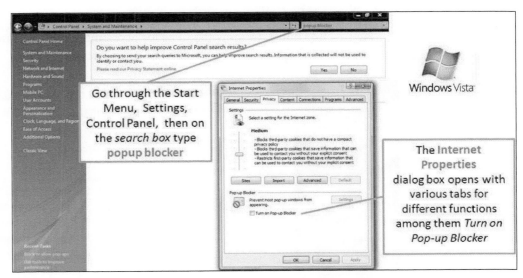

Figure 1.43
Computer maintenance—steps to access the Pop-up Blocker (Windows Vista users)

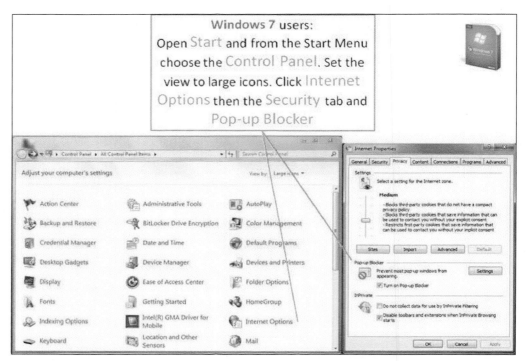

Figure 1.44

Computer maintenance—steps to access the Pop-up Blocker (Windows 7 users)

- **Access and set up Security settings**—You can set security settings, such as:

  - Check for security updates

  - Select the settings for the Windows Firewall

  - Check for Windows software updates

  - Scan for spyware and other potentially unwanted software

  - Change Internet security options

  Figures 1.45 and 1.46 show the steps for accessing security settings in Windows Vista and Windows 7.

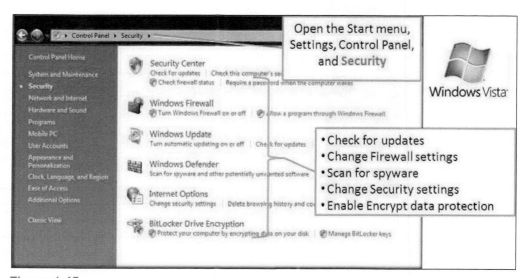

Figure 1.45

Computer maintenance—steps to access the Security settings (Windows Vista users)

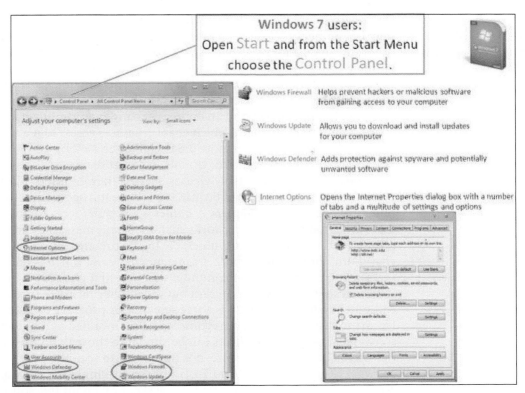

Figure 1.46

Computer maintenance—steps to access the Security settings and other functions (Windows 7 users)

Viruses

Establishing the habit of performing regular maintenance on your computer is one way to protect it, and yourself, from data loss. But there are many other dangers you need to be aware of too. Viruses, spyware, and **hackers** are all out there waiting to pounce on the unwary computer user. The term *hacker*, as used here, signifies an expert in computers and programming languages who uses his/her expertise to obtain unauthorized access to computer systems with the purpose corrupting data and/or stealing information.

What are viruses and how do they get on the computer? Computer **viruses** are malicious codes or software designed to invade your computer system and alter or destroy data without your knowledge and against your wishes. The severity of a virus can vary. Some viruses merely seem to be nuisances or might not even be obvious to the user; some cause files to be corrupted or erased; and others are capable of shutting down a computer and erasing the entire hard drive. Viruses infect a system and then attach themselves to a program or file to spread to other users.

Viruses can be distributed in several ways. In the early days of computers, viruses were spread by sharing infected floppy disks. Now, due to the ease in which files can be shared over the Internet, viruses are able to spread much more quickly. One of the most common ways to send a virus is through e-mail attachments. Security experts recommend that you never open an e-mail attachment unless you have first scanned it with antivirus software to determine that it is virus-free. Experts also recommend that unless you know the sender and have been expecting the e-mail attachment, it is best to delete the attachment without ever opening it. File-sharing services are another source for these types of problems.

Are viruses and worms the same thing? Worms are similar to viruses because they are also malicious programs that spread from computer to computer; however, unlike viruses, worms are able to do this without any human interaction and are able to replicate themselves so numerous copies can be sent. Worms can burrow into your e-mail address book, or locate e-mail addresses on files saved on your hard drive, then send themselves out without any help from you. When it reaches the e-mail recipient, it does the same thing to the recipient's address book. Also, because worms can quickly replicate themselves, they can repeat this scenario over and over. Just the sheer amount of traffic they cause on a network can be enough to bring an entire company to a grinding halt. Worms can also open a "back door" to your system, which enables hackers access to it and gives them the ability to control your computer remotely. Sasser, Blaster, NetSky, and MyDoom are all worms that have created a great deal of trouble in recent years.

Trojan horses are not truly viruses because they do not duplicate themselves or infect other files; however, they can be just as problematic because they open your system for other intruders such as *botnets*. A *botnet* is a popular term for a group of software robots that run automatically in networks such as instant massagers, chat rooms, and discussion groups that have been made vulnerable by the presence of Trojan horses. Once inside a chat room, for instance, a botnet can generate *spam,* which is bulk unsolicited e-mail messages to random lists of computer users. At first glance, a Trojan horse often appears to be a desirable software program but in fact they facilitate unauthorized access to a computer system. Perhaps it is a free screensaver program or a set of animated cursors. Unfortunately, these programs come with an unwanted and hidden agenda. After the software is installed, the effects can be similar to those that viruses or worms cause. Before you install new software, it is important to scan the program files with antivirus software to ensure there are no Trojan horses lurking there. And, as with unknown e-mail attachments, it is important to be skeptical about free software; it's not often that you really get something for nothing!

Spyware

How is spyware different from viruses? **Spyware** is software designed to capture personal and confidential information that resides on your system and send it elsewhere. It has quickly become as large a problem as viruses. Spyware's primary threat is to your privacy and confidentiality. Although spyware is not usually intended to harm your system, it can sometimes have that effect on it. *Adware* is spyware that tracks your Internet browsing and can install malicious cookies on your computer. A *cookie* is a small text file that contains information that can identify you to a website. Cookies are not necessarily bad. They are useful when they are used to help personalize your Web browsing experience, but cookies can threaten your privacy if they are used to reveal too much information.

How can you tell if spyware is on a computer? One symptom that indicates adware is on a computer is an increase in the number of pop-up ads the user receives, some of which might even address the user by name! Adware can generate pop-up ads even when you're not online. Some types of adware can also reset a Web browser's home page to a page of its choosing and take control of the search engine, directing you to websites that have been predetermined by the adware.

Are there other privacy threats? **Key loggers** are another type of spyware. In this case, a software program records every keystroke made on the computer. Key loggers can capture all sorts of confidential information this way—passwords, credit card numbers, bank account numbers, and so on—and then relay this information elsewhere. Entire e-mail messages and instant messaging conversations can be recorded this way too. Some key loggers are hardware, rather than software, although they perform the same devious function. Such hardware devices can be attached between the keyboard and the computer. The information stolen through the use of key loggers can easily make you a victim of identity theft. Trojan horses can be used to distribute key loggers and other types of spyware just as easily as they deliver viruses.

How can you avoid being a victim? To minimize the risk of having spyware installed on your computer, there are some practical precautions you can take. One of the most prevalent methods of spreading spyware is through file-sharing services, such as Morpheus or Kazaa. Not only can the file-sharing software include spyware, but often the files you think you are downloading for free are infected too. Although it's tempting to get the newest song or video for free from such a site, don't risk it!

This problem can be avoided if you use one of the legitimate, pay-as-you-go file-sharing services such as iTunes or the reincarnated Napster. Do not trust files or software sent by friends or acquaintances. Additionally, be cautious when you download and install freeware or shareware software. Make sure you deal with a reputable software publisher, scan the downloaded software for viruses and spyware, and read the licensing agreement. Some licensing agreements actually include information about additional software that will be automatically installed if you accept it.

Another way to prevent spyware is to avoid pop-up and banner ads whenever possible. You should never click on them. Often the "No Thanks" button is just a ruse to get you to click it and enable the spyware installation. Close pop-up ads by clicking the Close button in the top right corner. Installing pop-up blocking software can help to eliminate this risk almost entirely.

If you are running the most recent version of Windows, you already have a pop-up blocker available to you. You can view the pop-up blocker settings for Windows Vista in Figure 1.43 and access this dialog box through Internet Explorer's Tools menu. Many popular search engines, such as Google and Yahoo!, also include pop-up blocking features in their toolbars, which you can download at no charge. It is also wise to avoid questionable websites, because some of them can install spyware on your system just by visiting the site.

Protecting Yourself and Your Computer

In addition to being cautious in your Internet travels, there are some proactive measures you can take to protect yourself and your computer from viruses and spyware. These include:

- **Software updates** and **patches**—Keeping your operating system and software up to date is critical. Software manufacturers are constantly on the lookout for security threats, and they issue updates and patches to help protect your system. Check for these and install them regularly. Software manufacturers have begun to implement automated procedures to check and install such updates. If your computer has this capability, it's a good idea to use this feature.

- **Antivirus and antispyware software**—*Antivirus software* is a utility program used to search your hard drive and files for viruses, and remove those that are found. *Antispyware software* works in a similar fashion, but searches for spyware rather than viruses. No computer should be without this protection. Many users erroneously think that because they aren't regularly online or use only a slow dial-up connection, they aren't a target. Nothing could be further from the truth! Recent studies show more than two-thirds of all computer users have some form of virus or spyware on their system.

There are a variety of antivirus and antispyware products available. Unfortunately, there are also a lot of dishonest companies purporting to offer these products. Too often, these are really scams that will actually install spyware or viruses on your system! To avoid being scammed or downloading something malicious, you should never respond to offers that are received in a pop-up ad or unsolicited e-mail. To obtain legitimate products, it is best to purchase them from the manufacturer's website or from a local retailer. Additionally, some internet service providers are beginning to provide some of these products as part of their services.

Some well-known antivirus products include Norton AntiVirus (*www.symantec.com*), McAfee VirusScan (*www.mcafee.com*), and AVG Anti-Virus (*www.grisoft.com*).

Antispyware products include eTrust PestPatrol (*www.pestpatrol.com*), Ad-Aware (*www.lavasoft.com*), and Spybot Search & Destroy (*www.safer-networking.org*). You can search for other products at popular download sites such as Download.com (*www.download.com*) or Tucows (*www.tucows.com*) but you should be sure to read the software reviews and evaluate their usefulness before downloading or installing them.

It is best to use only one antivirus product, because running more than one can cause conflicts between the programs. However, because there are so many different types of spyware, antispyware products may address these problems in different ways. Experts recommend running at least two different antispyware applications in order to catch as many spyware programs as possible. It's not enough to install antivirus and antispyware software on your system; you need to update it frequently, at least once a week. Doing so will protect you against any new viruses or spyware created since the last time you checked. Software should be set to scan incoming data files, e-mail, and so on but regular full-system scans should be conducted on a weekly basis as well.

Personal firewalls—Firewalls may be software programs or hardware devices, although their purpose is the same to prevent unauthorized access to your computer. When a firewall is installed properly, it can make your computer invisible to hackers and other invaders. Not only can a good firewall help prevent infections and identity theft; it can also prevent hackers from accessing your computer and turning it into a ***zombie***. A zombie computer is one that can be controlled remotely and can be used to help spread viruses, spyware, or junk e-mail known as spam. Zombie computers can also be used in ***denial of service (DoS)*** attacks. DoS attacks occur when a large number of computers try to access a website at the same time, effectively overloading it and causing it to shut down. If you are using Windows XP or Windows Vista, you already have a firewall available to you.

You can access the firewall settings by clicking the Start button, settings, Control Panel, Security, and Windows Firewall.

What else should I look for? It might sound simple, but when online, do not give out personal information unless it is for legitimate purposes. It is important to avoid spam e-mail and ***phishing*** attacks e-mails that masquerade as authentic entities, such as banks and credit card companies, and ask for confidential information. Legitimate organizations will not ask for passwords, bank account numbers, or credit card details through e-mail. It is also possible to check for hoaxes and scams at a variety of websites, including many of the antivirus and antispyware sites. When in doubt, do some research to see if the request you've received is legitimate. If necessary, make a telephone call to the agency in question. Viewing such requests with a critical eye can help you avoid online scams and hoaxes.

Summary

In this chapter, you examined the benefits of computer fluency and identified the four basic functions of computing. You explored the various types of computers and their components, including CPUs, RAM, and storage devices. This chapter also discussed how to evaluate a computer system and understand the terminology used to measure storage capacity, memory, and microprocessor speed. Various hardware and peripheral devices were reviewed, including input and output devices, and different types of storage devices and media. You explored the basic types of computer software system software and application software and the different uses for each type. You identified various types of networks and the different ways networks can be configured. You also reviewed ways to maintain your computer and keep it safe from various threats, including viruses and spyware.

Key Terms

Adware	Compact disk	DVD drive
Antispyware software	Computer	DVD-ROM
Antivirus software	Computer fluent	DVI port
Application software	Configuration	Embedded computers
Arithmetic logic unit (ALU)	Connectivity port	Ethernet port
Arrow keys	Control keys	Firewall
Audio port	Control unit	FireWire port
Backup tape drive	Cookie	Flash drive
Bluetooth	CPU	Flash memory
Boot	Data	Flat-panel displays
Botnet	Database software	Floppy diskette
Boot process	Data mining	Floppy disk drive
Browser	Dedicated server	Function keys
Burn	Denial of service (DoS)	Gaming computers
Bus topology	Desktop computer	Gigabyte (GB)
CD	Device	Gigahertz (GHz)
CD burner	Dialog box	Graphical user interface (GUI)
CD drive	Digital camera	GUI
CD-ROM	Digital video recorder	Hackers
CD-R	Digital Video Interface (DVI) port	Handheld computers
CD-RW	Docking station	Hard copy
Central processing unit (CPU)	DOS	Hard disk drive
Click	Dot matrix	Hardware
Client	Dot pitch	Hyperlinks
Client/server network	Dots per inch (dpi)	Icon
Clock speed	Double-click	IM
Communication and organizational software	Drag	Impact
	DSL	Information
	DVD	Information processing cycle

Ink-jet

Input

Input devices

Insertion point

Internet control key

Intranet

IrDA port

Joysticks

Key logger

Keyboard

Kilobit

Kilobyte

LAN

Laser printer

LCD

LightScribe

Linux

Liquid crystal display (LCD)

Local area network (LAN)

Mac OS

Magnetic

Mainframe computers

Megabit (Mb)

Megabyte (MB)

Megahertz (MHz)

Memory

Menu

MFD

Microcomputer

Microphones

Microprocessor chip

Microsoft Windows

MIDI port

Mobile devices

Modem port

Monitor (or display screen)

Monitor port

Motherboard

Mouse

Mouse pointer

Multifunction device (MFD)

Multimedia control key

Multimedia projectors

Multitask

Network

Network topology

Node

Nonimpact

Nonvolatile

Notebook computer

Numeric keypad

Open-source

Operating system (OS)

Optical

OS

Output

Output device

P2P network (Peer-to-peer)

Parallel port

PDA

Peripheral

Permanent memory

Personal digital assistant (PDA)

Personal firewall

Phishing

Pixel

Port

Ppm (pages per minute)....19

Presentation software

Printer

Printout

Process

Program

Programmable

RAM

Random Access Memory (RAM)

RDBMS

Read-Only Memory (ROM)

Read/write

Refresh rate

Resolution

Restore point

Right-click

Right-drag

Ring (or token-ring) topology

ROM

S-video port

Scanners

Scroll

Scroll wheel

Sectors

Serial port

Server

Shortcut menu

Smartphones

Soft copy

Software patches or Software updates

Spam

Speech recognition

Speakers

Splash screen

Spreadsheet software

Spyware

Star topology

Storage

Storage devices

Stylus

Suite

Supercomputer

System software

System unit

Tablet computer

Toggle key

Temporary memory

Terabyte

Token-ring topology

Touch screen

Tracks

Trojan horse

Universal serial bus (USB) port

User friendly

User interface	WAN	Wireless network
Utility program	Web browser	Word processing
Video conferencing	Wide area network	software
Virus	(WAN)	Worm
VoIP	Windows	Zombie
Volatile	Wireless	

Matching

A Application software

B Computer

C Computer network

D Console/system unit

E CPU

F Hardware

G DVDs or CDs

H Memory (RAM)

I Motherboard/ system board

J Peripherals

K Port

L Server

M Software

N Spyware

O Topology

Match each term in the second column with its correct definition in the first column. Write the letter of the term on the blank line in front of the correct definition.

_____ 1. Computer programs.

_____ 2. Programs that enable you to accomplish a specific tasks or solve a specific need.

_____ 3. Two or more computers connected together to enable resource sharing.

_____ 4. Used to manage network resources, this type of computer can be dedicated to a specific task.

_____ 5. Optical disk drives use this type of storage media.

_____ 6. The layout or design/arrangement of computers connected to a network.

_____ 7. A peripheral device uses this to attach to the computer.

_____ 8. A programmable electronic device that can input, process, output, and store data.

_____ 9. The physical components of a computer system.

_____10. Hardware connected outside the computer's system unit.

_____11. The hardware unit that typically contains the CPU, RAM, a hard disk, and a power supply.

_____12. A large printed circuit board to which all the other components are connected.

_____13. The temporary storage that holds data and instructions waiting to be processed.

_____14. The processing unit.

_____15. This type of program threatens a user's privacy.

Multiple Choice

Circle the correct response.

1. Which of the following requires one byte of storage?
   a. Page   **b.** Paragraph   **c.** Sentence   **d.** Character

2. Which of the following units represents the fastest CPU clock speed?
   a. 733 MHz   **b.** 286 MHz   **c.** 2 GHz   **d.** 2 GB

3. Which of the following is not an input device?
   a. Keyboard   **b.** Speaker   **c.** Mouse   **d.** Stylus

4. Which of the following is an example of optical storage media?
   a. Disk drive   **b.** Flash card   **c.** RAM   **d.** Compact disc

5. Which of the following is not a type of computer?
   a. Mainframe   **b.** Multitask   **c.** Server   **d.** Supercomputer

6. Before a computer can process data, where must data be stored?
   a. In RAM   **b.** On a disk   **c.** In the control unit   **d.** On the monitor

7. What term, related to computers, means billions?
   a. Byte   **b.** Mega   **c.** Giga   **d.** Hertz

8. Which of the following is not a type of microcomputer?
   a. Desktop   **b.** Notebook   **c.** Personal digital assistant   **d.** Microprocessor

9. Which of the following can prevent the easy and casual connection to your computer by a nonauthorized user?
   a. Disk defragmenter   **b.** Antivirus software   **c.** Firewall   **d.** Key logger

10. Which of the following is capable of opening a "back door" on a computer and is able to spread without human interaction?
    a. Trojan horse   **B.** Worm   **c.** Adware   **d.** Zombie

Glossary

Command bar The toolbar located immediately above the right side of the browser window that can provide quick access to commands such as Home, Page, Safety, and Tools.

Domain name The part of a text-based URL that identifies the company or organization that owns the Web site.

Downloading To request a copy of a file or program from a remote server, such as a Web server, and then to save it on your local system or storage device.

Favorites bar The toolbar located immediately above the left side of the browser window that provides quick access to favorite Web sites.

Favorites Center An Internet Explorer feature that enables you to view the Favorites, Feeds, and History lists.

File Transfer Protocol (FTP) A protocol that enables individuals to copy files from one computer to another on a network.

Frames The method used to divide a Web page into separate panes that appear to be one complete Web page. Navigation is controlled by one of the panes while viewing several different pages of content displayed within a single browser window.

FTP *See* File Transfer Protocol.

History An Internet Explorer feature that tracks recently visited Web pages and sites.

Home page The Web page that displays every time you start Internet Explorer—it can be any Web page.

Hyperlinks Text, buttons, pictures, or other objects displayed on Web pages that, when clicked, access other Web pages or display other sections of the active page.

Internet Explorer 8 A Microsoft software program that enables you to view the contents of the World Wide Web.

Internet Service Provider (ISP) A company that provides an Internet connection through a regular telephone line, a special high-speed telephone line, or a cable.

Link Select pointer The mouse pointer view that displays as a pointing hand when you point to an item that links to another Web page.

MHTML A format used to save Web pages into a single archive, including all the page elements such as text and graphics.

Path The sequential description of the storage location of the HTML documents and files making up the Web page and stored in the hierarchy of directories and folders on the Web server.

Portal Home pages that contain links to frequently visited sites, up-to-the-minute news, weather reports, maps, and directories.

Protocol A set of rules for transferring data over the Internet.

Public domain Works that are created with the intention of letting anyone use them for any reason; also a work becomes public domain when the copyright has expired.

ScreenTip A small note that displays information about a screen element and is activated by pointing to a button or other screen object.

Search engine A program that searches for keywords in files and documents or other Web sites found on the Internet.

Sponsored link A site that pays to be displayed with results at a search engine site.

Tabs A browser feature that enables you to have multiple Web pages open at the same time without having to open multiple browsers.

Top-level domain (TLD) The highest level of the Domain Name System expressed as the last part of the domain name and represented by a period followed by three or four letters.

Uniform Resource Locator (URL) The unique address used to locate a Web page or Web site.

Web browser Software that enables you to use the World Wide Web and navigate from page to page and site to site.

Web page A document on the World Wide Web that displays as a screen with associated links, frames, pictures, and other features of interest.

Web site A group of related Web pages published to a specific location on the World Wide Web.

Glossary

Glossary

Adware Spyware that tracks your Internet browsing and can install malicious cookies on your computer.

Antispyware software A utility program used to search your hard drive for spyware, and remove those that are found.

Antivirus software A utility program used to search your hard drive for viruses, and remove those that are found.

Application software Programs that accomplish specific tasks, such as word processing, photo editing, or sending e-mail, and using the computer in a productive manner.

Arithmetic logic unit (ALU) Handles addition, subtraction, multiplication, and division, and also makes logical and comparison decisions.

Arrow keys Keys located at the bottom right of the keyboard between the standard keys and the numeric keypad that enable the user to move the insertion point around the active window.

Audio port Similar to video ports, these ports connect audio devices, such as speakers, headphones, and microphones to the computer's sound card.

Backup tape drive A storage device used to save data to tape media resembling audiocassettes.

Bluetooth A type of wireless technology that relies on radio wave transmission and doesn't require a clear line of sight. It is typically limited to less than 30 feet.

Boot The process of starting up a computer; the computer begins when power is turned on.

Botnet Term associated with malicious software or software *robots*.

Browser See Web browser.

Burn The process that saves data by using a laser beam that burns tiny pits into the storage medium.

Bus topology In a computer network, it connects each node to a single, central high-speed line known as a bus.

CD Acronym for compact disk; a polycarbonate material with one or more metal layers capable of optically storing digital information.

CD burner Type of optical drive capable of reading and writing data from and to a CD (provided the media is recordable, like CD-Rs and CD-RWs).

CD drive Type of optical drive that can read CDs (compact disks).

CD-ROM CD media that was burned once and from that moment on can only be read.

CD-R Also known as CD-Recordable, a type of compact disk that can be recorded using a CD burner (drive).

CD-RW A rewritable disc that enables data to be recorded, revised, or deleted, and new data written to the disc, similar to magnetic media.

Central processing unit (CPU) The part of the computer responsible for controlling all the commands and tasks the computer performs, acting as the brain of the computer.

Click A mouse function in which you point at an object, press and release the left (or primary) mouse button once.

Client In a client/server network, the computer used at a desk or workstation to write letters, send e-mail, produce invoices, or perform any of the many tasks that can be accomplished with a computer.

Client/server network A network in which two different types of computers have different functions. See also Client and Server.

Clock speed A measure of the speed at which a CPU processes data (number of instructions per second).

Communication and organizational software A program such as Microsoft Outlook 2007, used to send and retrieve e-mail, manage day-to-day tasks such as appointments and contacts.

Compact disk See CD

Computer A programmable electronic device that can input, process, output, and store data.

Computer fluent Describes a person who understands the capabilities and limitations of computers and knows how to use computer technology to accomplish tasks.

Configure To put together by selecting a combination of components, features, and options.

Connectivity port Ports such as Ethernet and modem that are used to connect a computer to a local network or to the Internet.

Control keys Keys such as the Ctrl, Alt, and the Windows key that provide shortcuts or increased functionality to the keyboard when used in combination with other keys.

Control unit In the CPU, the component responsible for obtaining and executing instructions from the computer's memory.

Cookie A small text file that contains information that can identify you to a website.

CPU See Central processing unit

Data Represents text, numbers, graphics, sounds, and videos entered to the computer's memory during input operations.

Database software Programs, such as Microsoft Access 2007, used to store and organize large amounts of data and perform complex tasks such as sorting and querying to generate specialized reports.

Data mining A function is some database software that looks for hidden patterns in the data to anticipate future trends.

Dedicated server A server in a network that is assigned to handle only specific tasks.

Denial of service (DoS) Attacks that occur when a large number of computers try to access a website at the same time, effectively overloading it and causing it to shut down.

Desktop computer A class of microcomputer, such as a PC or a Mac, that typically occupies a working area around a desk.

Device A hardware component that attaches to a computer. Includes disk drives, printers, mice, keyboards, and modems.

Dialog box A frame or window that shows the presets or defaults for a specific function and enables the user to make changes before moving ahead.

Digital camera A device that stores pictures digitally rather than using conventional film.

Digital video recorder Devices that let you capture digital images and movies and transfer them directly to your computer.

Digital Video Interface (DVI) port Ports that transmit a pure digital signal, eliminating the need for digital-to-analog conversion and resulting in a higher quality picture on an LCD monitor.

Docking station Device that enables the user to connect a notebook to a full-size keyboard, monitor, and other devices in an office setting.

DOS The original OS for personal computers in the early 1980s. This was a text-based or keyboard-driven operating system.

Dot matrix Printers that have small hammers, similar to a typewriter's, that strike a ribbon against paper, leaving behind the image of a character or symbol.

Dot pitch A display characteristic in monitors that refers to the diagonal distance between two pixels of the same color. The smaller the dot pitch results in a crisper viewing image because there is less blank space between the pixels.

Dots per inch (dpi) How resolution is expressed. The higher the dpi, the better the print quality.

Double-click The action of clicking and releasing the left mouse button twice in rapid succession while keeping the mouse still.

Drag The action of moving something from one location on the screen to another; the action includes pointing and clicking (releasing the mouse button at the desired time or location).

DSL Acronym for digital subscriber line. Type of communications line in which signals travel through copper wires between a telephone switching station and a home or business.

Dual-boot A computer that can run more than one operating system.

Dual-core Processors that have several advantages over a single processor CPU, including improved multitasking capabilities, system performance, and lower power consumption.

DVD Acronym for Digital Video Disk or Diversified Video Disk; media that holds data written by an optical device.

DVD drive Digital Video Disk drive capable of reading and writing DVD media.

DVD-ROM DVD media that was burned once and from that moment on can only be read.

DVI port See Digital Video Interface.

Embedded computers Small specialized computers built into larger components such as automobiles and appliances.

Ethernet port A port, slightly larger than a telephone jack, that can transmit data at speeds up to 1,000 megabits per second (Mbps) and is usually used to connect to a cable modem or a network.

Firewall A combination of hardware and software used to prevent unauthorized access to your computer.

FireWire port A port used to send data at rates up to 800 megabits per second (Mbps), frequently used for digital cameras or digital video recorders.

Flash drive A small, portable, digital storage device that connects to a computer's USB port (Universal Serial Bus); also called a thumb drive, jump drive, or USB drive.

Flash memory Portable, nonvolatile memory that uses electronic, solid-state circuitry.

Flat-panel displays Flat-panel displays or LCD monitors that use a liquid crystal display and are thin and energy efficient.

Floppy diskette Magnetic media used for data storage.

Floppy disk drive Device used to read and write to floppy diskettes media.

Function keys Keys that are located above the standard row of number keys and numbered F1 through F12. These keys are generally associated with certain software-specific commands.

Gaming computers Computers that are mostly used by video game enthusiasts. They are usually configured with a fast CPU, large size memory, a special video card, sound card, and surround sound speaker system.

Gigabyte (GB) Approximately one billion bytes; a unit used to measure memory size and storage space.

Gigahertz (GHz) One billion hertz; a hertz is one of the units used to measure processor speed. One hertz is one cycle (instruction read) per second.

Graphical user interface (GUI) Today's operating systems provide a *user-friendly* way to operate a computer with their graphical user interface. The user controls the action using the keyboard, a mouse, or a touch screen to make selections from onscreen objects such as icons, menus, or dialog boxes.

GUI See Graphical user interface.

Hackers Derogatory term to describe individuals who gain unauthorized access to computer systems for the purpose of corrupting or stealing data.

Handheld computers Small portable computers that might include personal productivity software and enable the user to play music, take photos and video, make phone calls, and access the Internet. PDAs, Pocket PCs, and smart phones fall in this category.

Hard copy The output of a printer (synonymous with printout).

Hard disk drive A combination of a device and media used as the main storage in most computers.

Hardware The physical or tangible components of the computer and any equipment connected to it.

Hyperlink A connection to another area of a document or a connection to an Internet URL.

Icon A graphic representation of an object on the screen. Icons can be selected with the mouse or using your fingers on a touch screen.

IM Acronym for instant messaging, software that enables users to communicate in real time like a phone conversation but using text only.

Impact A type of printer that resembles a typewriter; a key punches an inked ribbon to imprint a characters on paper.

Information Data that has been organized in a useful manner.

Information processing cycle The cycle composed of the four basic computer functions: input, process, output, and storage.

Ink-jet A nonimpact printer that uses a special nozzle and ink cartridges to distribute liquid ink on the surface of the paper.

Input During this step of the information processing cycle, the computer gathers data or allows a user to enter data onto memory.

Input devices Computer hardware used to enter data and instructions into a computer; examples include the keyboard, mouse, stylus, scanner, microphone, and digital camera.

Insertion point A blinking vertical line on the screen that shows where the next typed character will appear.

Internet control key Typically located at the top of certain keyboards, these keys enable the user to assign to each key a unique Web browser functions such as sending e-mail, browsing a specific site, or accessing their online bank account.

Intranet A network or part of a network in which access is restricted to authorized users only.

IrDA port A port that is used to allow devices such as PDAs, keyboards, mice, and printers to transmit data wirelessly to another device by using infrared light waves.

Joysticks Game controls that are input devices used to control movement within video games.

Key logger A type of spyware that records every keystroke made on the computer and can capture all sorts of confidential information this way such as passwords, credit card numbers, bank account numbers, and so on.

Keyboard The primary input device for computers.

Kilobit One thousand bits. It takes eight bits to make one byte.

Kilobyte Approximately one thousand bytes.

LAN Acronym for local area network. A network that connects computers that are reasonably close together.

Laser printer A type of nonimpact printer that uses a drum, static electricity, and a laser to distribute dry ink or toner on the surface of the paper.

LightScribe A disc-labeling technology that burns text and graphics onto the surface of a specially coated LightScribe CD or DVD.

Linux An alternative operating system. It is open source software, which means it is not owned by a single company and some versions are available at no cost.

Liquid crystal display (LCD) Technology used in flat panel monitors, resulting in thinner, lighter monitors that consume less energy.

Local area network (LAN) A network in which the nodes are located within a small geographic area.

Mac OS An operating system designed specifically for Apple's Macintosh computers.

Magnetic A type of storage process using magnetized film to store data; used by devices such as hard disks, or media such as tape cartridges.

Mainframe computers Computers often found in large businesses, organizations, and government agencies where thousands of users need to simultaneously use the data and resources for their everyday operations.

Megabit (Mb) Approximately one million bits. It takes eight bits to make a byte.

Megabyte (MB) Approximately one million bytes; a unit of measure for memory and storage space.

Megahertz (MHz) One million hertz; a hertz is one of the units used to measure processor speed. One hertz is one cycle (instruction read) per second.

Memory A generic term that signifies storage.

Menu A list of commands that perform specific tasks within a program.

MFD Acronym for Multi-Function Devices.

Microcomputer The computer most users are familiar with and that ranges in size from large desktop systems to handheld devices. The name comes from its main component or brain called the "microchip" or microprocessor.

Microphones Input devices used to capture and record sounds.

Microprocessor chip A microcomputer's main component; it is a tiny but powerful chip compared to a mainframe or a supercomputer.

Microsoft Windows The operating system that runs most microcomputers today and provides a graphical user interface to make the computer "user friendly."

MIDI port Ports used to connect electronic musical devices, such as keyboards and synthesizers, to a computer.

Mobile devices These devices fall into the category of handheld computers; they are small enough to fit in the palm of your hand and enable users to access personal productivity software, send and read e-mail, navigate the Internet, and some are capable of wireless communications.

Modem port Ports used to connect a computer to a local network or to the Internet.

Monitor (or display screen) Display devices that show images of text, graphics, and video once data has been processed.

Monitor port A port that is used to connect the monitor to the graphics-processing unit, which is usually located on the motherboard or on a video card.

Motherboard A large printed circuit board located in the system unit to which all other boards are connected; the motherboard contains the central processing unit (CPU), the memory (RAM) chips, expansion card slots, and ports.

Mouse An input device (pointing device) used to enter commands and user responses into a computer. This device controls a symbol on the screen (mouse pointer) used to manipulate objects and select commands.

Mouse pointer In a graphical user interface environment, a pointer is a small arrow or other symbol on the screen that moves as you move the mouse. This lets the user make selections from objects on the screen such as icons, menus, or dialog boxes.

Multifunction device (MFD) Hardware devices such as All-in-One printers that provide a number of functions in one unit.

Multimedia control key Some modern keyboards have at least a few keys or buttons that can be used for such tasks as muting or adjusting speaker volume, opening a Web browser, and sending e-mail.

Multimedia projectors Output devices used to display information on a screen for viewing by a large audience.

Multitask To perform more than one task simultaneously.

Network A group of two or more computers (or nodes) connected together via cables or wirelessly, to share information and resources.

Network topology The layout and structure of a computer network.

Node Any object connected to a network that is a computer or a peripheral device.

Nonimpact Printers that generate hard copies by means other than striking elements on to a ribbon and paper. They do not touch the paper when printing.

Nonvolatile Permanent storage; type of storage that holds its contents even when power is shut down. "Read Only Memory" (ROM) is a type of permanent storage.

Notebook computer Also known as a laptop, this microcomputer is smaller than a desktop and designed to be portable.

Numeric keypad A cluster of keys located at the right of the keyboard. This provides an alternative method of quickly entering numbers.

Open-source An operating system not owned by any company and that can be changed by people with the appropriate programming knowledge.

Operating system (OS) The software that controls the way the computer works from the time it is turned on until it is shut down.

Optical A type of storage process that uses a laser to read and write data; used to burn media such as CDs and DVDs.

OS See Operating system.

Output Data that has been processed and converted into information.

Output device Computer hardware components used to display information (show it) to the user; examples include the monitor, printer, and speakers.

P2P network (Peer-to-peer) A type of network in which each node can communicate with every other node. No PC has control over the network.

Parallel port A port that sends data in groups of bits as opposed to one bit at a time.

PDA See Personal digital assistant.

Peripheral A hardware device connected to a computer but not inside the system unit, such as a monitor, printer, a scanner, or mouse.

Permanent memory Type of memory that retains data and information even if the computer's power is turned off.

Personal digital assistant (PDA) These handheld devices vary in size and purpose, but they are all ultra-lightweight and portable. Initially designed to maintain and organize calendar appointments and business contacts, they enable users to access personal productivity software, send and read e-mail, and navigate the Internet.

Personal firewall Software or hardware that, when installed properly, can make your computer invisible to hackers and other invaders.

Phishing The process of attempting to acquire sensitive information such as usernames, passwords, and credit card details by pretending to be as a reputable entity.

Pixel An abbreviated name for "picture element." Tiny dots that make up images on computer monitors.

Port An interface or a connecting point by which peripherals are connected to the computer's system unit.

Ppm Acronym for "pages per minute." A measure of the speed of a printer.

Presentation software A program, such as PowerPoint 2007, used to create dynamic slideshows and generate speaker notes and audience handouts.

Printer An output device used to generate hard copy or printout.

Printout The output of a printer (synonymous with hard copy).

Process A CPU function in which data is converted into information.

Program Also known as software, sets of instructions or commands that tell the computer what to do and are used by the computer to perform certain tasks.

Programmable A device that can be programmed or instructed to perform a specific task guided by commands or instructions.

RAM Acronym for Random Access Memory.

Random Access Memory (RAM) The computer's temporary storage space (short-term memory). It stores data on chips connected to the motherboard. This data is held just before processing by the CPU.

RDBMS Acronym for Relational Database Management System and is database software that stores information in tables, which enable users quick access to the data by connecting tables with common fields.

Read Only Memory (ROM) See ROM.

Read/write Read is the action of retrieving or opening existing data and write is the action of saving or storing data.

Refresh rate The speed at which the screen's (monitor) image is redrawn.

Resolution The measurement used to assess the clarity and sharpness of an image on a monitor; determined by pixel density.

Restore point A file in which all your computer system settings are stored. It's similar to taking a picture of how everything is currently set up. If there is a system failure, Windows can come to the rescue.

Right-click The action of pressing and releasing the right mouse button.

Right-drag A mouse function done by pressing the right mouse button and continuing to hold it while dragging, or moving, the mouse pointer to another location.

Ring (or token-ring) topology A network layout that connects each node to the next, forming a loop or a circle.

ROM Acronym for Read Only Memory. A type of memory prerecorded on a chip that the computer can only "read," not write or change its contents.

S-video port Short for Super-Video, a technology for transmitting video signals over a cable by dividing the video information into two separate signals, color and brightness.

Scanners Input devices used to convert hard copy documents or images into digital files.

Scroll The action of moving up or down within a window to access any part of that window.

Scroll wheel A button on some mice, useful when scrolling within a document; rolling the wheel enables you to quicky move up or down within a window. Also, holding the Ctrl (Control) key while moving the wheel button lets you zoom in or out for closer or more distant viewing.

Sectors Wedge-shaped sections of a hard disk drive on a hard disk drive or any magnetic storage media (ZIP disks and floppy disks), each measured from the center point to the outer edge.

Serial port Ports that can send data only one bit at a time.

Server In a client/server network, a server is the computer that manages shared network resources and provides access to the client computer when requested.

Shortcut menu A type of menu that is displayed when the user right-clicks at an onscreen object. These menus are *context sensitive.* That means they display commands and options specifically related to the object that is being pointed at.

Smartphones Handheld devices that combine mobile phone capabilities with other features typically associated with pocket PCs and PDAs.

Soft copy The image generated by a display monitor as the result of output.

Software patches or Software updates Software manufacturers are constantly on the lookout for security threats, and they issue updates and patches to help protect your system. Check for these and install them regularly.

Spam Unwanted or unsolicited bulk e-mail messages.

Speech recognition Technology that enables the user to record discussions or lectures, or to control the computer functions using voice commands.

Speakers Output devices that enable the user to hear any auditory signals the computer sends.

Splash screen A window used to inform the user of what kind of software is necessary in order to view a specific website. Also a window shown before a user is given the option to continue to the content of a website.

Spreadsheet software A program such as Microsoft Excel 2007 used to organize data in rows and columns, perform calculations, create charts, and perform numerical analyses.

Spyware Software designed to capture personal and confidential information that resides on your system and send it elsewhere.

Star topology Each node in this type of network is connected to a special device known as a switch, which is centrally located. Each node must go through the switch to communicate with the other nodes.

Storage To retain data or information for future use.

Storage devices Hardware components that retain data and information to be used in the future.

Stylus A "pen-like" input device used to write on a tablet computer or PDA.

Suite A collection of application software programs developed by the same manufacturer, bundled together and sold at a price that is usually less than the cost of purchasing each program individually. One example is Office 2007.

Supercomputer A large, powerful computer typically devoted to specialized tasks.

System software The set of programs that enables a computer's hardware devices and program to work together; it includes the operating system and utility.

System unit The tower, box, or console that contains the critical hardware and electrical components of a computer. Typically, the motherboard, the CPU, RAM, and the hard drive are contained within the system unit.

Tablet computer A portable computer that features a screen that swivels and can be written on using advanced handwriting recognition software.

Temporary memory Short-term memory that stores data and program instructions that are waiting to be processed.

Toggle key Keystroke combinations that activate a function or, if pressed again, de-activate that function.

Terabyte One trillion bytes; a unit of measure for memory and storage space.

Token-ring topology A network topology that connects each node to the next, forming a loop or a circle.

Touch screen A part of tablet computers that swivel and enable the tablet to be used like a standard notebook computer in one position or like a clipboard in the second position. These screens are considered input/output devices.

Touch screen technology A type of display screen that has a touch-sensitive panel, which enables the user to touch and make selections from onscreen objects using the tip of the finger.

Tracks Concentric circles on a hard disk drive or any magnetic storage media that together with sectors provide the storage space for data and information.

Trojan horse A destructive program that presents itself as a genuine application.

Universal serial bus (USB) port A type of port able to interface with several different peripheral devices, which reduces the need for individual, dedicated ports.

User friendly A user interface that can be used easily with minimum training because it provides visual aids and onscreen help for novice users.

User interface The feature of a computer's operating system that enables you to interact with the computer. Also see GUI (graphical user interface) and DOS (disk operating system text-based interface).

Utility program A component of system software, typically small programs used to perform routine maintenance and housekeeping tasks for the computer.

Video conferencing The use of networks to communicate audio and/or video between two or more individuals in different locations, optimizing communications, information sharing, and decision making.

Virus Malicious programs that are usually installed on your computer without your knowledge. Viruses can cause files to be corrupted or erased, are capable of shutting down a computer, or erasing the entire hard drive.

VoIP Acronym for Voice over Internet Protocol. Allows voice, facsimile, and voice-messaging communications over networks and the Internet.

Volatile Nonpermanent memory; type of storage that is lost when the computer is turned off.

WAN Acronym for Wide area network.

Web browser Software used to locate and display Web pages and navigate through them.

Wide area network (WAN) A network composed of local area networks connected over long distances.

Window A frame on the computer screen that holds a program, a dialog box, or an object.

Wireless Technology that transmits and receives data without a physical cable connection.

Wireless network A network that connects using radio waves instead of wires or cables.

Word processing software A program such as Microsoft Word 2007 used to create, edit, print, and save documents such as term papers, letters, forms, posters, and resumes.

Worm Similar to viruses, malicious programs that spread from computer to computer; however, unlike viruses, worms are able to do this without any human interaction and are able to replicate themselves.

Zombie A computer that can be controlled remotely by a hacker and can be used to spread viruses, spyware, or spam.

Glossary

Active window The window in which the mouse pointer's movements commands, or text entry occur when two or more windows are open.

Address bar A toolbar that displays the organizational path to the active file, folder, or window.

Aero See Windows Aero.

All Programs Command at the bottom of the Start menu that takes you to all available programs on your computer.

Archive To back up files and store them somewhere other than the main hard drive.

Ascending order Files or folders listed from *a* to *z* when sorted.

Background See Desktop background.

CD A compact disc—an optical storage device used to store data and which can be read-only or read-write.

Click To press the left mouse button one time.

Clipboard A temporary storage area in Windows that stores the most recently copied item.

Close button A shortcut button in a title bar that closes a window or a program.

Command bar The area at the top of a window that displays commands relevant to the open window.

Compress Reduce the size of a file or combine several files into one.

Computer icon An icon that represents the computer on which you are working, and that provides access to the drives, folders, and files on your computer.

Content pane Displays files and folders stored in the selected disk drive or folder in the Navigation pane.

Context-sensitive command A command associated with activities in which you are engaged; often activated by right-clicking a screen item.

Descending order Files or folders listed from *z* to *a* when sorted.

Desktop The working area of the Windows 7 screen, consisting of program icons, a taskbar, a sidebar, and a Start button.

Desktop background The picture, pattern, or color that displays on the desktop.

Details pane Displays details about the drive, folder, or file selected in the Content pane.

Dialog box A box that asks you to make a decision about an individual object or topic. Dialog boxes do not have Minimize buttons.

Double-click Press the left mouse button two times in rapid succession, using caution not to move the mouse.

Drag Move the mouse pointer while holding down the left mouse button, and then release at the appropriate time.

Drive An area of storage that is formatted with the Windows file system and that has a drive letter such as C.

DVD A digital video (or versatile) disc—an optical storage device used to store data, and which can be read-only or read-write.

Edit mode A Windows mode that enables you to change the name of a file or folder, and works the same in all Windows applications.

Favorites The top part of the Navigation pane that displays favorite destinations associated with the current user.

File Work that you save and store on a drive, such as a Word document or a PowerPoint presentation.

File extension The three or four characters to the right of the period in a file name. Extensions tell the computer the program to use to open the file. File extensions can be displayed or hidden.

File list Displays the contents of the current folder or library.

Flash drive A small storage device that plugs into a computer USB port; also called a thumb drive or a USB drive.

Folder Storage area, represented on the screen by a picture of a paper file folder, used to store files or other folders.

Gadget A dynamic program—such as a clock, a stock market ticker, or a weather window—that displays on the desktop, usually in the Windows Sidebar.

Gadget controls A set of tools that includes a Drag gadget button in the shape of 12 small dots, an Options button in the shape of a wrench, a Larger/Smaller size button, and a Close button.

Graphical user interface (GUI) A computer interface that shows documents as they will look in their final form and uses icons to represent programs.

Hard drive A large disk drive inside your computer, also referred to as a Local Disk.

Hardware The computer memory, disk drive space, attached devices such as printers and scanners, and the central processing unit (CPU).

Horizontal scroll bar The bar at the bottom of a window that enables you to move left and right to view information that extends beyond the left and right edges of the screen.

Icon A graphic representation; often a small image on a button that enables you to run a program or program function.

Jump list A shortcut menu from an icon on the taskbar that displays frequent destinations you might want to visit from that program.

Libraries Folders used to sort files by file type.

Library pane Displays above the file list when a library is selected in the Navigation pane.

Local disk A large disk drive inside your computer, also referred to as a hard disk.

Maximize To increase the size of a window to fill the screen.

Menu A list of commands within a category.

Menu bar The bar near the top of a window that lists the names of menu categories.

Metadata Information about a file, such as tags, a title, a rating, the file name, and the file size.

Minimize To remove the window from the screen without closing it. Minimized windows can be reopened by clicking the associated button in the taskbar.

Mouse pointer The arrow, I-beam, or other symbol that shows the location or position of the mouse on your screen. Also called the pointer.

Navigation pane The pane on the left side of the Computer or Windows Explorer window that contains Favorites, Libraries, access to personal files and folders, and other items.

Notification area Area on the right side of the taskbar that keeps you informed about processes that are occurring in the background, such as antivirus software, network connections, and other utility programs. It also displays the time.

Operating system A set of instructions that coordinates the activities of your computer. Microsoft Windows 7 is an operating system.

Paint A program included with Windows in which graphics are created or edited.

Peek Use the *Show desktop* button to make the open windows transparent so you can see the desktop.

Pinned programs area An area at the top of the Start menu that is reserved for programs that you want to display permanently, although you can also delete programs from this area.

Pointer See mouse pointer.

Recycle Bin A storage area for files that have been deleted. Files can be recovered from the Recycle bin or permanently removed.

Restore Return a window to the size it was before it was maximized, using the Restore Down button.

Right-click Click the right mouse button to activate a shortcut menu.

Screen saver A picture or animation that displays on your screen after a set period of computer inactivity.

ScreenTip A small box, activated by holding the pointer over a button or other screen object, that displays the name of a screen element.

Scroll box The box in the vertical and horizontal scroll bars that can be dragged to reposition the document on the screen. The size of the scroll box also indicates the relative size of the document.

Search box A box in which you type a search word or phrase.

Search folder Retains all of the search conditions you specified during your search, and recreates the search every time you click the search folder.

Shake Use the title bar to move a window back and forth quickly to hide all other open windows.

Shortcut menu A menu activated by placing the pointer over an object and clicking the right mouse button.

Snip A screen or part of a screen captured using the Snipping Tool.

Snipping tool A program used to capture a screen or part of a screen.

Start button The button on the left side of the taskbar that is used to start programs, change system settings, find Windows help, or shut down the computer.

Start menu A menu that enables you to access the programs on your computer, and also enables you to change the way Windows operates, to access and configure your network, and to get help and support when it is needed.

Status area Another name for the notification area on the right side of the taskbar.

Submenu A second-level menu activated by selecting a menu option.

System tray Another name for the notification area on the right side of the taskbar.

Tags Custom file properties such as names, places, and descriptions that are added to files to enable you to categorize and find files more quickly.

Taskbar Displays the Start button and the name of any open documents. The taskbar also displays shortcut buttons for other programs.

Thumb drive A small storage device that plugs into a computer USB port; also called a USB drive or a flash drive.

Thumbnail A miniature representation of the contents of a window or file.

Title bar Displays the program icon, the name of the document, and the name of the program. The Minimize, Maximize/Restore Down, and Close buttons are grouped on the right side of the title bar.

USB drive A small storage device that plugs into a computer USB port; also called a thumb drive or a flash drive.

Vertical scroll bar The bar at the right side of a window that enables you to move up and down to view information that extends beyond the top and bottom of the screen.

Wildcard A character, such as an asterisk, that can be used to match any number of characters in a file search.

Window A box that displays information or a program, such as a letter, Excel, or a calculator. Windows usually consist of title bars, toolbars, menu bars, and status bars. A window will always have a Minimize button.

Window name The name that displays in a window's title bar.

Windows An operating system that coordinates the activities of a computer.

Windows Aero The Windows user interface that features a three-dimensional look, with transparent window frames, live previews of open windows, and multiple color schemes. Aero is an acronym for **A**uthentic, **E**nergetic, **R**eflective, **O**pen.

Windows Explorer A program that enables you to create and manage folders, and manage copy, move, sort, and delete files.

WordPad A simple word processing program that comes with Windows 7.